OTHERWISE LAW-ABIDING CITIZENS

OTHERWISE LAW-ABIDING CITIZENS

A Scientific and Moral Assessment of Cannabis Use

Matt Stolick

LEXINGTON BOOKS

A division of
ROWMAN & LITTLEFIELD PUBLISHERS, INC.
Lanham • Boulder • New York • Toronto • Plymouth, UK

LEXINGTON BOOKS

A division of Rowman & Littlefield Publishers, Inc.
A wholly owned subsidiary of The Rowman & Littlefield Publishing Group, Inc.
4501 Forbes Boulevard, Suite 200
Lanham, MD 20706

Estover Road
Plymouth PL6 7PY
United Kingdom

British Library Cataloguing in Publication Information Available

Library of Congress Cataloging-in-Publication Data

Stolick, Matthew, 1969–
Otherwise law-abiding citizens: a scientific and moral assessment of cannabis use / Matthew Stolick.
p.; cm.
Includes bibliographical references and index.
ISBN-13: 978-0-7391-2745-2 (cloth: alk. paper)
ISBN-10: 0-7391-2745-4 (cloth: alk. paper)
eISBN-13: 978-0-7391-3161-9
eISBN-10: 0-7391-3161-3
1. Cannabis—Social aspects—United States. 2. Cannabis—Therapeutic use—United States. 3. Cannabis—Law and legislation—United States. I. Title.
[DNLM: 1. Cannabinoids—therapeutic use—United States. 2. Marijuana Smoking—legislation & jurisprudence—United States. 3. Legislation, Drug—United States. 4. Philosophy, Medical—United States. QV 766 S875o 2009]
HV5822.C3S76 2009
362.29'520973—dc22

2008029397

Printed in the United States of America

∞™ The paper used in this publication meets the minimum requirements of American National Standard for Information Sciences—Permanence of Paper for Printed Library Materials, ANSI/NISO Z39.48-1992.

To the hundreds of thousands of cannabis users who are otherwise law-abiding citizens: to ease your guilt and demonstrate your rationale.

Contents

Acknowledgments

I WOULD FIRST OF ALL LIKE TO THANK THE University of Findlay for the sabbatical leave in the Spring 2007 during which I was able to do a substantial amount of work on this text. I also thank many students over the years. They inquired, challenged, and helped conduct rigorous arguments on various aspects of *Otherwise Law-Abiding Citizens.* I thank those at the University of Tennessee–Knoxville philosophy department who attended and provided feedback at an early version of this book (as "Healing Plant in a Political Jungle" in recognition of the stellar career of Kathy Bohstedt). I am forever grateful for the training in philosophy I completed during graduate school at the University of Tennessee-Knoxville (1993–1998) and continue to benefit from those formative years. This book could not have been written without the courageous efforts of many advocates for scientific research into cannabis throughout the twentieth and into the twenty-first century. Although there are too many to list, I recognize Alfred Lindesmith, Lester Grinspoon, Ed Rosenthal, the late Tod Mikuriya, Ethan Russo, Wayne Hall and Louisa Degenhardt in Australia, Franjo Grotenhermen in Germany (and executive director of the current IACM—"International Association for Cannabis as Medicine"), Jon Gettman, Rob Kampia (current president of MPP—"Marijuana Policy Project"), and Robert Randall. I also recognize the countless victims of cannabis law, those who have "come out" and openly advocated and told their stories. I appreciate the opportunity Lexington Books (Rowman and Littlefield) has provided, with competent and professional editorial work of Joseph Parry and Alison Syring.

During the five-plus years of writing *Otherwise Law-Abiding Citizens,* I derived immense benefit from the spiritual and emotional support of Bob Baratta (and his entire family), Mike Shank, Ray Abraham, Jeannine Grimm, Steve Sherman, Jereme Bear (and family), Louis Stulman, and Dale Brougher. I am deeply appreciative of the emotional and spiritual support, continual feedback and provision of a listening-board, of love and caring and ever-enduring patience of my wife Randi. She has been there since the original inspiration and decision to go ahead with this work, compassionately allowing me the time to research, ruminate, and work to bring *Otherwise Law-Abiding Citizens* to fruition. I also thank our children, daughters Van and Simone and son Moses. I pray being constantly surrounded by books and journal articles has sparked an interest in reading, reflecting, and creating. Finally, I thank my Lord and Savior Jesus Christ, for existence, spiritual gifts, inspiration, ability to summon continual motivation through draft upon draft of this work, introducing various points at just the right time and seemingly out of nowhere throughout the writing of *Otherwise Law-Abiding Citizens.* I humbly offer this work to glorify Him.

Introduction: The Two Realities That Dictate the Meaning of Cannabis Use in the United States

THIS PROJECT BEGAN WITH MY MORAL revulsion at the utter callousness of arresting and criminalizing terminally ill patients because they used cannabis. In speaking with those who work in palliative care as nurses, social workers, oncologists, and hospice volunteers, the response is consistent: the law prohibiting cannabis to these patients is certainly unjust. In talking with those who use cannabis for various illnesses, including terminal illness, there is almost always expressed a fear of legal punishment and criminalization. My search for the truth about cannabis has been an extensive multidisciplinary attempt to locate credible accounts about the nature of cannabis use and the cannabis plant. I have come to conclude the essence of the current prohibition of cannabis use is one of the criminalization of "otherwise law-abiding citizens" in order to stifle social change in the United States. Otherwise law-abiding citizens are regular citizens and community members from all walks of life who but for using cannabis are law-abiding.

There emerge from the cannabis literature two sets of beliefs regarding the meaning of cannabis. I will throughout refer to these two ways of understanding cannabis as "Realities." I employ the term "Reality" in a sociological way as articulated in Peter Berger and Thomas Luckmann's *The Social Construction of Reality*. "Reality" is "a quality appertaining to phenomena that we recognize as having a being independent of our own volition (we cannot 'wish them away')." This quality involves *how we understand* the phenomena of cannabis and cannabis use.[1] One of the two Realities on cannabis use will be called the "Social Reality on Cannabis Use." The Social Reality "knows" cannabis as essentially a Schedule I drug, high abuse potential with no therapeutic uses. The other Reality on cannabis use is the "Scientific Reality on Cannabis Use." The Scientific Reality "knows" cannabis as 483 chemical components, a relatively safe recreational drug with various therapeutic uses.

There are three main benefits derived from a sociological approach to debates about cannabis use and cannabis law. First is the acknowledgement of social events as relevant to the meaning of cannabis. This "sociology of knowledge" as applied to cannabis allows a consideration of not only empirical facts about cannabis (e.g., its chemical composition, neurological effects) but also a Social Reality understanding of cannabis as Schedule I, dangerous with no therapeutic uses. I present historical events and processes by which the body of "knowledge" of Social Reality on cannabis use has come to be established *as* "Reality." It became readily apparent to me upon my historical research of cannabis that the meaning of cannabis would not be captured by recording merely therapeutic effects experienced by terminally ill patients. The twentieth-century United States created and launched "reefer madness," intentionally creating a Social Reality of cannabis. This Social Reality is not based upon what can be studied neurologically and experientially.

A second benefit of citing two Realities is that it acknowledges the convictions of each group before assessing them rationally and morally. In this way sociology of knowledge respects strong convictions about cannabis and its effects. One argument considered several times throughout cannabis literature is the "gateway argument," claiming cannabis use *leads to* heroin use (or other hard drug use). This argument is held very strongly by the Social Reality up to the present day. It will be shown upon examination, however, that the Scientific Reality considers the gateway argument a relic of propaganda from the past, "nonsense," and a political argument not based on empirical evidence. However, again, the Social Reality "knows" the gateway argument is a reason against the legalization of cannabis. Berger and Luckmann explain that in applying sociology of knowledge, "the sociology of knowledge must concern itself with whatever passes for 'knowledge' in a society, regardless of the ultimate validity or invalidity (by whatever criteria) of such 'knowledge'"(Berger and Luckmann 1966, 3). Although there is little of either scientific or rational validity to major claims made by the Social Reality on cannabis use this does not make non-existent many Americans who believe (or at least parrot) these claims. Berger and Luckmann recognize "the sociology of knowledge is concerned with the analysis of the social construction of reality." I too have found that in order to capture the meaning of cannabis use in the United States I had to go beyond the Scientific Reality into the construction of "marijuana" as it has developed historically in the United States (and more broadly in the West).

A third benefit of employing a sociology of knowledge is that it invites the emergence of an interdisciplinary discussion on the meaning of cannabis in the United States. Getting to the "Truth" about cannabis demands a consideration of different facets and nuances about the meaning of cannabis. Disciplines through which I consider the meaning of cannabis use include neurology, sociology, psychology, cultural studies, religious studies, therapy, Hinduism, Christianity, Judaism, Islam, political science, and others.

The Social Construction of Reality has three main parts: The Foundations of Knowledge in Everyday Life, Society as Objective Reality, and Society as Subjective Reality. In this way, knowledge (e.g., about cannabis) is built upon foundations, and is of both an objective social reality and of a subjective acceptance of this objective social reality. The Social Reality of cannabis use is foundational in U.S. society, one of Schedule I status with laws prohibiting its use and criminalizing users. Foundations start with the "everyday life" as a "taken for granted" reality by the "ordinary members of society in the subjectively meaningful conduct of their lives" (Berger and Luckmann 1966, 19–20). In this ordinary reality we most basically use language to demonstrate our understanding of each other and ourselves in expressing ourselves. This language includes "objectified institutions." I propose the current Social Reality on cannabis use in the United States is such an objectified institution. To have "objectivity" in this sense means that the Social Reality of cannabis use exists above and beyond any particular people defending the beliefs. "In other words, the institutions are now experienced as possessing a reality of their own, a reality that confronts the individual as an external and coercive fact" (Berger and Luckmann 1966, 58). Americans simply accept and take for granted that cannabis (for the Social Reality, "marijuana") is a dangerous Schedule I drug. The Social Reality labels cannabis-users deviants, pot heads, morally bad people with a negative stigma attached solely by virtue of using cannabis (regardless of motivations involved). Citizens are raised and indoctrinated to understand cannabis use as per the Social Reality, being trained to accept the "institution" of the Social Reality on cannabis use and appearing to the child as all does to a child, "as given, unalterable and self-evident" (Berger and Luckmann 1966, 59).

Today, growing into adolescence and young adulthood in the United States brings with it ample availability of cannabis, given the rampant black market of this ironically top-grossing cash crop of the United States. The natural maturing process has adolescents and young adults wanting reasons and an explanation for the beliefs they have been given as citizens. They want an explanation for the current legal status of cannabis. Given their adolescent way of thinking, if there is a law to criminalize, punish, and negatively stigmatize cannabis users, then it stands to reason cannabis must be dangerous. Berger and Luckmann would point out that even a powerful Social Reality on cannabis use still requires "legitimation, "that is, ways by which it can be 'explained' and justified" (Berger and Luckmann 1966, 61).

Legitimation involves a "double problem," one of keeping believers and excluding non-believers. In the case of cannabis use, this is to hold the line of the Social Reality against the emerging Scientific Reality, excluding the latter as non-believers. Historically it will be seen that this has been done through cannabis prohibition and criminalization throughout the twentieth and into our twenty-first century in the United States. The laws first targeting "marijuana" in 1937 effectively "excluded" Mexicans and African Americans as per the rather clear racist intent of the time.

For the institution rendering cannabis Schedule I by the Social Reality to continue it must be passed down from generation to generation against the emerging Scientific Reality on cannabis use. "The priority of the institutional definitions of situations must be consistently maintained over individual temptations at redefinition" (Berger and Luckmann 1966, 62). The pragmatic value of institutions such as the law forbidding and criminalizing cannabis use, consider that "The more conduct is institutionalized, the more predictable and thus the more controlled it becomes" (Berger and Luckmann 1966, 62).

Berger and Luckmann explain that to exclude non-believers the general strategy is to label them and treat them as deviant:

> Since this knowledge is socially objectivated as knowledge, that is, as a body of generally valid truths about reality, any radical deviance from the institutional order appears as a departure from reality. Such deviance may be designated as moral depravity, mental disease, or just plain ignorance. (Berger and Luckmann 1966, 67)

The Social Reality of cannabis use in the United States similarly considers cannabis users deviant solely by virtue of breaking the federal law criminalizing all use. Those who advocate for legalization are morally depraved, suffering from a mental disease, or just plain ignorant. Of these, the first and third have been mostly employed by defenders of the Social Reality of cannabis use. Consider again that the Social Reality of cannabis use is "Reality" in a sociological sense. To realize cannabis is a dangerous drug without therapeutic purposes is "a realization in the double sense of the word, in the sense of apprehending the objectivated social reality, and in the sense of ongoing production of this reality" (Berger and Luckmann 1966, 66). That is, by defending the Social Reality and continuing to prohibit cannabis use and criminalize users, beliefs about cannabis (e.g., the gateway argument) are made real. However, although indeed referring to the cannabis plant, it will be made clear that those who make claims on behalf of the Social Reality usually have no personal experience with the "objectivated social reality," and most basically with the cannabis plant itself.

The Social Reality is inculcated through an "educational" process whereby "The institutional meanings must be impressed powerfully and unforgettably upon the consciousness of the individual" (Berger and Luckmann 1966, 70). These are memorized and "reimpressed," "if necessary by coercive and generally unpleasant means" (Berger and Luckmann 1966, 70). In regards to cannabis use, the U.S. federal government has most notably, in the Nixon and Reagan "Wars" on drugs, launched such education presenting *marijuana* as very dangerous, of no therapeutic value and leading to harm for anyone who uses it. These meanings become "trivialized" and "routine." In addition, prison rates resulting from these wars have the United States ("the land of the free") now imprisoning one out of every 100 adult citizens, more than any other country in the world.

Difficult to trivialize is the mounting evidence of the therapeutic effectiveness of cannabis. The Social Reality response or strategy is what Berger and Luckmann would refer to as "negative legitimation" or "nihilation." Nihilation uses a "machinery" to "liquidate conceptually everything *outside* the same universe. . . . Legitimation maintains the reality of the socially constructed universe; nihilation *denies* the reality of whatever phenomena or interpretations of phenomena do not fit into that universe" (Berger and Luckmann 1966, 114). The contention that cannabis has therapeutic use is to this day referred to as "nonsense" by the defenders of the Social Reality in the United States. The extremely low toxicity of cannabis is simply ignored. Scientific research must be approved by the Social Reality so that what is ultimately approved will serve the function of "legitimation." Again, although powerful, this process has not been entirely successful against the Scientific Reality of cannabis use (which shows signs of life in the early-twenty-first-century United States). Berger and Luckmann cite two ways of nihilating: the first is to view as less-than-human those who do not support the institution and to simply reject as nonsense their claims. The second form of nihilation is to incorporate the deviant concepts within the legitimate institutions, "and thereby to liquidate them ultimately" (Berger and Luckmann 1966, 115). Of the first, this can be to reduce all cannabis users down to hedonistic users. Of the second, consider that the efforts of pharmaceutical companies to provide synthetic THC as a substitute for cannabis have been such an effort at nihilation. However, the Scientific Reality will present a very compelling argument rejecting this as an adequate therapeutic substitute for the cannabis plant in its entirety (483 chemical compound substances). Furthermore, this second form of nihilation may be offered as an acceptance of cannabis only for medicinal purposes (as at this time twelve U.S. states have so recognized—and all eyes await an eventual showdown between states rights and federal rights[2]) and a reluctant, politically savvy move from Schedule I to Schedule II. As will become apparent in the moral assessment chapters, this move is grossly insufficient. Moral reasoning strongly indicates cannabis must assume the same recreational status as alcohol, the latter clearly demonstrating the U.S. public can be quite tolerant of the right to use a substance.

Otherwise Law-Abiding Citizens is presented in three parts. Part I presents in three chapters the Scientific Reality on cannabis use. Part II presents in three chapters the Social Reality on cannabis use. The Part III Moral Assessment is a detailed presentation and application of the moral thinking of Aristotle, Immanuel Kant, J. S. Mill, the Old Testament, and Christianity to three questions (Is cannabis use ever morally justified? Is cannabis prohibition morally justified? Is cannabis criminalization morally justified?). A way of assessing and judging as moral or immoral particular uses and ways of using cannabis is provided as well as arguments against the prohibition and criminalization of adult cannabis users.

My basic aim in this book, beginning with my initial repulsion at terminally ill patients being criminalized for using cannabis, is to present the truth about cannabis use. Although not simply done overnight but rather taking several years of patiently sifting, reading, and reflecting, the result will leave readers in the end to face a personal and political choice: either demonstrating courage and faith in the moral character of U.S. citizens by adopting the Scientific Reality on cannabis use or continuing to invest in nihilating the Scientific Reality for the sake of preserving the false and destructive Social Reality of cannabis use.

Notes

1. Berger and Luckmann define "knowledge" as "the certainty that phenomena are real and that they possess specific characteristics" (Berger and Luckmann 1966, 1). As the polarized views on the nature of cannabis and cannabis use are held with such strong conviction ("certainty"), it seems each Reality would claim to know cannabis has effects claimed by each Reality.

2. In her article "Smokescreen," Jessica Berg nicely summarizes this point: "Clear away the smoke from the advisory and you will find that behind the battle over medical marijuana is the underlying power struggle pervading many of our health care discussions, from abortion to health care access to physician-assisted suicide. It's a battle over state's rights and federal authority. Politics is just the window dressing." Jessica Berg, "Smokescreen," Hastings Center Report, vol. 36 (4): July–August 2006, 49.

I

THE SCIENTIFIC REALITY ON CANNABIS USE

1

The Plant-Brain Connection: The Neurological Truth about Cannabis Use

By understanding the mechanisms of how drugs alter these body processes [nervous and endocrine systems], we are able to recognize drug benefits and risks and devise therapeutic strategies to deal with ensuing problems. (Hanson, Venturelli, and Fleckenstein 2002, 114)

Neurology . . . Revolutionary Science of the Twenty-First Century

IN THE JANUARY 6, 2000, ISSUE OF THE *New England Journal of Medicine*, the editors relented to the spirit of excitement and reflection moving into the new millennium by putting together their own list of the eleven most important medical developments of the past 1,000 years ("Looking Back on the Millennium in Medicine"). I present these to emphasize just how historically recent is our understanding of and therapeutic focus on neurons and brain chemicals (the foundation of the Scientific Reality of cannabis use). The eleven developments cited ("in rough chronologic order according to the first noteworthy step taken in a given area"):

1. Elucidation of Human Anatomy and Physiology
2. Discovery of Cells and Their Substructures
3. Elucidation of the Chemistry of Life
4. Application of Statistics to Medicine
5. Development of Anesthesia
6. Discovery of the Relation of Microbes to Disease

7. Elucidation of Inheritance and Genetics
8. Knowledge of the Immune System
9. Development of Body Imaging
10. Discovery of Antimicrobial Agents
11. Development of Molecular Pharmacotherapy

Presented in the first five hundred or so years (1000–1500) are largely mistaken (explanatory) theories in medicine. More essentially, consider that Western medicine was grounded in Greek medicine accepted as paradigmatic from approximately 400 BC until AD1500:

> Except for some early work by the ancient Greeks, much of it wrong, there were few advances in clinical medicine until the Renaissance. In the 1400 years between Galen and Vesalius, medicine was stagnant, dominated by the belief that illness reflected an imbalance in the four humors of the body—blood, phlegm, yellow bile, and black bile. Life was nasty, brutish, and short, and medical care did not help. ("Looking Back on the Millennium in Medicine" 2000, 42)

Anatomy is presented with Vesalius (1514–1564) and his "Seven Books on the Structure of the Human Body" (1543), William Harvey (1578–1657) "On the Motion of the Heart and Blood in Animals" (1628), and the invention of the microscope by Antony van Leeuwenhock (1632–1723) "set the stage for the era of cellular biology, which was to occupy the last 200 years of the millennium," although "the rich substructure of cells remained unexplored until the early 1930s" ("Looking Back on the Millennium in Medicine" 2000, 43).

The infancy of a Western medical explanation based in neurology is evidenced by the fact that it was only in the years 1659 to 1859 that there came to exist a scientific explanation of fermentation, one accounting for the actions of enzymes.[1] Included in this most recent medical expansion of knowledge was acceptance in 1860 of Avogadro's law, allowing for "the rapid elucidation early in the twentieth century of the interconnected enzymatic reactions that are responsible for the stepwise oxidation of foodstuffs that fuels the vital activity of cells" ("Looking Back on the Millennium in Medicine" 2000, 43). Today's clinicians commonly effect neurological changes in a patient's brain to treat disease in their bodies.

> The notion of such cascades of chemical reactions initiated by enzymes whose catalytic activity is determined by their complex structure and modulated by the products they generate is at the very root of modern biochemistry. Discovery of the inhibition or enhancement of the action of cellular enzymes by hormones, neurotransmitters, cytokines, and paracrine molecules, so that cells can communicate with each other, has led to an understanding not only of normal processes,

> but also of diseases such as diabetes mellitus. ("Looking Back on the Millennium in Medicine" 2000, 43)

And from the late nineteenth century to the present day, this understanding of biochemistry and neurology continues to lead the substantial medical development of therapies, bringing to bear the neurological concept of "receptors" of the brain on which much of pharmacology applies.

> The antimicrobial defense against infectious diseases marked the beginning of modern pharmacotherapy. Subsequent advances were made possible by new concepts in organic chemistry in the period before and just after World War II and by the recognition that the therapeutic effectiveness of natural products was due to specific constituents. The identification of these active constituents, coupled with the recognition that many drugs produce their effects by binding to specific macromolecules or receptors, made possible the search for more potent and specific therapies with improved efficacy and safety. ("Looking Back on the Millennium in Medicine" 2000, 48)

The editors present as relevant to early-twenty-first-century medicine the work of Sir James Black, first finding through a hypothesis that the "myocardial adrenergic receptor was of the beta subtype," which led to "the development of beta-blockers." Consider the authors' characterization of this discovery within pharmacology as setting off an explosion of exponential growth of drug therapies:

> The recognition of the gastric histamine receptor was not antagonized by traditional antihistamines led Black to propose that a novel antihistamine (that would block H2 receptors) would reduce gastric output.
>
> These strategies led to the development of drugs to antagonize or stimulate numerous other receptors and drug targets. The treatment of Parkinson's disease with levodopa, for example, is based on an understanding of dopaminergic receptors in the nigrostriatum. The revolution in molecular biology is now producing an explosion in the number and variety of potential drug targets, which is likely to ensure the continuation of the exponential growth in pharmacologic discovery, even while pharmacogenetics is beginning to explain variability among individual patients in the response to drugs. ("Looking Back on the Millennium in Medicine" 2000, 48–49)

To set the stage and context within which to move toward a scientific understanding of cannabis I will focus on the field of neurology as central to any explanation of its effects. In addition to presenting a neurological explanation of cannabis, I present the effects of four other major types of psychoactive drug. One comprehensive text I use is *Drugs and Society,* 7th ed.[2] As this title of the textbook suggests, drugs are considered not only from a toxicological/pharmacological perspective but also from a sociological perspective. This well-researched, clear, and comprehensive presentation of drugs and specifically cannabis sets a basic foundation upon which to develop the Scientific Reality of cannabis. The eighteen chapters of *Drugs and Society* can be broken down into two parts: the first part about drugs generally and second about specific drugs. I draw on basic information presented from the first part about drugs generally and then consider their presentation of five specific types of drug (sedatives, opioids/narcotics, stimulants, hallucinogens, and cannabis). This way of moving into a consideration of cannabis shows at the outset the unique nature of cannabis among all other drugs. This contextualization is also necessary to judge the harmfulness or dangerousness of cannabis use, as understanding the use of any substance as dangerous, in order to be meaningful, presupposes the existence of other substances not dangerous.

Within the brain are billions of neurons. Within these billions are chemical reactions that are understood by neurologists as receiving and sending information. This information received and sent results in a change physically and sometimes psychologically in the individual whose brain is so changed. Neurological changes are more precisely understood as of the state of the body so that the change is not merely "in the brain" but the neurons in the brain change bodily organs and the way they function.

Gahlinger (*Illegal Drugs: A Complete Guide to Their History, Chemistry, Use, and Abuse* 2004) presents a most comprehensive and readable book on a wide variety of drugs, much more than I include here. My purpose in here citing Gahlinger is only to provide a basic understanding of what neurons are and how they function as well as how neurotransmitters are relevant to changes in the brain resulting in specific experienced effects. Gahlinger explains:

> Each neuron can be thought of as an electrical wire with plugs at each end. A chemical signal stimulates the plug and starts the electrical current at one end. The current then runs along the wire to the other end where it produces another chemical signal. This signal, in turn, stimulates the next neuron in line. (Gahlinger 2004, 134)

He notes that this conception of a neuron as a wire is "greatly oversimplified" as, unlike wires, neurons are surrounded by other neurons. As of the brain they are affected by what happens in other parts of this most complex bodily organ: "Neurons are living, growing cells; they're not fixed like an electrical circuit. Almost every neuron is constantly changing its function by adapting to bodily demands, sensations, and environmental influences"

(Gahlinger 2004, 137). Gahlinger explains neurons act as "regulators," releasing or inhibiting the production of neurotransmitters, neurotransmitters that (for the purposes of ultimately understanding the Scientific Reality of cannabis use) cause the various effects experienced. Different neurotransmitters and neurological reactions are revealed by both the effects these chemicals have on the brain and on the experience of drug users:

> A neuron regulates the production of its neurotransmitters, making more or less of them as needed. It also continually changes the number of receptors on its cell surface according to the amount of stimulation it receives from other cells. If the circuit is overstimulated, the receptors are downgraded so that fewer and weaker signals get through. If there is too little stimulation, the receptors may be increased and made more sensitive.
>
> The synaptic space itself is also constantly modified. Each neuron's terminals feel and reach out like tentacles. They grow with stimulation and atrophy with disuse. Like muscles, the cells of the brain are "use it or lose it." (Gahlinger 2004, 137)

Note here that neurons, specifically "terminals" of neurons, can grow and also atrophy. This suggests, among other things, therapies may be created to either stop the loss of neurons or perhaps stimulate their growth (terms such as "neuroprotection" or "neuroregeneration" will be introduced with a consideration of the therapeutic benefits of cannabis in chapter 3).

And of the receptors of the neurons:

> Receptors are special proteins located in the membranes of receiving neurons and other target cells. They help regulate the activity of cells in the nervous system and throughout the body. These selective protein sites on specific cells act as transducers to communicate the messages caused by endogenous *messenger substances* (chemicals produced and released within the body), such as neurotransmitters and hormones. (Hanson, Venturelli, and Fleckenstein 2002, 118)

As for an explanation of how it was discovered that synthetic and non-synthetic chemicals can affect the same receptors causing the same effects on users of either of the chemicals, consider the example given of opiate receptors and the subsequent discovery of endorphins:

> Discovery of the opiate receptors suggested the existence of internal (endogenous) neurotransmitter substances in the body that normally act at these receptor sites and have effects like narcotic drugs, such as codeine and morphine. This finding led to the identification of the body's own opiates, the endorphins (Kandel et al. 2000b). Specific receptors have also been found for other drugs such as the CNS depressant diazepam (Valium) (Kandel et al. 2000a) and the active ingredient in marijuana (Fattore et al. 1999). (Hanson, Venturelli, and Fleckenstein 2002, 118)

A basic principle in neurology is here revealed. The principle holds that if a synthetic drug stimulates brain receptors, then the brain likely produces a similar chemical (i.e., an endogenous chemical) which stimulates the same receptors producing similar effects. Employing the most common analogy used by neurologists to explain neurological functioning, consider the chemical as a "key" and the receptor as a "lock":

> Receptors that have been isolated and identified are protein molecules; it is believed that the shape of the protein is essential in regulating a drug's interaction with a cell. If the drug is the proper shape and size and has a compatible electrical charge, it may substitute for the endogenous messenger substance and activate the receptor protein by causing it to change its shape, or conform. This process is like a "lock-and-key" arrangement, with only certain shapes of chemicals (the keys) being able to interact and activate a receptor (the "lock") (Goldstein 1994). (Hanson, Venturelli, and Fleckenstein 2002, 119)

A drug is either an agonist (produces a response in receptor) or antagonist (prevents response in receptor). A response or prevented response involves the increase or decrease in the release of various neurotransmitters. "Experimental evidence shows that many different neurotransmitters exist, although much remains to be learned about their specific functions. These biochemical messengers are released from specific neurons" (Hanson, Venturelli, and Fleckenstein 2002, 120). Common neurotransmitters considered in *Drugs and Society* as involved in the use of the major types of drugs include acetylcholine, norepinephrine, epinephrine, dopamine, serotonin, GABA, and endorphins.

Consider briefly the specific neurotransmitters dopamine and then epinephrine, to give a bit more of an idea about the distinct effects of different neurotransmitters on behavior. For dopamine, there is the implicit assumption that there are various levels of dopamine potentially existent in any individual's brain. As brains have various levels of dopamine, and assuming there is some sensible notion of a "normal" level of dopamine,[3] suggested are possibilities for neurological therapy. The goal is one of achieving normal levels of dopamine (and other neurotransmitters). "Dopamine neurons help control our appetites for both food and sex. Increased amounts of dopamine produce a feeling of pleasure or reward and encourage people to be more outgoing and exuberant. Too much dopamine is believed to be a feature of schizophrenia" (Gahlinger 2004, 139). As an example, consider the message of "fight or flight" sent by another neurotransmitter, epinephrine:

> Epinephrine is a neurotransmitter produced by the adrenal gland, located above the kidney. . . . This hormone alerts the entire body, preparing it for flight or flight:

the heart rate increases, blood is moved away from the digestive organs to the muscles, and the lungs open up to breathe faster. Body functions that are not necessary for emergencies are inhibited: appetite is suppressed and hunger disappears.

Drugs that mimic epinephrine, such as the amphetamines, are sought out by soldiers, athletes, people who need to stay awake, people trying to lose weight, and people who want to feel more physically and emotionally stimulated. (Gahlinger 2004, 139–40)

Five Major Types of Drug of Use and Abuse in the United States

In the second part of *Drugs and Society* various types of drugs are presented. To give a basic overview of the nature of the neurological and experienced effects of various drugs (but by no means an exhaustive consideration of the nature and effects of each of these types of drug), I will present basic information about the neurology of each of five types of substance: sedatives/depressants, stimulants, narcotics/opioids, hallucinogens, and marijuana/cannabis.

Sedatives: Anxiety, Sleep, Muscle Relaxation
Bromide-------------------Barbiturates-------------------Benzodiazepine
(From more to less dangerous)

Central Nervous System (CNS) Depressants: sedative-hypnotics (barbiturates such as amobarbital, pentobarbital, phenobarbital, seconbarbital).

As one would expect from the name of these drugs, the primary effect is to "sedate" in experience and inhibit neurologically. A primary motivation for using this type of drug is to ease anxiety and nervousness. Consider that the barbiturates depress more than do the benzodiazepines, which "selectively" depress neurological activity:

> In contrast to barbiturate-type drugs, which cause general depression of most neuronal activity, benzodiazepines selectively affect those neurons that have receptors for the neurotransmitter gamma aminobutyric acid (GABA) (Hobbs et al. 1995). GABA is a very important inhibitory transmitter in several brain regions: the limbic system, the reticular activating system, and the motor cortex. . . . In the presence of benzodiazepines, the inhibitory effects of GABA are increased. Depression of activity in these brain regions likely accounts for the ability of benzodiazepines to alter mood (a limbic function), cause drowsiness (a reticular activating system function), and relax muscles (a cortical function). (Hanson, Venturelli, and Fleckenstein 2002, 164)

Again consider the neurological principle whereby if a drug has a chemical effect in the brain then there is likely the same chemical produced by the brain itself (i.e., endogenous chemical). This principle also goes the other way, where if the brain produces a chemical then in theory it is possible to synthetically reproduce this chemical as a drug. The authors point out:

> As yet, no endogenous substance has been identified that naturally interacts with this so-called benzodiazepine site. It is very likely, however, that a natural benzodiazepine does exist that activates this same receptor population and serves to reduce stress and anxiety by natural means. (Hanson, Venturelli, and Fleckenstein 2002, 164)

Of some of the experienced effects of the sedatives, specifically benzodiazepines:

> Reported side effects of benzodiazepines include drowsiness, lightheadedness, lethargy, impairment of mental and physical activities, skin rashes, nausea, diminished libido, irregularities in the menstrual cycle, blood cell abnormalities, and increased sensitivity to alcohol and other CNS depressants (McEvoy 2000). (Hanson, Venturelli, and Fleckenstein 2002, 164)

And of the more severe but rare side effects, they explain:

> On rare occasions, benzodiazepines can have paradoxical effects, producing unusual responses such as nightmares, anxiety, irritability, sweating, and restlessness (McEvoy 2000). Bizarre, uninhibited behavior—extreme agitation with hostility, paranoia, and rage—may occur as well. (Hanson, Venturelli, and Fleckenstein 2002, 165)

The major distinction authors make in presenting sedative drugs is between barbiturates and benzodiazepines. Authors explain historically, and as indicated by the continuum presented at the outset of this sedatives section, that as one moves from bromide to barbiturates to benzodiazepines, the drugs are less dangerous and more medicinally used:

> Attempts to find CNS depressants other than alcohol that could be used to treat nervousness and anxiety began in the 1800s with the introduction of bromides. These drugs were very popular until their toxicities became known. In the early 1900s, bromides were replaced by barbiturates. . . . It was not until the 1950s that the first benzodiazepines were marketed as substitutes for the dangerous barbiturates. (Hanson, Venturelli, and Fleckenstein 2002, 161)

Sedative effects are regarded as therapeutically beneficial and implicitly passing a risk/benefit analysis by the U.S. society. However, even for these currently accepted benzodiazepines, the authors note that there are still risks similar to that of the bromides, as a risk never to be eliminated from the very nature of the sedative drugs: "Although relatively safe when used for short periods, long-term use can cause dependence and withdrawal problems much like those associated with their depressant predecessors (Trevor and Lay 1998)," (Hanson, Venturelli, and Fleckenstein 2002, 161).

Giving a general characterization of the social acceptability of the sedatives,

> Benzodiazepines are by far the most frequently prescribed CNS depressants for anxiety and sleep. In fact, 4 of the top-selling 100 prescription drugs in the United States during 1999 were benzodiazepines (Latner 2000). . . . The first true benzodiazepine, chlordiazepoxide (Librium), was developed for medical use and marketed about 1960; the very popular drug Valium came on the market about the same time. In fact, Valium was so well received that from 1972 to 1978 it was the top-selling prescription drug in the United States. (Hanson, Venturelli, and Fleckenstein 2002, 163)

And consider, in light of the current U.S. schedules of drug dangerousness and therapeutic usefulness (and of cannabis as a Schedule I, most dangerous and no therapeutic usefulness) that sedatives are considered to have low abuse potential and to be safe medicinally: "Because of dependence problems, the benzodiazepines are now classified as Schedule IV drugs" (Hanson, Venturelli, and Fleckenstein 2002, 163). And of their specific therapeutic uses, the authors explain that:

> Benzodiazepines are used for an array of therapeutic objectives, including the relief of anxiety, treatment of neurosis, relaxation of muscles, alleviation of lower back pain, treatment of some convulsive disorders, induction of sleep (hypnotic), relief from withdrawal symptoms associated with narcotic and alcohol dependence, and induction of amnesia, usually for preoperative administration (Longo and Johnson 2000). (Hanson, Venturelli, and Fleckenstein 2002, 163–64)

Especially relevant is that most effects listed here are also therapeutic effects of cannabis use (although, as will be seen, distinct neurologically and in experienced effects as well as in risks involved). Ultimately, however, only the middle range sedatives, the barbiturates, are subject to the significantly more regulated Schedule II status (implying significant dangerousness) while benzodiazepines continue to have Schedule IV status (low dangerousness and specifically because, among other things, they are "long-acting"):

> Concern about the abuse potential of barbiturates caused the federal government to include some of these depressants in the Controlled Substances Act. Consequently, the short-acting barbiturates, such as pentobarbital and secobarbital, are classified as Schedule II drugs, whereas the long-acting barbiturates,

> such as phenobarbital, are less rigidly controlled as Schedule IV drugs. (Hanson, Venturelli, and Fleckenstein 2002, 168)

Because barbiturates have "substantial abuse potential," specifically "lack selectivity and safety," "have a substantial tendency to create tolerance, dependence, withdrawal, and abuse," and "cause problems with drug interaction," they have been "replaced by benzodiazepines in most treatments; however, they are still included in a number of combination products for the treatment of an array of medical problems, such as gastrointestinal disorders, hypertension, asthma, and pain (Hobbs et al. 1995)" (Hanson, Venturelli, and Fleckenstein 2002, 169).

Alcohol/Ethanol: Recreational Sedative and "Social Lubricant"

> Alcohol alters the production and functioning of transmitters such as dopamine, serotonin, GABA and brain endorphins (Hettema et al. 1999). These neurochemical effects contribute to the fact that alcohol consumption can aggravate underlying psychiatric disorders such as depression and schizophrenia ("Centerpiece" 1993).
>
> Heavy drinking over many years may result in serious mental disorders and irreversible damage to the brain and peripheral nervous system, leading to permanently compromised mental function and memory. (Hanson, Venturelli, and Fleckenstein 2002, 191)
>
> Every part of the brain and nervous system is affected and in extreme cases can be damaged by alcohol. "Initially, alcohol depresses subcortical inhibitions of the control centers of the cerebral cortex, resulting in disinhibition. In higher doses, alcohol depresses the cerebellum, resulting in slurred speech and staggering gait. In very high doses, alcohol can depress the respiratory centers of the medulla, resulting in death" (Levin 1990, 23). (Hanson, Venturelli, and Fleckenstein 2002, 191)

Hanson, Venturelli, and Fleckenstein stress throughout their presentation of alcohol that it is properly understood as one of the CNS depressant drugs as similar neurologically and in experienced effects by users.[4] The authors spend two lengthy chapters working through history, pharmacology, and behavioral aspects of alcohol, forming a central part of *Drugs and Society*. Harkening back to my consideration of the process of fermentation, an age old process in human history and of our most recent understanding of the enzymes, that is the biochemistry explaining this process, consider that even before alcohol (wine) there was "mead":

> Alcohol has been part of human culture since the beginning of recorded history. The technology for alcohol production is ancient. Several basic ingredients and conditions are needed: sugar, water, yeast, and warm temperatures.

> The process of making alcohol, called fermentation, is a natural one. It occurs in ripe fruit and berries and even in honey that bees leave in trees. . . . In fact, fermented honey, called mead, may have been the first alcoholic beverage. (Hanson, Venturelli, and Fleckenstein 2002, 182)
>
> The Egyptians had breweries 6000 years ago; they credited the god Osiris with introducing wine to humans. The ancient Greeks used large quantities of wine and credited a god, Bacchus (or Dionysus), with introducing the drink. . . .
>
> The distillation device, or *still*, was developed by the Arabs around A.D. 800 and was introduced into medieval Europe around A.D. 1250. By boiling the fermented drink and gathering the condensed vapor in a pipe, a still increases the concentration of alcohol, potentially to 50 percent or higher. (Hanson, Venturelli, and Fleckenstein 2002, 182–83)

And further explaining the neurological risk associated with heavy and prolonged alcohol use, the authors explain that:

> As with other psychoactive drugs, tolerance to alcohol encourages increased consumption to regain its effects and can lead to severe physical and psychological dependence (O'Brien 1995). Tolerance to alcohol is similar to that seen with CNS depressants, such as the barbiturates and benzodiazepines. It consists of both an increase in the rate of alcohol metabolism (due to stimulation of metabolizing enzymes) and a reduced response by neurons and transmitter systems (particularly by increasing the activity of the inhibitory neurotransmitter, gamma-aminobutyric acid [GABA]) to this drug. (Hanson, Venturelli, and Fleckenstein 2002, 188)

As a recreationally used sedative drug (and socially tolerated), alcohol is here revealed as including the dangerous combination of "increased rate of metabolism" as well as a "reduced response by neurons." Consider further the risks from consumption of alcohol:

> At low to moderate doses, disinhibition occurs; this loss of conditioned reflexes reflects a depression of inhibitory centers of the brain. The effects on behavior are variable and somewhat unpredictable. . . . At higher doses, the social setting has little influence on the expression of depressive actions of the alcohol. The CNS depression incapacitates the individual, causing difficulty in walking, talking, and thinking. These doses tend to induce drowsiness and cause sleep. If large amounts of alcohol are consumed rapidly, severe depression of the brain system and motor control area of the brain occurs, producing uncoordination, confusion, disorientation, stupor, anesthesia, coma, and even death. (Hanson, Venturelli, and Fleckenstein 2002, 189)

Death occurs through the use of alcohol, crucial for distinguishing the sedative drugs generally from other types of drugs. This most basically is due to the location of the relevant neurological receptors in the medulla (which includes respiratory centers). In the case of alcohol, "The lethal level of alcohol is between 0.4 percent and 0.6 percent by volume in the blood. Death is caused by severe depression of the respiration center in the brain stem, although the person usually passes out before drinking an amount capable of producing this effect" (Hanson, Venturelli, and Fleckenstein 2002, 189).

Judging the danger of alcohol use and specifically abuse, consider this drug in light of the larger category of which it is a part, the sedatives. At the outset of the sedatives section I presented the continuum of the sedatives in order of their discovery as well as in order of their dangerousness to users. Consider that the effects of alcohol cover this continuum, potentially as dangerous as bromide and as safe as benzodiazepines, depending on (among other things) the amount of alcohol used.

Bromide----------Barbiturates----------Benzodiazepine
<------------------------Alcohol---------------------------->
(From most dangerous to least dangerous)

The following are given as the "major components of alcoholism":

Craving: an overwhelming compulsion to drink even when not feasible, such as at work, driving a car, mowing a lawn, and so on.
Very impaired or loss of control: an inability to limit one's drinking once drinking has begun; for example, one drink only before going to bed is impossible to control.
Physical dependence: presence of withdrawal symptoms when attempting to abstain from usage. Such symptoms as nausea, sweating, shakiness, and anxiety about the availability of alcohol are common.
Tolerance: a need to continually increase the amount of alcohol consumed to maintain its effects (or to maintain the "buzz"). (Hanson, Venturelli, and Fleckenstein 2002, 213)

Note here the existence of *physical* dependence resulting from the regular consumption of large quantities of alcohol. This indicates a withdrawal syndrome. Significant and potentially severe withdrawal symptoms become apparent when use is abruptly interrupted. The severity of withdrawal can vary according to the length and intensity of the alcohol habit. The prototypic withdrawal patterns are as follows:

Stage 1 (minor): restlessness, anxiousness, sleeping problems, agitation, tremors, and rapid heartbeat.

Stage 2 (major): "minor" symptoms plus hallucinations, whole-body tremors, increased blood pressure and vomiting.
Stage 3 (delirium tremens): fever, disorientation, convulsions, seizures, and fatality in 3 percent to 5 percent of cases.
((NIDA Diagnosis 2000). Hanson, Venturelli, and Fleckenstein 2002, 191)

As a general summary of the various and significant negative *social* effects of alcohol use, consider the litany of harms (including *to others*) strongly associated with recreational use of CNS depressant alcohol:

> Although many consider the effects of alcohol enjoyable and reassuring, the adverse pharmacological impact of this drug is extensive, and its effects are associated with more than 100,000 deaths each year in the United States (Special Report 1997). It is estimated that at some time during their lives, almost 50 percent of all Americans will be involved in an alcohol-related traffic accident. The pharmacological effects of alcohol abuse cause severe dependence. . . . These effects also disrupt personal, family, social, and professional functioning and frequently result in multiple illnesses and accidents, violence, and crime (Eronen et al. 1996). Alcohol consumed during pregnancy can lead to devastating damage to offspring and is a principal cause of mental retardation in newborns (Larroque and Kaminski 1998). Next to tobacco, alcohol is the leading cause of premature death in America. Experts have estimated that in the United States, approximately $167 billion is spent annually dealing with social and health problems resulting from the pharmacological effects of alcohol (Quindien 2000). However, such estimates fall short of assessing the emotional upheaval and human suffering caused by this drug ("Centerpiece" 1993). (Hanson, Venturelli, and Fleckenstein 2002, 184)

Although alcohol/ethanol, a drug widely used and abused in the United States, costs $167 billion annually in health care and premature death, as well as significant suffering to family and friends, and injuries to innocent others through the irresponsible use of alcohol, it continues to be an unscheduled drug, legal and acceptable and tolerated by the U.S. public.

To further elaborate upon the dangerousness of alcohol abuse for users, consider that significant damage is potentially done to most every organ system of the body. One example is the liver, as "Among alcoholics, liver disorders are responsible for 10 percent to 15 percent of deaths (Worman 2000)" (Hanson, Venturelli, and Fleckenstein, 2002, 191). The stomach and pancreas can also be damaged, as "one out of three heavy drinkers suffers from chronic gastritis"; drinking "also can cause pancreatitis, pancreatic cirrhosis, and alcoholic diabetes (NIAAA 1997)" (Hanson, Venturelli, and Fleckenstein 2002, 194). And "[h]eavy drinking appears to affect the bone marrow, where various blood cells are formed. The suppression of the bone marrow can contribute to *anemia*, in which red blood cell production cannot keep pace with the need for those cells. Heavy drinkers are also likely to develop alcoholic bleeding disorders because they have too few platelets to form clots (NIAAA 1997)" (Hanson, Venturelli, and Fleckenstein 2002, 194). Heavy drinking can also cause cardiovascular damage:

> Chronic intense use of alcohol changes the composition of heart muscle by replacing it with fat and fiber, resulting in a heart muscle that becomes enlarged and flabby. Congestive heart failure from alcoholic cardiomyopathy often occurs when heart muscle is replaced by fat and fiber. Other results of alcohol abuse that affect the heart are irregular heartbeat or *arrhythmia*, high blood pressure, and stroke. A common example of damage is "holiday heart," so called because people drinking heavily over a weekend turn up in the emergency room with a dangerously irregular heartbeat. Chronic excessive use by people with arrhythmia causes congestive heart failure. Malnutrition and vitamin deficiencies associated with prolonged heavy drinking also contribute to cardiac abnormalities. (Klatsky 1995). (Hanson, Venturelli, and Fleckenstein 2002, 194)[5]

Endocrine system and hormones

Alcohol abuse alters endocrine functions by influencing the production and release of hormones, and affects endocrine regulating systems in the hypothalamus, pituitary, and gonads. Because of alcohol abuse, levels of *testosterone* (the male sex hormone) may decline, resulting in sexual impotence, breast enlargement, and loss of body hair in men. Women experience menstrual delays, ovarian abnormalities, and infertility (NIAAA 1997; Hanson, Venturelli, and Fleckenstein 2002, 195).

Renal problems and kidney damage

"Frequent abuse of alcohol can also severely damage the kidneys. The resulting decrease in kidney function diminishes this organ's ability to screen blood and properly form urine and can result in serious metabolic problems" (Hanson, Venturelli, and Fleckenstein 2002, 195).

Cognitive functions

Long-term heavy drinking can severely affect memory, judgment, and learning ability (NIAAA 1997). Wernicke-Korsakoff's syndrome is a characteristic psychotic condition caused by alcohol use and the associated nutritional and vitamin deficiencies. Patients who are brain-damaged (Hobbs et al.

1995) cannot remember recent events and compensate for their memory loss with *confabulation* (making up fictitious events that even the patient accepts as fact) (Hanson, Venturelli, and Fleckenstein 2002, 195).

Finally, consider that unlike other drugs, the use of alcohol by pregnant women shows demonstrable harms done to those infants born, specifically Fetal Alcohol Syndrome (FAS), "a condition affecting children born to alcohol-consuming mothers that is characterized by facial deformities, growth deficiency, and mental retardation" (Hanson, Venturelli, and Fleckenstein 2002, 195). "The incidence of FAS is one in three infants born to alcoholic mothers actively consuming during pregnancy (Hobbs et al. 1995)" (Hanson, Venturelli, and Fleckenstein 2002, 196).

Although a quite dangerous drug, there exists a conception of "responsible drinking" among the U.S. public. This justification for tolerating alcohol even includes health *benefits* from moderate consumption:

> The long-term effects of alcohol on the cardio-vascular system are dose-dependent. Recent studies have demonstrated that regular light to moderate drinking (two drinks or fewer of wine a day) actually reduces the incidence of heart diseases such as heart attacks, strokes, and high blood pressure by 20 percent to 40 percent in some populations. The type of alcoholic beverage consumed does not appear to be important as long as the quantity of alcohol consumed is moderate (1–2.5 ounces per day) ("Your Health" 1999). Although the precise explanation for this coronary benefit is not known, it appears to be related to the effects of moderate alcohol doses in relieving stress and increasing the blood concentration of high-density lipoproteins (HDL). (Hanson, Venturelli, and Fleckenstein 2002, 194)

Consider that perhaps the main reason for tolerating the recreational use of alcohol by adults is to *relieve stress*. This is important in that, regardless of whether or not this is a good or bad reason to recognize a right to consume alcohol, the reason is a legitimate one for using alcohol (one would assume it would also support using cannabis).

Narcotics (Opioids): Numbing and Deadening Pain

> The word *narcotic* has been used to label many substances, from opium to marijuana to cocaine. The translation of the Greek word *narkoticos* is "benumbing or deadening." The term *narcotic* is sometimes used to refer to a CNS depressant, producing insensibility or stupor, and at other times to refer to an addicting drug. Most people would not consider marijuana among the narcotics today, although for many years it was included in this category. Although pharmacologically

> cocaine is not a narcotic either, it is still legally classified as such. Perhaps part of this confusion is due to the fact that cocaine, as a local anesthetic, can cause a numbing effect. (Hanson, Venturelli, and Fleckenstein 2002, 238)

The wide use of the term "narcotic" to label many different substances has among other things the practical value of being able to treat various substances the same way (e.g., in law and policy). The term "narcotic" has been stretched so far as to mean *any* addicting drug. However, neurologically much clearer distinctions can be made.

> Narcotic Drugs:
> heroin (schedule I),
> morphine (Schedule II, III),
> methadone (Schedule II),
> meperidine, fentanyl (Schedule II),
> oxycodone, propoxyphene, codeine (Schedule II, III, V)
> (Hanson, Venturelli, and Fleckenstein 2002, 244)

As this book will several times bring up the gateway drug argument, whereby cannabis use is said to cause the use of "hard drugs" such as Schedule I heroin, consider that with cannabis the most used illicit drug in the United States one would logically expect to see at least increased if not rampant heroin use as well. However, "There are an estimated 600,000 active heroin addicts in the United States, a figure that has remained relatively stable despite changes in the number of infrequent and moderate users (NIDA Infofax 2000)" of cannabis (Hanson, Venturelli, and Fleckenstein 2002, 246).

opium--------morphine--------codeine--------heroin
(Historical order of pharmaceutical discovery)

Narcotics were pharmacologically identified in the early nineteenth century:

> In 1803, a young German named Frederick Serturner extracted and partially purified the active ingredients in opium. It was 10 times more potent than opium itself and was named *morphine* after Morpheus, the Greek god of dreams. . . . In 1832, the second compound was purified and named *codeine*, after the Greek word for "poppy capsule" (Maurer and Vogel 1967). (Hanson, Venturelli, and Fleckenstein 2002, 240)

A post–Civil War United States treated pain with these narcotics in the midst of the widespread sale and use of unregulated patent medicines, many containing narcotics. The crucial change made by the 1906 Pure Food and

Drug Act was the requirement to list all ingredients in any patent medicine (distinct from controlling what can and cannot be legally consumed). The turn of the twentieth century in the United States would bring a legislative response to what had come to be perceived as the "narcotic problem." "By 1900, an estimated 1 million Americans were dependent on the opiates (Abel 1980)" (Hanson, Venturelli, and Fleckenstein 2002, 240). This was also a time when heroin came on the market as a cough suppressant:

> Looking for better medicines, chemists found that modification of the morphine molecule resulted in a more potent compound. In 1898, diacetylmorphine was placed on the market as a cough suppressant by Bayer. It was to be a "heroic" drug, without the addictive potential of morphine—it thus received the name *heroin.* (Hanson, Venturelli, and Fleckenstein 2002, 241)

At the outset of this sub-section on narcotics the descriptive words used for narcotics were "benumbing" or "deadening." A better understanding of these words comes with an appreciation for the powerful effect these particular drugs have on visceral and somatic pains, pains primarily resulting from damaged organs and tissues of the body.

> The most common clinical use of the opioid narcotics is as analgesics to relieve pain. These drugs are effective against most varieties of pain, including *visceral* (associated with internal organs of the body) and *somatic* (associated with skeletal muscles, bones, skin, and teeth) types. Used in sufficiently high doses, narcotics can even relieve the intense pain associated with some types of cancer (Way et al. 1998).
>
> The opioid narcotics relieve pain by activating the same group of receptors that are controlled by the endogenous substances called *endorphins* (Way et al. 1998). (Hanson, Venturelli, and Fleckenstein 2002, 241)

Hanson, Venturelli, and Fleckenstein focus on the significant release of dopamine in the limbic system as a notable response to opioids: "the opioid receptors are present in high concentration within the limbic structures of the brain. Stimulation of these receptors by narcotics causes release of the transmitter, dopamine, in limbic brain regions (Reisine and Pasternak 1995)" (Hanson, Venturelli, and Fleckenstein 2002, 243). Narcotics work to effectively treat pain because of their neurological effectiveness. They block the transmission of pain but do not cure the injury which is the source of the pain. It stands to reason that by stopping narcotics, one who had internal organ damage would have the experience of pain return.

> Activation of opioid receptors by either the naturally released endorphins or administration of the narcotic analgesic drugs blocks the transmission of pain through the spinal cord or brain stem and alters the perception of pain in the

> "pain center" of the brain. Because the narcotics work at all three levels of pain transmission, they are potent analgesics against almost all types of pain. (Hanson, Venturelli, and Fleckenstein 2002, 242).

The potency of narcotics makes them effective, but also includes significant risks. "Although narcotics are very effective analgesics, they do cause some side effects that are particularly alarming; thus, their clinical use usually is limited to the treatment of moderate to severe pain (Reisine and Pasternak 1995)" (Hanson, Venturelli, and Fleckenstein 2002, 242). Of the significant and serious nature of narcotic dependence, consider the especially negative withdrawal symptoms. Rather than "irritability" and "anxiety" as will be seen as the most severe withdrawal symptoms of cannabis users abruptly ceasing use, here are *physical* effects definitive of a withdrawal *syndrome*:

> The development of psychological and physical dependence makes breaking the narcotic habit very difficult. Abstinence from narcotic use by a long-term addict can cause severe withdrawal effects such as exaggerated pain responses, agitation, anxiety, stomach cramps and vomiting, joint and muscle aches, runny nose, and an overall flu-like feeling. Although these withdrawal symptoms are not fatal, they are extremely aversive and encourage continuation of the narcotic habit (Colapinto 1996; Reisine and Pasternak 1995). Overall, the narcotics have similar actions; there are differences, however, in their potencies, severity of side effects, likelihood of being abused, and clinical usefulness. (Hanson, Venturelli, and Fleckenstein 2002, 244)

Consider that for heroin, "Approximately 3000 to 4000 deaths occur annually in the United States from heroin overdoses (Leland 1996)" (Hanson, Venturelli, and Fleckenstein 2002, 246). Of those who become dependent on heroin, consider the following regarding the significant harm users pose to themselves and others[6]:

> Although many young heroin addicts come from affluent or middle-class families (Weiss 1995), research shows most heavy users are poorly educated with minimal social integration. Because of these disadvantages, heroin addicts often have a low level of employment, exist in unstable living conditions, and socialize with other illicit drug users (Bourgois 1999; Hall et al. 1993). Clearly, such undesirable living conditions encourage criminal activity; however, three other factors also likely contribute to the association between heroin use and crime:
>
> 1. The use of heroin and its pharmacological effects encourages antisocial behavior that is crime-related. Depressants such as heroin diminish inhibition

and cause people to engage in activities they normally would not. The effects of heroin and its withdrawal make addicts self-centered, demanding, impulsive, and governed by their "need" for the drug.

2. Because heroin addiction is expensive, the user is forced to resort to crime to support the drug habit (Weiss 1995).
3. A similar personality is driven to engage in both criminal behavior and heroin use. Often, heroin addicts start heroin use about the same time they begin to become actively involved in criminal activity. In most cases, the heroin user has been taking other illicit drugs, especially marijuana, years before trying heroin (Hall et al. 1993). (Hanson, Venturelli, and Fleckenstein 2002, 247)

Here there are significant reasons for laws prohibiting heroin use, primarily on the grounds that users pose a danger to society. Use "encourages antisocial behavior" and "causes people to engage in activities they normally would not." This has users lose control and seems a prime example of an effect of a drug a society rightfully refuses to tolerate. Also a similar personality is driven to both criminal behavior and *heroin* use (note: not cannabis use). Were heroin legally available and affordable, it is not clear whether or not there would still be associated criminal behavior. This is very important in light of arguments for legalization of heroin so as to eliminate crime, as crime will inevitably happen by routinely losing control, as a result of using this particular drug. The third reason here, citing the "personality" that engages in both heroin use and criminal behavior, suggests that recreational heroin use poses a threat of harm to society in addition to significant threat of harm to the user.

Finally, consider that on the safer side of the narcotic continuum is codeine, the same type of drug as heroin but less potent and most frequently prescribed: "Codeine is a naturally occurring constituent of opium and the most frequently prescribed of the narcotic analgesics. It is used principally as a treatment for minor to moderate pain and as a cough suppressant" (Hanson, Venturelli, and Fleckenstein 2002, 256). And this narcotic drug is scheduled among the safest of drugs: "Codeine-containing cough syrup is currently classified as a Schedule V drug" (Hanson, Venturelli, and Fleckenstein 2002, 256).

Stimulants: Fight or Flight Performance Drugs

Amphetamines are synthetic chemicals that are similar to natural neurotransmitters such as norepinephrine (noradrenaline), dopamine, and the stress hormone epinephrine (adrenaline). The amphetamines exert their pharmacological effect by increasing the release and blocking the metabolism of these catecholamine substances as well as serotonin, both in the brain and nerves associated with the sympathetic nervous system. Because amphetamines cause release

> of norepinephrine from sympathetic nerves, they are classified as sympathomimetic drugs. The amphetamines generally cause an arousal or activating response (also called the *fight-or-flight response*) that is similar to the normal reaction to emergency situations or crises. (Hanson, Venturelli, and Fleckenstein 2002, 265)

The move from the sedatives and the narcotics to the stimulants has us consider effects quite contrary to these first two groups. Generally speaking, rather than bringing one down these pick one up (as experienced and described by users). The amphetamines activate the "fight or flight" response, putting one on edge and acutely aware and prepared for action. Here we also see the stress hormone epinephrine (adrenaline) introduced, which along with the blocking of its reuptake puts the user of amphetamines in a state of tense readiness.

Historically and medically,

> Until 1970, amphetamines were prescribed for a large number of conditions, including depression, fatigue, and long-term weight reduction. In 1970, the Food and Drug Administration (FDA), acting on the recommendation of the National Academy of Sciences, restricted the legal use of amphetamines to three medical conditions: (1) narcolepsy, (2) attention deficit hyperactivity disorder, and (3) short-term weight reduction programs (DSM-IV-TR 2000). (Hanson, Venturelli, and Fleckenstein 2002, 266)

The third primary medical use of amphetamines, weight reduction programs, is thought to be used to justify a significant amount of recreational use: "Many experts feel that the euphoric effect of amphetamines is the primary motivation for their continued use in weight reduction programs" (Hanson, Venturelli, and Fleckenstein 2002, 266). Of the risks that accompany the use of amphetamines, "The effects include increased heart rate, elevated blood pressure, and damage to vessels, especially small veins and arteries (Max 1991; Swan 1996). In users with a history of heart attack, coronary arrhythmia, or hypertension, amphetamine toxicity can be severe or even fatal" (Hanson, Venturelli, and Fleckenstein 2002, 266). And of the current use of the stimulant Ritalin to treat Attention Deficit Hyperactivity Disorder (ADHD), consider that although it is less potent, it basically blocks reuptake of adrenaline (again, a definitive chemical of stimulant use).[7]

Of the stimulant cocaine:

> Most of the pharmacological effects of cocaine use stem from enhanced activity of catecholamine (dopamine, noradrenaline, adrenaline) and serotonin transmitters. It is believed that the principal action of the drug is to block the reuptake and inactivation of these substances following their release from neurons.

> The consequence of such action is to prolong the activity of these transmitter substances at their receptors and substantially increase their effects. The summation of cocaine's effects on these four transmitters cause CNS stimulation (Woolverton and Johnston 1992). The increase of noradrenaline activity following cocaine administration increases the effects of the sympathetic nervous system and alters cardiovascular activity. (Hanson, Venturelli, and Fleckenstein 2002, 282)

And of the significant risk of Schedule II cocaine, "high chronic doses alter personality, frequently causing psychotic behavior that resembles paranoid schizophrenia" (DSM-IV-TR 2000; Nathan et al. 1998; Hanson, Venturelli, and Fleckenstein 2002, 282). Consider the significant withdrawal syndrome demonstrated by chronic (and recreational) users of the stimulant cocaine, one not merely for days (as with cannabis, see below) but for weeks and months, with an "indefinite" extinction implying reluctance to indicate a former user is no longer at risk for subsequent abuse or dependence:

> Of particular importance to treatment of the chronic cocaine users is that abstinence after bingeing appears to follow three unique stages, each of which must be dealt with in a different manner if relapse is to be prevented. These phases are classified as phase 1, or "crash" (occurs 9 hours–4 days after drug use is stopped); phase 2, or withdrawal (1–10 weeks); and finally, phase 3, or extinction (indefinite). (Hanson, Venturelli, and Fleckenstein 2002, 283)

In their *New England Journal of Medicine* review article on drug addiction, Jordi Camf and Magi Farre distinguish between various types of stimulants employing a neurological explanation:

> Cocaine is a potent blocker of the dopamine-, norepinephrine-, and serotonin-uptake transporters. Amphetamines have a more complex mechanism of action. Amphetamines cause neuronal storage vesicles in the cytoplasm to release neurotransmitters to the synapse; inhibit the uptake of dopamine, norepinephrine, and serotonin by membrane transporters; and act as mild inhibitors of monoamine oxidase. Amphetamine and methamphetamine seem to be more selective for dopamine and norepinephrine than for serotonin transporters, but MDMA and designer amphetamines are more selective for the serotonin transporter. (Camf and Farre 2003, 978)

Consider also the stimulant caffeine, one quite unique among the stimulants in its chemical structure and effects experienced by individual users (especially long-term):

> Caffeine belongs to a group of drugs that have similar chemical structures and are known as the xanthines. Besides caffeine, other xanthines are *theobromine*

> (means "divine leaf"), discovered in cacao beans (used to make chocolate) in 1842, and *theophylline* (means "divine food"), isolated from tea leaves in 1888. These three agents have unique pharmacological properties, with caffeine being the most potent CNS stimulant. (Hanson, Venturelli, and Fleckenstein 2002, 288)

Of the effective dose of caffeine, "although the CNS responses of users can vary considerably, in general, 100 to 200 milligrams of caffeine enhances attention, causes arousal, and diminishes fatigue (Daly and Fredholm 1998)" (Hanson, Venturelli, and Fleckenstein 2002, 290). And of risk-related doses of caffeine:

> Adverse CNS effects usually occur with doses greater than 300 milligrams per day. Some of these include insomnia, increased tension, anxiety, and initiation of muscle twitches. Doses over 500 milligrams can be dysphoric (unpleasant) and can cause panic sensations, chills, nausea, and clumsiness. Extremely high doses of caffeine, from 5 to 10 grams, frequently result in seizures, respiratory failure, and death (DSM-IV-TR 2000). (Hanson, Venturelli, and Fleckenstein 2002, 290)

Caffeine is not scheduled but available over the counter ("OTC") without a prescription, therefore deemed safe enough for adults to use. However, note that the dangers of this particular drug include seizures, respiratory failure, and death. Note also the somewhat serious withdrawal symptoms involved (e.g., panic sensation, nausea, and clumsiness). Actually the DSM-IV-TR includes a section of "Caffeine-Related Disorders." These include "Caffeine-Induced Anxiety Disorder" and "Caffeine-Induced Sleep Disorder." It also is stated that:

> The consumption of caffeine is ubiquitous in the United States, with an average caffeine intake of approximately 200 mg/day, and up to 30 percent of Americans consuming 500mg or more per day. Some individuals who drink large amounts of coffee display some aspects of dependence on caffeine and exhibit tolerance and perhaps withdrawal. However, the data are insufficient at this time to determine whether these symptoms are associated with clinically significant impairment that meets the criteria for Substance Dependence or Substance Abuse. (DSM-IV-TR 2000, 231)

However, to justify the OTC availability of caffeine in the form of 200 mg capsules and tablets as well as in various other forms for consumption (e.g., coffee, soda, chocolate, tea) it would seem that experiencing such extreme effects would have caffeine users "cut back" on their own, realizing the limit to their use (perhaps for many people used to increase productivity during the day, so that taking too much is counterproductive). This nature of caffeine makes it similar to cannabis, in that "less is more" or that taking too much too often simply defeats any recreational, vocational, productive, or medicinal purpose of using it. Again, another similarity between caffeine and cannabis: "Caffeine causes limited dependence, which, for most people, is relatively minor compared with that of the potent stimulants; thus, the abuse potential of caffeine is also much lower and dependence is less likely to interfere with normal daily routines (Daly and Fredholm 1998)" (Hanson, Venturelli, and Fleckenstein 2002, 291–92).

The lack of dangerousness of caffeine includes the fact that people can go without it if they need to, demonstrating a limited dependence or craving specifically as contrasted with that of a more potent stimulant such as amphetamine. Also used as a criterion of dependence in the DSM-IV-TR are the "daily routines" of an individual, specifically whether or not one could fulfill various responsibilities and obligations without caffeine. This criterion represents a practical facet and test for dependence. It also allows some sense of what dangerous means.

Another widely popular stimulant is nicotine. Nicotine-containing tobacco is used in a variety of forms and ways including most prevalently cigarettes. Here we move from a consideration of the unique stimulant caffeine to the unique stimulant nicotine, having mentioned amphetamines and cocaine. To further complement the neurological revolution of the nineteenth century described at the outset of this chapter, nicotine was discovered in 1828 as one component of tobacco, "a colorless, highly volatile liquid alkaloid" (Hanson, Venturelli, and Fleckenstein 2002, 308). Furthermore, the neurological effects of nicotine are brought about by a release of dopamine, so that with a quick hit of a cigarette, users get an automatic release of dopamine, bringing about an immediate feeling of pleasure:

> Nicotine produces an intense effect on the central nervous system. Research has demonstrated that nicotine activates the brain circuitry in regions responsible for regulating feelings of pleasure. In particular, nicotine increases the release of the neurotransmitter, dopamine, in the so-called reward or pleasure pathways of the brain. This effect likely contributes to the abuse potential of the stimulant.
>
> The pharmacokinetic properties of nicotine also enhance its abuse potential. As just noted, cigarette smoking allows nicotine to enter the brain rapidly, with drug levels peaking within 10 seconds of inhalation. The acute effects of this rapid increase in brain concentration dissipate within a few minutes, causing the smoker to continue to dose frequently throughout the day in order to maintain the pleasurable effects of the drug. (Hanson, Venturelli, and Fleckenstein 2002, 314)

Here are two measures of the abuse potential of a drug, namely the length of time before experiencing effect in using a drug and the length of time the effects last. Both smoked and injected drugs produce rapid effects, so that both cannabis and tobacco as smoked are of higher abuse potential in that there is an experience of effects very quickly (within 10–15 seconds) as opposed to an orally ingested drug, which effects may not be experienced for an hour or more. Also, the shorter the effects last the more frequently one would use a drug. This fact should also be noted when the comparison and contrast is made between cannabis and tobacco. Although cannabis may be more potent in certain ways (e.g., tar content), the effects last much longer than those of nicotine, thereby making cannabis of less "abuse potential" than tobacco (based upon the duration of effects).

Consider the dangerousness of the currently available recreational drug of nicotine (primarily through cigarettes):

> Tobacco use is responsible for more than 430,000 deaths each year, or 1 in every 5 deaths—more than alcohol, cocaine, heroin, suicide, homicide, fire, car accidents, and AIDS combined. This includes 98,000 deaths from heart disease, 123,000 deaths from lung cancer, 32,000 deaths from other forms of cancer, 72,000 deaths from chronic lung disease, 24,000 deaths from stroke, and about 81,000 deaths from other diagnoses (CDC 2000). In fact, tobacco use is the leading preventable cause of death in the United States (NIDA 1998). (Hanson, Venturelli, and Fleckenstein 2002, 315)

Hanson, Venturelli, and Fleckenstein also explain, "Cigarette smoking is a major cause of cancers of the lung, bladder, pancreas, cervix, and kidney" (Hanson, Venturelli, and Fleckenstein 2002, 317). Furthermore, "Cigarette smoking is the leading cause of bronchopulmonary disease, which includes a host of lung ailments. Cigarette smokers have higher death rates from pulmonary emphysema and chronic bronchitis and more frequently have impaired pulmonary function and other symptoms of pulmonary disease than nonsmokers" (Hanson, Venturelli, and Fleckenstein 2002, 317).

Tobacco (nicotine) creates many more serious negative consequences for users than does cannabis. The essential neurological difference between tobacco/nicotine and cannabis is that tobacco smoking results in an immediate release of dopamine. Cannabis, however, primarily activates its own unique receptors and has a different neurological effect than nicotine. Experientially the difference would likely be described as between being wired and stimulated from smoking cigarettes while being relaxed and reflective under the influence of cannabis.

Hallucinogens: Mind Drugs and Experience of Alternate Reality

The fourth type of drug is described in the medical literature as a "mind drug," as users typically have the experienced effect of a change in their way of perceiving the outside world. These drugs are not easy to characterize in a precise way:

> Agreement has not been reached on what constitutes a hallucinogenic agent (O'Brien 1996), for several reasons. First, a variety of seemingly unrelated drug groups can produce hallucinations, delusions, or sensory disturbances under certain conditions. For example, besides the traditional hallucinogens (such as LSD), high doses of anticholinergics, cocaine, amphetamines, and steroids can cause hallucinations.
>
> What's more, responses to even the traditional hallucinogens can vary tremendously from person to person and from experience to experience. . . . The features of hallucinogens that distinguish them from other drug groups are their ability to alter perception, thought, and feeling in such a manner that does not normally occur except in dreams or during experiences of extreme religious exaltation (Jaffe 1990). (Hanson, Venturelli, and Fleckenstein 2002, 338)

Note here the comparison of the perceptions experienced through the use of hallucinogens to "dreams" or "experiences of extreme religious exaltation" that "do not normally occur." Unique to the hallucinogens is the effect of exposing what many users describe as an alternative (way of viewing) reality. This is in contrast to cannabis, which instead typically exposes a reality that was already there but to which one was not sensitive. In other words, one uninhibited is therefore more open but one hallucinating is also sensing in ways not available to the most open and uninhibited of states of consciousness.

As for the reasoning for the Schedule I status of hallucinogens (providing information useful for understanding reasons a drug would be placed in the most stringent Schedule I category):

> the Food and Drug Administration (FDA) has not approved any of these agents for psychiatric use. The psychedelics currently available are considered to be too unpredictable in their effects and possess substantial risks (Abraham et al. 1996). Not only is their administration not considered to be significantly therapeutic but also their use is deemed a great enough risk that the principal hallucinogenic agents are scheduled as controlled substances. (Hanson, Venturelli, and Fleckenstein 2002, 340)

Here note that the hallucinogens are deemed to be a risk to individual users because they are "unpredictable in their effects" and pose "substantial risks." These risks result from the changing of "perception, thought, and feeling" from what it is normally. Among the often-noted potential negative effects of hallucinations are panic states: "During these drug-induced panic states, which in some ways are schizophrenic-like, people have committed suicide and homicide. These tragic reactions are part of the risk of using hallucinogenics and explain some of the FDA's hesitancy to legalize or authorize them for psychotherapeutic use" (Hanson, Venturelli, and Fleckenstein 2002, 340–41).

Further justifying the scheduling and control of the hallucinogens on the ground of dangerousness as specifically unpredictable in effect on users, is the neurological complexity of the effects of hallucinogens in the brain:

> That LSD and similar drugs alter serotonin activity has been proven; how they affect this transmitter is not so readily apparent.
>
> Although many experts believe changes in serotonin activity are the basis of the psychedelic properties of most hallucinogens, a case can be made for the involvement of norepinephrine, dopamine, acetylcholine, and perhaps other transmitter systems as well. Only additional research will be able to sort out this complex but important issue. (Hanson, Venturelli, and Fleckenstein 2002, 341)

The dangerousness of the hallucinogenics is not because of their addictive or "abuse potential" but because of the type of unpredictable mental states caused by their use, "Because there are no withdrawal symptoms, a person does not become physically dependent, but some psychological dependency on LSD can occur (NIDA Infofax 1999)" (Hanson, Venturelli, and Fleckenstein 2002, 343).

Cannabis: Relaxation of an Active Placebo

Weil and Rosen, by indicating that cannabinoid molecules are "insoluble in water," they explain why the psychoactive chemical THC of cannabis was not discovered until 1964, over a hundred years after the discovery of the opioids, narcotics, and stimulants:

> Marijuana is unique among the psychoactive drugs, in a class by itself. The chemicals it contains resemble no other drug molecules. Unlike most of the substances discussed in this book, marijuana molecules are insoluble in water but very soluble in oil. Therefore, they are absorbed unevenly when eaten, and they stay in the body for a long time because they accumulate in body fat. Marijuana is neither a stimulant nor a depressant but has some features of both. Many people regard it as a mild psychedelic, but its effects are different from those of the true hallucinogens, and it is not necessarily mild. Moreover, the abuse potential of marijuana is considerably higher than that of psychedelics, because it can be used frequently or continually in combination with everyday activities. (Weil and Rosen 2004, 135–36)

Consider the only very recent discovery (1988) of neurological receptors in the brain to which THC of cannabis binds:

> In 1988 Allyn Howlett, a researcher at the St. Louis University Medical School, discovered a specific receptor for THC in the brain—a type of nerve cell that THC binds to like a molecular key in a lock, causing it to activate. Receptor cells form part of a neuronal network; the brain systems involving dopamine, serotonin, and the endorphins are three such networks. When a cell in a network is activated by its chemical key, it responds by doing a variety of things: sending a chemical signal to other cells, switching a gene on or off, or becoming a more or less active. . . .
>
> The cannabinoid receptors Howlett found showed up in vast numbers all over the brain (as well as in the immune and reproductive systems), though they were clustered in regions reasonable for the mental processes that marijuana is known to alter: the cerebral cortex (the locus of higher-order thought), the hippocampus (memory), the basal ganglia (movement), and the amygdala (emotions). Curiously, the one neurological place where cannabinoid receptors didn't show up was in the brain stem, which regulates involuntary functions such as circulation and respiration. This might explain the remarkably low toxicity of cannabis and the fact that no one is known to have ever died from an overdose. (Pollen 2001, 153)

Here again is the neurological reason why there are no recorded fatalities from the use of cannabis: the neurons involved in cannabis use are not located in the brain stem, not a threat to the involuntary functions of circulation and respiration. The major areas of THC receptors in the brain are the basal ganglia, cerebral cortex, hippocampus, and amygdala (more on the relevance of these areas for the experienced and therapeutic effects of cannabis in chapter 2).

Although there is no consensus on the exact number of species of cannabis (the argument involves one to three possible species) most indicate two species exist (cannabis sativa and cannabis indica). However, Grinspoon and Bakalar describe three species of cannabis: cannabis sativa, cannabis indica, and cannabis ruderalis (Grinspoon and Bakalar 1997, 1). Plants of highest potency grow "in hot regions like Mexico, the Middle East, and India" (Grinspoon and Bakalar 1997, 2). Grinspoon and Bakalar also distinguish between three potencies of cannabis in India: bhang (least potent, cheapest), ganja (two to three times as strong as bhang), and charas (also known as hashish; strongest) (Grinspoon and Bakalar 1997, 2). "Marijuana" is typically identified with the weakest, bhang. Perhaps worth noting here is that the vast majority of marijuana used in the United States is of the weakest potency, except on the West Coast, where there is more potent sinsemilla available. "The quantities of other more potent types of marijuana such as sinsemilla as well as hydroponic-types of marijuana (known as 'hydro') are more readily available in illegal drug markets. The actual potencies of the more generic types of marijuana have remained the same in the past 30 years" (Hanson, Venturelli, and Fleckenstein 2002, 373).

Of the "cannabinoids," consider that referred to could be either synthetically created or naturally occurring and produced by the brain, both alternatives to the plant cannabis:

> Cannabinoids refer to pharmaceutical extracts derived from *C sativa* and to synthetic substances that act on cannabinoid receptors in the brain. Endocannabinoids refer to endogenous cannabinoids that are found in the human brain and body.
>
> Research during the 1990s identified sites of cannabinoid receptors in the brain and the endogenous cannabinoid ligands—endocannabinoids—that act on these receptor cites. Cannabinoid receptors respond to THC and to endocannabinoids such as anandamide and 2-arachidonyl-glycerol. Two types of cannabinoid receptors, CB_1 and CB_2, have been identified to date. CB_1, which is found mainly in the brain, causes the psychological effects of THC because drugs that block the receptor inhibit many of its effects in humans; CB_2 is found in the immune system. CB_1 and CB_2 are G-protein-coupled receptors found in membranes of nerve cells and are involved in chemical signaling between cells. (Hall, Christie, and Currow 2005, 35)

Adding to the neurological explanation of how cannabis (specifically THC) effects the brain of medicinal users, Doweiko explains that perhaps THC inhibits the production of an enzyme which is involved in the transmission of pain messages: "Researchers attempting to isolate certain neuropeptides that transmit pain signals between cells discovered a process through which THC inhibits the function of the enzyme *adenylate cyclase*, which is involved in the transmissions of pain messages" (Doweiko 1996, 121).

Citing as evidence, pharmacologically, that "cannabis based medicine extracts (CBME)" "may offer a distinct advantage over THC alone," Russo provides five reasons for this advantage of cannabis over one (synthetic) compound of THC (e.g., Marinol):

> First, "Potentiation," which involves an "entourage effect" whereby having other compounds along with THC makes for better THC binding and effectiveness.
>
> Second "Antagonism," certain compounds of cannabis (e.g., CBD) may offset negative side effects of THC, ones present with mere THC alone.
>
> Third, "Summation," "a number of cannabis components may contribute to a certain therapeutic effect of THC,"
>
> Fourth, "Pharmacokinetic," exemplified by one compound (e.g., CBD) "altering the metabolism" of THC, and
>
> Fifth, "Metabolism," and "due to the co-evolution over the millennia, humans are better able to metabolize herbal preparations (i.e., cannabis) as

compared to synthetic pharmaceuticals (i.e., synthetic cannabinoids). (Russo 2003, 4)

Oral administration involving the synthetic drugs (dronabinol, marinol, e.g.), has "been relatively little employed." Reasons include expense, delayed onset of effects in the range of 90–120 minutes, lack of practical titration of dosage, and a pronounced tendency toward dysphoria or other mental complaints from being 'too high" (Russo 2003, 10). Hanson, Venturelli, and Fleckenstein further explain why smoking cannabis is therapeutically superior to orally ingesting cannabis:

> In smokers, lung absorption and transport of THC to the brain are rapid; THC reaches the brain within as little as 14 seconds after inhalation. Marijuana is metabolized more efficiently through smoking than intravenous injection or oral ingestion. Smoking is also three to five times more potent than these two methods (Jones 1980; Kaplan and Whitmire 1995; Kryger 1995). (Hanson, Venturelli, and Fleckenstein 2002, 384)

Of the general effects of cannabis, Hanson, Venturelli, and Fleckenstein explain:

> Usually, such exposure causes some euphoria, a sense of well-being, and relaxation. Marijuana smokers often claim heightened sensory awareness and altered perceptions (particularly a slowing of time), associated with hunger (the "munchies") and a dry mouth (Swan 1994; Hubbard et al. 1999). (Hanson, Venturelli, and Fleckenstein 2002, 384)

Now that I have presented some basic information about the brain and about the plant, consider next some basic risks and dangers associated with cannabis use (a topic I cover in detail in chapter 3).

Hanson, Venturelli, and Fleckenstein explain of the risks associated with cannabis use:

> Marijuana has been found to have a negative impact on critical thinking skills. Recent research by the NIDA shows that heavy marijuana use impairs crucial skills related to attention, memory, and learning. Another study showed that even alertness, coordination, and reaction time were impaired by marijuana usage (NCADI 1998). Impairment continues even after discontinuing this drug's use for at least 24 hours (Brown and Massaro 1996). (Hanson, Venturelli, and Fleckenstein 2002, 378)

They further cite as a risk of heavy cannabis use "amotivational syndrome": "*Amotivational syndrome* refers to a belief that heavy use of marijuana causes a lack of motivation and reduced productivity. Specifically, users show apathy, poor short-term memory, difficulty in concentration, and a lingering disinterest in pursuing goals (Abood and Martin 1992)" (Hanson, Venturelli, and Fleckenstein 2002, 379). Also, "Long-term, chronic users often show decreased interest in personal appearance or goals . . . as well as an inability to concentrate, make appropriate decisions, and recall information from short-term memory (Abood and Martin 1992; Block 1996)" (Hanson, Venturelli, and Fleckenstein 2002, 384).

And of the physical dangers involved in smoking cannabis, consider the significant amount of tar in the smoke of cannabis: "Smoke is a mixture of tiny particles suspended in gas, mostly carbon monoxide. These solid particles combine to form a residue called *tar.* Cannabis produces more tar (up to 50 percent more) than an equivalent weight of tobacco and is smoked in a way that increases the accumulation of tar (Jones 1980)" (Hanson, Venturelli, and Fleckenstein 2002, 385). And also, "The carcinogen benzopyrene, for example, is 70 percent more abundant in marijuana smoke than in tobacco smoke" (Hanson, Venturelli, and Fleckenstein 2002, 385). Furthermore, "users have a higher incidence of such respiratory problems as laryngitis, pharyngitis, bronchitis, asthma-like conditions, cough, hoarseness, and dry throat (Hollister 1986; Goldstein 1995)" (Hanson, Venturelli, and Fleckenstein 2002, 385). And, "In human beings, cannabis causes both *vasodilation* (enlarged-blood vessels) and an increase in heart rate related to the amount of THC consumed (Abood and Martin 1992; NIDA 2000)" (Hanson, Venturelli, and Fleckenstein 2002, 385). They also explain, in their section "Tolerance and Dependence":

> Frequent high doses of THC also can produce mild physical dependence. Healthy subjects who smoke several "joints" a day or who are given comparable amounts of THC orally experience irritability, sleep disturbances, weight loss, loss of appetite, sweating, and gastrointestinal upsets when drug use is stopped abruptly. However, all subjects do not experience this mild form of withdrawal. It is much easier to show psychological dependence in heavy users of marijuana (Abood and Martin 1992; Hollister 1986). (Hanson, Venturelli, and Fleckenstein 2002, 387)

Here note that even at the most extreme abruptly stopping a heavy chronic smoker's use of cannabis, is called a "mild form of withdrawal," the symptoms pale in comparison to those experienced by individuals withdrawing from CNS depressants and opioids and are more comparable to caffeine withdrawal along with the psychological dependence similar to the hallucinogens. In addition to not being a "narcotic," Doweiko explains that it is misleading to call marijuana a "hallucinogenic" (Doweiko 1996, 122). "In many parts of the country, marijuana is classified as a hallucinogenic by law enforcement officials, in spite of the fact that it rarely causes hallucinations at the dosage levels normally used in the United States" (Doweiko 1996, 123).

Conclusion: An Assessment of the Harmfulness of Cannabis Use

In their recent "Development of a Rational Scale to Assess the Harm of Drugs of Potential Misuse," Nutt et al. present the results of a rating of the harmfulness of twenty different drugs including cannabis by two sets of experts. As they describe their study:

> Our approach provides a comprehensive and transparent process for assessment of the danger of drugs, and builds on the approach to this issue developed in earlier publications but covers more parameters of harm and more drugs, as well as using the delphic approach, with a range of experts. The system is rigorous and transparent, and involves a formal, quantitative assessment of several aspects of harm. . . . We believe that our system could be developed to aid in decision-making by regulatory bodies—eg. The UK's Advisory Council on the Misuse of Drugs and the European Medicines Evaluation Agency—to provide an evidence-based approach to drug classification." (Nutt et al. 2007, 1052)

They suggest a new system of rating drugs based upon their harmfulness, as opposed to the current UK Misuse of Drugs Act of 1971. This act has drugs sorted into three classes, A, B, and C, with Class A being the most harmful and Class C being the least harmful. Although cannabis is of this writing Class B (having within the last year having been moved from Class C back up to Class B) this study concludes cannabis, given a thorough assessment of its harmfulness relative to 19 other drugs, should be Class C. Two independent groups of experts rated the drugs, one a national group of consultant psychiatrists considered specialists in addiction, the other group of experts one of a "wider spread of expertise" regarding addiction (e.g., chemistry, pharmacology, forensic science, legal and police services).

A major finding of this study is that cannabis is properly classified "C" in light of the UK system of classification into class A, B, and C, from most to least harmful. Nutt et al. criticize the current UK as falsely implying the ranking is based upon the relative harmfulness of the drugs. The study shows that the schedules used are not based on relative harmfulness, given expert responses. "Neither the rank ordering of drugs nor their segregation into groups in the Misuse of Drugs Act classification is supported by the more complete assessment of harm described here" (Nutt et al. 2007, 1051). In defining the "harmfulness" of a drug, Nutt et al. propose three main factors, and divide these three into three sub-classes. The first factor is physical harm caused by the drug (i.e., damage to organs or system, physiological functions) with three facets of physical harm being acute physical harm, chronic physical harm, and harms associated with intravenous drug use. The second factor is dependence, including a consideration of short-term and long-term dependence, withdrawal symptoms, with three facets of dependence, including the intensity of pleasure, psychological dependence and physical dependence. The third factor considered is social harms, including three facets of intoxication, other social harms, and health-care costs.

They point out that "if a three-category classification were to be retained, one possible interpretation of our findings is that drugs with harm scores equal to that of alcohol and above might be class A, cannabis and those below might be class C" (Nutt et al. 2007, 1051). In their ranking, this would have Class A include heroin, cocaine, barbiturates, street methadone, and alcohol; Class B include ketamine, benzodiazepines, amphetamine, tobacco, and buprenorphine; and class C include cannabis, solvents, 4-MTA, LSD, methylphenidate, anabolic steroids, GHB, ecstasy, alkyl nitrites, and khat. They also point out quite bluntly that "We saw no clear distinction between socially acceptable and illicit substances" (Nutt et al. 2007, 1052). This study in the UK strongly implies that the same move of cannabis from Schedule I to another schedule, or to making it a legally available recreational drug as is currently the case with alcohol, is strongly suggested.

Notes

1. Human beings have made and consumed wine for many thousands of years, the primary intoxicant to be considered in an Old Testament consideration of intoxication. Chapter 9 will consider the proper use of wine from an Old Testament perspective.

2. A second text I draw on is Paul Gahlinger, *Illegal Drugs: A Complete Guide to Their History, Chemistry, Use, and Abuse* (New: Plume, 2004). This text provides ample information and explanation of drugs from a variety of disciplinary perspectives, especially strong in the area of pharmacology and of the various drugs representing the various "types" discussed.

3. "Normal" at least for the purposes of being able to indicate an extreme lack or extremely high level of dopamine in any particular individual's brain.

4. The relevance of alcohol in this work will be that it is a legal recreational drug and therefore sets a precedent on the amount of "danger" society is willing to tolerate in acknowledgement of the right of adult citizens to consume alcohol. For the purposes of this chapter, however, the primary focus will be on the pharmacological nature of alcohol and also the effects of alcohol on the body.

5. The alcohol-related emergency room visit is one of congestive heart failure and very serious health conditions related to a "fat and fibrous" heart. Later, in light of cannabis use, there will also be reported emergency room visits, but these will be shown to be largely anxiety experienced by naïve users of cannabis, and in contrast to alcoholics with CHF seems hardly a medical problem at all.

6. Also, this is indirectly relevant to the gateway drug argument, claiming cannabis use causes heroin use.

7. "The stimulation potency of Ritalin lies between that of caffeine and amphetamine" (Hanson, Venturelli, and Fleckenstein 2002, 274).

2

Experienced and Therapeutic Effects of Cannabis Use

> The age distribution of marijuana users among the general population contrasts with that of medical marijuana users. Marijuana use generally declines sharply after the age of 34 years, whereas medical marijuana users tend to be over 35. That raises the question of what, if any, relationship exists between abuse and medical use of marijuana; however, no studies reported in the scientific literature have addressed this question. (Joy, Watson, and Benson 1999, 92–93)

> The age group reporting the highest lifetime use was 26- to 34-year-olds (47.9 percent). For past-year and past-month usage, 18- to 25-year-olds reported the highest use. Marijuana use sharply dropped in the 35 and older age group across all usage periods (lifetime 29.4 percent, past year 4.1 percent, and past month 2.5 percent). (Hanson, Venturelli, and Fleckenstein 2002, 368–369)

THE SHARP DECLINE IN MARIJUANA USE after age 35, coupled with the highest incidence of recent use reported in the 18–25-year-old age group, characterizes recreational cannabis users as primarily young adults. Medical marijuana users tend to be older, suggesting motivations and meanings for use different than those for young adults.

In this chapter I focus on the most commonly experienced effects of cannabis use, various motivations for using cannabis, and then various therapeutic effects of cannabis use. By first presenting the experienced effects, I attempt to avoid moral characterizations of the users and instead focus on describing the experience of cannabis users. The experienced effects suggest the therapeutic effects to be presented last. Listing several illnesses and diseases for which cannabis has been shown to have therapeutic benefits, as well as listing illnesses and diseases for which there is strong potential for therapeutic uses, I move into a consideration of the way cannabis is therapeutic for those suffering from various types of disease.

Most Commonly Experienced Effects by Regular Users

Bob Green, David Kavanagh, and Ross Young, in "Being Stoned: A Review of Self-reported Cannabis Effects," examine the frequency of self-reported cannabis effects so as to more rigorously identify effects that may contribute to continued cannabis use as well as to discuss factors that may explain the variation in self-reported effects. Consider their general yet comprehensive results citing effects most commonly experienced by users of cannabis:

TABLE 2.1
Most Commonly Experienced Effects of Cannabis Use

	Percentage	*Number Surveyed*
Time slows (vs. goes faster):	96.3	327
Appetite	90.9	372
Relaxation	90.7	3,197
Concentration	85.9	177
Thinking better (vs. confusion)	84.2	177
Goes to sleep easily	83.3	150
Talkativeness	82.7	295
Laughter and giggling	82	372
Dry mouth and throat	79.8	272
Sexual pleasure	73.5	377
Floating sensation	69.2	295
Sociability	68.4	3,010
Drowsy	62.9	2,913
Creativity	54.3	2,760
Memory	51.9	295
Paranoia	51.4	2,708
Sexual arousal	51.3	2,808
Anxiety	40.4	2,737
Depressed	27.4	3,084
Dizziness	24.6	2,658
Hallucinations/visions	19.8	3,082
Irritability	7.7	2,855

(Green, Kavanagh, and Young 2003, 454)

Most subjects report time slowing, a consistently cited effect of cannabis use throughout the literature; also increase in appetite and relaxation, each reported by over 90 percent of those surveyed. Relaxation is arguably the primary effect of cannabis use. Increase in appetite (what is referred to by recreational users specifically as "having the munchies") is also quite non-controversial throughout the literature on the experienced effects of cannabis use. Note also that approximately half of subjects surveyed report an increase in creativity, sociability, and memory, morally neutral effects which can be valued but not necessarily valued. "Anxiety" was reported by 40.4 percent, depression by 27.4 percent, dizziness by 24.6 percent, hallucinations/visions by 19.8 percent, and irritability by 7.7 percent of those surveyed. These responses indicate those for whom cannabis would not likely be a drug of preference. It should also be noted at this point that it is therefore not likely that the entirety of the United States will "go to pot" upon the legalization of cannabis in the United States, as a quarter to a half of those using cannabis (in this study) have what seem to be negative or undesirable effects.

Green, Kavanagh, and Young observe 9 of 10 cannabis users experience "slowed time perception": "Slowed time perception, increased appetite and increased relaxation were endorsed by over 90 percent of cannabis users in studies which included these items" (Green, Kavanagh, and Young 2003, 455). They also observe that the most frequently reported effect cited in studies using a format of open-ended questions has been "'enhanced relaxation' (Berke, 1974), 'more relaxed' (Goode, 1970), and 'relaxation' (Atha, 1998)" (Green, Kavanagh, and Young 2003, 455). They also explain that contextual factors influence effects of cannabis use. The drug itself, neurologically, does not produce the same effect every time as would other drug types (sedatives, narcotics, or stimulants). This helps explain the characterization of cannabis by some as an "active placebo." As a placebo itself is an inert substance with regards to some specific individual and disease, and "active" indicating that several chemical components of cannabis do in fact have neurological effects and are "psychoactive," the experience differs depending upon "contextual factors" and expectations, the mind-set, of the user. Here one example of a contextual factor is given, distinguishing between solitary use and use with others in a group situation:

> Contextual factors have also been reported as influencing cannabis effects. Study participants who smoked cannabis in a small group of four rated the effects differently to when they smoked alone. Participants who smoked alone reported a 'relaxed, slightly drowsy, undramatic' state, whereas in the group situation,

> reported 'elation, euphoria, uncontrolled laughter, and a marked *lack* of sedation'. (Green, Kavanagh, and Young 2003, 457)

Green, Kavanagh and Young also interestingly point out a dispute over whether euphoria is an *active* or *passive* experience. It is interesting to me as a philosopher as to why exactly this distinction is one worth arguing over. Perhaps this helps to elucidate Weil and Rosen's description of cannabis (from chapter 1) as neither and both depressant and stimulant.

> The ambiguity concerning whether euphoria is an elevated mood or a feeling of well-being is highlighted in a study of words describing emotions. In this study 58 coders did not agree whether euphoria was an active or a passive experience. The literature on what constitutes euphoria is sparse, and the few authors who discuss euphoria in detail describe the ambiguity associated with use of the term.
>
> Irrespective of method, relaxation was the effect most frequently reported by cannabis users in the naturalistic studies. (Green, Kavanagh, and Young 2003, 457)

And just as they point out the disagreement as to whether "euphoria" is an active or passive phenomenon, "cognitive impairments" is shown to be a similarly disputed term:

> The self-reported improvement in thinking and creativity is also of interest, given research linking cannabis to subtle cognitive impairments. It is possible, however, that some of these very impairments are considered as positive by cannabis users (e.g. less focused attention and attending to stimuli normally considered irrelevant). (Green, Kavanagh, and Young 2003, 458)

Pollen provides a revealing description of cannabis intoxication as an "intensification of all the senses":

> All those who write about cannabis' effect on consciousness speak of the changes in perceptions they experience, and specifically of an intensification of all the senses. Common foods taste better, familiar music is suddenly sublime, sexual touch revelatory. Scientists who've studied the phenomenon can find no quantifiable change in the visual, auditory, or tactile acuity of subjects high on marijuana, yet these people invariably report seeing, and hearing, and tasting things with a new keenness, as if with fresh eyes and ears and taste buds. (Pollen 2001, 168)

And in addition to this experience of keen sensation of ordinary objects, Pollen relates cannabis intoxication to the "romantics" and "transcendentalists" and the desire to experience "wonder":

> It is by temporarily mislaying much of what we already know (or think we know) that cannabis restores a kind of innocence to our perception of the world, and innocence in adults will always flirt with embarrassment. The cannabinoids are molecules with the power to make romantics and transcendentalists of us all. By disabling our moment-by-moment memory, which is ever pulling us off the astounding frontier of the present and throwing us back onto the mapped byways of the past, the cannabinoids open a space for moving nearer to direct experience. By the grace of this forgetting, we temporarily shelve our inherited ways of looking and see things as if for the first time, so that even something as ordinary as ice cream becomes *Ice cream!*
>
> There is another word for this extreme noticing—this sense of first sight unencumbered by knowingness, by the already-been-there and seen-that of the adult mind—and that word, of course, is *wonder.* (Pollen 2001, 168)

This sense of wonder can be used with creative intentions, intentions of greater self-awareness and self-consciousness, and as even a way of comprehending the metaphysics of Plato. Of Plato specifically his notion of the "Forms" and how these eternal Ideas relate to the material/physical world in which we human beings live, consider how cannabis intoxication facilitates such an understanding.[1]

> One of the things certain drugs do to our perceptions is to distance or estrange the objects around us, aestheticizing the most commonplace things until they appear as ideal versions of themselves. Under the spell of cannabis "every object stands more clearly for all of its class," as David Lenson writes in *On Drugs.* "A cup 'looks like' the Platonic Idea of a cup, a landscape looks like a landscape painting, a hamburger stands for all the trillions of hamburgers ever served, and so forth." A psychoactive plant can open a door onto a world of archetypal forms, or so they can appear. (Pollen 2001, 147)

Hall and Solowij provide a fruitful general description of the experienced effects of cannabis intoxication:

> Cannabis produces euphoria and relaxation, perceptual alterations, time distortion, and the intensification of ordinary sensory experiences, such as eating, watching films, and listening to music. When used in a social setting it may produce infectious laughter and talkativeness. Short-term memory and attention, motor skills, reaction time, and skilled activities are impaired while a person is intoxicated. (Hall and Solowij 1998, 1611–1612)

Doweiko further reinforces relaxation as the primary effect of cannabis intoxication and also makes a distinction between two phases of each instance of cannabis use (two general phases mirrored in the use of other psychoactive drugs as well). The first phase is commonly referred to as one of an initial "rush" and then experience of the "high":

> At moderate dosage levels, marijuana brings about a two-phase reaction (Brophy, 1993). The first phase begins shortly after the drug enters the bloodstream, when the individual experiences a period of mild anxiety, followed by a sense of well-being or euphoria and a sense of relaxation and friendliness (Kaplan & Sadock, 1990; Kaplan, Sadock, & Grebb, 1994). These subjective effects are consistent with the known physical effects of marijuana. (Doweiko 1996, 123)

Doweiko also reinforces several points about cannabis intoxication. These include the relevance of contextual factors for the specific effects experienced by the user, heightened self-awareness, the experience of what in common vernacular are called "pipe dreams," and the second major phase of cannabis intoxication, of sedation:

> As with many drugs of abuse, the individual's *expectations* will influence how he or she interprets the effects of marijuana. Marijuana users tend to anticipate that the drug will (1) impair cognitive function as well as the user's behavior, (2) help the user relax, (3) help the user interact socially and enhance sexual function, (4) enhance creative abilities and alter perception, (5) bring with it some negative effects, and (6) bring about a sense of food "craving" (Schafer and Brown, 1991).
>
> Individuals who are intoxicated on marijuana report an altered sense of time as well as mood swings (Kaplan, Sadock, & Grebb, 1994) and feelings of well-being and happiness (Abood & Martin, 1992). Marijuana also seems to bring about a splitting of consciousness, in which users may experience the sensation of observing themselves while under the influence of the drug (Kaplan, Sadock, & Grebb, 1994; Grinspoon & Bakalar, 1992).
>
> Marijuana users often report a sense of being on the threshold of a significant personal insight but are unable to put this insight into words. These reported drug-related insights seem to come about during the first phase of the marijuana reaction. The second phase of the marijuana experience begins when the individual becomes sleepy, which takes place following the acute intoxication phase (Brophy, 1993; Abood & Martin, 1992). (Doweiko 1996, 123)

The two general phases of cannabis use (for the regular user) are generally of relaxation and then of sleepiness, with the user's expectations playing a definitive role in how those effects are experienced. Increased self-consciousness and perceived sociability, although not harmful or dangerous in and of themselves, will be valued or devalued differently by different people (who live different ways of life). In other words, these and most of the primary effects of cannabis intoxication are harms or benefits only in light of the values and lifestyle of specific individual users.

Rosenthal, Gieringer, and Mikuriya (in the introduction to *Marijuana Medical Handbook: A Guide to Therapeutic Use*) further explain this subjective meaning attributed to the experienced effects:

> Marijuana appeals differently to different people. People who like it often use it to increase the intensity of their senses. They may smoke before eating, listening to music, watching plays or movies, or taking a walk or hike, or while spending time with others or just thinking. Many users report subjective feelings of creativity and inspiration, although these don't always stand up to later, sober analysis. Many devotees report feelings of euphoria, exhilaration, good will, empathy, and religious awe. They say marijuana helps them think about serious matters, to become introspective and spiritual, to get to the essence of things.
>
> People who don't like marijuana complain of anxiety, self-consciousness, paranoia, social withdrawal, irritability, dysphoria, and loss of self-control. They may also find that it interferes with their ability to work, concentrate, and function. (Rosenthal, Gieringer, and Mikuriya 1997, 22)

Some (poets, actors, writers, performers, philosophers, [jazz] musicians) may enjoy and use cannabis to enhance their gifts and abilities, relaxing and intentionally fostering a creative process with cannabis as a part of the larger scene/setting. For others, self-consciousness brings anxiety, a repulsive feeling of losing control, making negative the experience of cannabis intoxication. There are perhaps within these extremes a middle mass of users who take it or leave it (ultimately leaving it after age 35 and perhaps then again using medicinally later in life).

Weil and Rosen insightfully recognize habitual users of cannabis can and do learn to function under its effect and work use into their daily routines, a phenomenon they refer to as "adaptation."[2]

> Adaptation to marijuana enables users to learn to perform well under its influence. Unlike alcohol, it does not invariably depress reflexes and reaction times. People who aren't used to its effects will not be able to drive cars well or do any number of other routines tasks well while stoned. Even experienced users need time to practice a given task under the influence of marijuana in order to bring performance up to normal. Some users feel that marijuana helps them concentrate and enables them to work better, but even they have to learn to adapt to its effects. (Weil and Rosen 2004, 143)

Consider Weil and Rosen also on the distinction between experienced and inexperienced users and experienced effects:

> When people learn to get high on marijuana, their early experiences with it are often quite lively. Everything may strike them as funny, and all sensory experiences

> become novel and interesting. Listening to music, eating, and making love can become more than usually absorbing. Time seems long and drawn out. People sometimes have strange illusions, such as seeing a room expand or feeling as though their legs have become enormously long.
>
> With repeated use, these remarkable effects tend to fade away. Regular users may find that pot makes them relaxed or more sociable without greatly affecting their perceptions or moods. Very heavy users usually feel little from the drug, often smoking it simply out of habit. (Weil and Rosen 2004, 137)

Using "simply out of habit" is an initial way of understanding dependence, the major risk for chronic users and (as will be demonstrated in the Part III Moral Assessment, there articulated as a state of will having one act apart from any desire).

Specifically on "bad reactions" to cannabis use, consider that inexperienced users are likely involved and that such "simple panic reactions" harmlessly wear off hours after use:

> Bad reactions to marijuana are more likely when high doses of strong material are taken in bad settings, especially by inexperienced users. Most are simple panic reactions, easily treated with reassurance that everything will be all right as soon as the drug wears off. The effects of smoking marijuana usually diminish after an hour and disappear after two or three hours. Some people, if they have smoked a lot of pot, feel tired or "fuzzy" the next morning. (Weil and Rosen 2004, 137–38)

Motivations for the Use of Cannabis

Those with any knowledge at all of cannabis debates in the United States will recognize the usual two major motivations for using cannabis, either for "recreational" purposes or for "medicinal" purposes. It seems rather obvious that there are a multitude of other motivations for the use of cannabis in addition to subtle variations of each recreational and therapeutic use. Even if it is easier to divide users up into these two categories simple expediency does not determine the truth of the matter. This section aims to present a comprehensive overview of the myriad of motivations for using cannabis.[3]

First consider Weil and Rosen's list of motivations for people's using drugs (from their chapter 3, "Why People Use Drugs," which includes elaboration on each motivation):

Why people use drugs:

1. Reinforcing religious practices
2. Expanding awareness and exploring the self

3. Treating disease
4. Altering moods[4]
5. Escaping tedium and despair
6. Facilitating and enhancing social interaction
7. Enhancing sensory experience and pleasure
8. Stimulating creativity
9. Improving physical performance
10. Rebellion
11. Going along with the crowd
12. Establishing an identity and getting attention

Again, it is quite difficult to force all of these reasons into one of two categories, medicinal or recreational. Reasons 1 and 2 seem quite positive as they have individuals engaging their highest human faculty of reason and even spirit, beyond mere appetite and passive sensation. Reason 3, "treating disease," of course, is a major reason given for many users (and regular users) of cannabis. Reason 4 is quite general and could be either escape or medicinal use. Reason 5, "escaping tedium and despair," is a motivation involving psychological, cultural, and social factors that should be explored further with the individual. Reason 6, facilitating social interaction, represents the major motivation given by those in the United States who justify the legal and responsible use of alcohol, refers to it as a "social lubricant" and not a drug. This same reason is clearly applicable to cannabis. Reason 7, "enhancing sensory perception and pleasure," is primarily hedonistic. Reasons 8 and 9, "stimulating creativity" and "improving physical performance," are both applicable to cannabis as used by some in their "work," as artists, performers, writers, etc. These reasons do not neatly fit under either medicinal or recreational motivations (not recreational as the use of cannabis here is done in the very process of producing work). Of these reasons, it seems 10–12 are uses of cannabis as using cannabis as a means to acquiring something else rather than primarily for the effects of cannabis itself.

Weil and Rosen astutely question laboratory studies of the effects of drugs outside of their normal context of use, especially when contextual factors clearly influence the effects experienced in using a drug (especially cannabis). They also articulate the common term of "set" (as in "set and setting" of use, or the mind-set and the context of use):

> The laboratory is not the real world, and pharmacology can explain only certain aspects of the complex relationships that human beings have with drugs. When people take drugs in the real world, their experiences are often not what pharmacologists would predict. The reason is that outside the laboratory other factors can completely change the effects of drugs. One such factor is known as

> *set*; set is what a person expects to happen when he or she takes a drug. Expectation is shaped by all of past experience—what a person has heard about the drug read about it, seen of it, thought about it, and wants it to do. Sometimes it is not easy to find out what people expect of a drug because they may not consciously know their real feeling. A boy smoking marijuana for the first time may think that he is eager to have a new experience, whereas unconsciously he may be terrified of losing his mind or getting so stoned that he will never come down. Such unconscious fears can determine reactions to marijuana more than the actual effect of the drug. (Weil and Rosen 2004, 25–26)

To complement Weil and Rosen's list, and to consider an interesting difference of wording essentially the same reasons, Hanson, Venturelli, and Fleckenstein list the following reasons why one may use drugs:

1. Searching for pleasure and using drugs to heighten good feelings.
2. Taking drugs to temporarily relieve stress or tension or provide a temporary escape for people with anxiety.
3. Taking drugs to temporarily forget one's problems and avoid or postpone worries.
4. Viewing certain drugs (such as alcohol, marijuana, and tobacco) as necessary in order to relax after a tension-filled day at work.
5. Taking drugs to fit in with peers, especially when peer pressure is strong during early and late adolescence; seeing drugs as a *rite of passage.*
6. Taking drugs to enhance religious or mystical experiences (very few cultures teach children how to use specific drugs for this purpose).
7. Taking drugs to relieve pain and some symptoms of illness.

They also in the next chapter add as reasons "for enhancing recreational pursuits (such as the popular use of ecstasy at raves and music festivals)" and "to enhance work performance, such as the use of cocaine by stockbrokers, office workers, and lawyers" (Hanson, Venturelli, and Fleckenstein 2002, 38).

As a third list, Gahlinger presents the following "Top Ten Reasons Why People Use Illegal Drugs":

1. To numb the body
2. Recreation
3. To join a social group
4. Social functioning
5. Mind expansion
6. Religion
7. To improve performance

8. To change the body
9. Self-medication
10. Because they are illegal

Note that "recreation" is here its own reason, apart from (among others) "social functioning," "mind expansion," "religion," and "self-medication." "Mind expansion" is a reason distinct from religion and more akin to one's development and exploration of oneself, a goal intrinsically valuable to most if not all philosophers (and more generally those who value rational introspection and intellectual development). This reason is also distinct from recreational as many who are motivated intellectually may find a recreational setting ill-suited to such motivation. It is also distinct from medicinal, as mind expansion and self-development are not "medical conditions." "Mind expansion" seems a distinct motivation, neither recreational nor medicinal, but more similar to (though not synonymous with) religious or spiritual motivations. As such it seems mind-expansion and religious and spiritual uses of cannabis are specific examples of motivations neither recreational nor medicinal. Finally, the term "self-medication" is used (as opposed to "medication"). It is likely that many users of cannabis do not reveal their use to their physicians, who themselves are largely unaware of the medicinal benefits of cannabis use. It seems self-medication could reveal other more basic motivations for use.

Gahlinger uniquely presents in contrast the "Top Ten Reasons Why People Do *Not* Use Illegal Drugs":

1. Social agreement
2. Lack of purity
3. Toxicity
4. Lack of knowledge
5. Lack of supervision
6. Lack of availability
7. Impaired performance
8. Fear of addiction
9. Expense
10. Because they are illegal (Gahlinger 2004, 104–5)

When these reasons are applied to cannabis specifically reasons 1–9 are rejected by many regular users of cannabis. Reason 10, because it is illegal, is especially striking in the narratives of "otherwise law-abiding citizens" who use cannabis to alleviate their suffering. These users commonly and especially regret having to use cannabis, given it is against the law. However, they also come to find the first nine reasons simply irrational. These reasons once relinquished can leave only the last, because it is illegal. At that point it can seem illogical if not unfair to abide by a law simply because it is the law.[5]

Therapeutic Effects of Cannabis Use

> Cannabis, or marijuana, has a long history of medical use in India and the Middle East as an analgesic, anticonvulsant, antispasmodic, antiemetic and hypnotic. It was used for medical purposes in Europe and the US in the 19th century but was supplanted in the early 20th century by pharmaceutical opiates, aspirin (acetylsalicylic acid), choral hydrate and the barbiturates, which could be given in standardized doses to produce more dependable effects. International drug control agreements in the 20th century also discouraged medical use of cannabis by classifying it as a "narcotic" drug with no known medical use. (Hall and Degenhardt 2003, 689)

The most basic statement of the Scientific Reality definition of cannabis is of its 483 chemical compounds. Consider the following breakdown of these chemical compounds of cannabis:

Cannabinoids 66
Nitrogenous compounds 27
Amino Acids 18
Proteins, glycoproteins, and enzymes 11
Sugars and related compounds 34
Hydrocarbons 50
Simple Alcohols 7
Simple aldehydes 12
Simple ketones 13
Simple acids 21
Fatty acids 22
Simple esters and lactones 13
Steroids 11
Terpenes 120
Noncannabinoid phenols 25
Flavonoids 21
Vitamins 1
Pigments 2
Elements 9
TOTAL: 483 (ElSohly 2002, 28)

And consider that although the cannabis plant includes these 483 compounds, the only significantly psychoactive one of the 66 cannabinoids is "THC":

> The marihuana plant contains more than 460 known compounds, of which more than 60 have the 21-carbon structure typical of cannabinoids. The only cannabinoid that is both highly psychoactive and present in large amounts, usually 1–5 percent by weight, is (-)3, 4-trans-delta-1-tetrahydrocannabinol, also known as delta-1-THC, delta-9-THC, or simply THC. (Grinspoon and Bakalar 1997, 2)

Quite relevant to understanding the therapeutic superiority of cannabis over isolated synthetic THC is McPartland and Russo's "Cannabis and Cannabis Extracts: Greater Than the Sum of Their Parts?" Here elaborated upon are both various therapeutic effects of chemical compounds of cannabis *other than THC* and the recognition of the *synergy* involved among these various chemical compounds of the cannabis plant. It is crucial to appreciate synergy in order to understand the therapeutic superiority of cannabis plant material over synthetic THC. One significant example of the relevance of synergy to consider is that although there are carcinogenic elements of cannabis smoke, there are also chemicals such as CBD in cannabis that counteract these effects (one theory explaining the lack of evidence for lung cancer in cannabis-only smokers). McPartland and Russo explain there are two main advantages of "polypharmaceutical herbs" over single-ingredient synthetic drugs (e.g., synthetic THC). First, "therapeutic effects of the primary active ingredients in herbs may be synergized by other compounds" and second, "side effects of the primary active ingredients in herbs may be mitigated by other compounds" (McPartland and Russo 2002, 104). Going beyond THC, McPartland and Russo present information about six other cannabinoids, over twelve terpenoids, three flavonoids, and one phytosterol. Of cannabidiol (CBD), presented are sedative properties, reduction of anxiety and other unpleasant psychological side effects provoked by pure THC, antipsychotic benefits, increased dopamine activity, serotonin uptake inhibitor, enhancer of norepinephrine activity, protection of neurons from glutamate toxicity, antioxidant, reduces hippocampal Ach release (which correlates with loss of short-term memory), and an anti-convulsant "on par with phenytoin" (known as "dilantin," a standard antiepileptic drug). They also explain "The CBD in cannabis smoke may explain why inhaling it causes less airway irritation and inflammation than inhalation of pure THC (Tashkin et al. 1977)" (McPartland and Russo 2002, 106). As therapeutic for asthma, CBD "blocks lipoxygenase (the enzyme that produces asthma-provoking leukotrienes)" (McPartland and Russo 2002, 107). Emphasized elsewhere by Russo is that . . .

> cannabidiol stimulates vanilloid receptors (VR1) with similar efficacy to capsaicin, and inhibits uptake of the endocannabinoid anandamide (AEA), and weakly inhibits its hydrolysis (Bisogno et al. 2001). These new findings have important implications in elucidating the pain-relieving and anti-inflammatory effects of CBD. In a manner of interpretation, CBD may be considered the first clinical agent that modulates endocannabinoid function. (Russo 2003, 16, 18)

Of cannabinol (CBN), the "degradation product of THC," it enhances the production of testicular testosterone, has anti-convulsant activity, anti-inflammatory activity, and with a "three-fold greater affinity for CB_2 receptors than does THC, possibly affects cells of the immune system" (McPartland and Russo 2002, 107). Cannabichromene (CBC) decreases inflammation, has analgesic effects, and exhibits strong antibacterial activity and mild antifungal activity (McPartland and Russo 2002, 108). Cannabigerol (CBG) is present only in minor amounts, inhibits GABA uptake more effectively than CBD and THC, acts as an analgesic, blocks lipoxygenase, and inhibits the growth of human oral epitheloid carcinoma cells (McPartland and Russo 2002, 108). Tetrahydrocannabivarin (THCV) is predominant in cannabis *indica* and *afghanica* varieties of cannabis and may be clinically effective in migraine treatment (McPartland and Russo 2002, 109). They also explain the unique smell of cannabis to be attributed to the terpenoids that make up over 100 of the compounds of cannabis (McPartland and Russo 2002, 109).

> Terpenoids may also act on other receptors and neurotransmitters. Some terpenoids act as serotonin uptake inhibitors (as does Prozac), enhance norepinephrine activity (as do tricyclic antidepressants), increase dopamine activity (as do monoamine oxidase inhibitors and bupropion), and augment GABA (as do baclofen and the benzodiazepines). Recently, strong serotonin activity at the 5-HT1A and 5-HT2A receptors has been demonstrated (Russo et al. 2000; Russo 2001) that may support synergistic contributions of terpenoids of cannabis-mediated pain and mood effects. (McPartland and Russo 2002, 110)

Consider also of other terpenoids: myrcene is the most abundant terpenoid produced by cannabis and also occurs in high concentrations in hops and acts as a potent analgesic (McPartland and Russo 2002, 114). Limonene, a major constituent of citrus rinds, is the second most common terpenoid in cannabis. In one study, it "blocks the carcinogenesis induced by benz(alpha)anthracene (Crowell 1999), a component of the 'tar' generated by the combustion of herbal cannabis. Thus, this terpenoid may reduce the harm caused by inhaling cannabis smoke. Limonene blocks carcinogenesis by multiple mechanisms" (McPartland and Russo 2002, 116). Another study of other tepenoids found some deeply sedating, also that combinations of these terpenoids "are synergistic in their sedative effects. These terpenoids may mitigate the anxiety provoked by pure THC. Inhalation of such terpenoids also provides antidepressant effects (Komori et al 1995)" (McPartland and Russo 2002, 116). McPartland and Russo also explain that "reducing anxiety and depression will improve immune function via the neuroendocrine system, by damping down the hypothalamic-pituitary-adrenal (HPA) axis. Hence, inhalation of terpenoids reduces the secretion of HPA stress hormones" McPartland and Russo 2002, 116). Finally, consider that "pulegone, a monocyclic monoterpenoid, is a minor constituent of cannabis (Turner et al. 1980). Higher concentrations of pulegone are found in rosemary (Rosmarinus officinalis), 'the herb of remembrance.' Pulegone may alleviate a major side effect of THC—loss of short-term memory consolidation. THC causes acetylcholine (Ach) deficits in the hippocampus. Hippocampal Ach deficits are also seen in people with Alzheimer's disease" (McPartland and Russo 2002, 117). Therapeutically, consider that various strains of cannabis will differ in the amount of each of the 483 chemical compounds. Cannabis medicine will develop by measuring and studying the effects of various strains of cannabis as well as with various combinations and amounts of the 483 chemical compounds so as to match the most effective of these with various diseases.

Hall, Christie, and Currow (2005) indicate the locations of CB_1 and CB_2 receptors explain the effectiveness of cannabis for specific symptoms and diseases:

> The distribution of CB_1 and CB_2 in the brain, immune system, and reproductive tissues is consistent with many therapeutic and recreational effects of cannabis. CB_1 is mostly concentrated in brain systems involved in mood control, motor function, memory, food intake, pain, immune function, and reproductive functions. A high density of CB_1 in the basal ganglia and cerebellum explains why cannabinoids interfere with coordinated movement. The absence of cannabinoid receptors in the lower brainstem explains why high doses of THC are rarely lethal. (Hall, Christie, and Currow 2005, 36)

Most basic to understanding therapeutic use of cannabis is the fact that the CB_1 receptors specifically are mostly concentrated in brain systems correlated with symptoms of many chronic and debilitating diseases.[6]

> Receptors for anandamide (and THC) are located mainly in the cerebral cortex and in the basal ganglia and cerebellum, parts of the brain associated with body movements. The receptors in the cortex may explain the cognitive effects of cannabis, and those found in the basal ganglia and cerebellum may account for its effects on muscle spasms and other body movement disorders. (Grinspoon and Bakalar 1997, 3)

The IOM (1999) similarly suggests therapeutic effects given the neurological location of cannabis receptors in the brain:

> Cannabinoid receptors are particularly abundant in some areas of the brain. The normal biology and behavior associated with these brain areas are consistent with the behavior effects produced by cannabinoids. . . . The highest receptor density is found in cells of the basal ganglia that project locally and to other brain regions. These cells include the substantia nigra pars reticulate, entopeduncular nucleus, and globus pallidus, regions that are generally involved in coordinating body movements. Patients with Parkinson's or Huntington's disease tend to have impaired functions in these regions.
>
> CB_1 receptors are also abundant in the putamen, part of the relay system within the basal ganglia that regulates body movements; the cerebellum, which coordinates body movements; the hippocampus, which is involved in learning, memory, and response to stress; and the cerebral cortex, which is concerned with the integration of higher cognitive functions. (Joy, Watson, and Benson 1999, 48–49)

And reiterating why the location of the cannabinoid receptors in the basal ganglia has implications for treating movement disorders, Muller-Vahl et al. explain:

> Central cannabinoid receptors are densely located in the output nuclei of the basal ganglia. Cannabinoids have been found to modulate neurotransmission in the basal ganglia by increasing GABAergic transmission, inhibiting glutamate release, and affecting dopaminergic uptake. Furthermore, evidence suggests that an endogenous cannabinoid tone participates in the control of movement. Therefore, it has been suggested that the central cannabinoid system is involved in the regulation of motor activity and might play a role in the pathophysiology of movement disorders. (Muller-Vahl et al. 2002, 211)

Hanson, Venturelli, and Fleckenstein elaborate on the cerebral cortex and specifically the "associational areas":

> a layer of gray matter made up of nerves and supporting cells that almost completely surrounds the rest of the brain and lies immediately under the skull. It is responsible for receiving sensory input, interpreting incoming information, and initiating voluntary motor behavior . . . the most developed part of the cortex is called the *associative cortex.* The associative areas of the brain do not directly receive input from the environment nor do they directly initiate output to the muscles or the glands. Instead, these cortical areas may store memories, control complex behaviors, and help process information. (Hanson, Venturelli, and Fleckenstein 2002, 124)

They further explain that because of the basal ganglia involvement of dopamine, cannabis may be an effective treatment for neurodegenerative diseases, keeping the "dopaminergic" neurons functioning thereby keeping intact physical and psychological abilities. Cannabis would be therapeutic in preserving the functioning of neurons which produce neurotransmitters dopamine and Ach. The location of the endocannabinoids

> are the primary centers for involuntary and fine-tuning of motor functions involving, for example, posture and muscle tone. Two important neurotransmitters in the basal ganglia are dopamine and Ach. Damage to neurons in this area may cause *Parkinson's disease*, the progressive yet selective degeneration of the main dopaminergic neurons in the basal ganglia. (Hanson, Venturelli, and Fleckenstein 2002, 123)

On the potential for, in addition to slowing or stopping neurodegeneration, also improving the state of the brain by "enhancing the metabolism of dopamine," Green, Kavanagh, and Young (2003) begin their consideration of reported effects of cannabis by actual users with a consideration of *the neurology* of cannabis. There they relevantly explain:

> Cannabinoids, the active constituents of cannabis have been found to interact with specific G protein-coupled brain receptors, while endogenous ligands have been identified that bind cannabinoid receptors in the brain, functioning as neurotransmitters or neuromodulators. Cannabinoids have been also described as enhancing dopamine synthesis, release and turnover as well as the inhibition of dopamine reuptake in reward-relevant brain loci, activating the reward/reinforcement circuits of the mammalian brain. (Green, Kavanagh, and Young 2003, 453–54)

Of the several well-researched and articulated books describing the therapeutic uses of cannabis, one of the most outstanding is *Marihuana: The Forbidden Medicine* (1997) by Lester Grinspoon and James Bakalar. Grinspoon is an expert on the therapeutic effectiveness of cannabis after himself becoming convinced (or as he puts it, "converted") during his own rigorous research of cannabis use in the late 1960s culminating in his 1971 effort, *Marijuana Reconsidered.* After over thirty years of continuing research, this second edition (1997) is a concise and comprehensive presentation of various case studies of actual patients who describe in detail the therapeutic effects of cannabis. A recurring theme related throughout these narratives is the standard of care medications (assuming there are any for a particular disease) are ineffective or the standard of care medications come with unbearable side effects. Most stories of these otherwise law-abiding citizens have them try cannabis and experience undeniable relief. Cannabis is thereafter regularly used with clearly demonstrable therapeutic effectiveness.

Again the current U.S. federal law has cannabis a Schedule I drug, which means three things:

A. Cannabis has a high potential for abuse.
B. has no currently accepted medical use in treatment in the United States.
C. There is a lack of accepted safety for use of cannabis under medical supervision.

The first criterion of "abuse" will be considered in the next chapter as defined by the DSM-IV-TR. One main element there is "recurrent and significant adverse consequences related to the repeated use of substances." It seems the *medicinal* use of cannabis results in positive rather than adverse consequences. The second and third criteria applied to cannabis are especially relevant in this section. In a legal sense, these second and third criteria will be true as long as there is a federal law forbidding physicians to recommend or prescribe cannabis. In other words, it does not matter whether cannabis can be shown to have therapeutic effects. The U.S. federal government defines "accepted medical use" and "accepted safety" and simply finds that neither can be said of medicinal use of cannabis.

The key term of the part B criterion is "currently accepted," obviously inviting the question, "By whom?" Many procure cannabis through the currently vibrant U.S. black market in cannabis and as actual users attest to "currently accepting" cannabis in treating their diseases (including the several conditions to be considered in this chapter). Not only would a majority of oncologists prescribe cannabis were it legally permitted, the American College of Physicians is the largest medical specialty organization and second-largest physicians group in the United States. In 2008 it put forth a position paper to (among other things) re-consider and re-Schedule cannabis.[7] In the UK cannabis has already been re-classified to the lowest of classes, Class C (only to recently be rescheduled in Class B). These and many credible others "currently accept" medical effects of cannabis use.

Criterion C of Schedule I, "lack of accepted safety" under "medical supervision," is also ill-suited to the Scientific Reality of cannabis use. Given that no one has ever died from using cannabis and it is one of the least toxic substances a human being could possibly use, it would be challenging to articulate the meaning of "safety" as used here in a way rendering cannabis "unsafe." Such an articulation would logically also rule as even more dangerous alcohol, tobacco, valium, and most types of drugs currently Schedule II or lower. More importantly, these are *medicinal* users of cannabis. They measure the difference of their quality of life and state of their pain and suffering with cannabis versus without cannabis and consistently testify to relief of symptoms and added quality of life with cannabis.[8] Patients with various different diseases make different risk/benefit analyses regarding the effects of cannabis use so that the dangers that do exist as a result of cannabis use are outweighed by the benefits of using cannabis. It is not clear why medical supervision would be required for cannabis use any more than alcohol users should have a signed note as permission from their physicians allowing them to consume alcohol. If "medical supervision" means at least informing one's physician of one's cannabis use, then practically speaking, the legalization and decriminalization of cannabis use will better make this happen. Currently, without trust in one's physician, aware of the federal government criminalization of cannabis use, patients are not likely to reveal their use let alone the pattern and way of their using cannabis.[9] Still, medical supervision seems unnecessary. Cannabis is currently the most frequently used illicit drug in the United States, and there are no apparent medical problems resulting from cannabis use (e.g., a wave of people with diseases caused by cannabis use), it seems medical supervision is not necessary for safety reasons.

The Scientific Reality of cannabis is one based in neurology. It finds most compelling as evidence for the proposed medical uses of cannabis the location of the CB_1 and CB_2 receptors in the brain, the human behaviors correlated with those brain areas, and possible therapeutic applications of cannabis for those suffering from diseases involving these brain areas. Primary brain locations are the basal ganglia, substantia nigra pars reticulate (Parkinson's Disease, Hodgkin's Disease, generally coordinating bodily movements), hippocampus (learning, memory, response to stress), putamen.

To give a sense of just how broad and lengthy a list of the therapeutic effects for which cannabis is effective, consider that, "In examinations of 2,480 California patients, Dr. Tod Mikuriya recorded over 250 distinct ICD-9 indications, all of them for chronic conditions resisting conventional pharmacotherapy (Gieringer 2002)" (Gieringer 2003, 63).

Grinspoon and Bakalar present a variety of ailments for which cannabis has proven effective. Again, theirs is a presentation of quite compelling first-hand accounts of actual medicinal users of cannabis. The book concludes with three sections: "In Defense of Anecdotal Evidence," "Weighing the Risks," and "The Once and Future Medicine." In these concluding sections they argue for the scientific credibility of anecdotal evidence as "proof" of therapeutic effectiveness so as to essentially conclude that criterion B ("no accepted therapeutic use") has been shown to be falsely applied to cannabis (thereby indicating a Schedule change is merited for cannabis). For my purposes in this chapter, I use the information provided by Grinspoon and Bakalar along with that of other researchers as strong evidence for the therapeutic effectiveness of cannabis use as per the Scientific Reality of cannabis use.[10]

Grinspoon and Bakalar provide in their table of contents those diseases for which they present actual patient accounts of the effectiveness of cannabis use:

undergoing cancer chemotherapy,
HIV/AIDS symptoms,
epilepsy,
multiple sclerosis,
quadriplegia/paraplegia,
chronic pain,
migraine,
Rheumatic Disorders,
Pruritis,
Premenstrual Syndrome,
Menstrual Cramps,
Labor Pains,
Depression and Other Mood Disorders.

In addition to these they also list illnesses and diseases under the heading of "Less Common Medical Uses":

Asthma,
Insomnia,
Other Causes of Severe Nausea,
Antimicrobial Effects,
Topical Anesthetic Effects,
Antitumor Effects,
Dystonias,
Adults Attention Deficit Disorder,
Schizophrenia,
Systemic Sclerosis (Scleroderma),
Crohn's Disease,
Diabetic Gastroparesis,
Pseudotumor Cerebri,
Tinnitus,
Violence,
Post-Traumatic Stress Disorder,
Phantom Limb Pain,
Alcoholism and Other Addictions,
Terminal Illness.

In addition to various therapeutic applications of cannabis for currently recognized diseases, Russo hypothesizes the existence of a new disease category, what he calls "clinical endocannabinoid deficiency (CECD). The diagnosis of CECD is primarily suggested to explain therapeutic benefits for migraine, fibromyalgia, irritable bowel syndrome" (Russo, 2004a). Russo suggests employing a basic principle of neurology to support his hypothesis of this new disease category:

> For each neurotransmitter system there are pathological conditions attributable to its deficiency: dementia in Alzheimer disease due to loss of acetylcholine activity, Parkinsonism due to dopamine deficiency, depression secondary to lowered levels of serotonin, norepinephrine or other amines, etc. Should the situation be any different for the endocannabinoid system, whose receptor density is in fact greater than many of the others? (Russo 2004a, 32)

Russo also suggests potential therapeutic usefulness for spasmodic disorder and spasticity, causalgia, allodynia, phantom limp pain, glaucoma, asthma, cystic fibrosis, biopolar disorder, and PTSD. And proposing an alternative theory on depression, he suggests "deficiencies of serotonin and norepinephrine may be insufficient explanations of the disorder, but rather, innate neuroplasticity is inherently impaired and requires specific treatment. Cannabinoids certainly seem to enhance that plasticity with their neuroprotective abilities" Russo 2004a, 36).

As I said to begin chapter 1, there is currently a neurological revolution happening and this can be seen in recent blossoming of the numerous possibilities for cannabis research and therapy. *Chemistry and Biodiversity* recently dedicated an entire issue to cannabinoids. It begins with an editorial introduction which, "to illustrate the exceptional blooming of the research around cannabis and endocannabinoids," presents the results of a performed search of the Web of Science and Pubmed. Here revealed is that the current decade will see the most publications ever on cannabis. Consider that from 1940–1949 one article cited on cannabis, 1950–1959 there were 40 articles, 1960–1969 there were 399 articles, 1970–1979 there were 3,090 articles, 1980–1989 there were 1,390 articles, 1990–1999 there were 1,032 articles, and 2000–2007 there were 2,969 articles.[11]

As in the United States cannabis is essentially a Schedule I drug and practically unavailable for research purposes, researchers are forced to work with what they have and to creatively attempt to examine CB_1, CB_2 receptors, the naturally occurring anadimide and other endocannabinoids, synthetic THC, etc. Looking in from the outside, it seems researchers are pounding up against a wall behind which would exist a whole new understanding and appreciation of the various therapeutic uses of cannabis (this "wall" is the Social Reality of cannabis use).

Rather than accounting for the entirety of research on therapeutic uses of cannabis, I simply present a general account of the type of relief described by those suffering from several diseases (including those already recognized through acknowledgement of synthetic cannabinoids as Schedule II drugs for cancer chemotherapy patients, AIDS wasting syndrome patients). I attempt to highlight several basic points in light of the diseases listed and encourage the reader to delve into the growing literature regarding those therapies listed. The symptoms of diseases are considered in a way which compliments effects described in Section 1 (experience of relaxation, increased appetite, e.g.) to those symptoms experienced by patients (e.g., depression, lack of appetite).

Cancer Chemotherapy: Cannabis Reduces Nausea and Vomiting

> But the most common and for many patients the most troublesome side effect of these drugs is profound nausea and vomiting. Retching (dry heaves) may last for hours or even days after each treatment, followed by days and even weeks of nausea. Patients may break bones or rupture the esophagus while vomiting. The sense of loss of control can be emotionally devastating. Furthermore, many patients eat almost nothing because they cannot stand the sight or smell of food. As they lose weight and strength, they find it more and more difficult to sustain the will to live. (Grinspoon and Bakalar 1997, 24)

> If nausea and vomiting cannot be controlled, the patient's complaints may cause doctors to lower the dose and jeopardize the effectiveness of the therapy. For many patients, the side effects of chemotherapy seem worse than the cancer itself, and they discontinue treatment, not only to eliminate the discomfort, but also to regain control over their lives. (Grinspoon and Bakalar 1997, 24)

Chemotherapy patients who would alleviate nausea and vomiting through the use of cannabis could perhaps endure and complete treatment were they legally able. The use of cannabis in treating various effects of chemotherapy is well-attested to and an effect for which the U.S. federal government itself acknowledges in its Compassionate Use IND program as well as in its current recognition of synthetic THC as a legitimate treatment for nausea and vomiting for cancer chemotherapy patients.

> In 1985 the Food and Drug Administration (FDA) of the United States approved Marinol Capsules, which contain synthetic dronabinol (2.5 mg, 5 mg or 10mg), for nausea and vomiting associated with cancer chemotherapy in patients that had failed to respond adequately to conventional anti-emetic treatments. (Grotenhermen 2006, 13)

Citing evidence of the therapeutic effectiveness of cannabis for nausea and vomiting associated with cancer chemotherapy, Russo explains that in "pooling available data in some 768 patients, oral THC provided 76-88 percent relief of nausea and vomiting, while smoked cannabis figures supported 70-100 percent relief in the various surveys (Musty and Rossi 2001)" (Russo 2003, 20).

An essential point to make in considering cancer chemotherapy and cannabis use is not whether or not it is therapeutically effective. Rather it is of the superiority of using the cannabis plant rather than synthetic THC. Not only is there more effective relief to patients, but also quite significant reduction of cost to suffering patients for synthetic drugs. Researchers comment that the standard and most effective drug for nausea costs hundreds of dollars per treatment. Consider the following startling case presented by Grinspoon and Bakalar of a patient who used cannabis for nausea instead of standard medications to save $20,000:

> During the course of her treatment my wife consumed less than $200 worth of cannabis. The necessary dose of Zofran (ondansetron), the antiemetic our oncologist first recommended, would have cost one hundred times that amount. Not that cost was a factor in her choice of treatments. She simply decided that marihuana was more likely to be effective and less likely to have serious side effects. In fact, she did take Zofran intravenously once when she forgot her marihuana pipe, and the cost was $600. A friend whose wife had the same treatment says the total cost of Zofran and its administration was more than $20,000. (Grinspoon and Bakalar 1997, 42)[12]

This contrast in cost between Zofran and cannabis, $200 versus $20,000, should cause us to pause to reconsider what seems to be a major systematic money saver. However, pharmaceutical companies are hesitant in investing in cannabis research. Gahlinger points out:

> Pharmaceutical companies are not permitted to patent a natural drug for exclusive manufacture and sale. Therefore, with less potential profit, there is not much incentive to manufacture these drugs or push for their legal use. The pharmaceutical companies would rather develop, patent, and sell a synthetic drug on which they have exclusive rights. The result is the following:
>
> - There is little effort to evaluate the benefits of natural drugs, because these drugs cannot be patented.
> - Natural drugs that were declared illegal tend to remain illegal, unless there is a politically strong group to lobby for legalization.
> - New, synthetic drugs are aggressively marketed because there is a high profit potential
> - If a synthetic drug has abuse potential, resulting in injury to the user or to others, it is usually withdrawn from the U.S. market in order to avoid liability lawsuits. It may continue to be sold in other countries, however. These

drugs may then be illegally imported into the United States. (Gahlinger 2004, 143–44)

Grinspoon and Bakalar describe the disadvantages of dronabinol/Marinol, the synthetic THC provided in pill form and wrongly considered to be the equivalent in therapeutic effectiveness to smoked cannabis. Smoking cannabis provides immediate medicinal relief and allows one to control the effective dose in each use. In contrast after synthetic pills are metabolized through organs before reaching the brain, approximately an hour later, the effects are commonly either not enough (which means additional use and waiting another hour) or too much ingested and therefore drowsy and the experience of sub-par results. They emphasize cannabis has 460 plus compounds of which only THC is used in synthetic cannabinoids. Many of these 460 plus compounds have yet to be understood and it is likely the case some of these other compounds are therapeutically effective.[13]

> Since 1985 oncologists have been legally permitted to administer a synthetic THC, dronabinol (the common brand name is Marinol) orally in capsule form, and almost 100,000 doses were prescribed in 1989. But inhaled cannabis may be preferable for several reasons. For one thing, oral THC is subject to the vagaries of bioavailability. This means that two patients who take the same amount may absorb different portions of the dose, and a given patient may respond differently on different days, depending on the condition of the intestinal tract and other factors. Furthermore, the effects of smoked cannabis are perceived almost immediately, so that patients can smoke slowly and take only what they need for a therapeutic effect. Patients who swallow dronabinol may discover after an hour or so that they have taken too much for comfort or not enough to relieve their symptoms. In any case, a patient who is severely nauseated and constantly vomiting may find it almost impossible to keep the capsule down. (Grinspoon and Bakalar 1997, 43)

And further on oral administration of cannabis in general, in Baker et al. in the context of their consideration of "cannabis therapeutics" and "neuroprotection":

> oral administration is probably the least satisfactory route for cannabis owing to sequestration of cannabinoids into fat from which there is a slow and variable release into plasma. In addition, significant first-pass metabolism in the liver, which degrades THC, contributes to the variability of circulating concentrations of orally administered cannabinoids, which makes dose titration more difficult and therefore increases the potential for adverse psychoactive effects. (Baker, Pryce, Giovannoni, and Thompson 2003, 297)

In attempting to get to the "truth" about the use of cannabis for the treatment of cancer chemotherapy it seems uncontroversial to consider oncologists the experts. An oft-cited statistic in the medical literature is from a survey of oncologists conducted by Doblin and Kleiman in 1991. They there report that "48 percent of oncologists would prescribe smoked marijuana to some of their patients if it was legal, and 44 percent have recommended to some patients that they smoke marijuana illegally" (Doblin and Kleiman 1991, 2079–80). Given the seemingly modest epistemological and medical claim that oncologists are experts on the therapeutic efficacy of cannabis, this statistic itself is powerful scientific support for legally available cannabis for medical purposes.

However, given the legal situation in the United States, oncologists are left to routinely practice within a moral dilemma. In their every provision of informed consent to those treatments that are used for nausea and vomiting, they are in a catch-22 situation: they either provide an informed consent that includes all viable options for the treatment of nausea and vomiting associated with chemotherapy treatment and therefore include a consideration of cannabis, or purposely avoid any discussion let alone recommendation of cannabis for nausea and vomiting for fear of being legally reprimanded and therefore providing "uninformed" or "partially" informed consent (therefore not informed consent).[14] This moral bind for oncologists is one which in other imaginable worlds they would never have to face. However, at the present time in the United States the question is whether their primary allegiance is to the U.S. federal government or to their patients.

Glaucoma: Break the Law or Lose Your Sight?

> Glaucoma is a disorder that results from an imbalance of pressure within the eye. The eyeball must be almost perfectly spherical to focus light accurately on the retina. Its shape is maintained by the pressure of an internal fluid, the aqueous humor. If the eye produces too much of this fluid or the channels through which it flows out are blocked, the increasing pressure may damage the optic nerve, which carries impulses from the eye to the brain. Glaucoma afflicts 1.5 percent of the population at age fifty and about 5 percent at age seventy. Almost one million Americans suffer from the disorder, and every year 80,000 are blinded by it. . . .
>
> Today glaucoma is treated chiefly with eye drops containing betablockers such as timolol (Timoptic), which inhibit the activity of epinephrine (adrenaline). They are highly effective but may have serious side effects; they may induce depression, aggregate asthma, slow the heart rate, and increase the risk of heart failure. (Grinspoon and Bakalar 1997, 45–46)

Robert Randall's experience with glaucoma, given a prognosis of three years left for his having sight, and discovering cannabis would maintain his eye sight beyond this three-year prognosis, was convincing enough to justify the

U.S. federal government establishment of an Investigational New Drug Program ("IND") to justify the distribution of cannabis to Randall (and later several other patients) provided by the federal government at their single grow farm in Mississippi. Randall avoided blindness and treated his glaucoma successfully, seemingly an "accepted medical use" in the United States, one safely conducted under medical supervision. Given that every year 80,000 are blinded by glaucoma, Randall is not an isolated case from the past. Since his case established this IND in the mid-1970s, Randall's life work has been advocating for the therapeutic benefit of cannabis.

Grinspoon and Bakalar present much of Randall's personal history leading up to his case becoming a precedent for the therapeutic effectiveness of cannabis (for glaucoma). Consider, specifically relevant to this section on the therapeutic uses of cannabis, the physical situation Randall found himself in at the time he first used cannabis:

> In the phase known as end-stage glaucoma, the patient has already lost a substantial degree of vision, the condition is worsening, standard drugs are no longer effective, and blindness is imminent. . . . Robert Randall, had reached the stage when he began to smoke marihuana regularly as a medicine. He had used all the available glaucoma drugs at the highest permitted doses, and his intraocular pressure remained dangerously high. If nothing further had been done, he would have gone blind. (Grinspoon and Bakalar 1997, 48)

Any rational human being would at least recommend using cannabis to prolong a life of sight. Furthermore, any health care worker who accepts the legitimacy of palliation seems logically led to champion cannabis availability for glaucoma patients. Proselytizing against these patients to reconsider their use in light of the legal status of cannabis is a callous rather than compassionate response, one inconsistent with the practice of medicine.

For an unlikely source of evidence (in the mid-70s) of the therapeutic effectiveness of cannabis for decreasing interocular eye pressure, consider the following presented by Grinspoon and Bakalar:

> The discovery that marihuana reduces intraocular pressure occurred accidentally during an experiment at UCLA designed to determine whether, as the Los Angeles Police Department believed, cannabis dilated the pupils. The police claimed that this supposed dilation . . . was a sign of marihuana intoxication and therefore good grounds for searching and arresting a citizen. The subjects of the experiment were normal volunteers smoking government-grown marihuana. Their eyes were photographed as they smoked, and the pupils were found to be slightly constricted rather than dilated. An ophthalmological examination showed that cannabis also reduced tearing . . . and intraocular pressure. Further experiments indicated a similar effect in patients with glaucoma. Marihuana re-

> duced intraocular pressure for an average of four to five hours, with "no indications of any deleterious effects . . . on visual function or ocular structure." (Grinspoon and Bakalar 1997, 46–47)

Finally, consider the following by Pate regarding cannabis for the treatment of glaucoma:

> The overall implication for the sum of these studies is potentially significant. Cannabinoids may reveal themselves to be useful for the treatment of glaucoma in a quite comprehensive manner: lowering IOP, resorting micro-circulation, inhibiting apoptosis, and minimizing free radical damage. This hypothetical multiple mechanism would surpass that employed by any current ocular drug, and may help to explain why the use of marijuana has preserved the sight of those unresponsive to other glaucoma therapies. (Pate 2002, 220)

Wasting Syndrome: The Low Social Priority of the Pain and Suffering of AIDS Patients

> The term "cachexia" refers to the dramatic weight loss that is characteristic of several systemic diseases, including malabsorption, congestive heart failure, major trauma, severe sepsis, AIDS, and cancer. Cachexia is characterized by unintentional weight loss involving depletion of skeletal muscle mass and adipose tissue and contributes significantly to mortality. Anorexia (meaning loss of appetite)—as a frequent complication of these diseases—is a major contributor to the development of cachexia. (Schnelle and Strasser 2002, 153)

Although Schnelle and Strasser indicate that cachexia is potentially involved in several types of disease processes they only refer to anorexia/cachexia syndrome of cancer patients and to those suffering wasting syndrome of AIDS. Of cancer, consider the various causes of common effects associated with cachexia:

> Many other factors can be related to the multifactorial etiology of anorexia-cachexia, such as pain, learned food aversion, anxiety and depression, sensory changes including olfactory and taste abnormalities, decreased gastric emptying, nausea and vomiting, diarrhea and constipation, mucositis, and direct anatomic effect of tumors (impaired swallowing, obstruction, malabsorption). (Schnelle and Strasser 2002, 154)

And more generally of patients who are "cachetic,"

> Cachectic patients present with a number of devastating symptoms including anorexia, chronic nausea, early satiety, constipation, asthenia, decreased motor

> and mental skills, decline in attention span and concentration abilities, and change in body image. All these symptoms seem to have impact on the general quality of life of the patients. (Schnelle and Strasser 2002, 155)

Finally, regarding the use of cannabis as a therapy for cachectic patients,

> In the management of anorexia-cachexia in cancer and AIDS wasting there is growing evidence that patients need individual treatment, according to the main underlying metabolic abnormalities and accompanying symptoms. In this view, cannabinoids such as THC or standardized cannabis extracts might prove useful, either as single drugs or in combination with other drugs, in the palliative treatment of those patients with symptoms such as anorexia, chronic nausea, asthenia, and depression. (Schnelle and Strasser 2002, 161)

"Increasing appetite" is one of the most non-controversial effects of cannabis use. For those patients who have little if any appetite to the point of being repulsed by the smell and very thought of eating food, cannabis is medically indicated. Woolridge et al. in "Cannabis Use in HIV for Pain and Other Medical Symptoms" (2005) "measure the patterns and prevalence of cannabis use in patients presenting at a large HIV clinic" and "evaluate its beneficial or detrimental effect on symptom control." This study is an example of the clever way researchers have of studying the therapeutic effectiveness of the cannabis plant (vs. synthetic pills) without having readily available standardized supply of cannabis to provide to their patients. They have simply identified a group of 523 patients who are *already* using cannabis as therapy even though it is illegal to possess.[15]

First, consider the effects of the illegality of cannabis on the quality of treatment and health care relationship:

> The large number of patients using cannabis as medicinal therapy for symptoms related to HIV raises a number of issues. First, patients are being left with no alternative but to use a non-medical source of supply, which has potential for heterogeneity of active cannabinoids, toxic contaminants, inappropriate dose, and drug misuse. Second, if part of the plant material has therapeutic efficacy, the source of the material should be standardized and subjected to clinical trials so that safe and effective use is advocated. Third, the patient is unlikely to divulge cannabis use to their medical team, so that potential drug interactions with prescribed antireteroviral medications may be occurring. (Woolridge et al. 2005, 361–62)

Of their 523 patients, "27 percent used cannabis to treat symptoms associated with HIV. Of this 27 percent (143 patients), administration was by smoking for 101 (71 percent), eating or drinking for 39 (27 percent) and ingestion for 3 (2 percent) (Woolridge et al. 2005, 360). Of the specific therapeutic benefits:

> A lack of appetite was the most frequent symptom reported and 97 percent experienced improvement with cannabis use. Pain was the next most frequent, being present in 45 percent of patients and improved in 94 percent of them. The collective results demonstrated statistically significant improvement in half or more patients in symptoms of nausea, anxiety, nerve pain, depression, tingling, numbness, weight loss, headaches, tremor, constipation, and tiredness. Symptoms that were not improved included weakness and slurred speech, and statistically significant memory deterioration was recorded in 47 percent of users. (Woolridge et al. 2005, 361)

And to provide a general idea of the number of people who could potentially benefit therapeutically from the use of cannabis, the Woolridge group indicates:

> HIV or AIDS affects over 40 million people in the world and more than 49,500 in the UK. . . . Symptoms associated with HIV occur as both direct and indirect consequences of the disease process and as a side effect of the antiretroviral drugs used in the treatment of the disease. These symptoms include nausea and vomiting, pain (e.g., in a nerve distribution), reduced appetite, weight loss, headaches, diarrhea, constipation, anxiety, and depression. (Woolridge et al. 2005, 358)

As a broader consideration of the effects of cannabis valuable to these patients, consider the following common side effects of HIV treatment:

> Symptoms commonly occurring as a side effect of HIV treatment include renal colic from nephrolithiasis associated with the protease inhibitor, indinavir; painful peripheral neuropathy from use of stavudine, a nucleoside analogue; or sleep disturbances from the non-nucleoside inhibitor, efavirenz. Thus, a wide range of symptoms can significantly affect the quality of life of individuals living with HIV as a long-term chronic infection. (Woolridge et al. 2005, 359)

Researchers (and clinicians) recognize that the illegality of cannabis likely motivates some of their patients to not disclose use. In addition to frustrating any studies on the effects of cannabis use, lacking this information also confounds the accuracy and quality of the treatment plan and potentially the health of cannabis using patients. For example, researchers (or clinicians) could be attributing the increase in appetite resulting from cannabis to some other therapy or cause.

Grinspoon and Bakalar present this particular therapeutic effect of cannabis on wasting syndrome as already having been established, explaining:

> Patients with AIDS need to maintain their appetite and body weight because they may be in danger of wasting away. Furthermore, a good appetite greatly improves their quality of life. Recreational users know that marihuana is an appetite stimulant; it not only makes them hungrier but enhances the flavor of food and the pleasure of eating. (Grinspoon and Bakalar 1997, 101)

The event of discontinuing the federal government IND for using cannabis (in 1992) will be considered in historical context in chapter 4. However as many AIDS patients were thereafter denied access to cannabis for medicinal use, consider the legality of cannabis is not about scientific truth but about political symbolism.[16] As Dan Baum describes it,

> By 1991 the community of AIDS sufferers was organized and noisy, demanding access to marijuana to block the nauseating effects of AZT and other drugs, and to stimulate appetite to control "wasting syndrome." In addition to Bob Randall, only nine people in the country had experimental permits to smoke pot, receiving tins of 300 government-issue marijuana cigarettes every month. But between the court decision, the oncologists, and the AIDS patients, the government was starting to receive a stream of new applications to its Compassionate Investigative New Drug (IND) program and was expecting a tidal wave of them.
>
> So the government killed the program. On June 21, Dr. James O. Mason, chief of the Public Health Service, announced the government would no longer make marijuana available to desperately sick people—even on an experimental basis. Those who were getting the drug would continue to do so, but everybody else—including the thirty-odd patients who'd been accepted for the program but hadn't yet started receiving their tins—would be shut out. In his press reference, Mason acknowledged the decision was based on politics, not health. "If it's perceived that the Public Health Service is going around giving marijuana to folks," he said, "there would be a perception that this stuff can't be so bad." (Baum 1997, 314)

As nausea and vomiting involved with cancer chemotherapy can be legally treated with synthetic dronabinol, so too "in 1992 the FDA approved Marinol Capsules for the treatment of anorexia associated with weight loss in patients with AIDS" (Grotenhermen 2006, 13). This gave birth to a new belief of Social Reality, that if oral THC is available then sufferers have an adequate alternative to illegal cannabis. Given the clearly significant differences between orally ingested synthetic THC and smoking cannabis (e.g., with its 483 chemical compounds and the import of the synergy between these various chemicals of cannabis), such a stance seems motivated by expediency rather than either reason or compassion.

Epilepsy: Effective Seizure and Spasticity Control

> Although the anticonvulsant properties of cannabis have been known since ancient times and were explored in the nineteenth century, this therapeutic use of the drug has been largely ignored in the past hundred years. (Grinspoon and Bakalar 1997, 67)

The anticonvulsant properties of cannabis, along with muscle relaxation, are supported by the location of CB_1 receptors, in areas of the brain related to fine motor skills. Cannabis is effective for those with epilepsy by decreasing both the severity and frequency of seizures. The disease of multiple sclerosis shows a similar therapeutic effect of reduced spasticity:

> Why do these patients use cannabis? Some achieve relief from primary symptoms of their disease; individuals with epilepsy reported reduced seizure severity (65 percent) and frequency (54 percent), whereas about half of patients with multiple sclerosis had diminished pain or spasticity. However, roughly two thirds of respondents with multiple sclerosis claimed relief from psychological symptoms, and only 43 percent of patients with epilepsy were using marijuana for medical symptoms. These findings suggest that many active users could be treating secondary effects of their disease. (Wingerchuk 2004, 315)

And within their consideration of cannabis for epilepsy, Grinspoon and Bakalar emphasize the point that for these particular patients there are no therapeutic alternatives. This is important in light of those who insist on the current availability of the "equally effective" synthetic cannabinoid:

> But we do know from cases like those presented above that some people are helped by cannabis and nothing else. Furthermore, they do not have to pay a high price in toxic or even uncomfortable side effects. Many epileptic patients are unsuccessfully treated with three or more antiepileptic drugs taken simultaneously, a practice that greatly increases the severity of toxic effects. The value of cannabis—for some patients, a unique value—is especially clear when overall quality of life is considered as well as adequacy of seizure control. (Grinspoon and Bakalar 1997, 80)

Multiple Sclerosis

> Multiple Sclerosis (MS) is a disorder in which patches of myelin (the protective covering of nerve fibers) in the brain and spinal cord are destroyed and the normal functioning of the nerve fibers themselves is interrupted. It seems to be an autoimmune response in which the body's defense system treats the myelin as a

> foreign invader. The symptoms usually appear in early adulthood, then come and go unpredictably for years. Attacks last weeks to months, and remission is often incomplete, with gradual deterioration and eventual severe disability. Injury, infection, or stress may cause a relapse. The average survival time is thirty years, but some patients deteriorate much faster, and others stabilize after a few attacks. (Grinspoon and Bakalar 1997, 80)

Emphasizing the importance of the neurology in finding some treatment for disease, here is a disease essentially of the degeneration of the myelin which protects neurons. Were cannabis effective in interrupting this process of myelin degeneration it could be a substantial therapeutic drug for these patients.

> As if the muscle relaxant and anti-spasmodic benefits of cannabis were insufficient, it has recently been demonstrated that cannabinoid agonists positively influence the immunological parameters of demyelinating diseases such as experimentally allergic encephalomyelitis (Baker et al. 2000). (Russo 2003, 19)

In summarizing a case presentation of a patient with multiple sclerosis, Grinspoon and Bakalar present the symptoms potentially alleviated by the use of cannabis: "There are hints in this case and others that cannabis not only relieves the symptoms of multiple sclerosis—muscle spasms, tremor, loss of muscle coordination (ataxia) and bladder control, insomnia—but also retards the progression of the disease" (Grinspoon and Bakalar 1997, 93–94). It seems that given the potential for cannabis retarding the progression of multiple sclerosis itself gives those living with this disease some sort of hope, some way of actively taking a measure not only to improve their quality of their lives but lengthen their lives. Wingerchuk points out not only that cannabis has therapeutic benefits for MS and epilepsy but also that not everyone who uses it for therapeutic purposes becomes dependent. Here are presented statistics from people of several countries, all with MS, and approximately 20 percent are regular cannabis users, of whom only approximately 3 percent met dependence criteria:

> Although the purpose of cannabinoid receptors remains a mystery, two recent Canadian surveys indicate that many people with multiple sclerosis and epilepsy reportedly stimulate these receptors for symptom relief. Gross and colleagues surveyed patients with epilepsy and reported that 48 percent of 136 respondents had tried cannabis, 21 percent were active users (use within past 12 months), and 3 percent were dependent. Clark and colleagues found that 36 percent of 220 patients with multiple sclerosis had tried cannabis for any purpose. 14 percent regularly used it for symptom relief, and 3 percent met dependence criteria. These findings are similar to results of a previous Canadian survey in multiple sclerosis. General population surveys of young adults show similar or higher frequen-

> cies of experience of using cannabis (30–61 percent), but lower rates of regular use (8-10 percent) and dependence (<0.4 percent). Statistics from Canada, the USA, and the UK are strikingly similar despite differing political and legal climates. It would be surprising if rates in young people with epilepsy or multiple sclerosis in the UK or the USA were much different from the Canadian results. (Wingerchuk 2004, 315)

In another testimonial presented by Grinspoon and Bakalar revealed is the very real and serious quality of life concern of bladder control for many living with multiple sclerosis:

> Talshir notes that cannabis helps her to control her bladder, a problem for up to 90 percent of patients with multiple sclerosis. Sometimes cannabis enables them to lead normal lives after years of being housebound by fear of embarrassment. Three women with multiple sclerosis have told us that although they began using cannabis for the relief of muscle spasms, they found it equally helpful for bladder control. One says she would use it for that reason alone if necessary.
>
> Cannabis may also be helpful for loss of bowel control in multiple sclerosis. (Grinspoon and Bakalar 1997, 91)

Corey further substantiates the therapeutic effectiveness of cannabis use, suggesting cannabis as a therapeutic agent generally for neurological disorders. Of course, the research involves "cannabinoids" and not the cannabis plant itself, which means, among other things, that cannabis is likely to be *more* effective than indicated by these reports of the synthetic cannabinoid compounds. Reporting results from fifteen independent, qualifying clinical trials (of which only three had more than 100 patients each):

> Two large trials found that cannabinoids were significantly better than placebo in managing spasticity in multiple sclerosis. Patients self-reported greater sense of motor improvement in multiple sclerosis than could be confirmed objectively. In smaller qualifying trials, cannabinoids produced significant objective improvement of tics in Tourette's disease, and neuropathic pain. A new, non-psychotropic cannabinoid also has analgesic activity in neuropathic pain. No significant improvement was found in levodopa-induced dyskinesia in Parkinson's Disease or post-operative pain. No difference from active placebo was found for management of cachexia in a large trial. (Corey 2005)

Neurodegenerative Diseases

The number of people suffering from diseases involving neurodegeneration is continuing to increase, and cannabis use could potentially slow the neurological processes.[17] Consider the following by Baker et al., which suggests that cannabis may halt neurodegeneration in patients:

> Although the current clinical use of cannabinoids focuses on symptom management, the biology of the cannabinoid system suggests that there may be other benefits in the treatment of neurological disease, notably the slowing of progression in neurodegenerative disorders. Selective loss of CB_1 receptors in the striatum is associated with the onset of signs in Huntington's disease before significant axonal loss, both in human beings and in animal models, which suggests that some cannabinoid regulation is lost before significant pathology develops. However, activation of the remaining receptors through stimulation by endocannabinoids can limit experimental Huntington's disease. Neurodegeneration is the main cause of morbidity in several diseases such as Huntington's, Parkinson's, Alzheimer's, and motor-neuron diseases and stroke. (Baker, Pryce, Giovannoni, and Thompson 2003, 296)

Reinforcing the sense of revolution in the area of neurology (as conveyed earlier), Russo explains:

> One of the most exciting and pressing areas of neurological investigation surrounds the emerging concept of neuroprotection. If one were able to prevent the progressive cell death of parkinsonism, amyotrophic lateral sclerosis, Alzheimer and Huntington diseases, the inevitable deterioration and ultimate demise that these disorders eventuate might well be mitigated or arrested. (Russo 2003, 21)

Migraine: Effective Response to the Aura

> Migraine is a severe headache lasting hours to days and accompanied by visual disturbances or nausea and vomiting or both. Usually the attacks are recurrent. They can be brought on in a susceptible person by stress, by certain foods, and by certain types of sensory stimulation (bright light, loud noise, penetrating odors). The onset usually occurs before the age of twenty and rarely after the age of fifty. About 20 percent of the population has experienced migraine attacks; they are three times more common in women than in men. (Grinspoon and Bakalar 1997, 123)

Russo explains cannabis was used 3,000 years ago as a treatment for migraine.

> Cannabis has been a recognized treatment for migraine in the Ayurvedic medicine of India since the sixth and seventh centuries, and perhaps for as long as 3,000 years. An unequivocal account of parenteral application of cannabis (intranasal) was noted by Ibn Sahl, a Nestorean physician in Persia in the ninth cen-

> tury. Culpeper commended hemp for inflammations of the head in the seventeenth century.
>
> From Clendinning's trials on migraine patients published in 1843, to the observations of Fishbein (an American Medical Association president) in 1942, there was a century of sanctioned Western medical usage of cannabis for the indication of headache, both symptomatically and prophylactically. (Russo 2002c, 188)

He adds the neurological explanation for why cannabis would relieve migraine headaches: "THC minimizes the release of serotonin from the platelets of migraine suffers" (Russo 2002c, 189). And as evidence of therapeutic effectiveness, Russo's lengthy and comprehensive review of literature on the history of cannabis use for migraine has him conclude, "The information reviewed indicates that cannabis has a long-established history of efficacy in migraine treatment, with current supportive biochemical and pharmacological evidence" (Russo 2002c, 190). He furthermore reveals his own clinical research experience with this particular therapeutic effect: "This author's personal experience in talking to several hundred migraine suffers who have employed cannabis is that 80 percent have noted improvement, often with complete symptomatic relief" (Russo 2002, 191).

Grinspoon and Bakalar cite J. B. Mattison in an 1891 medical journal article: "Reviewing his own and earlier physician's experiences, he concluded that cannabis not only blocks the pain of migraine but prevents migraine attacks. Years later William Osler expressed his agreement, saying that cannabis was 'probably the most satisfactory remedy' for migraine" (Grinspoon and Bakalar 1997, 6).

Moving into a technical examination of how cannabis is effective for one suffering from a migraine, consider the study of Papanastassiou, Fields, and Meng (2004). In studying cannabinoid receptors, they found that neurons involved in pain responses could be inhibited. As they explain, "Electrophysiological studies have demonstrated that cannabinoid receptor agonists also inhibit nociceptive neurons in the lumbar spinal cord dorsal horn (SCDH)" (Papanastassiou, Fields, and Meng 2004, 267–68). And as to the connection between such neurological inhibition and the relief of migraine headaches, consider that these inhibited neurons include those of the head and face: "The direct action of cannabinoid receptor agonists in the SCDH suggests that they may also affect trigeminal neurons, suppressing nociceptive inputs from the head and face" (Papanastassiou, Fields, and Meng 2004, 268). They further explain relevant to craniofacial pain including that of migraine sufferers: "The spinal trigeminal nucleus caudalis (Vc) is the primary relay for craniofacial pain, and as such represents a likely target for the possible analgesic action of cannabinoids. CB_1 receptors are present in the trigeminal ganglia and trigeminal nucleus, consistent with their location in dorsal root ganglion and SCDH neurons (Herkenham et al., 1991; Richardson et al., 1998; Tsou et al., 1998)" (Papanastassiou, Fields, and Meng 2004, 268). And in their conclusion:

> The experiments presented here demonstrate that cannabinoid agonists applied directly to the brain stem have their greatest effect on neuronal hyperexcitability, as measured by C-fiber mediated PDC activity. . . . Cannabinoid inhibition of PDC is important because the same stimuli that produce PDC are sufficient to produce central sensitization, which may lead to features of persistent pain such as hypersensitivity, secondary hyperalgia, and allodynia (Li et al., 1999; Wall and Woolf, 1986; Woolf, 1983; Woolf and Wall, 1986). (Papanastassiou, Fields, and Meng 2004, 272)

Paraplegia and Quadriplegia

Currently many patients are not given an adequate option to the "numbing" and "deadening" narcotics. Cannabis is a different type of drug and one which does not have several of the significant negative side effects of the opioids. "Many paraplegics and quadriplegics have now discovered that cannabis not only relieves their pain more safely than opioids but also effectively suppresses their muscle jerks and tremors" (Grinspoon and Bakalar 1997, 94). Grinspoon and Bakalar also indicate that cannabis can restore the ability of paraplegic and quadriplegic users to achieve and maintain erections and to ejaculate. Of one such patient:

> A thirty-year-old patient had suffered from MS for six years and was wheelchair-bound because of muscle spasms and ataxia. His erections lasted less than five minutes, and he was unable to ejaculate. When he smoked marihuana, both his motor functions and his sexual functions improved immediately. He can now sustain an erection for more than half and hour and his sexual life is satisfactory. (Grinspoon and Bakalar 1997, 96)

Given the current early twenty-first-century marketing boom for the drug Viagra (for inability to maintain an erection), this reason itself is legitimate to the U.S. general public. The problem, again, is that cannabis is the drug being used to bring about these effects, and it is illegal. However, this still leaves paraplegics and quadriplegics with the knowledge that they could regain a sex life with the use of cannabis and would be able to do so but for its illegality.

Chronic Pain

> Severe chronic pain is usually treated with opioid narcotics and various synthetic analgesics, but these drugs have many limitations. Opioids are addictive and tol-

> erance develops. The most commonly used synthetic analgesics—aspirin, acetaminophen (Tylenol), and nonsteroidal anti-inflammatory drugs (NSAIDs) like ibuprofen—are not addictive, but they are often insufficiently powerful. Furthermore, they have serious toxic side effects, including gastric bleeding or ulcer and, in the long run, a risk of liver or kidney disease. Stomach bleeding and ulcers induced by aspirin and other NSAIDs are the most common serious adverse drug reactions reported in the United States (1996 study cited). These drugs may be responsible for as many as 76,000 hospitalizations and more than 7,600 deaths annually. (Grinspoon and Bakalar 1997, 109)

Escohotado explains the existence of a synthetic/non-synthetic distinction in the United States. With this distinction is the assumption of the value, medical and moral, of use of synthetic pills over non-synthetic drugs. His suggestion seems one way of understanding why patients of the twentieth- and early twenty-first-century United States rely on, trust, and have an irrational faith in synthetic drugs. Perhaps the "smokers cough" of a chronic cannabis user is preferable to bleeding ulcers and kidney and liver disease. Time and again in my research it is posited that because the use of cannabis involves smoking as the mode of administration, it is thereby not an acceptable medicine. It seems arbitrary whether one smokes and assumes associated risks or one swallows pills and assumes associated risks. "Medical researchers have estimated that patients who take one to three acetaminophen tablets a day for a year or more account for about 8–10 percent of all cases of end-stage renal disease, a condition that is fatal without dialysis or a kidney transplant" (Grinspoon and Bakalar 1997, 110). Aspirin is not considered "dangerous," although it has been proven to lead to significant damage to internal organs if not death.[18]

Also striking is the fact that opiate treatment for chronic pain, although accepted as standard of care in many cases, is more "addictive" and "debilitating" than is cannabis. If this is true, it is reasonable to conclude that patients who are provided informed consent for treatment of their chronic pain should at least be offered cannabis as an alternative, offering a different sort of pain relief which has less serious side-effects.

> The greatest irony in proscribing the use of cannabis to relieve pain is that the best alternatives are addictive and sometimes debilitating opioids. A woman who described her case to us suffers from melorheostosis, a rare and incurable condition that involves severe joint pain. When she first developed the disorder, her physician prescribed massive doses of Darvocet, a combination of propoxyphene (a synthetic opioid) and Tylenol #3 (codeine and acetaminophen). She needed up to fifteen Darvocets a day to control the pain until she started to smoke marihuana. She has found that "smoking marihuana when the pain first starts will round it off. Otherwise it increases very fast; I begin to feel nauseated and develop cold and hot sweats, simply from the pain." She could usually control the

> pain with one to two joints a day. "But it is a black-market item, and when we are paying an average of $75 for a quarter of an ounce and you only have an income of $444 a month, you don't buy very much. I feel I should not have to live like a criminal because of the ignorance of politicians. I have to be terrified about whether police will come and search my home. Am I going to lose my home and my children because I have found something that makes me able to cope?" (Grinspoon and Bakalar 1997, 122)

Here is an "otherwise law-abiding citizen" who has to live like a criminal in order to treat her chronic pain. Furthermore, she is practically invited to develop a dependence on the synthetic drugs she was in fact prescribed, ironically much more dangerous than cannabis. "This woman echoes the nineteenth-century understanding that cannabis, while it is not as powerful a pain reliever as the opioids, has fewer serious side effects and creates no risk of dependence" (Grinspoon and Bakalar 1997, 123).

Post-Traumatic Stress Disorder ("PTSD"): Extinguishing Adverse Memories

One interesting fact about cannabis and how it can be utilized therapeutically regards treating post-traumatic stress disorder (PTSD). In his fascinating book *The Botany of Desire: A Plant's-Eye View of the World* (2001), Michael Pollen examines in one of the four major parts of his book the cannabis plant. In considering cannabis intoxication and the effect on memory, Pollen explains that forgetting can be a therapeutic effect for some users. This seems counterintuitive. Although "euphoria" and "mental impairment" are understandably ambiguous, forgetting seems prima facie a bad thing. However, Pollen explains that:

> forgetting is vastly underrated as a mental operation—indeed, that it is a mental operation, rather than, as I'd always assumed, strictly the breakdown of one. Yes, forgetting can be curse, especially as we age. But forgetting is also one of the more important things healthy brains do, almost as important as remembering. Think how quickly the sheer volume and multiplicity of sensory information we receive every waking minute would overwhelm our consciousness if we couldn't quickly forget a great deal more of it than we remember. (Pollen 2001, 160)

And explaining how cannabis would help one forget:

> The THC in marijuana and the brain's endogenous cannabinoids work in much the same way, but THC is far stronger and more persistent than anandamide, which, like most neurotransmitters, is designed to break down very soon after its

> release. (Chocolate, of all things, seems to slow this process, which might account for its own subtle mood-altering properties.) What this suggests is that smoking marijuana may overstimulate the brain's built-in forgetting faculty, exaggerating its normal operations. (Pollen 2001, 162)

In addition to the value of forgetting traumatic experiences (thereby able to "move beyond them" and not let them control one's life) there is a deeper sense that forgetting is valuable. Pollen explains this as the idea of not simply memorizing and repeating what one has inherited from one's precursors but rather living creatively and moving beyond these:

> Without dismissing the value of memory or history, he argues (much like Emerson and Thoreau) that we spend altogether too much of our energy laboring in the shadows of the past—under the stultifying weight of convention, precedent, received wisdom, and neurosis. Like the American transcendentalists, Nietzsche believes that our personal and collective inheritance stand in the way of our enjoyment of life and accomplishment of anything original. (Pollen 2001, 163)

And more on the point of the positive value of forgetting, Pollen moves from therapeutic, medicinal effects to motivations of self-perception, creativity, productivity, and aesthetic uses of cannabis:

> For Nietzsche the "art and power of forgetting" consist in a kind of radical editing or blocking out of consciousness everything that doesn't serve the present purpose. A man seized by a "vehement passion" or great idea will be blind and deaf to all except that passion or idea. Everything he does perceive, however, he will perceive as he has never perceived anything before: "All is so palpable, close, highly colored, resounding, as though he apprehended it with all his senses at once."
>
> What Nietzsche is describing is a kind of transcendence—a mental state of complete and utter absorption well known to artists, athletes, gamblers, musicians, dancers, soldiers in battle, mystics, mediators, and the devout during prayer. Something very like it can occur during sex, too, or while under the influence of certain drugs. It is a state that depends for its effect on losing oneself in the moment, usually by training a powerful, depthless concentration on One Big Thing. (Or, in the Eastern tradition, One Big Nothing.) If you imagine consciousness as a kind of lens through which we perceive the world, the drastic constricting of its field of vision seems to heighten the vividness of whatever remains in the circle of perception, while everything else (including our awareness of the lens itself) simply falls away. (Pollen 2001, 164)

It seems obvious that for certain people who live this transcendence (as the examples Pollen presents and likely many others) cannabis use is part of their way of life. One who chooses this particular effect is perhaps a spiritual, artistic, or intellectual user of cannabis, rather than being either a "recreational user" or a "medicinal user." Here, applied to PTSD, part of getting over the traumatic stress of the disorder (perhaps a sort of "transcendence") has one "remember to forget":

> Cannabinoids adversely affect short-term memory processing and could be disadvantageous to cognitive ability. However, sometimes patients with disorders such as post-traumatic fear responses also have to "remember to forget" and here stimulation of the cannabinoid system may be useful to extinguish certain aversive memories. Thus, cannabis may have positive and negative outcomes, and therefore its clinical use must balance these effects against the nature of the disorder. (Baker, Pryce, Giovannoni, and Thompson 2003, 294)

Consider from recent literature two further accounts of cannabis and PTSD. First, Marsicano et al. elaborate upon the extinction of aversive memories. In their investigation of a cellular basis for extinction of aversive memories, they find CB_1 and endocannabinoids present in memory-related brain areas that modulate memories. They focus specifically on the basolateral amygdala complex, known to control extinction of aversive memories, and endocannabinoid involvement in the long-term suppression of GABA. They conclude, "Overall our findings support that the endogenous cannabinoid system could represent a therapeutic target for the treatment of diseases associated with inappropriate retention of aversive memories or inadequate responses to aversive situations, such as post-traumatic stress disorder, phobias, and certain kinds of chronic pain" (Marsicano et al. 2002, 533). Second, Hill et al. consider more broadly the effect of chronic unpredictable stress on endocannabinoids in the hippocampus. They explain that the endogenous cannabinoid system (what they refer to as eCB) is involved in stress circuitry and emotional regulation. CB_1 receptors are "found in abundance in the hippocampus," which seems "an important structure in the functional neuroactivation of depression (McEwen 2003)" (Hill et al. 2005, 509). They further point out CB_1 is also very abundant in the limbic forebrain. Here, "impairments in cognitive flexibility manifested in increased preservatory behaviors" where there was CB_1 deficiency. The authors hypothesize that alternations in eCB signaling contribute to the cognitive impairments induced by chronic stress (Hill et al. 2005, 509) They hypothesize that impairment can be reversed by activation of CB_1 receptors. In their study with mice, they found preservatory behavior with induction of stress, then an "attenuation of this behavior with pharmacological enhancement of CB_1 receptor activity." They go on to discuss, among other things, that leptin is elevated after chronic unpredictable stress leading to decrease in eCB content in the hippocampus and also state that the eCB system may be another system that could be disturbed in depression (Hill et al. 2005, 513). Like PTSD, depression (and many stress-related diseases) "is characterized by problems with forgetting and behavior flexibility that are manifested as pathological tendencies to ruminate or perseverate on negative information" (Hill et al. 2005, 513).

Rheumatic Diseases: Anti-Inflammatory Effects of Cannabis

> Rheumatic diseases, which are many and diverse, have the common feature of limiting the ability to move freely. Most of them also cause chronic pain and inflammation; marihuana is unquestionably a pain reliever, and it may also be anti-inflammatory. (Grinspoon and Bakalar 1997, 126)

Anti-inflammatory effects of various compounds of cannabis have been presented in chapter 2. Here, to reinforce the point that synthetic THC lacks medicinal effects potentially/likely existent in the 483 compounds of the cannabis plant (including, most relevantly, the chemical CBD) consider Russo (2003):

> The benefits of cannabis and cannabinoids on inflammation have been extensively documented. The following are suggested as reviews (Hampson et al. 1998; Pertwee 2001; Burstein 1992; Russo 2001). Both THC and CBD have important roles in these observations. Of increasing interest is the recent demonstration that CBD possesses both anti-inflammatory and immunomodulatory benefits in an animal model of rheumatoid arthritis (Malfait et al. 2000). (Russo 2003, 18)

> Although other analgesics may be able to manage acute pain, there is a need to manage chronic neuropathic pain that is unresponsive to standard analgesics; cannabinoid use for chronic pain is supported by several clinical studies. (Baker, Pryce, Giovannoni, and Thompson 2003, 295)

Depression: Decreasing Severity and Piercing the Black Cloud

> Cannabis first appeared in the Western medical literature as a suggested treatment for depression in the middle of the nineteenth century. In 1845, Jacques-Joseph Moreau de Tours proposed its use in melancholia (especially with obsessive rumination) and chronic mental illness in general. Over the next hundred years medical papers supported and disputed the utility of cannabis in the treatment of depression. (Grinspoon and Bakalar 1997, 141)

"Today, among the minority of depressed patients who do not respond to any of the standard antidepressants or who find the side effects unbearable, some have discovered that cannabis is more useful than any legal drug" (Grinspoon and Bakalar 1997, 142).

Depression is a brain disease. Cannabinoid receptors lead to a potential explanation for why there would be a therapeutic effect caused by cannabis (perhaps the CB_1 receptor related to mood regulation are activated and the symptoms of depression are thereby less severe).

Denson and Earleywine present the results of an internet survey of over 4400 participants. Notably they find that "those who consume marijuana occasionally or even daily have lower levels of depressive symptoms than those who have never tried marijuana. Specifically, weekly users had less depressed mood, more positive affect and fewer somatic complaints than non-users. Daily users reported less depressed mood and more positive affect than non-users" (Denson and Earleywine 2006, 741). They also point out this study is the first to "separately investigate depression in medical marijuana users relative to recreational users" (Denson and Earleywine 2006, 741).

Of one particular depressed patient of a psychiatrist who also suffered from chronic depression, consider the therapeutic use of cannabis as well as its superiority to synthetic alternatives:

> In the spring of 1990 I smoked marihuana for the first time since 1973. To my amazement, a quarter of a joint changed my self-perception to match the person others saw. It was like night and day. I had experienced a similar change only a few times before, when Elavil kicked in and lifted me out of the depths. But with Elavil it took four days of rapidly increasing doses; with marihuana it took less than five minutes, every time. Since then I have been using marihuana to think clearly, to concentrate, and simply to enjoy the beauty of the world in a way I couldn't for years. (Grinspoon and Bakalar 1997, 143)

And at the end of her testimonial: "It is unfair and cruel that the antidepressant that helps me most (and is probably, in its pure form, least toxic) is unavailable for legal prescription. I have to break the law to obtain it and pay exorbitant prices for a drug whose cost of production is minimal" (Grinspoon and Bakalar 1997, 144)

In another testimonial:

> The marijuana permitted me to function better than any licit drug. I didn't become drowsy, develop tremors, or have any of the side effects associated with the drugs I had previously taken. I gained an appetite I never had and put needed weight on an emaciated frame. I found myself having ideas that would not ordinarily have come to me, some practical, some not. I was able to pierce the black cloud that surrounded me and climb out far enough to meet my responsibilities. The use of marihuana makes it impossible for depressive thoughts to become the total focus of my life. (Grinspoon and Bakalar 1997, 147)

Finally, consider this anecdotal evidence of the benign nature of cannabis over the long term:

> As of this writing, I have smoked marihuana for more than two decades. In addition to dampening the pain of depression, I have found that it reduces nausea and burning in the stomach due to the production of acid. It allows me to sleep peacefully. It stimulates my imagination when working on creative projects. It enhances simple joys, such as eating M&Ms or walking in the woods. Since its use jeopardizes my freedom, I would prefer a legal substitute. So far I have found none. (Grinspoon and Bakalar 1997, 147)

Alcoholism

The basic approach in treating alcoholism with cannabis is to exchange one habit for another, so that one uses cannabis instead of alcohol. Testimonies of patients undergoing such treatment are presented by Tod H. Mikuriya, a physician who himself conducted a study of 92 of his own patients. Mikuriya based his approach upon the underlying principle of harm reduction. Given the neurological and bodily damage (indicated in chapter 1) resulting from alcohol abuse and dependence opposed to the lack of significant short- or long-term effects of cannabis use, the harm reduced is in the life of (and lives effected by) the user, previously an alcohol abuser and now a cannabis user. Mikuriya explains:

> The harm-reduction approach to alcoholism is based on the recognition that for some patients, total abstinence has been an unattainable goal. Success is not defined as the achievement of perpetual sobriety. A treatment may be deemed helpful if it enables a patient to reduce the frequency and quantity of alcohol consumption; if drunken episodes and/or blackouts are reduced; and if success in the workplace can be achieved; if specific problems induced by alcohol (suspended driver's license, for example) can be resolved; and if ineffective or toxic drugs can be avoided. (Mikuriya 2004, 89)

As to the uniqueness of this therapeutic approach Mikuriya explains: "No clinical trials of the efficacy of cannabis as a substitute for alcohol are reported in the literature, and there are no papers directly on point prior to my own account (Mikuriya 1970) of a patient who used cannabis consciously and successfully to discontinue her problematic drinking" (Mikuriya 2004, 80).

Mikuriya indicates "ample references" do exist for substituting cannabis for opiates as well as cannabis as a "treatment for delirium tremens" (Mikuriya 2004, 80). He concludes cannabis works for certain alcoholics as a substitute treatment for alcoholism. These certain alcoholics seem to have an underlying depression for which alcohol is used. And on the way cannabis is employed for this same underlying condition: "Somewhere in the experience of certain alcoholics, cannabis use is discovered to overcome pain and depression, target conditions for which alcohol is originally used, but without the disinhibited emotions or the physiologic damage. By substituting cannabis for alcohol, patients were able to reduce the harm their intoxication caused themselves and others" (Mikuriya 2004, 81).

Mikuriya explains the 92 patients of his study, alcoholic and willing to try substituting cannabis for alcohol, come from a wide variety of occupations and ways of life (in the U.S. Pacific Northwest):

> A majority of the patients identified themselves as blue-collar workers: carpenter (5), construction (3), laborer (3), waitress (3), truck driver (3), fisherman (3), heavy equipment operator (3), painter (2), contractor (2), cook (2), welder (2), logger (2), timber faller, seaman, hardwood floor installer, bartender, building supplies, house caretaker, ranch hand, concrete pump operator, cable installer, silversmith, stone mason, Boatwright, auto detailer, tree service-handyman-cashier, nurseryman, glazier, gold miner, carpenter layer, carpenter's apprentice, landscaper, river guide, screenprinter, and glassblower . . . others were in sales (5), musicians (5), clerical workers (3), paralegal, teacher, actor, actress, artists, sound engineer, and computer technician." (Mikuriya 2004, 83)

In his "Observations," Mikuriya also points out the following:

> A slight majority of patients (51) reported being raised by at least one alcoholic parent. This is not surprising. The children of alcoholics enter adulthood with two strikes. They have endured direct emotional abuse and/or abandonment by parent(s), and they lack role models for coping with uncomfortable feelings other than by inebriation. It is to be expected that many, when encountering problems early in life, are treated with, or seek out, mind-altering drugs. (Mikuriya 2004, 85)

Mikuriya further points out that "Twenty-six patients reported using cannabis to treat depression (44 if the category is expanded to include anxiety, stress, and PTSD), and their comments frequently touched on the negative synergies between mood disorders and alcoholism" (Mikuriya 2004, 87). One particular example of how effective cannabis can be as a treatment for alcoholism:

> A 33-year-old river guide (and decorated Army vet) put it this way: "I have had a problem with violence and alcohol for a long time and I have a rap sheet to prove it. None of the problems occurred while using cannabis. Not only does cannabis prevent my violent tendencies, but it also helps keep me from drinking." On his follow-up visit (12 months) this patient improved communication with family members and fewer problems relating to other people. His alcohol

consumption had decreased from 36 drinks/week to zero (one month of sobriety). (Mikuriya 2004, 87)

Quite relevant to the therapeutic use of cannabis is the inherent respect for the patient, a respect missing from the current situation where cannabis use is illegal and considered deviant and dangerous. The treatment employed by Mikuriya "creates a different doctor-patient relationship," and one of immense benefit to the well-being of medicinal cannabis users:

> Patients seek out the physician to confer legitimacy on what they are doing or are about to do. My most important service is to end their criminal status, Aeschalapian protection from the criminal justice system, which often brings an expression of relief. An alliance is created that promotes candor and trust. The physician is permitted to act as a coach or an enabler in a positive sense. (Mikuriya 2004, 90)

Making available medicinal cannabis is consistent with Mikuriya's understanding of the practice of medicine. He intentionally removes the moral judgment, the chastisement and paternalism. Cannabis substitution presents a rational way of addressing alcoholism where the physician is a partner in a cooperative effort of shared decision-making with the patient.

Mikuriya presents the potential positive effect when alcohol is successfully replaced with cannabis:

> As enumerated by patients, the benefits can be profound: self-respect is enhanced; family and community relationships improve; a sense of social alienation diminishes. A recurrent theme at follow-up visits is the developing sense of freedom as cannabis use replaces the intoxication-withdrawal-recovery cycle, freedom to look into the future and plan instead of being mired in a dysfunctional past and present; and freedom from crisis and distraction, making possible pursuit of long-term goals that include family and community. (Mikuriya 2004, 90)

Adding to a better understanding of the complexity of any particular individual's drug use, Mikuriya explains that "drug-of-choice is not simply a function of an individual's brain chemistry; social group plays a key role (Carstairs 1951)" (Mikuriya 2004, 91). Further citing Carstairs ("Bhang and Alcohol: Cultural Factors in the Choice of Intoxicants"[19]), Mikuriya concludes his paper with the following "two aspects of Carstairs' report" which "resonate strongly with my own observations":

1. The disinhibition achieved via alcohol is . . . a flight from reality, becoming "blotto," whereas the disinhibition achieved via cannabis is the result of focused or amplified contemplation.

2. "Drug of choice" tends to be—perhaps invariably is—determined by social factors, and, once determined, becomes a defining element of individual self-image, i.e., possible but not easy to change in adulthood. Undoubtedly, alcohol's status as a legal drug that is widely advertised and can be purchased virtually anywhere influences the number of college students and other young adults who make it their initial drug of choice. Perhaps the firmer implementation of California's medical marijuana law will make it possible to study whether young adults with a family history of alcoholism, given no legal obstacle to using cannabis as an alternative to alcohol, would do so, with positive results. (Mikuriya 2004, 92)

Terminal Illness: Cannabis and a Good Death

A particular examination of the broader field of medicine, "palliative medicine," which includes the terminally ill but more generally involves the "alleviation of suffering" ("palliation") from symptoms of an illness or disease for which there is no cure. Gallagher et al., in their "Attitudes and Beliefs about the Use of Cannabis for Symptom Control in a Palliative Population" conclude cannabis could very sensibly be used instead of opiates by many patients. In their survey of 68 patients in British Columbia, there were included 11 statements about cannabis, morphine, and analgesics in general. "To be eligible, the patient must have an advanced life-limiting illness and been aware of their diagnosis" (Gallagher et al. 2003, 43). Among these questions asked, results were recorded based on a five-point scale, with "strongly agree," "agree," "disagree," "strongly disagree," and "don't know." The results of this study indicate, among other things, that this population most strongly disagrees with the notions that "the use of cannabis for medical reasons will cause disagreements and relationship problems between my loved ones and me," and "Cannabis used for pain and nausea may lead to the use or abuse of harmful substances such as heroin." The latter shows this population rejects the "gateway argument." Ironically, for these patients, cannabis *may keep them from using* harder drugs. The gateway argument is strongly agreed to by only 2.9 percent, agreed to by 13.2 percent, disagreed to by 36.8 percent, strongly disagreed to by 27.9 percent (second-highest strongly disagree response of all eleven responses), and "don't know" by 19.1 percent. The strongest agreement (aside from their comfort with using cannabis to treat their own pain and/or nausea) was with the belief that "When using narcotics such as morphine for relieving pain, the risk of becoming addicted to the pain medication is extremely low," and also strong agreement that "because cannabis is a more natural substance, it is safer than morphine and other strong pain killers." On the question of whether cannabis used for the relief of pain or nausea is addictive, this was one of two questions where none of the respondents would "strongly disagree," and with roughly a quarter of respondents filling the four remaining categories. As to the question of whether cannabis used for the relief of pain and nausea will cause an inability to think and act clearly, 1.5 percent strongly agree, 23.5 percent agree, 35.3 percent disagree, 7.4 percent strongly disagree, and 32.4 percent don't know.

In their discussion the authors recognize support of use of medical cannabis "spans all demographics" and "the previous use of cannabis in our study population appears to have little or no bearing on willingness to use it as a medical therapy" (Gallagher et al. 2003, 48). Ultimately, the authors recognize that cannabis will be used by terminally ill patients if they have no other effective medicine and cannabis promises to provide symptomatic relief. They indicate that ideally scientific research and study would happen first and then a controlled, safe supply of cannabis provided, but implicitly recognize politics and other factors will likely prevent this from happening.

Conclusion: Cannabis Has Several Therapeutic Effects

Although there is much more to be said about the therapeutic uses of cannabis, my intention in this chapter was to provide essential points regarding the experiences, motivations, and various therapeutic uses of cannabis. Given the history of the prohibition of cannabis in the United States, in my research I came to stop and wonder how much research, data rational, and scientific explanation would be enough to demonstrate therapeutic effectiveness. It struck me (along the lines of the Jamaican study to be presented in chapter 4) that the status of cannabis has less to do with proving therapeutic effectiveness and more about what cannabis symbolizes to Americans.

Notes

1. Here is where it is appropriate to consider the use of cannabis for "spiritual" reasons, as Plato's metaphysical view could be just as well another metaphysical view, with the idea being that cannabis opens one to the possibility of appreciating the meaning of metaphysics itself, and of feeling in the marrow and heart the difference between appearance and reality in themselves and the world around them.

2. "Daily routines" will become crucial in the consideration of cannabis amotivational syndrome, and more generally consideration of psychological "addiction" in chapter 3.

3. As setting up for the Part III Moral Assessment of cannabis use, where it will be shown the "faculties" of desire, will, spirit, and reason will be ones used in reference to the motivations of individuals, making moral/normative judgments about various ways of using these faculties with a focus on cannabis use. Again, the purpose of this current section is to merely describe those motivations in fact cited by cannabis users, ones already reflected in the phenomenological/experiential presentation of the experience of cannabis intoxication.

4. "Many people take drugs to relieve anxiety, depression, lethargy, or insomnia or just because they feel bored. The view that unwanted moods are disease states that are treatable by taking medicines has now become widespread in our society" (Weil and Rosen 2004, 18).

5. More will be said regarding two senses of justice in Part III: Moral Assessment of Cannabis Use and Law.

6. Scientific research clearly and consistently points out not all people will experience the same effect from the use of cannabis. As with other medicines, cannabis can be seen to be of more benefit for certain personalities, diseases, life-situations.

7. American College of Physicians. "Supporting Research into the Therapeutic Role of Marijuana." A Position Paper, 2008.

8. The main question suggested is not whether or not these patients are "abusing" cannabis but rather of what reason would justify arresting such a user.

9. Of course, this information is important for physicians to know, but criminalization of cannabis use pushes it underground and makes it something to conceal for fear of criminalization, involving treatment, etc.

10. I take the concluding sections to argue that anecdotal evidence counts as evidence, and if there is evidence then there is proof; if there is proof then there should be a reconsideration of the Schedule I status of cannabis. Instead of using this tact to recommend legalization, I instead will present in Part III a moral assessment of cannabis use and cannabis law, specifically prohibition and criminalization of cannabis use. In other words, only after a moral assessment of cannabis use, cannabis prohibition, and cannabis criminalization, will I consider the justice/injustice of the Schedule I status of cannabis. Although in agreement with Grinspoon and Bakalar and supportive of their argument, I more broadly criticize the law regarding and all uses of cannabis by U.S. (adult) citizens. The "Schedule I" status of cannabis is dealt with as the essence of the Social Reality of cannabis use in the United States, symbolic of much more than the therapeutic use.

11. Lambert, Didier M. Editorial. "Cannabis and Cannabinoids: 'The Old Man and the Teenagers.'" *Chemistry and Biodiversity* 4(2007): 1610.

12. This economic point is obviously relevant to what Escohotado refers to as the definitive twentieth-century paradigm shift within U.S. society, one to an unfailing faith and dedication to synthetic drugs and a suspicion and rejection of non-synthetic drugs. More by Escohotado will be presented in chapter 4.

13. This of course is also relevant to much research which deals only with the legally approved synthetic cannabinoids, THC rather than cannabis. Namely, there is a jump or a generalization made from the synthetic to cannabis, where there is one compound, THC, being considered the equivalent of the 483 compounds of cannabis.

This is a false generalization, although understandably researchers are doing what they can with what they have legally available to further explore the various potential therapeutic uses of cannabis.

14. Even if cannabis is not the primary recommendation of a physician for a cancer chemotherapy patient (or any patient for whom cannabis would be a viable therapeutic option) physicians still have a moral duty to provide other possible recommendations for there to be "informed consent" to the treatment. In other words, informed consent to treatment requires a diagnosis, recommendation, possible medically viable alternatives to the recommendation, as well as the prognosis involved with each.

15. This point is morally relevant in two ways: first, in that it shows that cannabis is already accepted therapeutically; second, that the legalization for therapeutic purposes does more to bring to light the uses already being made rather than create a large number of new users.

16. See also Clinton A. Werner, "Medical Marijuana and the AIDS Crisis," *Journal of Cannabis Therapeutics* (2001): 17–33.

17. Such indications are the kinds that would dictate policy, were research dictating policy rather than policy dictating research.

18. Again, an appreciation for the meaning of the concept of "informed consent" would have one realize that a viable treatment alterative, one arguably preferable for certain patients through a risk/benefit analysis given their lifestyle and treatment goals, is not optional but mandatory for a competent physician to at least suggest if not recommend.

19. From David Solomon, ed., *Marihuana Papers* (New York: Bobbs Merill, 1951).

3

The Acute and Chronic Harms Associated with Cannabis Use

THIS CHAPTER ARTICULATES AND EXPLORES the nature of possible negative short-term and long-term effects of cannabis use. First I consider the present criteria of abuse and dependence in general and then those criteria for cannabis abuse and dependence in particular as per the *Diagnostic and Statistical Manual-IV-TR* (2000) (hereafter "DSM-IV-TR"). Second I briefly present several relevant points made by Weil and Rosen in their "Marijuana" chapter of *From Chocolate to Morphine.* Third I present a general "summary of adverse effects of cannabis" by Wayne Hall, including a focus on specific effects not covered by the DSM-IV-TR (i.e., "medical" rather than "mental" disorders). Fourth I consider adolescents as a group of particular concern regarding cannabis abuse, revealing those adolescents who are at most risk for cannabis abuse are those with preceding conduct disorders, peers who use cannabis and who are subject to one or more of four negative parenting styles. This presentation of the risk group of adolescents demonstrates, among other things, the relatively minor place the "message sent" by the federal law prohibiting cannabis use has on resulting cannabis abuse of adolescents.

DSM-IV-TR on Substance Dependence and Substance Abuse

Substance Dependence

The general definition of dependence focuses on symptoms and specifically the seven listed after the general definition of "Substance Dependence." Consider first a general account of dependence followed by the seven symptoms used to diagnose dependence:

> The essential feature of Substance Dependence is a cluster of cognitive, behavioral, and physiological symptoms indicating that the individual continues use of the substance despite significant substance-related problems. There is a pattern of repeated self-administration that can result in tolerance, withdrawal, and compulsive drug-taking behavior. A diagnosis of Substance Dependence can be applied to every class of substances except caffeine. The symptoms of Dependence are similar across the various categories of substances, but for certain classes some symptoms are less salient, and in a few instances not all symptoms apply (e.g., withdrawal symptoms are not specified for Hallucinogen Dependence). Although not specifically listed as a criterion item, "craving" (a strong subjective drive to use the substance) is likely to be experienced by most (if not all) individuals with Substance Dependence. Dependence is defined as a cluster of three or more of the symptoms listed below occurring at any time in the same 12-month period. (DSM-IV-TR 2000, 192)

Consider four points about what has been stated thus far about Substance Dependence as a clinical diagnosis. First, it involves a cluster of "cognitive, behavioral, and physiological" symptoms. This means dependence is not merely a matter of neurology neither one merely of psychology nor of any particular discipline. To diagnose Substance Dependence symptoms a myriad of facts of an individual user's life must be examined. Second, the phrase "despite significant substance-related problems" uses the ambiguous term "related." At the very least one must be careful to distinguish between a causal relationship, from the substance to these problems, and a correlation between the two (substance use and problems co-exist but neither causes the other to exist). Third, there is a pattern of use which "results in" symptoms of dependence. This indicates dependence does not happen automatically but over a period of time and through repeated use. Fourth, different symptoms are more pronounced in the use of different substances. This is particularly important to understanding *cannabis* dependence (as will be explained below).

Substance dependence is defined as a cluster of three or more of the symptoms listed below occurring at any time in the same twelve-month period.

The Seven DSM-IV-TR Criteria of Substance Dependence:

Criterion 1: Tolerance: the need for greatly increased amounts of the substance to achieved intoxication (or the desired effect) or a markedly diminished effect with continued use of the same amount of the substance. (DSM-IV-TR 2000, 192) "Individuals with heavy use of cannabis . . . are generally not aware of having developed tolerance. . . . Tolerance must also be distinguished from individual variability in the initial sensitivity to the effects of particular substances" (DSM-IV-TR 2000, 194).

Criterion 2a: Withdrawal: "a maladaptive behavioral change, with physiological and cognitive concomitants, that occurs when blood or tissue concentrations of a substance decline in an individual who had maintained prolonged heavy use of the substance. After developing unpleasant withdrawal symptoms, the person is likely to take the substance to relieve or to avoid those symptoms (Criterion 2b)." (DSM-IV-TR 2000, 194, emphasis added)

Dependence is much broader than is "addiction" (addiction typically defined as tolerance plus withdrawal symptoms). Consider that "Neither tolerance nor withdrawal is necessary or sufficient for a diagnosis of Substance Dependence." If neither is necessary, then that means that one can be properly diagnosed as substance dependent even though one had only withdrawal symptoms or development of tolerance (and therefore dependent but not addicted). This is especially important in light of cannabis disorders, as there is no withdrawal syndrome although usually tolerance. However, even without tolerance, one can still rightly diagnose a user as "cannabis dependent" if s/he meets at least three of the seven criteria of substance dependence. "Some individuals (e.g., those with Cannabis Dependence) show a pattern of compulsive use without obvious signs of tolerance or withdrawal" (DSM-IV-TR 2000, 194).

Throughout the medical literature not merely on cannabis but on drugs in general there is primarily use of "dependence" rather than "addiction," treating the latter as an essentially contested term which is variously misleading. Addiction is simplistic and politically speaking, if one can demonstrate tolerance and withdrawal one can use the claim a drug is *addictive* and therefore justify using the law against users of said substance. The problem with addiction is that it is way too narrow. There are seven different criteria of dependence, only two of which are tolerance and withdrawal symptoms. Dependence, therefore, allows a much broader consideration of the way of life of an individual (e.g., meeting or not meeting role responsibilities).

Consider here in light of cannabis use and an analysis of its effects, this term "addiction." Doweiko tentatively argues that marijuana "does appear to meet the criteria necessary to classify it as an addictive drug" (Doweiko 1996, 127) because there can be said to exist the development of tolerance to that chemical and the existence of merely withdrawal symptoms (not a syndrome with physiological dependence) upon discontinued use. Withdrawal symptoms are largely psychological not physiological/physical. This is of crucial importance for legitimately using the term "syndrome" in relation to symptoms of withdrawal for any drug, especially cannabis. If there are mere symptoms, psychological but not physiological, then there are at most withdrawal "symptoms" but not a withdrawal "syndrome."

Gahlinger explains the lack of withdrawal syndrome although symptoms from cannabis use:

> Most marijuana users—even those with long-term, heavy use—experience no withdrawal when they stop. Some people have reported generally mild symptoms, including insomnia, hyperactivity, decreased appetite, nausea, diarrhea, restlessness, irritability, depression, anxiety, salivation, sweating, and tremors. There may also be a slight increase in heart rate, blood pressure, and body temperature.
>
> If there are any symptoms at all, they usually occur within a day of withdrawal, peak in about two to four days, and then resolve within a week or two. (Gahlinger 2004, 333–34)

And as to the question of whether cannabis is addictive, Gahlinger explains:

> Marijuana does not cause a physical dependence. There is an active debate, however, about whether marijuana should be considered to cause psychological dependence. For reasons that are not clear, some users do develop the compulsive behavior that is characteristic of addiction, although to a much smaller degree than with other addictive drugs. (Gahlinger 2004, 335)

Gahlinger's tentativeness is partly due to the context of significantly more addictive nicotine, alcohol, heroin, barbiturates, benzodiazepines, amphetamines, cocaine, opiates and inhalants.

Criterion 3: Going over Limit

"The individual may take the substance in larger amounts or over a longer period than was originally intended (e.g. continuing to drink until severely intoxicated despite having set a limit of only one drink)" (DSM-IV-TR 2000, 194).

Criterion 4: Many unsuccessful efforts at quitting, at decreasing or discontinuing use. (DSM-IV-TR 2000, 194)

Criterion 5: "The individual may spend a great deal of time obtaining the substance, using the substance, or recovering from its effects. In some instances of Substance Dependence, virtually all of the person's daily activities revolve around the substance" (DSM-IV-TR 2000, 195).

Criterion 6. "Important social, occupational, or recreational activities may be given up or reduced because of substance use" (DSM-IV-TR 2000, 195).

Criterion 7: "Despite recognizing the contributing role of the substance to a psychological or physical problem (e.g., severe depressive symptoms or damage to organ systems), the person continues to use the substance." (DSM-IV-TR 2000, 195)

These seven criteria will be used throughout this book to indicate dependence. More articulation of each criterion will be made in applying them to cannabis use (which is to follow).

Substance Abuse

Moving from the more chronic, long-term condition of dependence, consider next the acute, short-term condition, abuse. Abuse is different from dependence in that abuse does not include tolerance, withdrawal, or a pattern of compulsive use. Abusers, unlike the dependent, have in general most recently started using the substance(s) in question and can "take it or leave it," not having developed a (long-term) relationship and attachment to the substance in question. Definitive of abuse are *adverse consequences* resulting from the use of a substance. To further articulate the term abuse, consider the DSM-IV-TR:

> The essential feature of Substance Abuse is a maladaptive pattern of substance use manifested by recurrent and significant adverse consequences related to the repeated use of substances. In order for an Abuse criterion to be met, the substance-related problem must have occurred repeatedly during the same 12-month period or been persistent. There may be repeated failure to fulfill major role obligations, repeated use in situations in which it is physically hazardous, multiple legal problems, and recurrent social and interpersonal problems (Criterion A). Unlike the criteria for Substance Dependence, the criteria for Substance Abuse do not include tolerance, withdrawal, or a pattern of compulsive use and instead includes only the harmful consequences of repeated use. A diagnosis of Substance Abuse is preempted by the diagnosis of Substance Dependence if the individual's pattern of substance use has ever met the criteria for Dependence for that class of substances (Criterion B). Although a diagnosis of Substance Abuse is more likely in individuals who have only recently started taking the substance, some individuals continue to have substance-related adverse social consequences over a long period of time without developing evidence of Substance Dependence. The category of Substance Abuse does not apply to caffeine and nicotine. The term *abuse* should be applied only to a pattern of substance use that meets the criteria for this disorder; the term should not be used as a synonym for "use," "misuse," or "hazardous use." (DSM-IV-TR 2000, 198)

As the more general definition of substance dependence is followed by specific criteria to apply to determine whether or not an individual user is dependent, so too the general substance abuse definition is followed in the DSM-IV-TR by criteria to be applied. Consider the "Criteria for Substance Abuse":

Criteria for Substance Abuse

A. A maladaptive pattern of substance use leading to clinically significant impairment or distress, as manifested by one (or more) of the following, occurring within a 12-month period:
   (1) recurrent substance use resulting in a failure to fulfill major role obligations at work, school, or home (e.g. repeated absences or poor work performance related to substance use; substance-related absences, suspensions, or expulsion from school; neglect of children or household)
   (2) recurrent substance use in situations in which it is physically hazardous (e.g., driving an automobile or operating a machine when impaired by substance use)
   (3) recurrent substance-related legal problems (e.g., arrests for substance-related disorderly conduct)
   (4) continued substance use despite having persistent or recurrent social or interpersonal problems caused or exacerbated by the effects of the substance (e.g., arguments with spouse about consequences of intoxication, physical fights)
B. The symptoms have never met the criteria for Substance Dependence for this class of substance

Again, rather than explaining these criteria in detail, I introduce these to emphasize the meaning of substance abuse in general. The consideration of cannabis abuse which follows will provide a more appropriate place to consider in more detail each of these features.

Substance Intoxication/Use

Having considered each dependence and abuse, consider next the meaning of "Substance Intoxication":

> The essential feature of Substance Intoxication is the development of a reversible substance-specific syndrome due to the recent ingestion of (or exposure to) a substance (Criterion A). The clinically significant maladaptive behavioral or psychological changes associated with intoxication (e.g., belligerence, mood ability,

> cognitive impairment, impaired judgment, impaired social or occupational functioning) are due to the direct physiological effects of the substance on the central nervous system and develop during or shortly after use of the substance (Criterion B). The symptoms are not due to a general medical condition and are not better accounted for by another mental disorder (Criterion C). Substance Intoxication is often associated with Substance Abuse or Dependence. This category does not apply to nicotine. (DSM-IV-TR 2000, 199–200)

Consider also that "intoxication" is quite complex and varies from drug to drug, person to person. The essence of intoxication for the DSM-IV-TR is the occurrence of "disturbances":

> The most common changes involve disturbances of perception, wakefulness, attention, thinking, judgment, psychomotor behavior, and interpersonal behavior. The specific clinical picture in Substance Intoxication varies dramatically among individuals and also depends on which substance is involved, the dose, the duration or chronicity of dosing, the person's tolerance for the substance, the period of time since the last dose, the expectations of the person as to the substance's effects, and the environment or setting in which the substance is taken. Short-term or "acute" intoxications may have different signs and symptoms from sustained or "chronic" intoxications. For example, moderate cocaine doses may initially produce gregariousness, but social withdrawal may develop if such doses are frequently repeated over days or weeks. (DSM-IV-TR 2000, 200)

Substance abuse includes maladaptive behaviors, whereas the broader category of intoxication focuses on physiological changes not necessarily maladaptive. This is a crucial point to recognize, namely that not all use of a substance equates to abuse of that substance (let alone dependence). When used in the physiological sense, the term intoxication is broader than abuse. Many substances may produce physiological or psychological changes that are not necessarily maladaptive. For example, an individual with tachycardia from excessive caffeine use has a physiological intoxication, but if this is the only symptom, and it is not "maladaptive," the diagnosis of Caffeine Abuse would not apply. The maladaptive nature of a substance-induced change in behavior depends on the social and environmental context. To make it clear that this is so, consider that all examples given of "adverse effects" involve harm to others: "The maladaptive behavior generally places the individual at significant risk for adverse effects (e.g., accidents, general medical complications, disruptions in social and family relationships, vocational or financial difficulties, and legal problems)" (DSM-IV-TR 2000, 200). "Maladaptive" is primarily a social term consisting in adverse effects in relationships with others be they immediate others or society at large. This is to be distinguished from pathological or physical state of someone who has a disease (or "dependence").

Having now briefly introduced dependence, abuse, and intoxication (i.e., use), consider that the DSM-IV-TR reminds clinicians to consider possible pathological, medical conditions, to account for substance use. This is an important point regarding the use of cannabis specifically. Many cannabis users who may appear to meet criteria for cannabis dependence do not in clinical reality for this very reason. Their medical conditions are likely being treated using cannabis (e.g., muscle spasms from a medical condition of Multiple Sclerosis). If patients are using cannabis for a medical condition, clinicians are advised by the DSM-IV-TR to "distinguish" such use from any non-medical use. To fail to account for pathological, medical conditions in labeling a user cannabis dependent is to misdiagnose (and negatively stigmatize, harm in other ways) a cannabis user.

> Substance-Related Disorders are distinguished from *nonpathological substance use* (e.g., *"social" drinking*) and from the *use of medications for appropriate medical purposes* by the presence of a pattern of multiple symptoms occurring over an extended period of time (e.g., tolerance, withdrawal, compulsive use) or the presence of substance-related problems (e.g., medical complications, disruptions in social and family relationships, vocational or financial difficulties, legal problems). Repeated episodes of *Substance Intoxication* are almost invariably prominent features of *Substance Abuse* or *Dependence.* However, one or more episodes of Intoxication alone are not sufficient for a diagnosis of either Substance Dependence or Abuse. (DSM-IV-TR 2000, 207)

DSM-IV-TR on Cannabis Use Disorders

Cannabis Use Disorders
- *30 Cannabis Dependence*
- *20 Cannabis Abuse*

Cannabis-Induced Disorders
- *292.89 Cannabis Intoxication*
- *292.81 Cannabis Intoxication Delirium*
- *292.11 Cannabis-Induced Psychotic Disorder, With Delusions*
- *292.12 Cannabis-Induced Psychotic Disorder, With Hallucinations*
- *292.89 Cannabis-Induced Anxiety Disorder*
- *292.9 Cannabis-Related Disorder Not Otherwise Specified*

(DSM-IV-TR 2000, 235–36)

Cannabis Dependence

Consistent with the more general definition of Substance Dependence is the DSM-IV-TR articulation of Cannabis Dependence.

304.30 Cannabis Dependence

> Refer, in addition, to the text and criteria for Substance Dependence. Individuals with Cannabis Dependence have compulsive use and associated problems. Tolerance to most of the effects of cannabis has been reported in individuals who use cannabis chronically. There have also been some reports of withdrawal symptoms, but their clinical significance is uncertain. There is some evidence that a majority of chronic users of cannabinoids report histories of tolerance or withdrawal and that these individuals evidence more severe drug-related problems overall. Individuals with Cannabis Dependence may use very potent cannabis throughout the day over a period of months or years, and they may spend several hours a day acquiring and using the substance. This often interferes with family, school, work, or recreational activities. Individuals with Cannabis Dependence may also persist in their use despite knowledge of physical problems (e.g., chronic cough related to smoking) or psychological problems (e.g., excessive sedation and a decrease in goal-oriented activities resulting from repeated use of high doses). (DSM-IV-TR 2000, 236)

Consider next the seven criteria of "Substance Dependence" as applied to cannabis use:

> *Criterion 1: Tolerance*: the need for greatly increased amounts of the substance to achieved intoxication (or the desired effect) or a markedly diminished effect with continued use of the same amount of the substance.

There exists strong evidence for this being a primary criterion for the diagnosis of Cannabis Dependence. Arguably, tolerance is achieved by most every chronic user who uses cannabis every day several times a day. It is not as clear there is a need for "greatly increased amounts" when applied to cannabis relative to other substances, so that some users continue to re-intoxicate but do not necessarily need more and more to achieve the same intoxication.

> *Criterion 2a: Withdrawal*: "a maladaptive behavioral change, with physiological and cognitive concomitants, that occurs when blood or tissue concentrations of a substance decline in an individual who had maintained prolonged heavy use of the substance. After developing unpleasant withdrawal symptoms, the person is likely to take the substance to relieve or to avoid those symptoms (*Criterion 2b*)."

There is no "withdrawal syndrome" as positing the existence of such a state requires "physiological concomitants" which are not existent in abruptly stopping the long-term use of cannabis. The psychological concomitants are typically not clinically significant relative to the withdrawal symptoms occurring after the long-term use of other drugs (e.g., narcotics, depressants, stimulants). When they do exist, they are relatively mild. It seems cannabis users can and will stop use when they have to (e.g., weeks or months prior to employment drug tests), so that a cannabis user would not clearly break down and use because the craving was so strong (therefore making Criterion 2b less significant for cannabis in contrast to other drugs). This indicates cannabis users can quit without significant withdrawal symptoms.

> *Criterion 3: Going over Limit*: "The individual may take the substance in larger amounts or over a longer period than was originally intended (e.g. continuing to drink until severely intoxicated despite having set a limit of only one drink)."

Applying this criterion as it is intended to be understood would have the cannabis user using large amounts at once, consistently going "over the limit" and moving quickly toward the second phase of cannabis intoxication, sedation or sleep (more likely to happen for early users/abusers of cannabis). Going over the limit would therefore have cannabis users moving beyond their intended amount of use. More relevant to cannabis users is the sense of "going over the limit" where one has been using over a longer period of time than was intended. Months and years of use could meet this criterion, given a violation of the "original intention." Weil and Rosen nicely capture this second sense of going over the limit by describing it as use "getting away from" the cannabis user.

> *Criterion 4*: Many unsuccessful efforts at quitting

This criterion seems pretty straightforward, and it is relevant to point out one of the subtleties of the way the majority of cannabis users end up in treatment. The percentage of those who voluntarily seek treatment for cannabis dependence is approximately 15–20 percent of all who attend treatment, with the rest being largely court-appointed or as an alternative to more substantial punishment. The staunch federal government stance against cannabis use, including its criminalization, can confuse this issue, with users contemplating quitting less because of the effects of the drug and more because of the significant legal risks assumed by "otherwise law-abiding citizens."

> *Criterion 5:* "The individual may spend a *great deal of time* obtaining the substance, using the substance, or recovering from its effects. In some instances of Substance Dependence, virtually all of the person's daily activities revolve around the substance."

This is a definitive criterion of cannabis dependence; as characterized by using several times a day every day, the individual is spending a great deal of time using and recovering from the effects of cannabis (although "recovering" here should be distinguished from experiencing, the latter indicating perhaps a use of the effects rather than using cannabis for itself). The time spent "obtaining" the substance is not as marked as with other drugs. For example, one could purchase an ounce of cannabis and as a regular user still not need to purchase again for several weeks as opposed to an alcohol or heroin user, who would be continually purchasing their drug as supply ran out daily.

> *Criterion 6: Important social, occupational, or recreational activities* may be given up or reduced because of substance use."

This is also a very significant criterion for cannabis dependence. Here one expects to see a user bypassing opportunities socially, with friends, family, co-workers, occupationally (perhaps not developing oneself, seeking further skills and promotion, etc.), and recreationally (this is a major one, and would include most generally not exercising regularly if not largely living an inert existence). Note that this criterion has us compare and contrast an individual (socially, occupationally, and recreationally) before and after cannabis use. The word used here is "because," so that this Criterion is citing changes occurring *after* and not before cannabis use. To be accurate in applying this particular criterion, astute clinicians would distinguish between cannabis use as "causing" major changes in these three areas of a person's life and recognizing when these changes *pre-exist* cannabis use. The latter may indicate a deeper alienation, perhaps mental illness, or in any event that cannabis is not the cause.[1]

> *Criterion 7:* Despite recognizing the contributing role of the substance to a *psychological or physical problem* (e.g., severe depressive symptoms or damage to organ systems), the person continues to use the substance." (DSM-IV-TR 2000, 195)

The physical effects from cannabis use will be examined in more detail below. As will be seen there, this criterion must be applied to specific individuals involved, as "risks" of cannabis use are especially relative to the circumstances of the use and mind-set of the user (e.g., difference between recreational and medicinal use). Rather than being measured through blood tests, as a pathological condition of the user, note that these criteria indicate cannabis dependence as a psychological disorder, one essentially involving the lifestyle, activities and way of spending time. Relative to other drugs (e.g., alcohol) cannabis is relatively safe in its physical effects.

Substance Withdrawal

Of the seven criteria for dependence, one of special importance for (among other things) demonstrating the dangerousness of a substance is the experience of withdrawal symptoms. Chapter 1 presented a variety of these for the five types of substance. Consider the DSM-IV-TR articulation of Substance Withdrawal (noting the absence of cannabis from examples presented):

> The essential feature of Substance Withdrawal is the development of a substance-specific maladaptive behavioral change, with physiological and cognitive concomitants, that is due to the cessation of, or reduction in, heavy and prolonged substance use (Criterion A). The substance-specific syndrome causes clinically significant distress or impairment in social, occupational, or other important areas of functioning (Criterion B). The symptoms are not due to a general medical condition and are not better accounted for by another mental disorder (Criterion C). Withdrawal is usually, but not always, associated with Substance Dependence. Most (perhaps all) individuals with Withdrawal have a craving to readminister the substance to reduce the symptoms. The diagnosis of Withdrawal is recognized for the following groups of substances: alcohol; amphetamines and other relate substances; cocaine; nicotine; opioids; and sedatives, hypnotics, or anxiolytics. The signs and symptoms of Withdrawal vary according to the substance used, with most symptoms being the opposite of those observed in Intoxication with the same substance. The dose and duration of use and other factors such as the presence or absence of additional illnesses also affect withdrawal symptoms. Withdrawal develops when doses are reduced or stopped, whereas signs and symptoms of Intoxication improve (gradually in some cases) after dosing stops. (DSM-IV-TR 2000, 201)

Essentially, Substance Withdrawal is a diagnosis of the condition of an individual (usually Substance Dependent) who has within the past couple of days abruptly stopped using the substance. The key term of the criteria for Substance Withdrawal seems "clinically significant distress."

Criteria for Substance Withdrawal

A. The development of a substance-specific syndrome due to the cessation of (or reduction in) substance use that has been heavy and prolonged.
B. The substance-specific syndrome causes clinically significant distress or impairment in social, occupational, or other important areas of functioning.
C. The symptoms are not due to a general medical condition and are not better accounted for by another mental disorder. (DSM-IV-TR 2000, 202)

The DSM-IV-TR purposely omits the existence of a withdrawal *syndrome* for cannabis users. This is the most powerful evidence for the non-existence of such a syndrome or of there existing "clinically significant" effects result from chronic users stopping their use.

> Symptoms of possible cannabis withdrawal (e.g., irritable or anxious mood accompanied by physiological changes such as tremor, perspiration, nausea, change in appetite, and sleep disturbances) have been described in association with the use of very high doses, but their clinical significance is uncertain. For these reasons, the diagnosis of cannabis withdrawal is not included in this manual. (DSM-IV-TR 2000, 235)

There has been considerable controversy regarding the non-existence of a cannabis withdrawal syndrome. Both sides of this controversy grant there exist observable symptoms for up to four days after a heavy cannabis user stops using. The true controversy is whether there is a "syndrome" which is caused to happen upon cessation of cannabis use. Along with the DSM-IV-TR finding, it seems there is lacking enough evidence to grant that such a "syndrome" exists. Consider Neil Smith on this point:

> That individuals suffer unpleasant effects when abstaining from cannabis is not in doubt. Although the literature is flawed it presents a picture of a set of symptoms that are brief and mild and centre around agitation, appetite change and sleep disturbance. These same symptoms can also be found in individuals who cease non-pharmacological addictions, which lends weight to the viewpoint that the withdrawal symptoms seen on ceasing cannabis use are not substance-specific and could be rebound phenomena which might be influenced by personality. (Smith 2002a, 629)

Not every symptom can be used to justify the claim that there therefore exists a "withdrawal syndrome." If this were the case it would absurdly follow that anything we stop doing after habitually doing it results in a psychiatric diagnosis of withdrawal. A longing for and desire to resume the previous habit, simply "out of habit," is accompanied by negative feelings not properly diagnosed as in themselves evidence of a *syndrome* but better described as simply missing an old habit, experiencing growing pains and the normal desires, thoughts, emotions associated with any significant change in routine.

> There is even a report by researchers in Prague who detail the cases of these individuals abstaining from excessive use of carrots (Cerny & Cerny 1992). These individuals reported symptoms very similar to those seen in the cannabis literature. The paper concludes with a discussion of the likely substances within carrots that may be causing these symptoms. (Smith 2002b, 916)

Smith's comparison of cannabis to carrots suggests the general conception of "withdrawal symptoms" is subject to abuse by those with political interests.[2] If one considers cannabis withdrawal symptoms evidence of a syndrome then the same must be done for carrots (and every other substance). Hall senses an underlying motive of policy makers who use withdrawal symptoms to justify cannabis prohibition.

> The implicit assumption often is that our policy towards cannabis depends upon whether a cannabis withdrawal syndrome exists: if cannabis has a withdrawal syndrome, then it is "addictive," and hence its use should continue to be prohibited; or if there is no cannabis withdrawal syndrome, then cannabis is not an addictive drug, and hence prohibition should be repealed. (Hall 2002, 754)

He importantly points out that there are perhaps 10 percent of all cannabis users who are dependent (a figure also cited by Gahlinger 2004, 97, and one used throughout this book):

> For a substantial minority of cannabis users (perhaps 10 percent) their lives revolve around using cannabis: they spend most of their waking time intoxicated; they continue to use it despite personal and social problems that their use causes; they find it difficult to stop or cut down when they try to do so; some report 'withdrawal symptoms' on cessation; and some say that these 'withdrawal symptoms' are one reason why they find it hard to stop using cannabis. Their dependence symptoms cohere in the same way that dependence symptoms do for other drugs (Swift, Hall & Teesson 2001) and the more of these symptoms users report the more psychological distress they report (Degenhardt, Hall & Teesson 2001). (Hall 2002, 754)

Here is a figure of 10 percent of all users as being diagnosed as cannabis dependent, a very important and significant fact for the Part III Moral Assessment. Doweiko similarly explains that most who use cannabis do not become dependent: "The majority of marijuana users experiment with the drug briefly and then discontinue its use. Only a minority of those who try marijuana go on to use the drug on a regular basis for an extended period of time" (Doweiko 1996, 120–21).

The 1999 IOM study reported: "More often than not, drug dependence co-occurs with other psychiatric disorders. Most people with a diagnosis of drug dependence disorder also have a diagnosis of a (sic) another psychiatric disorder (76 percent of men and 65 percent of women)" (Joy, Watson, and Benson 1999, 95). Such statistics lead to the conclusion that up to three-fourths of those 10 percent of users who are cannabis dependent likely have underlying psychiatric disorders. This is crucial to consider in light of possible therapeutic effects of cannabis, specifically for mental illnesses (e.g., depression, PTSD) as well as for the moral assessment of cannabis dependence (as three-fourths of cannabis dependent also have a mental illness and bear less moral culpability for their use).

Cannabis Abuse

305.20 Cannabis Abuse

> Refer, in addition, to the text and criteria for Substance Abuse. Periodic cannabis use and intoxication can interfere with performance at work or school and may be physically hazardous in situations such as driving a car. Legal problems may occur as a consequence of arrests for cannabis possession. There may be arguments with spouses or parents over the possession of cannabis in the home or its use in the presence of children. When psychological or physical problems are associated with cannabis in the context of compulsive use, a diagnosis of Cannabis Dependence, rather than Cannabis Abuse, should be considered. (DSM-IV-TR 2000, 236–37)

Also pointed out under the "Additional Information on Cannabis-Related Disorders," in the sub-section, "Associated physical examination findings and general medical conditions," are harms for cannabis users:

> Cannabis smoke is highly irritating to the nasopharynx and bronchial lining and thus increases the risk for chronic cough and other signs and symptoms of nasopharyngeal pathology. Chronic cannabis use is sometimes associated with weight gain, probably resulting from overeating and reduced physical activity. Sinusitis, pharyngitis, bronchitis with persistent cough, emphysema, and pulmonary dysplasia may occur with chronic, heavy use. Marijuana smoke contains even larger amounts of known carcinogens than tobacco. (DSM-IV-TR 2000, 239)

And in this same general section of additional information, under the subsection "Course,"

> Cannabis Dependence and Abuse usually develop over an extended period of time, although progression might be more rapid in young people with pervasive conduct problems. Most people who become dependent typically establish a pattern of chronic use that gradually increases in both frequency and amount. With chronic heavy use, there is sometimes a diminution or loss of the pleasurable effects of the substance. Although there may also be a corresponding increase in dysphoric effects, these are not seen as frequently as in chronic use of other substances such as alcohol, cocaine, or amphetamines. A history of Conduct Disorder in childhood or adolescence and Antisocial Personality Disorder are risk factors for the development of many Substance-Related Disorders, including Cannabis-Related Disorders. Few data are available on the long-term course of Cannabis Dependence or Abuse. As with alcohol, caffeine, and nicotine, cannabinoid use appears early in the course of substance use in many people who later go on to develop Dependence on other substances—an observation

> that has led to speculating that cannabis might be a "gateway drug." However, the social, psychological, and neurochemical bases of this possible progression are not well understood, and it is not clear that marijuana actually causes individuals to go on to use additional types of substances. (DSM-IV-TR 2000, 240)

Here again is a focus on tolerance, significant time spent with the substance and interference with significant roles. The physical damage done seems to amount to a smoker's cough/bronchial irritation, but relatively minor contrasted with the significant physical damage done by other drugs (as per chapter 1 discussion of alcohol). Note also that cannabis (as has already been shown) is unique neurologically, distinct in effect from hard drugs of narcotics (the benumbing, pain deadening drugs). Further, the DSM-IV-TR here rejects as unfounded the "gateway drug" argument. Finally, consider that there is not a clear distinction between cannabis use and cannabis abuse/dependence regarding cannabis use:

> The distinction between *occasional use of cannabis* and Cannabis Dependence or Abuse can be difficult to make because social, behavioral, or psychological problems may be difficult to attribute to the substance, especially in the context of use of other substances. Denial of heavy use is common, and people appear to seek treatment for Cannabis Dependence or Abuse less often than for other types of Substance-Related Disorders. (DSM-IV-TR 2000, 241)

Cannabis Use, Dependence as per Weil and Rosen

To complete this consideration of cannabis dependence and cannabis abuse, Weil and Rosen's *From Chocolate to Morphine: Everything You Need to Know About Mind-Altering Drugs* (2004) includes a well-articulated characterization of "Marijuana" and specifically the nature of cannabis dependence and abuse.[3] Of course, the "Marijuana" chapter will be the focus of our consideration here, but note an essential point made throughout Weil and Rosen's book, that there are not good or bad drugs but good or bad *relationships* with drugs. In this "Marijuana" chapter Weil and Rosen capture many other points revealed throughout this Scientific Reality chapter, in the Social Reality chapters to come, and especially in addressing cannabis dependence. Captured is cannabis dependence in common sense terms, acknowledging the danger of cannabis use, that it can "get away from users" and become a psychological dependency. This description matches up nicely with the DSM-IV-TR criteria of cannabis dependence.

To briefly present main points of this chapter and specifically those relevant to cannabis dependence and use, first recognize that in the United States cannabis was (as will be seen in chapter 4) "the drug of minority races and deviant subcultures even before it got mixed up with hippies and revolutionaries. Despite its status as the most widely used illegal drug today, the dominant culture still views it as a dangerous drug, worse than alcohol and tobacco, likely to lead to heroin" (Weil and Rosen 2004, 136). Further justifying my use of two different "Realities" in this book, one Social and the other Scientific, they relevantly indicate how effects of cannabis and the use of cannabis itself can mean vastly different things to different people (as was already indicated in the meaning, and specifically normative meaning, of the terms "euphoria" and "cognitive impairments"). This controversy is one which extends into the medical profession.

> In this highly charged atmosphere, arguments about marijuana tend to be more political than factual. And because pharmacologists and medical doctors are just as caught up in the politics of marijuana as other people, it's difficult to get neutral information about the drug. Much marijuana research sets out to prove preconceived ideas, and much of it is not worth reading. (Weil and Rosen 2004, 136–37)

And further strengthening the belief of the Scientific Reality that cannabis is relatively safe:

> Compared with other drugs, however, the physical effects of marijuana are not spectacular. It makes the heart beat somewhat faster, causes the mouth and eyes to become dry, and reddens the whites of the eyes. Of these, the most noticeable change is the dryness of the mouth. Only people who wear contact lenses are likely to notice the dryness of the eyes. Increased heart rate is easily ignored, although it can become the basis of a panic reaction in anxious first-time users, who may interpret it to mean that they are having a heart attack. (Weil and Rosen 2004, 137)

Some have begun to call attention to the rate of emergency room visits involving cannabis. Note here that these visits are generally the result of anxiety of ignorant users. "The medical safety of marijuana is great. It does not kill people in overdose or produce other symptoms of obvious toxicity. Occasional use is no more of a health problem than the occasional use of alcohol" (Weil and Rosen 2004, 139).

And of the risk of the oral and synthetic cannabinoids that is not assumed by those who instead smoke cannabis (and a major reason why synthetic oral THC is inferior to smoked cannabis):

> The main problem with oral use is the risk of overdose. Since the stomach absorbs the drug unevenly, the right dosage is hard to estimate, and it's easy to take too much. Overdoses of cannabis are unpleasant, though not dangerous medically.

They can make people extremely disoriented and delirious, as if suffering from a high fever, and are often followed by stupor and hangover. Perhaps because oral use requires more preparation and produces stronger effects, people who eat marijuana are less likely to become dependent on it than people who smoke it. (Weil and Rosen 2004, 138)

As an initial characterization of the negative physical effects of cannabis use, ones to be focused upon in the sections to follow in this chapter, consider "respiratory irritation" as the only clearly observable "medical problem" from the use of marijuana:

Aside from respiratory irritation, heavy marijuana use does not seem to cause other medical problems. Of course, warnings of the medical dangers of cannabis have been well publicized, with reports of everything from brain damage to injury to the immune and reproductive systems, but these are based on poor research, often conducted by passionate foes of the drug. Studies of populations that have smoked cannabis for many years do not reveal obvious illnesses that can be linked to marijuana. (Weil and Rosen 2004, 139)

And further on risks to be considered in sections that follow:

Psychological problems related to regular use of marijuana are also controversial. Opponents of the drug charge that it interferes with memory and intellectual functioning and leads to an amotivational syndrome in which people lose their initiative and will to work. There is no question that young people who lack motivation often smoke a lot of pot and do very little else, but it is doubtful that marijuana made them that way. Heavy pot smoking is more likely to be a symptom of amotivation than a cause, and those same young people would probably be wasting their time in other ways or with other drugs if pot were not available. (Weil and Rosen 2004, 140)

And moving into a focus on cannabis abuse and dependence, consider again the effect on memory as per the discussion of therapeutic use for PTSD, but now in the context of recreational use: "As for its effects on memory and intellect, regular users often say that marijuana makes their minds fuzzy and can interfere with memory. These effects disappear when people cut down on their use of their drug or stop using it altogether" (Weil and Rosen 2004, 140–41).

And providing a good idea of what "cannabis dependence" looks like:

At its worst, marijuana dependence consists of chain smoking, from the moment of getting up in the morning to the time to falling asleep—a pattern similar to that of many cigarette smokers. But dramatic withdrawal syndromes don't occur when people suddenly stop using marijuana, and craving for the drug is not nearly as intense as for tobacco, alcohol, or narcotics. (Weil and Rosen 2004, 141)

Of the seven criteria of substance dependence, withdrawal symptoms and "intense craving for drug when not available" (leading to re-dosing) are not significant relative to the other types of drug (this leads to a focus on the five remaining criteria of dependence as definitive of cannabis). One major criterion for cannabis dependence is "tolerance":

> Tolerance for marijuana also occurs. Even the strongest varieties seem to lose their power if people smoke them day in and day out. This leads heavy users to keep searching for more potent pot so that they can feel stoned again. In fact, all they really need to do is cut back on their frequency of use; even a twenty-four-hour break from the routine of smoking all day long will allow a heavy user to become sensitive again to the psychoactive properties of marijuana. (Weil and Rosen 2004, 141)

Further characterizing how such a "tolerance" and life of continual use can happen, Weil and Rosen explain:

> Marijuana dependence can be sneaky in its development. It doesn't appear overnight like cigarette addiction, or in a matter of weeks like heroin addiction, but rather builds up over a long time. In most cases, people begin smoking pot only in special, usually social, situations. At first, because the drug causes such strong effects, they cannot imagine smoking it at other times. With increasing use, however, tolerance develops, and also people learn to adapt to being high. Soon they can perform normal activities while under the influence of marijuana. Users may then begin to smoke during the day, perhaps by themselves. With time, and unless precautions are taken, marijuana smoking can gradually pervade all their waking hours. At that point, the habit is not easy to break. (Weil and Rosen 2004, 142)

As described here, cannabis dependence is psychological and not one of physical dependence: "The main danger of smoking marijuana is simply that it will get away from you, becoming more and more of a repetitive habit and less and less of a useful way of changing consciousness" (Weil and Rosen 2004, 145). Cannabis use and abuse can become dependence, if one has no "rules" for use one may find oneself stuck with an "unproductive habit": "Unless you set rules for when and where you will smoke, you are likely to find yourself using pot more than you should—to the point where all the interesting and useful effects of the drug disappear and you are left with a stubborn, unproductive habit" (Weil and Rosen 2004, 146).

Among Weil and Rosen's fourteen "suggestions about the use of marijuana":

> If you find the effects that you like from marijuana are becoming less intense or are disappearing altogether, *stop using it.* You can resume after a break and get them back. The trick is to keep frequency of use below the level where you become insensitive to marijuana's interesting effects on consciousness. Odd as it may sound, less is more, and you can easily prove that to yourself. (Weil and Rosen 2004, 146–47)

And using the term *control*, one especially relevant to the Part III Moral Assessment of cannabis use and most relevant virtue of temperance:

> If you find that you are using marijuana more than you want to and are not getting useful effects from it, consider the possibility that it is controlling you more than you are controlling it. Try to do without it for a while. If you cannot, you may need outside help in breaking the habit. (Weil and Rosen 2004, 147)

Weil and Rosen unequivocally reject the "gateway argument" which concludes that cannabis use leads to the use of harder drugs:

> Even the heaviest usage of marijuana does not lead to heroin or any other drug. Many junkies smoked marijuana before they tried opiates, but few marijuana users take narcotics. Many junkies also drank alcohol heavily, sometimes at very young ages, before they discovered heroin, yet no one argues that alcohol leads to heroin. The reason, of course, is that alcohol enjoys general social approval, while marijuana is a "bad" drug and so invites false attributions of causality. Perhaps marijuana users are more likely than nonusers to try psychedelics and cocaine, because the distribution networks of these drugs overlap somewhat, but there is no quality of marijuana that induces its users to become consumers of other substances. The concept of marijuana as a "gateway drug" is nonsense. (Weil and Rosen 2004, 142–43)

They also emphasize several medicinal uses of cannabis:

> Both THC and marijuana are good treatments for nausea and vomiting. Doctors have used them successfully with cancer patients receiving chemotherapy, which involves very toxic drugs that often cause intense stomach upset. This effect was first discovered by teen-agers with leukemia who happened to be pot heads. Cannabis may also help asthma patients breathe easier, but if it is smoked, the smoke will probably make them worse. It also relaxes stiff muscles in a condition called spastic paralysis that results from brain injuries and diseases such as multiple sclerosis. Finally, it stimulates appetite in wasting conditions that accompany

> serious chronic diseases like AIDS and cancer. Conventional medicine does not have good remedies for these conditions. (Weil and Rosen 2004, 144)

Also reinforcing the point that THC is not the same thing as cannabis, the latter composed of 483 compounds and THC being a synthetic version of one of these 483 compounds:

> Although many patients prefer the effect of marijuana to that of pure THC, federal agencies won't permit doctors to prescribe the natural plant. Yet THC is not the same as whole marijuana and may not be as safe. Recently, several pharmaceutical companies have come up with synthetic drugs related to THC and have tried to market them as antinausea remedies. In general, they are less effective and more toxic than marijuana. (Weil and Rosen 2004, 144–45)

Assessing the Potential Harms of Cannabis Use

In his 1998 "Adverse Effects of Cannabis," Hall and Solowij provides a comprehensive overview of the risks of cannabis use:

Summary of Adverse Effects of Cannabis

Acute Effects

1. Anxiety and panic, especially in naïve users
2. Impaired attention, memory, and psychomotor performance while intoxicated
3. Possibly and increased risk of accident if a person drives a motor vehicle while intoxicated with cannabis, especially if cannabis is used with alcohol
4. Increased risk of psychotic symptoms among those who are vulnerable because of personal or family history of psychosis.

   Chronic effects (uncertain but most probable)
5. Chronic bronchitis and histiopathological changes that may be precursors to the development of malignant disease
6. A cannabis dependence syndrome characterized by an inability to abstain from or to control cannabis use
7. Subtle impairments of attention and memory that persist while the user remains chronically intoxicated, and that may or may not be reversible after prolonged abstinence

   Possible adverse effects (to be confirmed)
8. Increased risk of cancers of the oral cavity, pharynx, and oesophagus; leukaemia among offspring exposed in utero

9. Impaired educational attainment in adolescent and underachievement in adults in occupations requiring high-level cognitive skills

Groups at Higher Risk of Experiencing these Adverse effects

- Adolescents with a history of poor school performance, who initiate cannabis use in the early teens, are at increased risk of using other illicit drugs and of becoming dependent on cannabis.
- Women who continue to smoke cannabis during pregnancy may increase their risk of having a low-birthweight baby.
- People with asthma, bronchitis, emphysema, schizophrenia, and alcohol and other drug dependence, whose illnesses may be exacerbated by cannabis use.

In what follows I will focus on the four acute and three chronic effects listed, adding to what has already been presented in the DSM-IV-TR to explain the meaning of each risk involved. I pay special attention to the effects of cannabis use on the "group at higher risk," adolescents, presenting various facets of cannabis use by this particular age group including risk factors of possible use, correlations between peers, parents, and cannabis use, and attempt to determine what specific harms are done to adolescents as a result of using cannabis.[4]

Acute Effects of Cannabis Use

1. Anxiety and panic, especially in naïve users
2. Impaired attention, memory, and psychomotor performance while intoxicated
3. Possibly and increased risk of accident if a person drives a motor vehicle while intoxicated with cannabis, especially if cannabis is used with alcohol
4. Increased risk of psychotic symptoms among those who are vulnerable because of personal or family history of psychosis.

1. Anxiety and Panic, Especially in Naïve Users

First, consider that the anxiety and panic experienced by naïve users, first-time users or inexperienced users, will result in "coming down" in three to four hours and having these symptoms abate. There is no clear harm done other than the uncomfortable experience, a risk seemingly assumed by those who voluntarily use cannabis. Second, this may also indicate that for particular individuals cannabis is not an agreeable drug (something already shown by the Green et al. study at the outset of chapter 2 on the experienced effects of cannabis use). These effects are not likely for experienced users (unless caused by fear of being arrested or otherwise punished for using an illegal drug). Third, consider that such a reaction can reflect the (mind) set and/or setting in which one is using cannabis. In short, anxiety and panic seem to be inherent in the naïve user's experience; this especially given the existence of an expectation of such a (possible) result in these users and an ill-suited setting of use (e.g., in unknown place with unknown people).

To better appreciate the significance of a staunch U.S. law against cannabis use on the experienced effects of cannabis use, consider Pollen's experience of using cannabis legally in Amsterdam. Social acceptance and tolerance of cannabis use itself provided an environment which made anxiety and paranoia much less likely. This indicates a confounding variable for any study of the United States which attributes such reactions to cannabis alone (with no regard to the effect of the U.S. legal criminalization and negative stigma associated with cannabis use):

> Remember that I was in a country where one can smoke marijuana openly and without fear. The effect of the American drug war on the experience of smoking marijuana—a drug notoriously susceptible to the power of suggestion—cannot be overestimated. Writing in *The Atlantic Monthly* in 1966 about the intellectual "uses" of marijuana (now, there's a topic that's moved beyond the pale; these days one may speak of marijuana's medicinal uses, perhaps, but intellectual?) Allen Ginsberg suggested that the negative feelings marijuana sometimes provokes, such as anxiety, fear, and paranoia, are "traceable to the effects on consciousness not of the narcotic but of the law." . . . Smoking in a comfortable coffee shop with a dozen other people doing the same thing, I had no reason to feel paranoid, which is probably why I didn't. (Pollen 2001, 150–51)

2. Impaired Attention, Memory, and Psychomotor Performance while Intoxicated

One major effect of using cannabis as consistently revealed in the medical and psychology literature is on short-term memory. This involves losing one's train of thought, forgetting something on one's mind only seconds before and an impaired retention of events experienced while intoxicated. As the phenomenological studies clearly show, a major effect of cannabis intoxication is the perception of time slowing. Psychomotor performance would be affected by cannabis use. However a major qualification must be made here and that regards the amount of experience of the user. Experienced, chronic users of cannabis can perform most roles under the influence, having adjusted to cannabis intoxication (as already explained by Weil and Rosen).[5]

Impaired attention and short-term memory are not clearly "dangers" in the sense of harms in themselves, but rather are such they could conceivably have a negative influence on individuals who have specific responsibilities and routines no longer being completed due to cannabis use (e.g., high school students, college students). Consider the major age-group of cannabis users are the 18–25-year-old range, with a "maturing out" or sharp drop-off after 35. These young adults are not clearly put in danger as a result of the impairment of short-term memory and attention. It does seem this effect is a serious concern for adolescents and late-teens in school that would benefit greatly in their adults lives from a reliable and sober use of their short-term memory and attention. As such, these effects are of serious concern for adolescents using cannabis, but not as much so for young adults.

3. Possibly and Increased Risk of Accident if a Person Drives a Motor Vehicle while Intoxicated with Cannabis, Especially if Cannabis Is Used with Alcohol

My literature search has shown no definitive proof that cannabis use has caused any significant motor vehicle-related harm. Again, a lot of this research is dictated by policy, to establish a causal relationship between cannabis use and motor vehicle accidents. However, after controlling for alcohol in these various studies there is no evidence of cannabis use causing increased risk of motor vehicle accidents. It is crucial that alcohol use be controlled and accounted for in studies attempting to establish a correlation between cannabis use and motor vehicle accidents. This also reiterates there is a serious alcohol-related risk of motor-vehicle accidents. Relevant research would involve no other substance but cannabis in accidents considered. It is difficult for researchers to even locate accidents involving only cannabis without alcohol.

Consider the recent study by Stephanie Blows et al. "Marijuana Use and Car Crash Injury." Conducted in the Auckland region of New Zealand, with a population of approximately 1.1 million, the group reveals that "recent literature reviews conclude that overall the evidence for the role of marijuana use in car crashed remains inconclusive" (Blows et al. 2005, 606; the group cites five studies here). And again focusing on the point credible studies consistently reveal, namely that when alcohol is controlled for there is no clear correlation between cannabis use and motor vehicle accidents: "Acute use of marijuana prior to the crash was associated with four times the risk of car crash injury with adjustment for non–risk taking variables, but after adjustment for speed, seat-belt use, blood alcohol level and sleepiness this association was no longer present" (Blows et al. 2005, 609).

4. Increased Risk of Psychotic Symptoms among Those Who Are Vulnerable Because of Personal or Family History of Psychosis

Those especially late adolescents who have a family history of psychosis are more likely to experience psychosis after smoking cannabis. Literature on cannabis use and psychosis shows that cannabis can bring about symptoms of a pre-existing brain susceptibility to development of schizophrenia. However, cannabis use is not causing a schizophrenia that would not have occurred but for cannabis use. Rather, cannabis use may bring about symptoms or foretell schizophrenia likely to surface in early adulthood. This risk has been a major item of discussion in certain quarters of the medical community, specifically those interested in the neurological discovery of cannabis receptors and the implications for the control of chronic and acute pain and suffering. Ultimately, the research shows that those who are vulnerable to schizophrenia (i.e., have brains that, given certain experiences in the world, may become schizophrenic in a clinically diagnosable sense) can have psychotic episodes associated with or perhaps resulting from (acute) cannabis use. Cannabis use is just one of many different experiences or brain events that would bring a perhaps inevitable schizophrenia.

Aside from psychotic reactions foretelling the potential future development of schizophrenia, consider the research on psychotic reactions of those who do not later become schizophrenic. Leweke, Gerth, and Klosterkotter point out such reactions are short-term and tend to disappear on their own[6]:

> Transient psychotic reactions due to cannabis use tend to disappear as soon as the short-term drug effect decreases, and thus no particular pharmacological intervention is necessary in most cases. In those cases that do require treatment, benzodiazepines are the psychopharmacological treatment of first choice and may also be useful to support short-term psychotherapeutic interventions. This is in line with reports of the effectiveness of benzodiazepines in the early treatment of psychotic symptoms. (Leweke, Gerth, and Klosterkotter 2004, 905).

And they conclude their comprehensive literature review on "cannabis psychosis":

> Despite the limitations of the data, it can be concluded that there is no convincing evidence from controlled and open studies that "cannabis psychosis" can be identified as a nosological entity of its own. Because of the variety of psychopathological symptoms associated with acute or chronic cannabis consumption, the data

> gathered so far do not indicate that cannabis use produces a clearly defined disease that would justify the term "cannabis psychosis." Therefore, we would like to suggest the more neutral term "cannabis-associated psychosis," implying that with regard to psychopathology, there are several states that may all be induced or, at least, intensified by cannabis use. The term "cannabis-associated psychosis"points to the potential role of cannabis consumption in psychosis but does not imply a simple causal association between the clinical disorder and the use of cannabis. (Leweke, Gerth, and Klosterkotter 2004, 900)

The key term in this article is "transient," a term employed to distinguish the psychotic symptom of acute use from those of schizophrenia (perhaps triggered by cannabis use). The authors indicate this important distinction must be made in a differential diagnosis ruling out a pathological or medical condition (e.g., schizophrenia) to account for psychotic reaction as opposed to arguing cannabis caused the psychotic reaction.

Given the revolutionary discovery of CB_1 and CB_2 brain receptors, hypotheses are being made to explain why cannabis smoking would cause psychotic reactions for a person vulnerable to schizophrenia. "The distribution of CB_1 receptors overlaps with the putative neural circuitry of schizophrenia" (Leweke, Gerth, and Klosterkotter 2004, 902). Giuffrida et al. ("Cerebrospinal Anadamide Levels Are Elevated in Acute Schizophrenia and Are Inversely Correlated with Psychotic Symptoms") offer a neurological explanation for the increased risk of a psychotic reaction. From using cannabis for those with schizophrenia, citing a different level of endocannabinoids in schizophrenic patients:

> The hypothesis that a dysfunction in endocannabinoid signaling may be associated with schizophrenia is further supported by studies showing that endocannabinoid levels in cerebrospinal fluid (CSF) (Leweke *et al*, 1999b) and plasma (Yao *et al*, 2002; De Marchi *et al*, 2003) as well as CB_1 receptor expression (Dean *et al*, 2001) are abnormal in schizophrenic patients. (Giuffrida et al. 2004, 2108)

And furthermore on the naturally occurring THC, anandamide, which activates C1 and C2 neurotransmitters, for schizophrenic patients it may be that, given an already elevated level of anandamide, using cannabis overloads their systems, so to speak, resulting in a psychotic reaction. "We found that the CSF levels of anandamide are markedly elevated in neuroleptic-naïve acute schizophrenic patients" (Giuffrida et al. 2004, 2111). And, "Pharmacological experiments in the rat have suggested that anandamide release may serve as an inhibitory feedback signal countering dopamine activation of motor behavior (Giuffrida *et al*, 1999; Beltramo *et al*, 2000)" (Giuffrida et al. 2004, 2112).

Ferdinand et al. (2005) ("Cannabis Use Predicts Future Psychotic Symptoms, and Vice Versa") explain the title of their article:

> Although previous studies provided some evidence for the role of cannabis as a risk factor for psychotic symptoms, psychosis may also constitute a risk factor for cannabis use. Individuals with incipient psychosis might use substances to self-medicate their symptoms (Noordsy *et al.* 1991; Hambrecht & Hafner 1996). Hambrecht and Hafner (1996), for instance, investigated 232 first-episode schizophrenia patients and found that the first symptom of schizophrenia was more often followed than preceded by use of illicit drugs. (Ferdinand et al. 2005, 613)

And in the conclusion to their study, "It is remarkable that in the present study, links between psychotic features and cannabis seemed to run in both directions, from cannabis use towards psychotic symptoms, and vice versa." This further refutes the claim that cannabis causes psychotic reactions. They propose that "the finding that psychotic symptoms predicted cannabis use may be considered as supportive for the self-medication hypothesis (Hambrecht & Hafner 1996)" (Ferdinand et al. 2005, 619). However, Hall and Degenhardt ("Cannabis Use and Psychosis: A Review of Clinical and Epidemiological Evidence") point out a psychological variable which must be controlled by the self-medication hypothesis. They observe that those who will later develop schizophrenia first used cannabis for the same reasons as the majority of other adolescents (e.g., experimentation, peer-pressure). This puts into question the hypothesis there was something about the (pre) schizophrenic brain which draws an individual to use cannabis:

> The self-medication hypothesis is superficially plausible but the evidence in its favour is not very compelling. The reasons that most persons with schizophrenia give for using alcohol, cannabis and other illicit drugs are similar to those given by persons who do not have schizophrenia, namely, to relieve boredom, to provide stimulation, to feel good and to socialize with peers. The drugs that are most often used by patients with schizophrenia are also those that are most readily available, namely tobacco, alcohol, and cannabis. (Hall and Degenhardt 2000, 31)

In their "overall evaluation" psychotic disorders involve increased dopamine levels, something observed with very heavy, high potency cannabis use (rare in the United States):

> Psychotic disorders involve disturbances in the dopamine neurotransmitter systems as evidenced by the fact that drugs that increase dopamine release produce psychotic symptoms when given in large doses and neuroleptic drugs that reduce psychotic symptoms also reduce dopamine levels. Cannabinoids, such as

> tetrahydrocannabinol (THC), increase dopamine release. (Hall and Degenhart 2000, 32)

And on the question of cannabis causing schizophrenia, consider this evidence against such a causal relationship:

> The most contentious issue is whether cannabis use can cause schizophrenia that would not have occurred in its absence. Although one cannot rule out this hypothesis, if true it is unlikely to account for more than a minority of cases. Most of the 274 conscripts in the study of Andreassen *et al.* who developed schizophrenia had not used cannabis. Only 21 of those who did develop schizophrenia were heavy cannabis users, and at most 7 percent of cases of schizophrenia could be attributed to cannabis use. Moreover, the treated incidence of schizophrenia, and particularly early onset, acute cases, declined (or remained stable) during the 1970s and 1980s despite very substantial increases in cannabis use among young adults in Australia and North America. (Hall and Degenhart 2000, 32)

Chronic Effects (Uncertain But Most Probable)

5. Chronic bronchitis and histopathological changes that may be precursors to the development of malignant disease
6. A cannabis dependence syndrome characterized by an inability to abstain from or to control cannabis use
7. Subtle impairments of attention and memory that persist while the user remains chronically intoxicated, and that may or may not be reversible after prolonged abstinence

5. Chronic Bronchitis and Cancer/Malignant Disease

Bronchitis, inflammation, and irritation of the lungs can be observed in heavy users. As Hall describes this effect:

> Chronic heavy cannabis smoking is associated with increased symptoms of chronic bronchitis, such as coughing, production of sputum, and wheezing. Lung function is significantly poorer and there are significantly greater abnormalities in the large airways of marijuana smokers than in non-smokers. Tashkin and colleagues have reported evidence of an additive effect of marijuana and tobacco smoking on histopathological abnormalities in lung tissue. (Hall and Solowij 1998, 1612)

And moving from bronchitis to a consideration of lung cancer, consider first the logical hypothesis that since cannabis smoke and tobacco smoke both have similar carcinogens, and tobacco smoke causes lung cancer, that therefore cannabis smoke likely causes lung cancer.

> In view of the adverse effects of tobacco smoking, the similarity between tobacco and cannabis smoke, and the evidence that cannabis smoking produces histopathological changes that precede lung cancer, long-term cannabis smoking may also increase the risks of respiratory cancer. (Hall and Solowij 1998, 1613)

On the question of cancer specifically, Hall, Christie, and Currow (2005) reveal that although the negative effects of tobacco smoke would lead one to assume that cannabis smoke causes lung cancer, "There is a conspicuous lack of evidence on the association between cannabis smoking and lung cancers" (Hall, Christie, and Currow 2005, 37). In theory, one would expect to observe and demonstrate lung cancer, throat cancer, but these theories have not been borne out in the scientific literature. In fact, a study presented at the 2006 Annual Meeting of the American Thoracic Society revealed cannabis use does not cause lung cancer.

> The study, which compared the lifestyles of 611 Los Angeles County lung cancer patients and 601 patients with head and neck cancers with those of 1,040 people without cancer, found no elevated cancer risk for even the heaviest pot smokers. It did find a 20-fold increased risk of lung cancer in people who smoked two or more packs of cigarettes a day. (Taskin, 2006)

As a physiological explanation for why cannabis would not be carcinogenic:

> THC and other cannabinoids can change cell metabolism, DNA synthesis, and cell division in vitro, but these events stop cell division rather than lead to cancer. There is no evidence that THC and other cannabinoids are mutagenic in standard microbial assays of mutagenicity such as the Ames test, and THC is not carcinogenic in skin tests on mice. (Hall, Christie, and Currow 1998, 36)

And also on cannabis *smoke*:

> Cannabis smoke is mutagenic in vitro, in the Ames test, and in skin tests done on mice. Carcinogens found in cannabis smoke are similar to those in tobacco smoke; however, cannabis smoke contains cannabinoids whereas tobacco smoke contains nicotine. (Hall, Christie, and Currow 1998, 36–37)

They advocate for further research on the anti-cancer (here "antineoplastic") potential of cannabinoids and other chemical components of cannabis. In a section called "Anticancer Effects of Cannabinoids":

> Evidence suggests that THC, other naturally occurring cannabinoids (e.g., cannabidiol, and cannabinol), synthetic cannabinoid agonists, and endocannabinoids have antineoplastic effects in vitro against lung carcinomas, gliomas, thyroid epithelioma, lymphomas, skin carcinomas, uterine carcinoma, breast cancer, prostate carcinoma, and neuroblastoma. (Hall, Christie, and Currow 1998, 37)

Russo presents cannabis as potentially anti-carcinogenic in the context of his article which emphasizes CBD and other compounds of the cannabis plant are therapeutic in their own right and demonstrate synergy together:

> Whereas, governmental pronouncements have long sought to indict marijuana and THC as contributors to the incidence of cancer, closer analysis has failed to demonstrate epidemiological support for significant danger, even with smoked cannabis (Ware and Tawfik 2001). Little publicity, in contrast, has accrued to an increasing number of studies that demonstrate anti-carcinogenesis by THC.
>
> Legitimate concerns surround the use of smoked cannabis, and its contribution to pulmonary irritation, bronchitis symptoms, and possible neoplastic sequelae (Tashkin 2001). However, recent study indicates that THC and even cannabis smoke blocks the activity of a key enzyme in pulmonary carcinogenesis (Roth et al. 2001), perhaps explaining the observation that there are still no documented cases of lung cancer in cannabis-only smokers.
>
> THC also has been demonstrated to promote apoptosis (programmed cell death) in malignant conditions including: leukemia (McKallip et al. 2002) via CB2 stimulation, gliomas (Sanchez et al. 1998), and melanoma (Casanova et al. 2003), in which tumor angiogenesis is also inhibited. Additionally, two types of breast tumor cell lines were inhibited by THC (De Petrocellis et al. 1998), apparently via prolactin receptor effects. This is obviously a fertile area for further research. (Russo 2003, 22)

6. A Cannabis Dependence Syndrome Characterized by an Inability to Abstain from or to Control Cannabis Use

> It has been proposed that chronic cannabis use leads to an amotivational syndrome (McGlothlin & West 1968; Smith 1968; Kolansky & Moore 1971; Tennant & Groesbeck 1972; Millman & Sbriglio 1982; Brill & Nahas 1984), but this has not been supported by field studies conducted in societies where heavy cannabis use is widespread (Carter, Coggins & Doughty 1980; Rubin & Comitas 1975) or by laboratory studies (Mendelson, Rossi & Meyer 1974; Edwards 1976). Furthermore this syndrome, if it exists, is extremely rare (Halikas *et al.* 1982) and has been reported only in those with a chronic history of prolonged, heavy cannabis use. (Lynskey et al. 2003, 690)

As cannabis dependence is defined by the DSM-IV-TR seven criteria of dependence, here cannabis dependence is qualified with the term "syndrome." It would be illegitimate to suggest a physical dependence to cannabis, something not shown in physiological/neurological studies (again, where the consensus is that cannabis is primarily a drug of *psychological* dependence). Doweiko points out that the logical fallacy of *post hoc ergo proper hoc*, after the fact therefore because of the fact, by challenging the assumption that the symptoms described as "amotivational syndrome" may have proceeded rather than anteceded cannabis use. He directs the focus to the personality of the user and away from cannabis as a cause of a syndrome. He presents a motivational syndrome as a "research artifact":

> It has been suggested that the amotivational syndrome is a research artifact. Individuals who use marijuana on a regular basis are also likely to be those individuals who are already bored, depressed, listless, alienated from society, and cynical—some of the very characteristics thought to be a result of the marijuana-induced amotivational syndrome (Grinspoon & Bakalar, 1992). Thus, it is not clear at this time whether marijuana causes observed personality characteristics, or whether people with these personality traits are most likely to use marijuana regularly. Obviously, further research is necessary to determine once and for all whether the amotivational syndrome does indeed exist and what role chronic marijuana use may play in its development (Schwartz, 1987). (Doweiko 1996, 126–27)

Working Men and Ganja is a study supporting the conclusion that amotivational syndrome is a social artifact rather than a diagnosable condition caused by cannabis use. This work makes clear amotivational syndrome is a concept relative to the U.S. society and not Jamaican society, with (the meaning of) cannabis inexorably intertwined with culture. This is demonstrated in the fact that the opposite of amotivational syndrome can be observed of chronic users in Jamaica.

> The interrelatedness of work life and ganja use described in this volume reinforces the earlier reports on Jamaica (Rubin and Comitas 1975) which challenge the universality of an "amotivational syndrome." This syndrome was described by D.E. Smith (1968:43) as "the loss of the desire to work, to compete, to face challenges. Interests and major concerns of the individual become centered on marihuana and drug use becomes compulsive." Whether or not ganja enhances individual productivity as users claim, it is clear that it often provides the impetus for both individuals and groups to accomplish work; ganja functions both ideologically and operationally to permit the user to face tasks in competitive work environments. Thus, the claims of Smith and others (Marcovitz and Myers 1944, Wilson 1968, Maugh 1974, Jones 1976, Hart 1976) that the consequences of routine smoking of cannabis include impairment of the ability to work, apathy, lethargy, unsound judgment, and detachment from reality simply are not supported by the evidence from rural Jamaica; in fact, the evidence indicates that ganja functions in just the opposite manner. (Dreher 1982, 197)

Consider several points here: first, several studies of ganja use in Jamaica have demonstrated the opposite of an amotivational syndrome in users. Users claim ganja *enhances* productivity, a claim mirrored by slaves and crop workers in the early United States Second, ganja is viewed in Jamaica as alcohol is viewed in the United States, as an intoxicant "permitting users to face tasks in the competitive work week." It may be hypothesized that cannabis use in the United States indicates a correlation between the industrial, technological explosion of the twentieth century as impacting individuals in ways making cannabis use more desirable.

Further countering the existence of an amotivational syndrome as well as the gateway theory and the characterization of ganja users as deviant or inherently base:

> Societal comparisons, for instance, reveal that theories about cannabis use such as deviance, rebellion, relief of boredom, and the stepping-stone hypothesis also fail to hold up cross-culturally. Nor can these ethnocentric theories account for the ritual and medicinal consumption of marihuana which occurs in societies such as Jamaica's, but which is generally absent in North American culture. Thus, in the process of testing some commonly held notions about marihuana, the overseas studies have raised serious questions about the way in which culture influences the nature and extent of cannabis consumption. (Dreher 1982, 198)

Consider here the failure of the gateway or "stepping stone" hypothesis to explain cannabis use in Jamaica. This is yet another reason for rejecting the gateway argument. Furthermore, the Jamaica studies reveal that a mere neurological, phenomenological, and psychiatric presentation of cannabis use cannot adequately explain cannabis use. These are all focused on only the individual and not the cultures involved. Merely focusing on individual effects, in other words, fails to adequately capture the meaning of cannabis use. Again, in the United States considerations must also be given to American culture to understand the meaning of cannabis use.

> despite long-standing affirmations that cannabis usage cannot be properly understood without reference to the sociocultural context in which it occurs (Weil 1968, Blum 1969, Goode 1969, Grinspoon 1971), the majority of sociocultural research focuses on the individual user and the marihuana experience rather than on the society and the marihuana complex. (Dreher 1982, 198)

Dreher next articulates two "models" for explaining cannabis use, each criticized as being too narrow and not accounting for the motivations for using cannabis in many users (e.g., Jamaican users). She explains that "two models have dominated this body of research: predisposing background model and deviant sub-culture model."

In the predisposing background model:

> "Certain common characteristics of marihuana users are considered to influence both their initiation to cannabis and the later patterns that use will take.

> That is, given the availability of marihuana, some people are predisposed to use and continue using the drug by virtue of psychological, social, and cultural characteristics expressed in their individual behavior. . . . Various populations are thus surveyed and explanations derived from statistical correlations between patterns of use and individual life styles. Through these correlations, researchers attempt to explain phenomena such as motivation, patterns of use, and differences between types of users. According to this conceptual model, sub-populations maintain differing patterns of drug use by nature of the sociocultural and psychological characteristics of their members. (Dreher 1982, 198–99)

As for the failure of the predisposing background model to provide an adequate explanation of cannabis use:

> In the predisposing background model, this arbitrary separation of cannabis use from the other aspects of an individual's total behavior often leads to monocausal, or at least inadequate, explanations of the relationship of cannabis to society. Cannabis activities, like culture, are reduced to a listing of individual traits—the amount of use, frequency of use, age first smoked, etc.—which researchers then correlate with other individual traits. This methodology invites them to overlook the context of cannabis use and the way in which it is linked to other social, cultural, and economic behavior. Thus researchers attempt to explain a sociocultural phenomenon in terms of individual characteristics and values. (Dreher 1982, 199)

> A qualitative analysis of the apparent quantitative correlation between ganja-smoking and anti-social, or even violent, behavior on Deerfield Estate reveals that, far from creating discord and hostility, the smoking and exchange of ganja are actually attempts to deal with a highly charged, competitive work environment. (Dreher 1982, 200)

Furthermore, relevant to the U.S. portrayal of cannabis users as *ipso facto* deviant:

> This study has demonstrated the almost insurmountable difficulty of sorting out the relationship between marihuana and anti-social behavior in societies where cannabis is often used as a convenient whipping boy for various kinds of untoward behavior. (Dreher 1982, 200)

Further challenging the conception of cannabis users as defining themselves by their use of cannabis, the very existence of a "cannabis sub-culture":

> If persons convene primarily to smoke marihuana, why are such groupings often structured along age, class, occupational, or ethnic dimensions? How does this

> model account for the fact that these sub-cultures flourish in some segments of the society and not in others? The argument that a cannabis sub-culture exists, therefore, is neither very convincing nor particularly useful. Even if a sub-culture does indeed exist, it cannot be understood in isolation from the mainstream culture that to a large extent defines and structures it. To describe smoking men from Leyburn, Deerfield, or Buckland as a sub-culture whose ideological stance is at odds with the wider society would completely misinterpret the function and role of such groupings. Far from expressing deviant goals and objectives, ganja smoking often serves as an initial strategy for attaining goals held by the wider society. (Dreher 1982, 200–201)

Although perhaps difficult for the current U.S. society to imagine, consider that ganja plays essentially the same role in segments of Jamaican society as alcohol does in American society. Just as one in the United States meets others at a bar and restaurant after work and consumes alcohol, so too many in Jamaican society use ganja:

> In fact, while ganja smoking is a regular activity of adult male groupings, it is incidental to the major purpose of the gathering. The men do remark occasionally on the quality of the ganja being smoked or lament its legal constraints. However, conversation among smoking men generally centers around issues relevant to daily life in their respective communities—farming, politics, religion, and local gossip. (Dreher 1982, 201)

Further indicating the problem with any theory proposing to explain *the* motivation behind cannabis use (e.g., reducing it down to a deviant or other sub-cultural phenomenon), researcher expectations lead to results presupposed and reflect a selection bias on the part of the researcher.

> Relying (again) on correlational evidence, whatever the researcher defines as the most notable value orientation of the population in question then serves as both the motivation for and the effects of cannabis use. Thus, in low-income laboring groups cannabis is used for relief of tedium and monotony; among students, it is to relieve tensions and symbolize alienation and rebellion; within intellectual and artistic communities it is used to expand awareness and heighten experience; among ascetic, spiritual Brahmin, it produces passive spirituality, and so forth. These theories do not, however, explain why the cause-effect complex varies from group to group or how or why marihuana came to be the vehicle for achieving these various objectives. (Dreher 1982, 202)

Concluding her point on the problem with explaining cannabis use by referring merely to deviant values or a sub-culture, Dreher concludes, "while the sociological interest in values is legitimate, explanations which center on values as a mechanism for explaining the existence of cannabis in society have serious shortcomings"(Dreher 1982, 203). Just as the current U.S. society offers a variety of venues at which to consume alcohol and a general "institution" of alcohol use, so too the Jamaican society demonstrates the same distinctions with ganja. Therefore, just as an adequate understanding of why and how individuals use alcohol in the United States must include a consideration of the larger social institution of drinking, so too is the case with ganja smoking in Jamaica.

> In the Jamaican working class the ganja complex is already a well-established institution complete with norms, personnel, and a set cycle of activities. Consequently, any interpretation of ganja must include social phenomena such as the structure and organization of the community or neighborhood, work group cohesion, partner relations, the necessity for reinforcing and maintaining a group identity, and the manner in which all of these articulate with the ganja complex. For example, values in Jamaica are attached to the mode of consumption as well as the substance itself. Thus, it is common to find Jamaican housewives who eschew smoking but prepare ganja infusions regularly or men who smoke ten to fifteen spliffs a day but berate chillum smokers. Although at first blush the contradictions may appear illogical or even hypocritical, they are not; the mode of consumption has symbolic social significance that engenders either acceptance or disapproval. (Dreher 1982, 203–4)

Further explaining that any explanation of ganja smoking in a society must include more than the effects of a drug but must account for the social meaning of ganja use:

> This is another indication that ganja-linked behavior is related at least as much to the social characteristics of the substance as to its physical properties. Once marihuana has assumed this kind of symbolic significance, individual drives and perceptions centered on reputed properties or effects of the substance become less useful for explaining the nature and degree of cannabis use in a society. There is no evidence that ganja consumption in Jamaica moved outside institutionally defined limitations and became a mechanism for personal belief. (Dreher 1982, 204)

Here is provided further attention to researchers biased by virtue of the social policy they support. This point is quite relevant to and necessary for understanding and interpreting research studies on cannabis in the United States Consider how a researcher's value system can determine the nature of the observed effects of cannabis:

> Perhaps part of the reason that sociocultural research has fallen short in bringing a closer understanding of the relationship between cannabis and society lies in the desire of social scientists to justify a point of view for the formulation of

> social policy. Depending on which side of the cannabis debate the researcher stands, the effects of cannabis are euphoria, a better appetite, more energy, increased sociability, and expanded awareness—or nausea, dizziness, loss of memory, an amotivational syndrome, and psychotic episodes. *For some, cannabis users are enlightened, sensitive, politically aware free spirits, while for others they are debauched, hedonistic, anti-social, and potential hard drug users.* (Dreher 1982, 205; emphasis added)

Here are captured major descriptions of the Social Reality and the Scientific Reality of cannabis use. The Social Reality considers cannabis users to have negative moral character, to be hedonistic, to be anti-social/deviant, rejects therapeutic arguments for using cannabis, and also holds the gateway drug argument. The Scientific Reality considers each individual cannabis user separately and describes some users as here described, "enlightened, free spirits, sensitive." The Social Reality, defending the Schedule I legal status of cannabis as unchangeable is not able to acknowledge users of cannabis as "enlightened," "free spirits," or "sensitive," disallowing the very possibility of such people existing.

When research is driven by policy rather than driving policy, the result is a weaker understanding of cannabis use:

> The importance of having social policy well-grounded in rigorously obtained research findings cannot be overemphasized. The ethnocentric focus on public issues as research topics, however, tends to narrow rather than broaden our range of understanding. Researchers caught up with supporting or negating popular notions about cannabis may overlook other, less sensational, aspects of behavior which ultimately could be more germane to a sociological understanding of cannabis and more useful for the formulation of policy. (Dreher 1982, 205)

The move to characterize the U.S. policy in 1982 is still applicable today. Of research which is legally allowed to continue and is granted funding, one essential characteristic is that the hypothesis and conclusion will further support and not call into question the federal government Schedule I stance on cannabis. In this way, *policy dictates research rather than research dictating policy.* Were research determining policy, scientists would most likely find compelling the discovery of CB_1, CB_2 receptors in the brain as well as the myriad of therapeutic effects potentially enjoyed by a diverse and substantial range of medical patients.

> Even the most cursory look at marihuana policy in the United States shows that it is shaped by multifarious forces and, in turn, is probably more influential in determining the nature and extent of cannabis research than is cannabis research in shaping policy. A case in point is the recent shift on the part of government

> agencies from a comparatively liberal to a strongly conservative posture on the issue of marihuana. This dramatic reversal appears to have been effected in spite of, rather than because of, any new evidence and probably reflects a score of social, political, and economic factors unrelated to any intrinsic features of the substance itself. (Dreher 1982, 205)

A final recommendation for trying to overcome researcher bias to establish accurate information about cannabis use would have researchers more conscious of methodological considerations, moving beyond narrow models of explaining cannabis use:

> The argument raised here is whether many of the differences between the United States and Jamaica in cannabis activity are attributable not to culture but to methodological considerations—considerations that include the techniques used, the populations studied, and the question asked. The characterization of North American usage as deviant, hedonistic, episodic, and recreational and of Jamaican usage as integrated, functional, and strongly associated with work life may well reflect a research bias rather than a cultural difference. It is quite likely that employing a community-based institutional analysis would transcend the first-level correlational analysis and permit cannabis researchers to find the same integration of cannabis with other social institutions, the same situational expression of values, the same contradictions and rationalizations and scapegoating of marihuana as found in Jamaica. (Dreher 1982, 207)

I find the Jamaica research quite convincing as a counter to the veracity of "amotivational syndrome." This concept seems much more a cultural label than a medical diagnosis. The fact that the same drug and the same effects are considered hedonistic and immoral in the United States and productive and functional in Jamaica gives pause to rational thinkers who want to get to the "truth" about the effects of cannabis (let alone the justification existing for the legal prohibition of all uses of cannabis).

7. Subtle Impairments of Attention and Memory That Persist while the User Remains Chronically Intoxicated, and that May or May Not Be Reversible after Prolonged Abstinence.

Consider one critical report on the proposed long-term effects of cannabis use by Harrison Pope ("Cannabis, Cognition, and Residual Confounding"). In his response is to a recent and poorly designed study that reported harms from long-term use, Pope counters:

> The weight of evidence from other studies seems tilted in the opposite direction. For example, a recent meta-analysis of neuropsychological studies of long-term

> marijuana users found no significant evidence for deficits in 7 of 8 neuropsychological ability areas and only a small effect size (ie, 0.23 SD units; 99 percent confidence interval, 0.03–0.43) for the remaining area of learning. Another recent study from our laboratory, published subsequent to this meta-analysis, found virtually no significant differences between 108 heavy cannabis users and 72 controls—screened to exclude those with current psychiatric disorders, medication use, or any history of significant use of other drugs or alcohol—on a battery of 10 neuropsychological tests after 28 days of supervised abstinence from the drug. (Pope 2002, 1173)

This risk of cannabis use again employs the ambiguous "impairments." As has already been discussed, "impairments" can be positive or negative depending on the nature of the impairment and the individual (and values, lifestyle, motivations) involved.

Understanding Adolescent Cannabis Abuse: Focus on Parents not Plants

To finish this chapter focused on the risks of cannabis use I present results of my research focused on adolescents and cannabis use. As moral analysis of cannabis use and legal prohibition will follow in later chapters, it is imperative to establish a scientific understanding of youth cannabis use. By and large adolescents who experiment with cannabis are not demonstrably harmed in either the short or long term by cannabis. Most will "mature out" of use. My research has revealed two major risk factors for adolescent cannabis use: cannabis using friends/peers and certain parenting styles.

Adolescents with a history of poor school performance, who initiate cannabis use in the early teens, are at increased risk of using other illicit drugs and of becoming dependent on cannabis. Articulated here are two separate points: one is that cannabis using teens are at risk of using other illicit drugs; the other is that teens may later become dependent on cannabis. Recognize there is no neurological explanation for why activating CB_1 and CB_2 receptors would cause one to activate opioid receptors. When considering any form of the gateway argument, where it is believed that cannabis "leads to" harder drugs, one should recognize two different possible meanings of "leads to": either cannabis use *itself causes* hard drug use so that if one uses cannabis one will eventually use heroin, cocaine, or some "hard drug"—this is the *causal* "leads to"; or cannabis use is found to "lead to" later use of hard drugs (using hard drugs significantly more often than those adolescents who did not use cannabis). This latter way of cannabis "leading to" harder drugs is not a causal claim about the neurology/physiological effects of cannabis but a *correlation* that may have nothing to do with cannabis. Rather it may be that cannabis use also necessarily involves the black market/criminal element, and that the stronger correlation is between those who use drugs from the black market/illegally versus those who use legally obtained alcohol (e.g.). It could be argued that alcohol is less of a gateway to harder drugs because it, unlike cannabis, does not necessitate contact with the black market/criminal element, where hard drugs are available (along with profit motive of dealers).

> The gateway analogy evokes two ideas that are often confused. The first, more often referred to as the "stepping stone" hypothesis, is the idea that progression from marijuana to other drugs arises from pharmacological properties of marijuana itself. The second is that marijuana serves as a gateway to the world of illegal drugs in which youths have greater opportunity and are under greater social pressure to try other illegal drugs. The latter interpretation is most often used in the scientific literature, and it is supported, although not proven, by the available data. (Joy, Watson, and Benson 1999, 99)

Quite bluntly defining the "gateway theory" as a social and not causal theory, the 1999 IOM report states:

> Whereas the stepping stone hypothesis presumes a predominantly physiological component of drug progression, the gateway theory is a social theory. The latter does not suggest that the pharmacological qualities of marijuana make it a risk factor for progression to other drug use. Instead, the legal status of marijuana makes it a gateway drug. (Joy, Watson, and Benson 1999, 99)

Further clarifying this crucial distinction between the physical, causal hypothesis and the social correlation hypothesis regarding the gateway argument:

> In the sense that marijuana use typically precedes rather than follows initiation into the use of other illicit drugs, it is indeed a gateway drug. However, it does not appear to be a gateway drug to the extent that it is the *cause* or even that it is the most significant predictor of serious drug abuse; that is, care must be taken not to attribute cause to association. The most consistent predictors of serious drug use appear to be the intensity of marijuana use and co-occurring psychiatric disorders or a family history of psychopathology (including alcoholism). (Joy, Watson, and Benson 1999, 100–01)

In *Drugs and Society*, Hanson, Venturelli, and Fleckenstein include a section titled "The Role of Marijuana as a Gateway Drug." They there state:

> Gateway drugs, or drugs-of-entry, serve to initiate a novice user into the drug-using world. Although the linkage is not biochemical, common gateway drugs

> include tobacco, inhalants, alcohol, and anabolic steroids. The claim that marijuana use leads to the use of other more serious drugs, such as heroin, is controversial (Gardner 1992). Although it is true that many heroin addicts began drug use with marijuana, it is also true that many, if not most, also used coffee and cigarettes. Millions of marijuana users never go beyond the gateway drugs used. "There are only a few thousands opiate addicts in Great Britain, yet there are millions who have tried cannabis" (Gossop 1987, 9). (Hanson, Venturelli, and Fleckenstein 2002, 372)

And also,

> Much more important factors are the personality of the users as well as their social environment . . . youths who turn to drugs are usually slightly to seriously alienated individuals. Thus, progression from marijuana to other drugs is more likely to depend on peer group composition, family relationships, social class, and the age at which drug use begins (Indiana Prevention Resource Center 1996). (Hanson, Venturelli, and Fleckenstein 2002, 372)

Hanson, Venturelli, and Fleckenstein further suggest that a stronger gateway argument could be made for tobacco. In their section "Social Issues: Looking to the Future," "Tobacco as a Gateway Drug," the authors reveal:

> Just recently, several research findings have indicated that tobacco is more of a serious gateway drug than previously expected. For example, nearly all heroin addicts initially begin using gateway drugs such as alcohol and/or tobacco products (Granted, most people who drink alcohol and use tobacco do not become heroin addicts.).
>
> Biochemical evidence proving that the use of gateway drugs leads to the abuse of others is weak. However, some findings are quite interesting. "The decision to use tobacco or other gateway drugs set up patterns of behavior that make it easier for a user to go on to other drugs" ("Non-smoking Youth" 1991). In other words, smokers have developed the behavioral patterns that may lead them to experiment with and use other licit and illicit drugs.
>
> Research indicates that cigarette smokers are more likely to use alcohol, marijuana, and cocaine than are nonsmokers (Giovino et al. 1994). "[I]n the 12- through 17-year-old group . . . those who smoked daily were approximately 14 times more likely to have binged on alcohol, 114 times more likely to have used marijuana at least 11 times, and 32 times more likely to have used cocaine at least 11 times than those who had not smoked" (USDHHS 1994)." (Hanson, Venturelli, and Fleckenstein 2002, 329–30)

Also consistently stated by those researchers studying adolescent cannabis use (and drug use generally) is that there exist two general stages for parents: one prior to puberty where children are to be monitored and steered away from drug use (and more concretely, be presented with positive role models), given positive reinforcement and attention, and after puberty where peers challenge parents for primary influence over an adolescent and his/her use of cannabis.

> As discussed in the beginning chapters of this text, the mass media and parental role models directly influence the development of youths' attitudes regarding drug use. However, beginning several years before age 13 (early adolescence), peers and peer groups exert the most influence (Greenblatt 1999; Heitzeg 1996; Tudor et al. 1987; Venturelli 2000). (Hanson, Venturelli, and Fleckenstein 2002, 371)

Reinforcing the idea that cannabis use varies with the motivations of the individual involved, consider the array of relevant factors other than peer influence:

> In addition to peer influences, four additional factors must be taken into account as influencing factors responsible for drug use:
>
> 1. Structural factors, such as age, gender, family background, religious beliefs.
> 2. Social and interactional factors, such as type of interpersonal relationships, friendship cliques, and drug use within the peer group setting.
> 3. Setting (physical location of drug use).
> 4. Attitudinal factors, such as personal attitudes toward the use of drugs. (Hanson, Venturelli, and Fleckenstein 2002, 371)

Very important to those who wish to direct educational and instructional materials at the most at-risk age groups, the authors find that the group at most risk of non-completion because of cannabis use were those in year 10 or 14–15 years old.[7] Consider the decrease in drop-out rate between year 10 (14–15) and year 11 (15–16):

> Interestingly, the association between weekly cannabis use and early school-leaving appeared strongest at younger ages and diminished progressively with increasing age: in year 10 weekly cannabis users were 5.8 times more likely to leave school, in year 11 they were 3.2 times more likely to leave school and by year 12 they were 2.0 times more likely to leave school. (Lynskey et al. 2003, 689)

Also, for those high-risk, early experimenters with cannabis (age 14 and below), there are indicated many other significant problems:

> We found that the association between weekly cannabis use and school-leaving diminished with age, with no evidence of an effect of weekly cannabis use upon educational attainment once participants had reached the final year of high

school. This finding is consistent with previous literature indicating that it is *early onset* substance use that is associated with a range of other problems such as later problematic substance use (Fergusson & Horwood 1997; Grant & Dawson 1997, 1998; Brook *et al* 1999), risky sexual behavior (Brook *et al* 1999; Newcomb & Bentler 1988) and criminal activity (Brook *et al.* 1999) and research indicating that the effects of cannabis use diminish with age (Fergusson, Horwood & Swain-Campbell 2002; Solowij & Grenyer 2002). (Lynskey et al. 2003, 690)

The Tims et al. study of 600 adolescent cannabis users (2002) succinctly makes the point that "For most adolescent treatment clients the problem is not 'just drugs'" (Tims et al. 2002, 56). This is the ultimate conclusion from their investigation of 600 adolescents in cannabis treatment programs. They go further into an account of the importance of many other variables in the lives of those adolescents who use cannabis. In this study, adolescents were referred to treatment in clinics in four metropolitan areas of the United States in what the authors call the Cannabis Youth Treatment (CYT) study. Striking to the authors is the need for providing effective interventions where obvious risk factors pre-exist cannabis use in the lives of these adolescents:

The risk factors evident in the CYT sample, such as psychiatric co-morbidity and life stress indicators, together with drug-using peers, earlier initiation of drug use and possibly lower parental support among more severe cases underscore the need for providing effective interventions in a timely way. (Tims, et. al. 2002, 54)

As well as being cannabis users, consider the striking predominance of drugs and alcohol in the lives of these adolescents:

Over half the CYT sample was referred to treatment by the criminal justice system. Moreover, the co-morbidity of CD [cannabis dependence] with other disorders, especially ADHD, and also with greater drug diagnosis severity underscores the heterogeneity of adolescent treatment populations, and the need for comprehensive treatments. Regular peer use of alcohol and drugs in school, work and social activities was reported by most adolescents, indicating the likelihood of frequent exposure to drugs and peer pressure. (Tims et al. 2002, 54)

The authors characterize cannabis not as a menace drawing in innocent children but rather as one small part of the complicated psychological and social problems (including abuse, psychological issues) evident in the general lifestyle of the adolescents who are cannabis users in this study:

In the CYT sample there are clearly many co-occurring problems (behavioral, psychological and health) associated with adolescent substance use. The high prevalence of experienced physical, sexual, or emotional abuse and psychiatric

> symptoms indicates a need for treatment that is comprehensive and not based simply on an acute care model. (Tims et al. 2002, 54)

These authors also step back to astutely recognize the adolescent years are for *any* individual quite stressful and involve major psychological change:

> The adolescent is at the threshold of developing autonomy and separating somewhat from the family, yet still is dependent on the family for physical security and social support. Family members, especially the parents, can help in the treatment process by becoming involved themselves. Family therapy and family support approaches have been developed, and can be useful in improving parenting skills, improving family cohesion and functioning and helping parents to better understand adolescent behavior and positive responses. Effective family treatment should result in support for both client motivation and coping. (Tims et al. 2002, 55)

Hanson, Venturelli, and Fleckenstein point out that the majority of young drug users simply "mature out" of such use: "It is important to note, however, that many, if not most, young drug users do eventually leave drug-using groups and abandon their drug-using behavior, a process sometimes called *maturing out*" (Hanson, Venturelli, and Fleckenstein 2002, 372). As adolescents go through these stressful times of major life changes the challenge for parents is to detect that their adolescent child is demonstrating risk factors for teen cannabis use and not pubescent growing pains. The IOM study presents the following risk factors that apply especially to adolescents:

- Peer norms favoring use
- Misperception of peer norms (users set the tone)
- Power of age group (peer norms versus other societal influences)
- Conflicts that generate anxiety or guilt, such as dependence versus independence, adult maturational tasks versus fear, new types of roles versus familiar safe roles
- Teenage risk-taking, sense of omnipotence or invulnerability
- Use defined as a rite of passage into adulthood
- Use perceived as glamorous, sexy, facilitating intimacy, fun, and so on

In addition to these factors, note conduct disorders are visible, observable risk factors for future cannabis use. That conduct disorders *precede* cannabis use is distinct from conduct disorders being caused by cannabis use:

> A strong association between drug dependence and antisocial personality or its precursor, conduct disorder, is also widely reported in children and adults

> (reviewed in 1998 by Robins). Although causes of the association are uncertain, Robins recently concluded that it is more likely that conduct disorders generally lead to substance abuse than the reverse. (Joy, Watson, and Benson 1999, 95)

Parents themselves, not wanting to take responsibility for an adolescent cannabis user, can provide (fabricate) reasons other than leaving conduct disorders unaddressed during childhood and pre-pubescent years, a significant factor leading to subsequent adolescent cannabis abuse. What is consistently revealed in the literature is that those adolescents who abuse cannabis also most likely had unaddressed conduct disorders prior to abuse. In challenging parental accounts that cite cannabis as the cause of various behavioral problems (rather than the parents being a causal factor themselves):

> Although parents often state that marijuana caused their children to be rebellious, the troubled adolescents in the study by Crowley and co-workers developed conduct disorders *before* marijuana abuse. That is consistent with reports that the more symptoms of conduct disorders children have, the younger they begin drug abuse, and that the earlier they begin drug use the more likely it is to be followed by abuse or dependence. (Joy, Watson, and Benson 1999, 97)

Consider as another facet to be considered in explaining the use of cannabis the genetic factor. Here it is suggested that one with a cannabis-using parent is perhaps genetically predisposed to use cannabis himself:

> Family and social environment strongly influenced the likelihood of ever using marijuana but had little effect on the likelihood of heavy use or abuse. The latter were more influenced by genetic factors. Those results are consistent with the finding that the degree to which rats find THC rewarding is genetically based. (Joy, Watson, and Benson 1999, 98)

At puberty an adolescent changes physically, psychologically, and socially and many of the risk factors associated with cannabis abuse are quite similar to these normal changes. Patton et al., in "Puberty and the Onset of Substance Use and Abuse," state:

> The strongest social factor associated with substance abuse was the report of best friends being substance users. Associations with this risk factor differed across pubertal stages, with almost threefold higher odds of most friends being substance users for those in late puberty, compared with those in early puberty. . . Puberty has long been noted as a time of greater emphasis on relationships with peers and greater distances from parents, a pattern consistent with the current findings. Receiving less attention, however, is the possibility that puberty spurs the development of new patterns of friendship, which then affect health-related attitudes and behavior. (Patton et al. 2004, e305)

Consider the neurological explanation for why a pubescent adolescent may use cannabis or engage in any risk behavior at all:

> Sex hormones do act at receptors in the hippocampus and hypothalamus, areas of the brain implicated in novelty-seeking and social interaction.
>
> Puberty is also a time of psychologic[al](sic) changes, with shifts to higher levels of risk-taking and sensation-seeking, which is a possible alternative explanation for changes in substance abuse with pubertal stage. (Patton et al. 2004, e305)

And a relevant conclusion to the study:

> This study suggests that pubertal changes are more directly implicated in the development of substance abuse than previously understood. Changes in patterns of affiliation, with increasing numbers of friends who are substance users in later puberty, seem to represent an important mediating pathway, one that has implications for the prevention of substance abuse. (Patton et al. 2004, e305)

It is important to distinguish cannabis use by adolescents from use by adults in the motivations for using of each. Hanson, Venturelli, and Fleckenstein make this point in their section "Adolescent versus Adult Drug Abuse":

> Adolescent patterns of drug abuse are very different from drug use patterns in adults (Moss et al. 1994). The uniqueness of adolescent drug abuse means that drug-dependent teenagers usually are not successfully treated with adult-directed therapy. For example, compared with adults who abuse drugs, drug-using adolescents are (1) more likely to be involved in criminal activity and at earlier ages; (2) more likely to have other members of the family who abuse drugs; (3) more likely to be associated with a dysfunctional family that engages in emotional and/or physical abuse of its members; and (4) more likely to begin drug use because of curiosity or peer pressure (Bahr et al. 1995; Daily 1992b; Hoshino 1992; Steinberg et al. 1994; Teen Challenge 2000). Such differences need to be considered when developing adolescent-targeted treatment programs. (Hanson, Venturelli, and Fleckenstein 2002, 462)

Given family members who encourage the use of various substances, criminal activity at young ages, physical and other abuse committed by family members, focusing on the treatment of cannabis use is to focus on surface symptoms of unfortunate, chaotic lives with serious problems leading to abuse of cannabis and much else. Hanson, Venturelli, and Fleckenstein explain for adolescents drugs are typically not the problem leading to other major problems but are better understood as a symptom of other problems.

> Researchers have concluded that the problem of adolescent drug use is a symptom and not a cause of personal social maladjustment. Even so, because of the

pharmacological actions of drugs, routine use can contribute to school and social failures, unintended injuries (usually automobile-related), criminal and violent behavior, sexual risk taking, depression, and suicide (Curry and Spergel 1997). (Hanson, Venturelli, and Fleckenstein 2002, 462)

In their section "Prevention, Intervention, and Treatment of Adolescent Drug Problems," Hanson, Venturelli, and Fleckenstein present concrete warning signs of adolescent drug use. This puts the primary onus on parents to perceive and address these risk factors and to distinguish them from pubescent age-appropriate change:

> As with most health problems, the sooner drug abuse is identified in the adolescent, the greater the likelihood that the problem can be resolved. It can be difficult to recognize signs of drug abuse in teenagers because their behavior can be erratic and unpredictable even under the best of circumstances. In fact, many of the behavioral patterns that occur coincidentally with drug problems are also present when drugs are not a problem. However, frequent occurrence or clustering of these behaviors may indicate the presence of substance abuse. (Hanson, Venturelli, and Fleckenstein 2002, 468)

The behaviors that can be warning signs include the following (Archambault 1992):

Abruptly changing the circle of friends
Experiencing major mood swings
Continually challenging rules and regulations
Overreacting to frustrations
Being particularly submissive to peer pressure
Sleeping excessively
Keeping very late hours
Withdrawing from family involvement
Letting personal hygiene deteriorate
Becoming isolated
Engaging in unusual selling of possessions
Manipulating family members
Becoming abusive toward other members of the family
Frequently coming home at night "high" (Hanson, Venturelli, and Fleckenstein 2002, 468)

Addressing these when they first occur (around age 15) seems the most effective way of addressing and resolving adolescent cannabis use. Given the myriad of problems in the lives of adolescents who abuse cannabis along with the fact that they likely have first-hand experience of the effects of cannabis, it becomes clear that scare tactics based on fictional or overblown dangers of cannabis will only further alienate an adolescent. Such an approach can actually validate an adolescent who is "continually challenging rules and regulations." Primary prevention (preventing the problem from even starting) is one major strategy in itself in stopping adolescent cannabis use. This strategy is best served by the institution of the family, parents who are actively involved in raising their children. Here the prevention is being delivered by other-than family members, already attempting to address the problem of drug use in light of a family failure to do so. It should be noted that the assumption here is that such teaching can in fact be effectively delivered through other-than-parents and families. This major assumption aside, consider that in such educational efforts directed at adolescents it must be done in the right way to be effective:

> Informational scare tactics are frequently used as component of primary prevention strategies. These messages often focus on a dangerous (although in some cases, rare) potential side effect and presenting the warning against drug use in a graphic and frightening fashion. Although this approach may scare naïve adolescents away from drugs, many adolescents today, especially if they are experienced, question the validity of the scare tactics and ignore the message. (Hanson, Venturelli, and Fleckenstein 2002, 468)

To further explain the way parents can make it more or less likely their adolescent uses cannabis, consider the following three studies addressing the first chance to use cannabis, the risk of continuing to use cannabis, and a sense of how risks of using cannabis are diminished. In "Influences of Parenting Practices on the Risk of Having a Chance to Try Cannabis," Chen, Storr, and Anthony present their study as "the first to investigate whether early parenting practices might help shield youths from early-onset cannabis involvement, which seems to be more hazardous than onset of use in adulthood, with a focus on a youth's first opportunity to try cannabis" (Chen, Storr, and Anthony 2005, 1631). They found less chance of having a first chance of trying cannabis if parents were involved in the lives of their children and provided reinforcement to their children as well as for parents who also used lower levels of coercive parental discipline:

> we were able to observe delayed and reduced occurrence of the first chance to try cannabis among the children who had had the highest levels of parental involvement/reinforcement, as well as those with lower levels of coercive parental discipline, through the years of adolescent and early adulthood; however, the evidence did not remain statistically robust for parental monitoring. (Chen, Storr, and Anthony 2005, 1636)

It is striking that "monitoring" by parents was not related to the lesser incidence of an opportunity to use cannabis. Merely knowing where one's adolescent is does not prevent the use of cannabis. Consider this point along with NIDA statistics that indicate the black market has provided ample opportunity for 8th through 12th graders to acquire cannabis in the United States from 1975 to the present (see p. 138).

Further on their point about monitoring:

> Previous studies suggested that higher levels of parental monitoring were related to lower risks of alcohol, tobacco, and cannabis use and other health-compromising behaviors in adolescence. Extending the outcome to the earliest stage of cannabis involvement, our study suggests that higher levels of parental monitoring (eg, parents' knowledge of their child's whereabouts), measured midway through primary school, might have had little or no impact on delaying or reducing the risk of exposure to try cannabis after early adolescence. (Chen, Storr, and Anthony 2005, 1637)

Parental involvement, reinforcement, and low-levels of coercive discipline from the middle years of childhood may shield adolescents from their first cannabis use opportunity. Early adolescence into young adulthood is the at-risk period for first-time opportunity to use cannabis. This crucial point is that the disposition of an adolescent for using/not using cannabis is formed prior to puberty so that older children who are being parented in a positive way are acquiring a foundation to reject opportunities to experiment with cannabis or to go on to abuse cannabis in adolescent years:

> Certain parenting practices in the middle years of childhood may have a durable impact, shielding youths from having a chance to try cannabis throughout adolescence and into young adulthood, the at-risk period during which most individuals start to engage in drug-related activities. (Chen, Storr, and Anthony 2005, 1637–38)

To consider those adolescents who do go on to use cannabis multiple times, Hanson, Venturelli, and Fleckenstein indicate that even in the case of adolescent cannabis use, there seem to be no negative, long-term effects:

> Most of these adolescent users will not go on to develop problematic dependence on drugs and, for the most part, should be watched but not aggressively confronted or treated. The adolescents who usually have significant difficulty with drug use are those who turn to drugs for extended support as coping devices and become drug-reliant because they are unable to find alternative, less destructive solutions to their problems. Several major factors can contribute to serious drug dependence in adolescents (Archambault 1992; Johnson et al. 1996; Walsh and Scheinkman 1992). (Hanson, Venturelli, and Fleckenstein 2002, 460)

Very relevant to consider as a factor correlated with an increased risk of adolescent cannabis use are certain parenting styles:

> It has been suggested that certain types of parents are more likely to raise children at high risk for substance abuse (Archambault 1992). For example, an alcoholic adolescent usually has at least one parent of the following types:
>
> *Alcoholic.* This parent serves as a negative role model for the adolescent. The child sees the parent dealing with problems consuming drugs. Even though drinking alcohol is not illegal for adults, it sends the message that drugs can solve problems. The guilt-ridden alcoholic parent is unable to provide the child with a loving supportive relationship. In addition, the presence of the alcoholic parent is often disruptive or abusive to the family and creates fear or embarrassment in the child.
>
> *Nonconsuming and condemning.* This type of parent not only chooses to abstain from drinking but also is very judgmental about drinkers and condemns them for their behavior. Such persons, who are often referred to as teetotalers, have a rigid, moralistic approach to life. Their black-and-white attitudes frequently prove inadequate and unforgiving in an imperfect, grey world. Children in these families can feel inferior and guilty when they are unable to live up to parental expectations and they may resort to drugs to cope with their frustrations.
>
> *Overly demanding.* This type of parent forces unrealistic expectations on his or her children. These parents often live vicariously through their children and require sons and daughters to pursue endeavors in which the parents were unable to succeed. Particular emphasis may be placed on achievements in athletics, academics, or career selections. Even though the parents' efforts may be well intended, the children get the message that their parents are more concerned about "what they are" than "who they are." These parents frequently encourage sibling rivalries to enhance performance, but such competitions always yield a loser.
>
> *Overly protective.* These types of parents do not give their children a chance to develop a sense of self-worth and independence. Because the parents deprive their children of the opportunities to learn how to master their abilities within their surroundings, the children are not able to develop confidence and a positive self-image. Such children are frequently unsure about who they are and what they are capable of achieving. Parents who use children to satisfy their own ego needs or who are trying to convince themselves that they really do like their children tend to be overly protective. (Hanson, Venturelli, and Fleckenstein 2002, 461)

To conclude this section focused on adolescents, it has been argued that adolescents going through puberty, specifically 14–15 years old, are at highest risk for developing long-term dependence. Various risk factors, although challenging to distinguish from "normal pubescent change," do exist prior to cannabis use (e.g., conduct disorders). Parents play a crucial and seemingly irreplaceable role as the ones who keep adolescents away from cannabis and drugs generally.

Beyond effective monitoring by parents as a way to keep their adolescent son or daughter from using drugs, consider "the most important factor influencing drug use among adolescents is peer drug use (Bahr et al. 1995; Kandel 1980; NIDA 1999; Swadi 1992; Winters 1997)"; also, "Research has identified a correlation between strong family bonds and non-drug-using peer groups (NIDA 1999)" (Hanson, Venturelli, and Fleckenstein 2002, 460). As to the experience of a cannabis using adolescent, consider that "Many adolescents use drugs to help cope with boredom, unpleasant feelings, emotions, and stress or to relieve depression, reduce tension, and reduce alienation (Teen Challenge 2000)" (Hanson, Venturelli, and Fleckenstein 2002, 460). And also, "Sociological factors that damage self-image can also encourage adolescent drug use. Feelings of rejection cause poor relationships with family members, peers, school personnel, or co-workers" (Hanson, Venturelli, and Fleckenstein 2002, 461).

Perceptions of Risk, Availability, and Prevalence of Cannabis Use by Adolescents

Among the points established in this chapter regarding adolescent cannabis use is that conduct disorders in childhood precede adolescent cannabis abuse, four specific parental styles are associated with increased chance of cannabis abuse, and that having cannabis-using friends increases chances of adolescent cannabis use. One (Social Reality) belief is that were cannabis legalized, adolescents would perceive cannabis as safe to use (thereby legalization of cannabis for adult use would "send the wrong message" to adolescents). It is unclear and unproven that making cannabis legal for adult use would overcome positive parental influence and have adolescents with no previous conduct disorders abusing cannabis. Valuable here to consider are data regarding current and past perceived risk by adolescents. The Monitoring the Future Study ("MTF") conducted at the Institute of Social Research at the University of Michigan for the National Institute on Drug Abuse provides this valuable data. In what follows I present results on marijuana specifically, focused on the perceived risk (one of the four general questions posed in the study). These provide some idea of the perceptions of "great risk" from using cannabis by adolescents from 1975 to the present. My main reasons for presenting these data is to have something to work with in considering the question of what effect, if any, the legalization of cannabis would have on the perceived risk of cannabis by adolescents. As I understand the "sending the wrong message" argument, with the legalization of cannabis for adult use the result would be significantly less perceived risk by adolescents. This prediction has no U.S. precedent, as the use of cannabis as an intoxicant is a twentieth-century phenomenon (as will be shown in chapter four). Only in the 1960s in the United States was there widespread use of cannabis as a whole new drug amid a unique and politically charged context. Cannabis was scheduled as one of several of the most controlled substances in 1973, and before that from 1937 on was treated as a producer of violence (assassin myth). All this is to say social and political context must be appreciated and somehow factored into a prediction of how harmful adolescents will think cannabis to be.

In the "National Results on Adolescent Drug Abuse: Overview of Key Findings, 2007," contents include Introduction, Study Design and Methods, Overview of Key Findings, Specific Results by Drug (subsections: any illicit drug, marijuana, inhalants, LSD, cocaine, crack, amphetamines, methamphetamine and crystal methamphetamine (ice), heroin, narcotics other than heroin, tranquilizers, sedatives (barbiturates), ecstasy (MDMA) and other "club drugs," alcohol, cigarettes, smokeless tobacco, steroids), Subgroup Differences, and Tables Covering All Drugs. In the introduction they explain that "The 2007 MTF survey encompassed nearly 50,000 eighth-, tenth-, and twelfth-grade students in over 400 secondary schools nationwide" (Johnston et al. 2007, 1). They also explain that the figures presented are based upon the overall proportions of students who: 1. use a drug, 2. see "great risk" associated with its use, 3. disapprove of its use, and 4. say they think they could get the drug "fairly easily" or "very easily" if they wanted to. Also, "The years for which data on each grade are available are 1975–2007 for 12th graders and 1991–2007 for 8th and 10th graders, who were first included in the study in 1991" (Johnston et al. 2007, 1). They also relevantly explain in their Overview of Key Findings a general principle they gleaned from data on all drugs. The principle about drugs in society at large (as percentages in the study bear out) is as perceived risk of a drug decreases use of that drug increases. This point makes quite important the perceptions of the risk of cannabis use (and other drugs) *by adolescents.*

Of "Perceived Risk" of marijuana (and several other drugs), the following question is asked: How much do you think people risk harming themselves (physically or in other ways) if they . . . followed by three scenarios (note that the question is of "people" and not other adolescents). Consider the actual perception of risk by 12th graders for each of the three scenarios:

Of "great risk" of trying marijuana once or twice, 12th graders responded as low as 8.1 in 1978 and as high as 27.1 in 1991. Of the "great risk" of smoking marijuana occasionally there were as few as 12.4 percent of 12th graders answering "great risk" in 1978 and as many as 40.6 percent answering "great risk" in 1991. Of the "great risk" of smoking marijuana regularly, there were as few as 34.9 percent in 1978 and as many as 78.6 percent answering "great risk" in 1991. It is fascinating these two years (1978, 1991) are the two extremes for

TABLE 3.1
Document: 12th Grader Perception of Risk of Marijuana Use

Year	*Try Marijuana Once Once or Twice*	*Smoke Marijuana Occasionally*	*Smoke Marijuana Regularly*
1975	15.1	18.1	43.3
1976	11.4	15.0	38.6
1977	9.5	13.4	36.4
1978	8.1	12.4	34.9
1979	9.4	13.5	42.0
1980	10.0	14.7	50.4
1981	13.0	19.1	57.6
1982	11.5	18.3	60.4
1983	12.7	20.6	62.8
1984	14.7	22.6	66.9
1985	14.8	24.5	70.4
1986	15.1	25.0	71.3
1987	18.4	30.3	73.5
1988	19.0	31.7	77.0
1989	23.6	36.5	77.5
1990	23.1	36.9	77.8
1991	27.1	40.6	78.6
1992	24.5	39.6	76.5
1993	21.9	35.6	72.5
1994	19.5	30.1	65.0
1995	16.3	25.6	60.8
1996	15.6	25.9	59.9
1997	14.9	24.7	58.1
1998	16.7	24.4	58.5
1999	15.7	23.9	57.4
2000	13.7	23.4	58.3
2001	15.3	23.5	57.4
2002	16.1	23.2	53.0
2003	16.1	26.6	54.9
2004	15.9	25.4	54.6
2005	16.1	25.8	58.0
2006	17.8	25.9	57.9
2007	18.6	27.1	54.8

Johnston, L. D., P. M. O'Malley, J. G. Bachman, and J. E. Schulenberg. *Monitoring the Future National Results on Adolescent Drug Use: Overview of Key Findings, 2007* (NIH Publication No. 08-6418). Bethesda, MD: National Institute on Drug Abuse, 2007.

all three of these questions from 1975 to 2007. If one reflects on the social and political climate and defined issues and trends in these two years, perhaps one could seize upon some factors (e.g., generational beliefs of the parents in each year) between the perceived "great risk" of cannabis use by adolescents. Remember that the "sending the wrong message" argument predicts the percentage of those who perceive a "great risk" of using cannabis in each of the three scenarios would plummet upon the legalization of cannabis use for adult use. Again, it is far from clear one could with confidence make such a prediction if for no other reason than the incredible complexity of various factors to take into account in making such a prediction.

In 2007, notice the decline in the percentage of 8th, 10th, and 12th graders who answered "great risk" to the same questions. Given the onset of puberty, adjusting and preparing to enter adulthood, all of the significant changes in personality and overall development, it seems those most relevant and to be considered in sending the right message are again parents, peers, conduct disorders, etc. (as discussed in the previous section).

Consider also the perception by 12th graders of "great risk" resulting from using once or twice the following drugs (compared and contrasted with the 18.6 percent of 12th graders who think using marijuana once or twice is a "great risk" of harm):

LSD: 37
PCP: 48
MDMA: 58.1
Cocaine: 51.3
Crack: 47.3
Heroin: 58.4
Amphetamines: 41.3
Crystal Meth: 60.2
Sedatives (barbiturates): 27.9
Try one or two drinks of an alcoholic beverage (beer, wine, liquor): 10.5
Smoke one or more packs of cigarettes per day: 77.3
Take steroids: 57.4

Determining how adolescents come to view drugs as a "great risk" is a complex matter. It is important to also point out that cannabis, although a Schedule

TABLE 3.2
Document: 8th, 10th and 12th Grader Perception of Risk of Marijuana Use (2007)

Grades	*Try Marijuana Once Once or Twice*	*Smoke Marijuana Occasionally*	*Smoke Marijuana Regularly*
8th:	32.8	50.7	74.3
10th:	22.2	36.0	64.5
12th:	18.6	27.1	54.8

Johnston, L. D., P. M. O'Malley, J. G. Bachman, and J. E. Schulenberg. *Monitoring the Future National Results on Adolescent Drug Use: Overview of Key Findings, 2007* (NIH Publication No. 08-6418). Bethesda, MD: National Institute on Drug Abuse, 2007.

I drug and therefore controlled as much as a drug can be controlled and eradicated using law, is readily available to adolescents. The MTF study also includes in three tables "Trends in Availability of Drugs" for each 12th, 10th, and 8th graders. Consider for 2007 the perception of availability of marijuana for each of these three age groups:

> How difficult do you think it would be for you to get each of the following types of drugs, if you wanted some?
>
> Marijuana: 8th grade, 37.4; 10th grade, 69.0; 12th grade, 83.9.

Again, note the significant increase in availability within these several years. The percentage of 12th graders who perceive marijuana to be fairly easy to get has remained steady from 1975 to 2007, ranging from 82 to 90 percent throughout these years. This quite significant data shows, among other things, that making cannabis legal for adult use *would not significantly increase the availability* of cannabis (as it is available to virtually any 12th grader who wants it under the current absolute prohibition of cannabis). Given this availability, it also stands to reason that the perception of risk of cannabis use is one informed by actual experience with cannabis, either using oneself or experiencing the use and observing effects in peers (or adults). In "Trends in Annual Prevalence of Use of Various Drugs in Grades 8, 10, and 12 (Table 2)," consider for marijuana/hashish the following percentage of students have used marijuana in the last year: 8th, 10.3; 10th, 24.6; 12th, 31.7. And from annual use to use within the past month: 8th, 5.7; 10th, 14.2; 12th, 18.8. Finally, consider percentages reporting daily use of marijuana: 8th, 0.8; 10th, 2.8; 12th, 5.1.

These numbers suggest that of those adolescents who do use cannabis, it is not likely they will continue to use repeatedly. Although 31.7 have used in the past year, 18.8 have used in the past month and then there is a quite significant drop to 5.1 using daily. Rather than indicating a problem with cannabis dependence, these numbers show marijuana use as one of experimentation during the year, less likely during the past month, and quite unlikely used daily.

Notes

1. This same point is crucial to appreciate in the context of "amotivational syndrome" as well, with symptoms of this syndrome (e.g., bored, listless) many times preexisting cannabis use, rather than being caused by cannabis use.

2. To add one final attack on the potential for misuse of the term "withdrawal symptoms," Ashton skeptically concludes that "Clinical definitions of supposedly drug-specific withdrawal syndromes can only be arbitrary (Ashton 1991)." Heather Ashton Defining the Indefinable: Comments on Smith Letters to Editor *Addiction* 97 (2002): 756.

3. In *From Chocolate to Morphine*, Weil and Rosen present fourteen chapters, including "Straight Talk at the Start," "What Is a Drug?," "Why People Use Drugs," "Relationships with Drugs," "Types of Drugs," "Stimulants," "Depressants," "Psychedelics, or Hallucinogens," "Marijuana," "Solvents and Inhalants; Deliriants; PCP and Ketamine," "Medical Drugs: Herbal Remedies; Smart Drugs," "Problems with Drugs," "Alternatives to Taking Drugs," "Final Words."

4. Low-birth weight research revealed little to demonstrate any significant concern for pregnant women. Cannabis use actually has a long history of use by midwives and those in what we now refer to as the medical field of obstetrics and gynecology. The second group listed by Hall here, of those who generally have a pre-existing condition which may be exacerbated by the use of cannabis, go beyond the more general risks I am primarily interested in presenting in this section.

5. Again, this is the 10 percent of those diagnosable as dependent; those new to cannabis use would likely display more inability to perform various psychomotor tasks

6. This matches my own discussions with several ER physicians who consistently told me of marijuana using ER visits: we just talk them down and they usually leave in three or four hours.

7. As this study is in Victoria (Australia) year 7–12 for secondary school with year 7 having children ages 11–12; year 8, 12–13; year 9, 13–14; year 10, 14–15; year 11, 15–16; year 12 (last year of secondary school): 16–17).

II

THE SOCIAL REALITY ON CANNABIS USE

4

Western Responses to the Unknown: Foundational Events Creating the Social Reality of Cannabis Use

> It is impossible to understand an institution adequately without an understanding of the historical process in which it was produced. (Berger and Luckmann 1966, 54–55)

> But what is so unusual about cannabis's coevolution (compared to that of the rose, say, or the apple) is that it followed two such divergent paths down to our time, each reflecting the influence of a completely different human desire. Along the first path (which appears to have begun in ancient China and moved west toward northern Europe, then on to the Americas), the plant was selected by people for the strength and length of its fibers. (Up until the last century, hemp was one of humankind's main sources of paper and cloth.) Along the other path (which began somewhere in central Asia and moved down through India, then into Africa, and from there across to the Americas with the slaves and up to Europe with Napoleon's army), cannabis was selected for its psychoactive and medicinal powers. Ten thousand years later, hemp and cannabis are as different as night and day: hemp produces negligible amounts of THC and cannabis a worthless fiber. (In the eyes of the U.S. government, however, there is still only one plant, so that the taboo on the drug plant has, pointlessly, doomed the fiber.) It is hard to conceive of a domesticated plant more plastic than cannabis, a single species answering to two such different desires, the first more or less spiritual in nature and the other, quite literally, material. (Pollen 2001, 157–58)

IN THIS CHAPTER I PRESENT SEVERAL HISTORICAL events relevant to the twenty-first-century Social Reality of cannabis use.[1] This story about cannabis begins in the East several thousands of years ago. This is by no means an exhaustive presentation of the history of cannabis. My modest purpose is to develop two points: First, present and make clear the significance of cannabis having origins in the East and of how this fact led to a general rejection of cannabis by the West. This point provides a backdrop against which to focus on the birth of the U.S. federal government prohibition of cannabis (as "marijuana"), especially in the twentieth century up to the present day. Second, demonstrated is that the law against cannabis has virtually nothing to do with the physical, neurological, or therapeutic effects of cannabis but has to do with those who use cannabis.

Earliest Recorded History of Cannabis Use

Cannabis is very new to the West and specifically the United States. Although cannabis/hashish has been used for over 3,000 years in the East, we in the United States have only in the past 100 years or so come to experience the use of cannabis/marijuana as an intoxicant. The name "marijuana" itself is Spanish/Mexican, a socially constructed label created by the U.S. federal government inviting the false assumption that cannabis as a plant is of Mexican origin even though it is not a native plant to Mexico. Vivienne Crawford explains how the name "marijuana" came to be used for cannabis: "The Spanish word first gained currency in the USA in the 1920's, as part of a deliberate attempt to associate the plant with Mexican migrants" (Crawford 2002, 40–41). These deliberate attempts included the popular press drawing connections between Mexican migrants and "culturally subversive attitudes and anti-social behaviour" (Crawford 2002, 41).

Earliest Recorded History of Cannabis Use

Hemp has been used for several millennia to make durable rope, sails for ships, and clothing, and cannabis has been used for millennia to serve religious, medicinal, therapeutic, and recreational ends. The earliest history of cannabis is in the East. Hanson, Venturelli, and Fleckenstein cite the *Book of Drugs* as arguably the first known record of cannabis:

> The *Book of Drugs* written about 2737 B.C. by the Chinese Emperor Shen Nung; he prescribed marijuana for treating gout, malaria, gas pains, and absentmindedness. The Chinese apparently had much respect for the plant. They obtained fiber for clothes and medicine from it for thousands of years. The Chinese named the plant *ma* (maw), which in the Chinese language can also mean "valu-

> able" or "endearing." The term *ma* was still used as late as 1930. (Hanson, Venturelli, and Fleckenstein 2002, 365)

In 2000 B.C., "nomadic tribes started to spread out from central Asia. The first were the Aryans from whom it is thought the Indians acquired the name *bhang* (or *bhanga*) for cannabis" (Booth 2004, 20). The Hindu *Vedas*, specifically the fourth of four books, the Atharva Veda, considers cannabis one of five sacred plants through which mankind is cleansed of sin, and presents the god Shiva bringing cannabis down from the Himalayas for the pleasure of mankind (Booth 2004, 20). The Aryans also influenced the Assyrians who in 900 B.C., "used cannabis for religious purposes, calling it *qunubu*, meaning 'the drug for sadness'" (Booth 2004, 22). Then in 800 B.C. "another migration of Aryans occurred" known as the Scythians, "they came from the region of the Altai mountains in southern Siberia. . . . They were also trading partners with the Semites in the Middle East, who referred to them as the Ashkenaz, a war-mongering race who, in the seventh century BC, invaded the area now covered by Israel, Jordan and southern Syria. They brought cannabis with them and it is through contact with them that Europeans first came to know of it" (Booth 2004, 24).

Escohotado begins *A Brief History of Drugs: From the Stone Age to the Stoned Age* by emphasizing the significance of the ancient Greek Hippocratic School of medicine for how we today understand and practice medicine. As focused on disease as a part of natural physical processes an epistemological and metaphysical change is made from prior beliefs of the involvement of gods, spirits, and unobservable supernatural entities. This basic Greek understanding of medicine provided the most basic assumptions that ground current Western scientific conception of the practice of medicine and healing. This initial move is one commonly described in Western philosophy as a shift from myth to reason. The defining characteristics of the first philosophers, the pre-Socratics, are their questions of cosmology and use of reason to come to conclusions about the origin of the cosmos, ultimate reality, and of all that exists. Escohotado explains the move to rationality within the practice of medicine as Aristotelian, where there was believed to exist an order of pre-existing categories in nature that the human mind could grasp. There exist ways of ordering and categorizing, therefore understanding through reason and not revelation, the essence of plants, animals, and human beings. Escohotado characterizes the subtle but quite significant change from *pharmakos* to *pharmakon*:

> In distancing his acts from magic and religion, the Hippocratic adeptly negated the validity of any cure based on a symbolic transference of the malady from one person to another, thus breaking up with the institution of the scapegoat. Instead

> of using some *pharmakos* or goat to absorb the alien impurity, the new medicine used *pharmakon*, or a suitable drug. (Escohotado 1999, 12)

Of the use of cannabis medicinally by the Greeks and Romans, James L. Butrica ("The Medical Use of Cannabis among the Greeks and Romans") clarifies significantly the Scythian ritual (as described by Herodotus) of tossing "cannabis seeds onto red-hot rocks and inhale the vapors that were released" (Butrica 2002, 54). A main point of his presentation is that this was not recreational but rather the end of a typically forty-day ritual following the death of a family member. The mood was one of mourning. Of the Scythians, they would actually "crawl under small tents 18 inches high" and insert their heads into "a structure at ground level." The use of cannabis in such a structure within this ritual is not one of pleasure and hedonism.

Still focusing on the Greco-Roman world, Butrica points out that "Probably the earliest surviving account of the medical use of cannabis is the entry in the *Materia medica* of the Greek physician Dioscorides, published around 65 CE, followed closely by the one in the *Historia naturalis* of Pliny the Elder, finished in 77 CE and dedicated to the emperor Titus" (Butrica 2002, 56). Among the treatments recorded by Pliny, Butrica cites use of seeds to "extinguish the semen" (as in drying up leaking semen), in treating the ears (vermin out of the ears), for the bellies of farm animals, using the cooked root on joints and against gout, and use of the raw root on burns" (Butrica 2002, 57–58). Galen cites, as did Pliny, the effects of "drying up the semen" and also for use against earaches, also referencing uses as a mosquito repellant, for nosebleeds, gonorrhea (as a condition of the spermatic ducts, therefore making more sense of the use of "drying the semen").

The most basic of terms of our current understanding of drug use and abuse, tolerance, was free of the negative moral connotations it carries today. The Greeks also perceived the phenomenon we today call tolerance, even though they saw it not as part of an undesirable habit but as a positive mechanism of "autoimmunization." Escohotado cites Theophrastus explaining 'familiarity robs them of their venom'" (Escohotado 1999, 13).

Within Greece "the social and individual danger of drugs in their case was concentrated on wine" (Escohotado 1999, 15; more to be said on wine in chapters 9 and 10). There was little if any use of cannabis as a (recreational) intoxicant during the five hundred years before and after Christ. With the fall of the Roman Empire and birth of sea trade, conquest, and exploration, a need for rope, sails, and other materials ideally provided by sturdy hemp materials had the cultivation of hemp dominate European countries (perhaps introducing cannabis to North America through the Vikings). This sixth-century use of hemp qua fiber would continue up through the nineteenth century.

Gnostic Rejection of Intoxication

An early sect of Christianity in Ethiopia used cannabis in their rituals, "Ethiopia . . . became a Christian nation from the fourth century. A Monophysite form of Christianity, the Ethiopian Coptic faith has used cannabis in its rituals for centuries" (Booth 2004, 43). And further, on Africa generally,

> As cannabis smoking developed into a communal social activity, earth pipes were constructed, a sort of hybrid between hand-held pipes and primitive incense burners. A small hole was dug in the ground and filled with a mixture of dried herbivore dung and dagga. Once this was alight, the smokers cupped their hands over the whole and inhaled through a gap between their thumbs. This method of smoking was common amongst bush tribes until the advent of the cigarette. (Booth 2004, 45)

The differing beliefs of the Social Reality on cannabis use emerge as the Roman Empire is Christianized in the fifth century. Escohotado points out the radical extent to which the meaning of drugs changed at this time as "rigorously abstemious sects" began to impose and intermingle a moral standard into Christianity. This turn to rigidity and self-denial was new even to those who adhered to the Law of the Old Testament, and includes a rather idiosyncratic read of the Pauline Letters of the New Testament:

> the "relaxation" introduced by inebriation, had been one of the pagan's gifts from Dionysius, accepted as well by the Old Testament. But now it became necessary—as St. Paul says—to liquidate all stimulus toward a "relaxed behavior." That gave rise to rigorously abstemious sects, such as the Encratics, Tatians, Marcionites, and Aquarians. . . .
>
> This turn of events required erasing any point of comparison, any communion not based on autosuggestion. All other mystery rites in the Mediterranean swiftly became "dealings with Satan." God was no longer to have any vegetable mystery or multiplicity; it was to be one, and transcendent, in the same manner as the authority of the faith itself. (Escohotado 1999, 25–26)

And in light of my chapter 2 consideration of the controversy over whether euphoria is an active or passive experience, consider the same controversy seemingly alive in the early Christian Church:

> Not only were the magical and religious uses stigmatized; all inebriation implied guilty weaknesses. Euphoria, whether positive (by providing contentment) or negative (by relieving pain) constituted an end in itself for the pagan. Euphoria is simply therapeutic, healthy. The Christian faith, however, desired a considerable measure of affliction, since pain was welcome to God as long as it

"mortified the flesh": that which didn't relieve momentary pathologic states was seen as unworthy flight from the misfortunes affecting human beings. (Escohotado 1999, 26)

Here is a pivotal point in history, during the rise of the institution of the Church in the world approximately five hundred years after Christ. It seems there also emerges a Gnostic belief in asceticism or total self-denial, a rejection of all drugs and a welcoming of suffering and mortification of the flesh. Here is the origination of the Western belief in an absolute prohibition on wine and all intoxicants. Gnosticism, a fifth-century B.C. sect essentially held Jesus was not actually in bodily form but that a total separation existed between mind and body. This belief led them to practice asceticism in order to completely deny the body (with no distinction made between "flesh" and "body"). After the fall of the Roman Empire and subsequent rise to power of the Church a Western conception and symbolism was created— linking cannabis with other religions and heresy. Note that by the tenth century heresy included any medicinal use of drugs, so of course this would include not merely cannabis but any medicines:

> Successive councils decreed that drug sellers be exterminated or else sold as slaves. The Frankish king Childeric declared in an edict that the use of "diabolic plants" was treason to the Christian faith, and Charlemagne defined opium as "the work of Satan." By the tenth century—when the church and the state formed a unity without fissures—the use of drugs for therapeutic purposes could be a synonym for heresy. (Escohotado 1999, 27)

Crusades and Advent of the Assassin Myth

The relevance of references to drugs as "diabolical" and of "treason to the Christian faith" to the current meaning in twenty-first-century United States is of course difficult to determine, given the massive number of intervening developments. However, this belief seems resilient and existent in events which follow in the West from the year A.D. 1000 on. These events I relate after considering another highly significant happening for the meaning of cannabis in the West, the advent of the major world religion of Islam. Regarding hashish/cannabis, it will be within the Crusades and in the myth of the assassins where a second relevant belief (in addition to asceticism regarding cannabis use) in the West will emerge.[2]

Booth's presentation of the Islamic faith within his consideration of cannabis (a presentation much more detailed than what I present here) emphasizes alcohol use is abhorred and forbidden while hashish was permitted by some fringe sects.[3] Booth points out the rationale behind the rejection of alcohol use and acceptance of hashish use is one based upon the effects on users of each:

> The Koran (2: 219) specifically prohibits *intoxicants, gambling, the altars of idols and games of chance.* The word used for intoxicants, *khamar,* is open to interpretation. The root word from which this comes is the verb *khamara* meaning 'to cover'. The implication, therefore, is that any substances that 'covers' the mind is sinful. The teaching adds that this prohibition includes the use of intoxicants in medicine. The morality of hashish imbibing in Islam is, therefore, somewhat ambiguous. (Booth 2004, 39)

The ambiguity involves the claims by those who use hashish that such use is mind-uncovering, mind-expanding, and further develops and deepens the faith of believers. Booth explains the "mystical Sufi" sect, an early and exceptional sect of Islam accepted the use of hashish: "The mystical Sufi Muslims believed spiritual enlightenment was attainable through a state of ecstasy or altered consciousness and used hashish specifically for that purpose. To them, hashish was sacramental"(Booth 2004, 40). And of this late-seventh-century sect, "as it developed, it increasingly came under attack from orthodox Islam and increasingly disseminated itself over the Arabic world, taking with it its use of hashish" (Booth 2004, 41).

A sect of Shiite Nizari Ismaili founded in 1090 came to practice secret assassinations, "Such judicious (or religious, judicial) murder was commonplace in the Islamic world, homicide being a well-tried political modus operandi." This practice was carried out by a small unit of men, an "elite commando force," and Booth points out "Many considered it a terrorist organization" (Booth 2004, 50). The *fida'i* ('the devoted ones') "saw themselves as religious soldiers earning their place in Heaven. Their enemies regarded them as fanatical criminals" (Booth 2004, 51).

The Christian Crusaders came into conflict with these sects in the late 1100s. Booth explains "Chroniclers of the Crusades wrote at length of the Islamic sect with its dissident views, ruthless terror tactics and strange, mythical leader. The legend of the Assassins was born and a new verb, to assassinate, entered the dictionaries of Europe" (Booth 2004, 52). The assassins were ultimately invaded and overcome by Mongols in the 1250s. Booth explains "There is simply no historical basis for the assumption that the assassins were driven to assassinate by being in a hashish-induced state of mind" (Booth 2004, 53).

It seems important to emphasize that Marco Polo and others spread through Europe the story of assassins along with the embellishment that hashish caused ruthless, cold-blooded murder.

> So it was that, gradually, by association with the Assassins, about whom little was really known and who had been inaccurately tarred with a barbarous brush by

> their enemies, hashish came to be considered a drug capable of generating bedlam, undermining society, creating chaos and turning otherwise merciful men into merciless murderers. And this grossly erroneous myth has been perpetuated ever since, right up to the modern day, by those who would proscribe or prohibit anything to do with cannabis. (Booth 2004, 55)

Booth puts this point quite bluntly (especially to Christians who would attempt to indict hashish as causing violence and cold-blooded murder): "Religion leads to assassinations, not hashish. The supposed hashish-induced 'visions of paradise' are as responsible for assassinations as the religiously fortifying drinking of wine and eating of wafers are responsible for the bloody crusades" (as cited by Booth 2004, 53).

Escohotado also includes in his *A Brief History of Drugs* the introduction of the plant intoxicant hashish/cannabis into the consciousness of many Westerners through "assassins." He points out within the sect of assassins there was a myth of the "old man on the mountain" and the foundation of the order of "haschishins" "with an Ismailian lineage and strong Sufi influence" (Escohotado 1999, 31). He also notes that later European orders also took large amounts of hashish before going off to battle, "But the French and English chroniclers of those wars saw things only from their own side" (Escohotado 1999, 31). Contrary to the quite narrow Western rejection of hashish as having no medicinal value, Escohotado points out the "Arabic physician Rhazes attributed it [hashish] the capacity to deal with grave cases of melancholy or depression" (Escohotado 1999, 31).

At the same time as the Crusades were to enter their final years, Booth also points out cannabis was used by sorcerers as well as physicians and herbalists, with use by the former resulting in its again being deemed heretical by the Church. "In 1231 Pope Gregory IX outlawed hemp use as heresy, branding users as witches" (Booth 2004, 58). Furthermore, "Pope Innocent VIII banned the use of hemp in ritual to prevent the celebration of the Black or Satanic Mass." And then, "With the Inquisition came the next demonization of cannabis which was said to be a vital ingredient of witches' brews" (Booth 2004, 58).

Before the slave trade brought cannabis into the Americas consider the tension between Western medicine and Church in the Middle Ages. Although the Church stance was rigidly against the use of drugs and branded drug use heretical at the same time Dioscorides' *Materia medicas* was

> considered a central medical text until well into the seventeenth century. The ailments treated with cannabis were many: it was used as an analgesic or anaesthetic to combat earache, toothache (it was believed it drugged or put to sleep the worms that caused the pain), rheumatism, arthritis, menstrual and labour

pains, headaches and migraines and a large number of similar discomforts. It was also prescribed for epilepsy, inflammation, coughs, convulsions, fever and jaundice. (Booth 2004, 57)

Slave Trade and Entrance of Cannabis into North America

As a psychoactive drug, cannabis has a much longer history in other parts of the world than it does in Western countries. Europeans and Americans grew the plant exclusively for its fiber for many years, and even when tincture of cannabis was widely used in Western medicine in the 1800s, few people took it to get high or reported that they felt high when they did take it. The knowledge of how to smoke hemp was probably brought to Brazil by black slaves who used the plant in Africa; the practice traveled north to Mexico and, finally, reached the United States. (Weil and Rosen 2004, 136)

Here Weil and Rosen trace cannabis back from the United States through Mexico, Brazil, and ultimately Africa. Booth similarly explains that black slaves from Africa brought cannabis with them into the newly established sugar plantations of what would be the U.S. states of Virginia south to Louisiana as well as Brazil in the first half of the sixteenth century. In the colonies and northern United States there is no clear evidence of cannabis use for its intoxicating effects although there was an essential use of hemp for various purposes: "In North America, hemp was planted near Jamestown in 1611 for use in making rope. By 1630, half of the winter clothing at this settlement was made from hemp fibers. There is no evidence that hemp was used medicinally at this time" (Booth 2004, 129).

At this same time the Native American plant of tobacco was discovered. Similar to how cannabis has been treated, so too tobacco was treated, as an evil plant of a heretical nature.[4]

Opponents of tobacco use disputed its medical value. They pointed out that tobacco was used in the magic and religion of Native Americans. Tobacco was attacked as an evil plant, an invention of the devil. King James I of England was fanatically opposed to smoking. In an attempt to limit tobacco use, he raised the import tax on tobacco and also sold the right to collect the tax (Austin 1978; O'Brien et al. 1992). (Hanson, Venturelli, and Fleckenstein 2002, 304)

In the seventeenth century a papal decree was issued against tobacco, one which was ultimately "annulled":

In 1642, Pope Urban VIII issued a formal decree forbidding the use of tobacco in church under penalty of immediate excommunication. This decree was in

> response to the fact that priests and worshippers had been staining church floors with tobacco juice. One priest in Naples sneezed so hard after taking snuff that he vomited on the altar in full sight of the congregation. In response, Pope Innocent X issued another edict against tobacco use in 1650, but the clergy and the laity continued to take snuff and smoke. Finally, in 1725, Pope Benedict XIII, himself a smoker and "snuff-taker," annulled all previous edicts against tobacco (Austin 1978). (Hanson, Venturelli, and Fleckenstein 2002, 304)

Napoleon Bonaparte and the Entrance of Cannabis as an Intoxicant into France

Booth presents 1798 France and Napoleon Bonaparte's invasion of Egypt as a critical point for the entrance of cannabis as an intoxicant into Western consciousness. Hashish was introduced into France through returning French troops and became of interest and availability to broader social circles (e.g., intellectuals). The use of hashish and other narcotics by French Romantics (who were "creating art for art's sake") formed the "Hashish-Eaters' Club." This would influence new generations, including a spread into the United States in the form of the New York "Bohemians" of the mid-1850s.

At about the same time of the Hashish Eater's Club in France in the mid-1800s, there was also growing use of pharmaceuticals, tonics, and medicines of all sorts in the United States. Focusing on the medicinal use of cannabis in the United States, Booth points out that cannabis was available in 1842 in England as "Squire's Extract" (as an analgesic) and in America as "Tilden's Extract." Implicit here (THC was isolated and identified in 1964, neurological understanding in 1988, early 1990s) is that THC had not yet been isolated (primarily because the substances identified in the early nineteenth century were ones soluble in water, whereas cannabis is not an alkaloid nor soluble in water).

> Whilst Squire was almost certainly the first person to manufacture a medicinal tincture of cannabis, he was by no means the only pharmacologist experimenting with and investigating cannabis, the work encouraged by the recent successes in isolating morphine, nicotine and caffeine. All these substances, however, were alkaloids but, as cannabis contains no active alkaloidal compounds—and it was these for which the searchers were hunting—little progress was made.
>
> Squire's Extract and medicines like it quickly became widely used. Doctors were keen to prescribe them because the only other effective painkiller they could offer was highly addictive opium and, it was soon realized, cannabis-based extracts were not physically addictive. Furthermore, opium was expensive and produced side effects such as chronic constipation, a lowering of respiratory and heart rates, excessive pruritis (itching) and loss of appetite. Cannabis appeared

> to have no adverse side effects whatsoever other than feelings of euphoria, drowsiness and hallucinations. By 1850, it was listed in a number of British and European pharmacopoeias and was, that year, included in the *United States Pharmacopoeia* with its application being appropriate for the treatment of neuralgia, tetanus, typhus, cholera, rabies, dysentery, alcoholism and opiate addiction, anthrax, leprosy, incontinence, snake bite, gout, virtually any disease that induced convulsions, tonsillitis, insanity, menorrhagia (excessive menstrual bleeding) and uterine hemorrhaging. (Booth 2004, 92–93)

Furthermore, American Hobart Amory Hare suggested in 1887 "how cannabis calmed the anxiety felt by sufferers of terminal illnesses." However, pharmaceutical companies were poised to revolutionize the practice of medicine at the turn of the twentieth century, offering very pragmatic, efficient, synthetic, standardized treatments. Booth describes the situation as does Escohotado as the pivotal moment leading to the way we continue to understand drugs, specifically cannabis, in the early twenty-first century. Cannabis was no longer a "viable medical product" with "the emergence of synthetic drugs created from the massive advances in chemistry made especially during the last thirty years of the nineteenth century. That these synthetics were often far more harmful than natural cannabis was considered by the way" (Booth 2004, 97). Organization of prescription systems, dispensing chemists, and the advent of aspirin took the focus of medicine away from cannabis.[5] Escohotado seizes on this particular move at the end of the nineteenth century as quite profound, away from natural medicines and toward wholesale acceptance of synthetic medicines in twentieth-century United States.

The question of the effects of the use of hashish was investigated rigorously in India in 1894 by the Indian Hemp Drugs Commission. This study of over 3,500 pages was published in seven volumes. Booth echoes most if not all twentieth-century commissions appointed to investigate the nature of cannabis use and its effects when claiming of this report, "Those who conducted the study were specifically unpartisan and objective and remain to the present day the most thorough official study of cannabis ever conducted" (Booth 2004, 115). Escohotado echoes Booth here on the authority and credibility of the Indian Hemp Drugs Commission Report: "But no text of the period comes close to the solidity of the seven volumes of the Indian Hemp Drugs Commission, published by the British Government in 1894" (Escohotado 1999, 72). This is a precedent commissioned study, one cited by several studies on cannabis conducted in the United States in the twentieth century, (including LaGuardia, Shafer Commission Study, and IOM study). "The Indian Hemp Drug Commission Report in the 1890s and the 1930 Panama Canal Zone Report on marijuana stressed that available evidence did not prove marijuana to be as dangerous as it was popularly thought; these reports were given little publicity, however, and for the most part disregarded" (Hanson, Venturelli, and Fleckenstein 2002, 367).

Escohotado presents the United States at the turn of the twentieth century as highly suspicious and fearful of psychoactive substances. He presents two major factors behind the change in attitude toward hashish and drugs in general, two factors still integral to the current Social Reality opposing cannabis use in the United States:

1. A vigorous puritan reaction in the United States, which viewed the mass of new immigrants and the growth of big cities with distrust. Different drugs became identified with groups defined by social class, religious belief, or race: the first alarms regarding opium coincided with the corruption of children attributed to the Chinese; the anathema of cocaine was related to sexual crimes by blacks; condemnation of marijuana was connected with the immigration of Mexicans, and the objective of abolishing alcohol was related to immoralities of Jews and Irish. All of these groups represented "infidels"—pagans, papists, or killers of Christ—and all were characterized by a moral and economic inferiority. Other psychoactive and supertoxic drugs, such as barbiturates, did not become identified with marginal or immigrant social groups, and as such were ignored by moral reformers.
2. Progressive liquidation of the minimal state and recourse to enlarged bureaucracies as a response to explosive relations between capital and labor, a process during which the therapeutic establishment gradually began to assume the functions formerly held by the ecclesiastical establishment. The last decades of the nineteenth century witnessed a fierce battle between doctors and pharmacists against healers and herbalists, with the objective of establishing a monopoly on drugs by the former groups. (Escohotado 1999, 74–75)

Racist Opium Prohibition as Model for Racist "Marijuana" Prohibition

Addiction lingered after the Civil War and into the twentieth century, while medicine was making incredible advances and on the brink of revolutionary discoveries. With medicine showing such promise and taking off as a scientifically grounded profession, culturally at the turn of the twentieth century cannabis use was beginning to be viewed as a dangerous social menace, fueled by a dislike for and distrust of foreigners and their cultural ways:

> There was a growing condemnation of drug use. With an estimated 3 percent of the American population medicinally addicted to opiates in 1900, there now ex-

> ists a climate of considerable caution: and with caution came fear. In addition, drugs were identified in the public consciousness with foreigners and ethnic minorities who, in the strongly xenophobic and racist white portion of American society from which the administration and ruling class were drawn, were regarded with suspicion and already subjected to considerable social exclusion and repression. Drugs were, in short, deemed un-American.
>
> Two ethnic groups in particular were disenfranchised: The Chinese and the Negroes. (Booth 2004, 127)

It is amazing and breathtaking to read accounts from less than one hundred years ago, revisiting such incredible and explicit passion and personal investment in racism. Social policies were openly and expressly used as tools of racism, of suppressing others based upon their race alone not on their moral character and value as citizens.

> These early opium prohibitions, the first drug legislation to criminalize the consumer for his indulgence, clearly had more to do with the drug's users than with the drug itself—most (eleven) were passed in western states where there was little pretense of assimilating the newly immigrated Chinese populations: Nevada (1877), South Dakota and North Dakota (1879), Utah (1880), California and Montana (1881), Wyoming (1882), Arizona (1883), Idaho and New Mexico (1887), and Washington (1890). The violence of the anti-Chinese agitation during the seventies and eighties was matched only by the viciousness of the rhetoric; in 1882 the federal government responded by forbidding further Chinese immigration. Called upon to test the constitutionality of opium prohibition, even the appellate judiciary recognized the law's ethnic origins: "Smoking opium is not our vice, and therefore, it may be that this legislation proceeds more from a desire to vex and annoy the 'Heathen Chinee' in this respect, than to protect the people from the evil habit." (Bonnie and Whitebread 1999, 14)

So with early opium prohibition efforts in the late 1880s–1890s, it was recognized that "we" do not use opium and "they" do, and the law proceeded from this racist belief. Cannabis laws were similarly created to justify punishing minorities (primarily Mexicans).[6] As a quite informative statement of the state of the United States at the turn of the century, specifically focused on immigrants and on the atmosphere in which the first cannabis legislation was to be created, consider Booth here:

> The influx of Mexican migrant workers in the first thirty years of the century, not to mention Pancho Villa's occasional attacks, damaged US–Mexican relations which had been historically weak for a century. Many Americans looked on these newcomers with disdain and racial distrust: a Mexican was regarded by definition as a thief and ne'er-do-well. Yet America needed them. The country was expanding and the Mexicans were cheap labour. Traditionally employed as

> *vaqueros* on the ranches of Texas, they soon spread to become fruit and vegetable pickers in east Texas, Arizona and California, laborers on the Colorado and Montana sugar beet farms, cattle wranglers on the railroad as far north as Chicago and horse wranglers in northern Texas, Oklahoma and Kansas. For a while, this was accepted but was not long before it was the cause of more racial bitterness. Corporate landowners began to squeeze small farmers out of business by hiring the low-waged Mexicans and labour unions hated them because they were non-union and took union members' jobs. They were commonly robbed, beaten, murdered, driven out of town and generally accused of being un-American because of their language, their willingness to accept poor wages and their use of marijuana which was blamed whenever the Mexicans struck back. As the Chinese had suffered half a century before over their opium use, so now did the Mexicans over cannabis. Marijuana was labeled an alien drug, the fact that it was grown in America and had been an ingredient of patent medicines for decades was conveniently overlooked. (Booth 2004, 132–33)

To think of these fellow human beings being abused and mistreated, disrespected, and that this treatment was ultimately justified under the ruse of dangers of cannabis is a primary reason for suspicion of the injustice of cannabis law at its inception in the United States.

> Once the potential of marijuana legislation for suppressing the migrants was realized, other cities and districts were quick to imitate it. Soon, the south-western and southern state legislatures started to lobby in Washington for federal action against what was now being termed "killer" or "loco weed." (Booth 2004, 133)

Congressman Francis Burton Harrison would have his name given to the act that would attempt to first criminalize marijuana:

> In early drafts of the Harrison Act, cannabis had been fully included, but the federal lawyers later excluded it as it was so common as a medicine, especially for glaucoma and migraine sufferers. The drug companies pressured for its exception. It was argued that the availability of a drug used in corn plasters and veterinary preparations should not be so restricted. It was, the lobbyists pointed out, ridiculous for a pharmacist to have to record every sale of a sticking plaster because it contained a listed narcotic. Even some anti-drug reformers allowed the point that cannabis was hardly as significant a problem as opiates and cocaine. The downside to the legislation was that physicians and druggists felt put upon by the bureaucracy and, on the now illegal market, prices rose sharply for opiates and cocaine, so many addicts, who had previously been good citizens, turned to petty crime to meet the rising cost of their habituation. (Booth 2004, 134)

Along with the racist subjection of Mexicans was continued racist subjection of blacks, including jazz musicians, who became a clear target for anti-marijuana legislation.

> The jazz musicians, who were mostly black and played in the brothels or saloons, avoided alcohol because it dulled the senses and opiates because they sent the taker to sleep. Marijuana, on the other hand, with which they were all familiar, kept them alert and fought off exhaustion. It also enhanced their musical creativity. Jazz and blues evolved with the help of marijuana. (Booth 2004, 138)

In Bonnie and Whitebread's *The Marijuana Conviction: A History of Marijuana Prohibition in the United States* (1999), focused on sixty years from the first U.S. federal government marijuana legislation in 1937, it is extremely clear that marijuana was perceived by many as foreign, different, and unknown and *therefore* considered a threat to "the American way of life." Arguably the crucial legislative move made during this time was the definition of marijuana as a "narcotic." After being made, based upon no scientific evidence or credible testimony, but rather on horror stories fabricated in the press, justification legally existed for society to condemn cannabis (narcotic status would remain for cannabis until the early 1970s in the United States). The stark realization from reading *The Marijuana Conviction* is that legislation penalizing cannabis/marijuana use was anti-Mexican and anti-immigrant in nature. There was neither first-hand nor scientific knowledge about cannabis use among those legislating against marijuana. Marijuana prohibition was about neither science nor morality but rather an exercise of legal means to arrest, imprison, and control Mexicans specifically and immigrants generally.[7]

Enter Harry Anslinger, arguably the major figure in the criminalization of marijuana use in the United States. Through the use of political savvy, propaganda, and a motivation to keep his agency funded and himself employed, he in effect created business by creating criminals out of cannabis-users. He was the first commissioner of the Federal Bureau of Narcotics (FBN) (assuming the post August 12, 1930, and not leaving until 1962).

> Prior to the 1930s, those who knew of the drug, and were neither Mexican nor black, usually referred to it as hemp. Marijuana, as it gained common parlance, came to stand for a criminal substance, a foreign drug set to undermine mainstream American culture. (Booth 2004, 148)

The changing of the name of cannabis to marijuana is crucial to its new symbolic meaning. This meaning was created and disseminated by the FBN. Booth explains the bureaucratic motivations of the FBN that would create criminals out of cannabis users by first setting the political context within the first two years of its establishment:

> The Depression caused a considerable fall in tax revenue and government spending plummeted. The FBN budget was substantially cut. In order to boost his organization, Anslinger had to find a new target—a new drug menace—upon

> which to peg a budget increase. Although he had previously given marijuana little thought and deferred putting it under federal legislation, he now set about demonizing it, circulating pamphlets and planting stories in the press about murders committed whilst under marijuana intoxication. He also started pushing for marijuana to be included as a dangerous drug alongside opiates and cocaine in the Uniform State Narcotic Acts then widely under consideration by a large number of state legislatures. (Booth 2004, 149)

The atmosphere post–alcohol Prohibition included a "public worried about the crime wave prohibition had set in motion" while "brewers and distillers became concerned that marijuana—cheap and easily grown—would dent their profits" (Booth 2004, 149). As for Anslinger, Booth points out the extra pressures of holding his position in the FBN, namely that he had seemingly gotten his job through connections his wife's family had in government (Booth 2004, 150). In light of Roosevelt's initiative to "root out favouritism" in government:

> under pressure to be seen to be proactive, Anslinger began to focus on marijuana, writing articles about how it induced rapes and murders in which the perpetrators were almost always black or Mexican, the victims white. These were issued by the FBN to the press or sourced by the newspapers to Anslinger.
>
> Not surprisingly, public awareness of marijuana increased very sharply and a wide range of lobby groups such as the YWCA and YMCA, the Women's Christian Temperance Union and the national association of parent-teacher associations joined in the demand for the drug to be included in the Uniform State Narcotic Acts. FBN annual reports, which had hitherto concentrated on opiates or cocaine, suddenly started to concentrate on marijuana. The 1935 publication held thirteen pages on the subject, with photographs. (Booth 2004, 150)

In Escohotado's account of the history of drugs, this move to cast cannabis/marijuana as dangerous to individuals and society, a social menace, is entirely consistent with the "pharmacratic peace" developed with acceptance and reliance on synthetic drugs, drugs made distinct from the dangerous (non-synthetic, natural) cannabis. He casts this period of pharmacratic peace from 1930–1960, after which there occurs an "openly rebellious phase" (1960–1975) (Escohotado 1999, 125). These years of pharmacratic peace are also the years Anslinger wielded considerable power within the federal government, specifically in keeping alive his personal project of convincing society that marijuana was a social menace. He consciously and intentionally orchestrated a propaganda campaign to create a meaning of "marijuana" so as to use language to ensure the connection was made between this plant and Mexicans who threatened the American way of life. There neither was nor is scientific or medical evidence to justify his claims (rooted in claims based in an "assassin myth" which has cannabis use causing violence) but rather was a perversion of justice, the use of legislation to oppress and control certain minorities of the American population. His standard modus operandi was to have people from around the country send him stories about the most vicious accounts of violent crimes and then to link marijuana to these, suggesting if not outright claiming a causal link between the use of marijuana and the vicious crimes. He typically included pictures of the victims so as to relate marijuana to these events, sullying cannabis and lying in the name of his own pre-conceived strategy to maintain his own job as well as that of his department. Consider, for example, a standard description of marijuana use by Anslinger: "It is almost impossible to estimate the number of murders, suicides, thefts, muggings, extortion, and misdemeanors of manic insanity provoked by marijuana each year" (Escohotado 1999, 88). Booth also points out that the propaganda movies of the 1930s included one "partly financed by a major distilling company" which has students exposed to cannabis and one sent to an insane asylum for life (Booth 2004, 151)! This is the rotten root of the current U.S. marijuana law.

It is crucial to realize and consider as various authors on cannabis law have readers do, that the laws we live under today were born out of this falsity, propaganda, and racism. Perhaps the very same "needs" of security on the part of the majority in the United States by means of rhetoric and fear are still in the twenty-first century deemed appropriate by the federal government justification of the absolute ban of cannabis for any use. The effectiveness in the U.S. consciousness of the mid-to-late 1930s of the marijuana propaganda cannot be overstated. Upon it was built the twentieth-century U.S. "wars on drugs." The world had not seen the likes of the newspaper and propaganda machine that would overwhelm the national consciousness of the United States.

Jack Herer notably and substantially argues (in *The Emperor Wears No Clothes: Cannabis and the Conspiracy against Marijuana*) that behind the opposition to marijuana and specifically its use as hemp and not merely as intoxicant, lie substantial commercial interests, most notably those of newspaper owners who also had personally commercial interests in timber and use of paper over hemp. Booth cites Herer, "hemp products posed a threat to established financial and industrial interests. . . . He argues that the petrochemical and pulp paper industries stood to lose billions of dollars if the commercial potential of hemp was fully realized" (Booth 2004, 152). "William Randolph Hearst and Lammont DuPont, head of the multinational pharmaceutical and petrochemical conglomerate that bore his name," are cited by Booth as "the main orchestrators of the anti-hemp movement" (Booth 2004, 153). Further, Herer (and others) also point out that at this time in the 1930s when Anslinger was working to establish a law to suppress cannabis use, Edward Scripps, of

"Scripps Newspaper Company in San Diego . . . owned massive timber interests in the states of Washington and Oregon" (Booth 2004, 153).

The culmination of Anslinger's efforts was the creation of the Marihuana Tax Act of 1937. He and "the spreaders of alarm and despondency produced no scientific evidence to support their claims, although this did little to dilute the reputation of the killer weed that drove you mad. Whenever voices of moderation spoke out, they were suppressed or dismissed" (Booth 2004, 154). Booth points out that "From the mid-1930s onwards, he [Anslinger] engaged upon a vigorous and sustained anti-marijuana campaign without a reason justification other than his personal prejudice" (Booth 2004, 154).

A major occurrence during the preliminary hearings for the Marihuana Tax Act of 1937 was the sole medical expert, Dr. William C. Woodward, testifying on behalf of the American Medical Association. Woodward clearly pointed out the lack of scientific evidence to support claims made to justify this legislation, but his voice was literally ignored. These hearings are the stuff of Orwellian nightmare, with Anslinger's invented refer madness having been planted and propagated by others in power in order to suppress minorities, insisting on the cannabis assassin myth. The one person who would seem to know the most about cannabis, Dr. Woodward, is dismissed as simply not with the program. This dismissing the "scientific truth" of the effects of cannabis has continued into the twenty-first century.

The 1937 Marihuana Tax Act was the first federal legislation controlling marijuana, essentially through repressive taxation. The Orwellian nightmare continues when Anslinger removed cannabis from the American pharmacopoeia. The current early-twenty-first-century debates concerning the Schedule I status of cannabis has the Social Reality claiming there are no "scientifically or medically recognized therapeutic uses" of cannabis. In the early 1940s this one bureaucrat laid the foundation for today's Schedule I claim concerning cannabis and shifted the burden of proof for medical efficacy from those who would criminalize such use to those who would advocate cannabis for medicinal purposes.

> Three years later, just before the USA entered the Second World War, cannabis was dropped from the American pharmacopoeia, it is said at Anslinger's request. Although American doctors were still theoretically allowed to prescribe medicinal cannabis, they did not because of the over-regulation and cost in tax. (Booth 2004, 156)

The current status of marijuana in the U.S. Schedule I "recognized as having no therapeutic value" is a major tenet of current U.S. Social Reality to retain the prohibition and criminalization of cannabis use. This claim of cannabis having no therapeutic uses was born through political sleight of hand, not rational argument and scientific proof. As Booth describes it, two immediate results of the Marijuana Tax Act of 1937 were the demand for more arrests and "the alienation of a large section of the ethnic-minority population of the USA which was, marijuana aside, largely law abiding. This in turn caused them to become secretive and closed" (Booth 2004, 157). Here are the original "otherwise law-abiding citizens."

In 1944 Mayor LaGuardia in New York presented the results of a thorough investigation of the effects of cannabis called "The Marihuana Problem in the City of New York." One of the major studies in the past 100 years on marijuana, "LaGuardia's committee had completely debunked Anslinger's proselytizing" (Booth 2004, 169). In 1946 the United Nations "decided no further study needed be conducted into cannabis. Not surprisingly Anslinger, in his role as US representative to the Commission, disagreed" (Booth 2004, 169). LaGuardia's study was a statement of the Scientific Reality of cannabis use, but instead of being heeded and used to reassess cannabis law during the post-WWII years, it was ignored and instead a move in the opposite direction was made (Boggs Act of 1951), significantly *increasing* penalties (to the point of the death penalty) for the use and possession of marijuana.

The Move from Assassin Myth: Gateway Drug Argument Is Born

Booth leads into the 1950s with Anslinger retooling his arguments against marijuana, attempting to link it to Communism. The retooling also included arguments and facts about the effects of cannabis that were contrary to those cited by him in the late 1930s, especially in his move from the assassin myth:

> He stressed that marijuana could turn America into a nation of compliant pacifists; this, when ten years before he had been preaching how it induced violence. The label of docility was to remain attached to marijuana for another two decades.
>
> To associate marijuana with heroin, Anslinger stated that the heroin addict's first taste of drugs was with cannabis, from which he graduated to more dangerous substances. That in 1937 he had said quite bluntly, during the debate leading up to the Marihuana Tax Act that marijuana did not lead to heroin use, was now conveniently forgotten. This was to be a backbone of his anti-marijuana argument for the remainder of his career at the FBN and was given credence in 1951 when a US Senate committee declared marijuana led to a use of other drugs. (Booth 2004, 177)

Here is the historical birth of the "gateway argument," one rejected in the 1930s and then accepted in the 1950s by the same Anslinger, apparently for reasons of providing some justification for the continuation of the criminalization of cannabis users in the context of Cold War United States. The Boggs Act of 1951 set harsh sentences for possession and use of cannabis, with a first offense resulting in two to five years. The 1956 Narcotic Control Act "reassessed the maximum terms for possession of marijuana as laid down by Boggs and increased them to ten, twenty and forty years" (Booth 2004, 178). The 1950s had even the mention of illegal drugs taboo.

The post-WWII period had the United States move toward more rampant and routine use of synthetic drugs while further demonizing the use of non-synthetic drugs. Escohotado cites a 1958 report entitled "Drug Addiction: Crime or Disease?" which "maintained that the crusade was a pseudomedical and extrajudicial enterprise that could only result in crime and marginalization" (Escohotado 1999, 108). Furthermore, one could hardly ignore the ever-present double standard with the legality of alcohol:

> Alcohol drinkers, however, did not need to be "treated and rehabilitated," while the user of opiates, cocaine, and hemp turned out to be ill, and identical to a sufferer from ulcers or pneumonia, except that the disease was considered an epidemic, treatable by quarantine. (Escohotado 1999, 109)

And on the synthetic/natural distinction:

> But chemists and laboratories found and offered legal alternatives to the banned drugs, and their efforts supplied the pharmacies of the planet with an astonishing variety of drugs. In fact, the number of people who habitually used a pharmacy product multiplied eight- or tenfold, even though the majority of them were unaware of being dependent on a psychoactive compound. It was a time when official toxicologists, beginning with Anslinger, enjoyed full public confidence; they substituted one pharmacopoeia for another, with the criterion of preferring the synthetic over the natural, the patented over the unpatentable. (Escohotado 1999, 112)

Consider that the current, twenty-first-century UN resolution controlling cannabis was born of Anslinger's late career efforts, putting into question the justice of this current reigning world law. "In 1954, Anslinger finally forced the UN to agree that cannabis had no medical use whatsoever and it was, consequently, proposed to be internationally banned. . . . Seven years later, the UN Single Convention on Narcotic Drugs was ratified on 10 March 1961" (Booth 2004, 205).

Beat Subculture Rejects Social Reality of Cannabis Use

The early 1960s in the United States was the time of Anslinger's retirement and the beginning of what Escohotado describes as a move out of pharmacratic peace and into a time of "rebellion" (1960–1975). Of the beat subculture and use of cannabis (and drugs generally), Booth says, "It might be said to have given birth to, or at least been the progenitor of, the modern drug culture" (Booth 2004, 201). To better appreciate the relevance of the beats to the meaning of cannabis use in the United States consider the classic sociological work by Ned Polsky, *Hustlers, Beats and Others.* Polsky writes from the very perspective and time of the beats and presents a discerning account of the ideals, motivations, and philosophy of those who lived as beats. It may be that what Polsky reveals is, in addition to immigrants and minorities, another group specifically targeted by federal government laws and propaganda against the use of cannabis.

In attempting to relate the ideals and way of life of the majority of the beats, Polsky takes the focus off of that small minority who are known as the beat writers and poets, ("it would be charitable indeed to say that a tenth of the beats are concerned to write," 174).[8] Consider the three characteristics of the "typical beat":

1. "Nearly all Village beats most of the time and most of them all of the time want not even a hostile relationship with squares. They restrict their relations with squares to that bare minimum needed to live at all."
2. "Moreover, the large majority of beats do not flaunt their physical presence before the public gaze."
3. "A substantial minority, between a fourth and a third, also wear various kinds of badges (beards, typically) but usually do so as a ready means of identifying themselves to one another and to promote a "we" feeling, not out of a desire to call the attention of outsiders to themselves." (Polsky 1985, 147)

Rather than openly and intentionally threatening society, the beats basically wanted to be left to themselves. Polsky also offers a description of a lifestyle that may be translated by the Social Reality on cannabis use as symptoms of "amotivational syndrome": "Beats avoid work . . . almost always a matter of conviction pure and simple. This conviction is so strong that many beats are willing to starve for it." And on their "retreatism" from job norms, they "voluntarily choose not to work" in such situations. "Furthermore, their ideological refusal to work is not essentially a product of neurosis . . . [but] is largely cultural in origin" (Polsky 1985, 154). Consider also a possible underlying rationale for the alienated, disaffected of today, specifically in their kind of reflection upon social conditions:

> Unlike most of their age-mates, beats are keen critics of the society in which they have grown up. Their anti-work ideology is not nearly so much a sign of inability

> to accept the reality principle as a sign of disaffiliation from particular, mutable realities. Sensible of America's inequitable distribution of income and its increasing depersonalization of work and leisure and its racial injustices and its Permanent War Economy, the beats have responded with the Permanent Strike. (Polsky 1985, 155)

A major point of emphasis by Polsky is that the philosophy of the beats is "retreatist" and not one of "conflict." In relation to politics, Polsky explains "it is wrong to describe the beats as apolitical *lumpen* who are potential fascists (Malaquais) or potential socialists (Mailer)" (Polsky 1985, 156). Rather, "They are not apolitical but consciously and deliberately *anti*political, which is something else entirely, and, as a common attitude, something new in American history" (Polsky 1985, 156). Furthermore, they are not "anarchists," as "the beat doesn't want to promote anarchism or any other ism" (Polsky 1985, 157). Finally, there seems little threat of civil disobedience in an organized way by beats: "Of course the beat is pleased to see beat attitudes spread, but he isn't interested in joining any organized social movement toward that end. Each of the three words 'organized social movement' sounds obscene to the beat's ears." Polsky further explains that although society attempts to identify the beats and the way of life with particular individuals (e.g., Allen Ginsberg, beat writers as speaking for the beats), "the beat's only spokesman is himself" (Polsky 1985, 158).

In his chapter on photographer Robert Frank's "Existential Vision," George Cotkin (in his *Existential America*) presents as especially influential Jack Kerouac's *On the Road*, experimentation and "living in the moment" as beat ideals, and a "culture of spontaneity." However, "unlike the existentialist, the beat did not work through a perspective of anguish and dread." Beats remained upbeat about America, with a precursor in Walt Whitman rather than nihilistic existentialists. Beats are "upbeat about America" although living a different way of life than the status quo. This involves a rejection of the political state of affairs, represented by Frank who "despised the dominant visions of the 1950s with their naïve suggestions that happiness could be found through consumer spending, military buildups, and the social status quo."

Moving back to Polsky and a focus on the beats and cannabis use, consider:

> For obvious reasons beat drug-taking is a furtive affair, and hence few outsiders realize that it is a totally pervasive part of beat life, both as an activity and as a topic of conversation. The illegal use of drugs is one of the handful of things that characterize all male beats with very rare exceptions, and a good majority of the females. But contrary to some popular views, (a) the majority use non-addicting drugs exclusively and (b) the majority of such users do not eventually go on to use addicting drugs and become junkies. (Polsky 1985, 160)

Consider further when cannabis is available alongside of alcohol, some choose cannabis instead of and not in addition to alcohol. The beats exemplify this: "Many younger beats have been thoroughly socialized to drug-taking without every having been socialized to drinking, and are teetotalers when it comes to alcohol" (Polsky, 160–61). Explaining sociologically why the gateway theory is not supported: "Although beat heroin users and beat marihuana smokers are part of one subculture, they tend to split into two separate groups when it comes to the specific activity of taking drugs, each developing its own customs" (Polsky 1985, 164) and that of marijuana user "has much more social quality than that of the heroin user" (Polsky 1985, 164).

In a footnote where he reflects on the "horde of teenage beats" many of whom "just arrived in the Village this summer" who "nearly all use marihuana," Polsky explains,

> The beats of the early 1960's, and their immediate "hippie" successors, went less and less for addicting drugs, and indeed developed an elaborate ideology which promulgated "mind" drugs and put down all "body" drugs (by which they meant not only the usually addicting drugs, such as heroin and the barbiturates, but also those drugs, non-addicting in ordinary use, that can produce physical dependence with prolonged use of heavy doses—such as alcohol and the amphetamines). About 1966, however, this ideology began to break down. (Polsky 1985, 166)

And when glancing back on the beats by 1966 or so being subsumed into many others sub-cultures (most notably those related to rock music) Polsky observes a point which, now forty years later, helps to explain the continual growth of the use of cannabis among U.S. citizens:

> The beats' most enduring imprint on American culture appears, in retrospect, to have been precisely this diffusion of marihuana use to many circles of middle- and upper-class whites outside the jazz world. Such contemporary white use, although now self-sustaining and still growing, stemmed largely from public attention given to beat practices and beat literary proselytizing on the matter. (Polsky 1985, 167)

The beats are of special significance to the distinction I have drawn between Social Reality and Scientific Reality. Although outcasts of the Social Reality, they understand cannabis as do the medical experts of the Scientific Reality:

> The beats managed to do what some scientific investigators of marihuana had tried but failed to do: they convinced many sectors of the American public that the Federal Narcotics Bureau's myths about marihuana—the notions that marihuana is a significant cause of crime, insanity, and heroin addiction—were indubitably myths. (Polsky 1985, 170)

Polsky further dismisses the gateway argument and also notes continuing perpetuation of the myth by the Federal Narcotics Bureau (a claim still an accurate characterization of federal cannabis strategy in the United States):

> Although the better-educated segment of the public is now aware of the myths for what they are—knows, for example, that the myriads of college students who currently smoke marihuana are not thereby "led to" heroin addiction—this has in no wise lessened the efforts of the Federal Narcotics Bureau to perpetuate the myths and otherwise to suppress the scientific evidence of marihuana's harmlessness. The Bureau's undiminished efforts have led a number of sociologists, including myself, to come round to the view long maintained in heroic isolation by Alfred Lindesmith of Indiana University, viz., that some Bureau officials are not dedicated truthseekers having honest differences of opinion with the academic investigators, but, on the contrary, dedicate themselves first and last to extending the power of the Federal Narcotics Bureau—to the extent of deliberate falsification of evidence. (Polsky 1985, 170)

Even with Anslinger completing in the UN an international prohibition of cannabis use (on behalf of the United States), the newly elected John F. Kennedy brought a different approach to cannabis law. Anslinger and the Social Reality he had helped construct were facing immediate rejection. Conider for example, the release of the Prettyman Report in 1962, conducted as a reassessment of cannabis law:

> In September 1962, as he had promised in his presidential campaign manifesto, Kennedy held a Conference on Narcotic and Drug Abuse. . . . The five-hundred-strong body of delegates accepted that there was much blether spoken about cannabis. Within eight weeks, a paper was published called "The Prettyman Report," named after its author, E. Barrett Prettyman, a retired US Supreme Court of Appeal Judge. Prettyman stated bluntly that marijuana was not proven to be linked to criminality and that reports of its dangers were grossly overstated, and suggested that federal drug laws be rewritten as far as marijuana was concerned, removing the harsh mandatory sentences for being *in poor social perspective.* (Booth 2004, 206)

Further evidencing what Escohotado refers to as the period of rebellion was the introduction of the use of cannabis (and other drugs) for intellectual reasons, reasons of mind-expansion and self-awareness. For example, prolific writer of the time Alan Watts used drugs not as recreational but as "a means towards redefining intellect and understanding," as did Aldous Huxley (Booth 2004, 208). "Their writing was objective and measured, promoting a natural herb not as an escapist drug but as a way to increase personal awareness and acuity" (Booth 2004, 209). In the *Atlantic Monthly*, November 1966, Allen

Ginsberg condemned cannabis law in "The Great Marijuana Hoax: First Manifesto to End the Bringdown." The Beatles, a band that signaled a core part of this rebellious period also advocated use of cannabis in their "Got to Get You Into My Life":

> The Beatles' use of marijuana was to impinge itself upon their music. In 1994, Paul McCartney commented upon his use of marijuana: "*I'd been a rather straight working-class lad, but when we started to get into pot it seemed to me quite uplifting. It didn't seem to have too many side effects like alcohol or some of the other stuff, like pills, which I pretty much kept off. I kind of liked marijuana and to me it seemed it was mind-expanding. Literally mind-expanding. So "Got To Get You Into My Life' is really a song about that. It's not about a person, it's actually about pot. It's saying, 'I'm going to do this. This is not a bad idea.' So it's actually an ode to pot, like someone else might write an ode to chocolate or a good claret . . .*" (Booth 2004, 218)

Escohotado portrays this cultural rebellion as including a rejection of synthetic pharmaceuticals and the life that came with them, a rebellion which "had shaken the pharmacratic structure that had been in place since the forties, with easy and comfortable distinctions between decorous psychopharmaceuticals ('medicines,' 'food supplements') and the not-so-decorous ones ('narcotics')."

> Before the 1960s, marijuana use was largely confined to small segments of African American urban youth, jazz musicians, and particularly artists and writers who belonged to the 1950s beat generation. Use rose tremendously in the 1960s, when it was closely associated with the hippie counterculture, in which marijuana was categorized as a psychedelic (consciousness-expanding) sacrament. It spread into other youth categories during the 1970s, until approximately 1978. In each year from 1978 until 1991, marijuana use fell. After 1991, researchers and prevention specialists were astounded to see a rise in usage among youth. (Hanson, Venturelli, and Fleckenstein 2002, 367)

Booth presents international effects of this rebellious period. Hippies and others of the marijuana culture began to sojourn to Eastern countries, and hashish and sophisticated drug smuggling operations were created. In addition, here the Social Reality seemed to show some awareness that "otherwise law-abiding citizens" were being criminalized by an unjust law:

> Although the US government was making strident efforts to combat drug smuggling, it was by 1970 having to admit that domestic drug control was not only a failure but also causing anger in the middle classes. Thousands of otherwise respectable citizens, most of them under the age of twenty-five, were being given

> prison sentences and criminal records for what many considered either a petty offense or nothing more than a moment of youthful foolishness. Under such pressure, legislators started to re-assess the criminality of marijuana taking and the penalties attached to it. (Booth 2004, 245)

Severe penalties from the 1950s laws were now being experienced by families of the Social Reality. No reasoning was necessary here to change the criminal punishments regarding cannabis use, but mere anger from those of the Social Reality caused law changes. Of course, the laws had been enforced throughout the fifties and sixties, so that presumably "otherwise respectable citizens" were being "given prison sentences and criminal records" for this petty offense. That there wasn't the kind of law-changing anger prior to the late sixties reveals a significant aspect of the Social Reality, disallowing injustice to the majority although accepting the exact same injustice done to the minority. "The 1970 Comprehensive Drug Abuse Prevention and Control Act . . . removed mandatory minimum sentences and reduced possession of marijuana to the level of a misdemeanor" (Booth 2004, 246).

In Britain the Wootton Report was published in January 1969. Its conclusions, reinforcing the findings of the 1894 Indian Hemp Study:

> The Government may have hoped for a controversial report that supported their line but they were to be disappointed. It confirmed earlier studies, announcing, *Having reviewed all the material available to us we find ourselves in agreement with the conclusion reached by the Indian Hemp Drugs Commission appointed by the Government of India (1893–1894) and the New York Mayor's Committee on Marihuana (1944), that the long-term consumption of cannabis in moderate doses has no harmful effects.* It went on to say that cannabis was *very much less dangerous than the opiates, amphetamines, and barbiturates, and also less dangerous than alcohol [and] it is the personality of the user, rather than the properties of the drug, that is likely to cause progression to other drugs.* The report recommended that the Government *bring about a situation in which it is extremely unlikely that anyone will go to prison for an offence involving only possession for personal use or for supply on a very limited scale.* (Booth 2004, 273)

And the response to the report by the British government was to instead *increase* criminal penalties for all cases of cannabis use:

> The Government ignored the report and, in 1971, increased the penalties for all cases involving cannabis under the Misuse of Drugs Act. In this legislation, which was reinforced in the mid-1980s and has remained in force ever since, illicit drugs were categorized in three classes: Class A included heroin, cocaine and morphine; Class B codeine, amphetamines, barbiturates and cannabis; Class C

substances were such drugs as the stimulants pemoline and mazindol, steroids and anti-depressants. (Booth 2004, 274)

War on Drugs: Social Reality Responds with Schedule I Status for Marijuana

The election of Richard Nixon was a staunch, conservative response to turmoil in the U.S. Vietnam, riots, demonstrations, too many events to list. Nixon intended to quell the storm, to suppress hippies and deviants of society. The strategy included the same strategy used against immigrants and minority groups in the 1930s: to attack them through the criminalization of cannabis.

Bonnie and Whitebread present the following example of an admitted forfeiting of logic in policy, specifically in prohibiting marijuana because it is "dangerous." This claim is made while alcohol remains legal yet far more dangerous to individual users and to society. This double standard is demonstrated by those who use the rationale of "dangerousness" to justify both the legal prohibition and criminalization of cannabis and legalization and lack of criminal penalty for alcohol use.

> Naturally, the rhetorical nature of this argument did not escape the challengers, who immediately countered with the alcohol comparison. Although harmful in at least every respect that marihuana might be, alcohol use was not criminal; in fact, its use was permitted and in some ways encouraged by the government. How then, the challengers contended, could the government justify criminal penalties for marihuana use?
>
> As late as April 1968 Giordano was responding officially to this argument in a manner which could have been written thirty years earlier: 'The purpose of the present drug laws is to prevent the incorporation of additional debilitating vices within our culture. The fact that other dangerous drugs, alcohol and tobacco, are not prohibited is irrelevant. This attitude may offend logic, but it results in the conservation of human values, and logic may be offended in such a cause.'" (Bonnie and Whitebread 1999, 234)

The reason being given here to justify the overriding of the most basic moral right and liberty of a citizen is that such overriding is "results in the conservation of human values." So the value liberty is in actuality violated in order to preserve a future yet non-existent liberty. Of course there is no clear way of measuring such conservation, of comparing and contrasting our society's current values against those of a separate world where cannabis is legal. Within this argument for prohibition of cannabis use is the assumption that there would be a cumulative effect with the legalization of cannabis, so that in addition to problems with nicotine and alcohol, there would be further *accumulation* of additional problems related to cannabis use. This accumulation cannot be assumed but should be demonstrated. That there is some question as to an "accumulation" of social and individual problems as a result of legalization of cannabis is suggested by (among other things) the existence and strong influence of what is known as the "forbidden fruit effect," whereby a law forbidding cannabis use (e.g.) can thereby make it more attractive and increase use. In addition, it may be that with the legalization of cannabis (as with the Jamaican society) alcoholism drops and along with it the various dangers to self and society so that there is a significant reduction rather than an accumulation of individual and social problems, and therefore a "conservation of human values." Finally, to merely express a personal preference for alcohol over cannabis as intoxicant of choice does not therefore necessitate refusing the use of cannabis to others who do not share this preference. It should be made explicit especially how the prohibition of cannabis use by adult citizens is consistent with the human value of liberty.

Nixon knew what he thought and would think about cannabis before he appointed experts to his Presidential Commission on the nature of cannabis use:

> The director of the National Institute of Mental Health, Bertram Brown, said in a speech he thought marijuana offenses should be treated "like a parking ticket." Nixon fired him. He ordered Haldeman to find a way to take all remaining responsibility for drugs away from HEW and give it to Justice, because at HEW "they're all on drugs anyway." Two days after firing Brown, Nixon exploded to Haldeman that he wanted "to put out a statement on marijuana that's really strong, one that really tears the ass out of them" (Baum 1997, 54)

As with Anslinger, Nixon simply used rhetoric if not outright fabrications in order to justify his strongly held position opposing cannabis use. Nixon's appointed commission to consider cannabis, The National Commission on Marihuana and Drug Abuse, tellingly titled their report, "Marihuana, A Signal of Misunderstanding." They conclude cannabis should be legalized and convincingly argue to the conclusion that there is more damage done to cannabis users by the law itself than from the effects of using cannabis:

> In its final report, released in 1973, it recommended that marijuana possession for personal use should be decriminalized, as should the selling or gifting of small amounts. No conclusive evidence was found that marijuana was a cause of crime, insanity, sexual aberration, promiscuity or led to other drug use. It also stated, *a careful search of literature and testimony by health officials has not revealed a single human fatality in the US proven to have resulted solely from the use*

> *of marijuana* . . . and that it . . . *is of the unanimous opinion that marihuana use is not such a grave problem that individuals who smoke marihuana, or possess it for that purpose, should be subject to criminal procedures.*
>
> National legal, medical, religious and public health professional bodies agreed. President Nixon did not. He had personally hand-picked nine of the thirteen commissioners in order to bias the findings. Furious, he ignored the report, accusing it of liberalist tendencies, and increased anti-drug policing budgets. (Booth 2004, 246)

And Baum's description of Nixon's response:

> The commission was telling Nixon, in effect, that the real marijuana problem wasn't the drug, but the war on the drug. The war was alienating young people, turning "straight" society against the counter-culture, and leading police to use pot laws as political weapons. Marijuana prohibition, the commission concluded, is not in the national interest.
>
> "I read it and reading it did not change my mind," Nixon told reporters during an impromptu Oval Office press conference a couple of days after its release. He offered no reason for his decision. None of the big newsweeklies reported on the commission's findings. After years of emotional back and forth about the medical, legal, and social implications of the boom in marijuana use, a commission of Nixon's own choosing recommended legalization, and the press let Nixon bury the story. (Baum 1997, 71–72)

Shafer Commission Report and Recommendations on Cannabis: Scientific Reality Ignored

Consider the official name of the Shafer Commission Report, *Drug Use in America: Problem in Perspective* (1973). In five chapters of over 460 pages, the Shafer Commission Report is structured as follows:

Chapter One. Defining the Issues
Chapter Two. Drug Using Behavior in the United States
Chapter Three. The Social Impact of Drug Dependence and Drug-Induced Behavior
Chapter Four. Toward a Coherent Social Policy
Chapter Five. Looking Ahead

After presenting a history of various drug acts and laws created in the twentieth century, emphasizing the social rather than scientific basis for these, the first chapter moves to a section called "The Social Response: False Premises and the Perpetuation of a Problem." Here, the problem being perpetuated is drug abuse and this is done through faulty assumptions and premises of the

Social Reality drug policy. Considered among these is the assumption that the goal of the policy should be to "eliminate 'non-medical' drug use." However, it is not clear whether this goal is "desirable or possible," nor is it clear how the drugs of alcohol and tobacco/nicotine should be dealt with in applying such a policy. Furthermore the commission astutely points out that just because there is no medical professional involved in the prescription of a drug does not mean therefore use is '"non-medical" or hedonistic" (*Drug Use in America* 1973, 20). It may be medical, as the use of cannabis may be done with a therapeutic intention by and effect experienced by individuals. And simply referring to any cannabis use as "hedonistic" is to commit the straw-man fallacy, presenting cannabis users in the weakest, least defensible light in order to condemn all cannabis use while ignoring meanings other than hedonistic motivations for cannabis use (e.g., creative, therapeutic, spiritual).

Furthermore, they point out the false premise (still existing today in the twenty-first century) that drugs can be distinguished by arbitrarily labeling some "medical" (licit) and others "recreational" (illicit). In the early 1970s the commission recognized this distinction as further problematic in light of the increasing number of "emotional ailments" considered as medical concerns. They would likely be struck aghast at the number of prescriptions being written in the early twenty-first-century United States for "emotional ailments" (especially among, ironically, not only adolescents but also young children). The authors ask the rather obvious question which leads to an open acknowledgement of the arbitrary division between licit and illicit drugs: "how does the daily use of a prescribed barbiturate to bring a person 'down' from the day differ from the similar use of a self-prescribed minor tranquilizer or, for that matter, a martini?" (*Drug Use in America* 1973, 21).

The commission report points out a further questionable premise: "Often cited in support of societal disapproval of non-medical drug use is the proposition that individuals should not risk their health by using drugs" (*Drug Use in America* 1973, 21). Among the responses to this line of argument the commission makes, consider one inviting a consideration of the question of who, exactly, is to be the relevant authority in weighing the "acceptable benefits" of using cannabis:

> If the standard for social policy were potential injury to individual health, barbiturates, alcohol, and tobacco would present the clearest cases for prohibition . . . and furthermore pushing the question (in a way similar to the way J.S. Mill does in *On Liberty*, regarding a rather logical point to consider in light of the attempt to stop people from harming themselves): "But individuals would not choose to use psychoactive drugs if they did not perceive some advantage to themselves. So the fundamental question arises: Who is to weigh the perceived advantages of drug use against the risk, the individual or society?" (*Drug Use in America* 1973, 22)

The Social Reality answer is "society," whereas the Scientific Reality answers "the individual." A further insight in the Shafer Commission Report is made in the next section of their chapter one, "Motivation for Mood Alteration." Here it is pointed out:

> Subsumed within the societal goal of eliminating non-medical drug use is the value judgment that use of drugs for the explicit purpose of mood alteration is *per se* undesirable. To harmonize this judgment with approved conduct, we avoid analyzing the motivations of similar behaviors. We do not think about the alcohol experience as an altered state of consciousness but rather as a means to some other end, such as promoting conviviality or stimulating conversation. (*Drug Use in America* 1973, 22–23)

The Social Reality defends the use of alcohol/ethanol as "a social lubricant" and as a useful means to an acceptable ends. However, the use of cannabis toward the same ends, effectively allowing the same social feelings, is rejected. Instead, cannabis is referred to by the Social Reality in different terms, as altering consciousness in a way somehow morally worse than doing so using alcohol. The report concludes this section by ruling out as a legitimate way of justifying the illegality of cannabis the mere fact that it "alters consciousness"[9]:

> Whatever the biological and psychological foundations for the common human desire to alter consciousness, policy makers must recognize that drugs have always been used for this purpose. Most societies have institutionalized at least one form of drug-induced mood alteration; only the drugs differ, not the essential purpose. Instead of assuming that mood alteration through some drugs is inherently objectionable, while similar use of others is not, the public and its leaders must focus directly on the appropriate role of drug-induced mood alteration. It is no longer satisfactory to defend social disapproval of use of a particular drug on the ground that it is a "mind-altering drug" or a "means of escape." For so are they all. (*Drug Use in America* 1973, 23)

In the following section, "Drugs and Individual Responsibility," the report continues: "Implicit in present policy is the concern that many individuals cannot be trusted to make prudent or responsible decisions regarding drug-taking" (*Drug Use in America* 1973, 23).

At the outset of their chapter four, the report once again comes back to the essentially philosophical question (one I will later consider from a moral perspective) from their chapter one:

> The issue of perspective, which is really a problem of description, leads to an issue of philosophy, which is a problem of prescription. As we noted in chapter

> One, the decision whether or not to use drugs is fundamentally a question of values. The question is: whose values should determine the answer?
>
> The American value system prizes self-reliance, productivity and community involvement. From this perspective, resort to drugs for unnecessary purposes poses undesirable risks, whatever immediate benefits the individual user may perceive. (*Drug Use in America* 1973, 202)

The report here captures an essential conflict between Social Reality and Scientific Reality. Although self-reliance could be considered consistent with the beat subculture, productivity and community involvement are perceived differently by the Social Reality and Scientific Reality. For the former, productivity and more generally consumerism is good, a community of consumers ideal, while for the beat subculture this is a herd mentality of thoughtlessly following along. This latter view is simply disallowed by the Social Reality, for which cannabis use cannot be logically related to self-reliance, productivity and community involvement.

The committee moves on to consider a "second dilemma" involving the "uneven application" of principle within the U.S. drug policy regarding alcohol and cannabis:

> Should public policy toward drug use reflect the prevailing morality of aspiration or the realities of individual and group behavior? This issue is most important when policy toward one substance, for example marihuana, involves the moral ideal, while policy toward another, alcohol, accommodates the way most people behave. Such uneven application of principle explains why some critics believe that present drug policy is no more than an assertion of majority preferences. (*Drug Use in America* 1973, 202–3)

This mere "assertion of majority preferences" is what Tocqueville warned of in the U.S. democracy, despotism and tyranny of the moral majority. Again, an obvious way to understand the Social Reality "uneven application of principle" is in on the one hand approving alcohol and on the other hand forbidding cannabis use. The result of such partiality in the administration of justice is the diminishing of the integrity of the federal government:

> An apparent double standard compromises the integrity of social institutions and interferes with efforts to deal with the consequences of excessive drug use.
>
> The Commission also believes that semantics must not blur the basic philosophical dilemma: when policy restricts individual choice for the common interests, the decision should be stated unequivocally. A determination that society suffers more from an easing of restrictive policy than from the use of a particular drug should be stated with equal candor. (*Drug Use in America* 1973, 203)

This last challenge has not yet been met. The most unequivocal reason given by the federal government for forbidding adults the use of cannabis is that legalization of cannabis would "send the wrong message to the youth." It is not clear anyone is sending such messages to the youth (certainly none who would be deterred by a law forbidding such action). To legalize cannabis for adult use would more likely send the same message to adolescents that continues to be sent by the federal government concerning cigarettes and alcohol: they are dangerous but it is an adult right to assume the risk of using them.

The committee presents policy recommendations for various types of drugs. For marihuana the following is stated:

> As promised in our first Report, the Commission has reviewed all of its findings and recommendations during this past year. We reaffirm all of our conclusions and recommendations. The risk potential of marihuana is quite low compared to the potent psychoactive substances, and even its widespread consumption does not involve the social cost now associated with most of the stimulants and depressants (Jones, 1973; Tinkenberg, 1971). Nonetheless, the Commission remains persuaded that availability of this drug should not be institutionalized at this time.
>
> The Commission's 1972 National Survey data suggest that the incidence and prevalence of marihuana use may indeed be peaking. Uncertainty about long-term effects of heavy use continues. Lastly, it is painfully clear for the debate over our recommendations the absence of a criminal penalty for private use is presently equated in too many minds with approval, regardless of a continued prohibition on availability. The Commission regrets that marihuana's symbolism remains so powerful, obstructing the emergence of a rational policy. (*Drug Use in America* 1973, 224–25)

Consider especially this commission's expression of regret, in 1973, that the symbolism remains so powerful, obstructing the emergence of a rational policy. This in response to pressure apparently placed on the committee to recommend criminalization of cannabis use, which they did not recommend. Further elaborating upon the "symbolism" of cannabis and cannabis users, consider from the section called "Symbolism,"

> If society feels strongly enough about the impropriety of certain conduct, it may choose to express this norm through the criminal law even though the behavior is largely invisible and will be reduced only through effective operation of other institutions of control. Laws against incest and child beating are good examples. To weigh the costs and benefits of such symbolism requires a special, no-quantitative method of measurement. The benefits consist of the value of society in reaffirming

> certain norms, together with a reinforcement of self-restraint by those who accept society's judgment. The costs include the effect on the integrity and functioning of the legal system of having a law that is largely unenforceable, plus the resentment of those who reject society's judgment. The scale that balances these two sets of intangibles indicates, among other things, how widely and deeply the values in question are held. (*Drug Use in America*, 1973)

Here the Shafer Commission recognizes the costs and benefits of maintaining the criminal symbolism of cannabis. Also recognize (quite significant to the Part III Moral Assessment of cannabis law) society does criminalize behavior in order to "reaffirm social norms" without providing either moral or scientific justification. Here one can sense the Social Reality desire for the government to act as a parent, one who will "send messages" for them via criminal law.

> Use of prohibited substances constitutes deviance from American social values in a very special sense. When alcohol is properly regarded as a psychoactive substance, it becomes evident that discouragement of drug-taking behavior in general does not rank particularly high on this nation's scale of values. Rather, concern is for use of particular substances by particular populations; but even here the American public appears willing to tolerate more deviance today than it did previously.
>
> In light of the ambivalent attitude toward drug use, the relative ineffectiveness of the possession penalty as a deterrent, and the high social costs of its enforcement, the Commission believes that the criminal law is not a very useful symbol of the discouragement policy. Yet, until society develops a replacement symbol and other institutions assume their share of responsibility for control, it may be a necessary codification of public policy. Unfortunately, 60 years of coercive policy have so exaggerated the symbolic importance of the criminal law that it has become interwoven with social attitudes regarding drug use. Removing it suddenly would connote a change in values rather than merely a shift in emphasis.
>
> Perpetuating a criminal law principally for its symbolism does not comport well with the fundamental purposes of the rule of law. The Commission is strongly of the opinion, however, that policy makers cannot abruptly displace criminal law as a central support for control of drug-using behavior. The common reaction of those opposed to our recommendation to remove the criminal sanction from personal possession of marihuana illustrates the difficulty of rearranging even a part of the structure. We observe in our First Report that a legal policy designed to curtail the availability of cannabis substances could no more be constructed as neutrality toward or approval of marihuana use than could a similar legal scheme employed during Alcohol Prohibition. Nevertheless, there has been a chorus of objections that the withdrawal of the criminal sanction would signify approval of use and encourage more consumption of the drug.

> In the case of marihuana use, though, the symbolic value is plainly outweighed by the philosophical, constitutional and functional considerations. The Commission reaffirms its view that a criminal proscription of possession of marihuana for personal use is self-defeating as a means of implementing a discouragement policy. Moreover, the Commission believes that in the long run a measure of success of this nation's drug policy will be how much we have been able to disengage the criminal law from concern with consumption. As long as the legality of using the prohibited drugs is the major symbol of disapproval, the law will continue to bear the sole burden of fulfilling public policy and, almost certainly, bear it badly. (*Drug Use in America* 1973, 255–56)

The Shafer Commission recommendation for decriminalization and legalization of cannabis for personal use is reiterated here, and yet entering the twenty-first century the United States thirty-five years later continues on with the same ineffective policy. Ignoring the Shafer Commission recommendation and understanding of the effects of cannabis as well as the weighty "philosophical, constitutional, and functional" considerations emphasized, Nixon formed the DEA in 1973 and then most importantly "Scheduled" drugs and made marijuana "Schedule I." Again, this means three things:

A. Cannabis has a high potential for abuse.
B. Cannabis has no currently accepted medical use in treatment in the United States.
C. There is a lack of accepted safety for use of cannabis under medical supervision.

This is still the U.S. law today, a law constructed upon a Social Reality suppression of those viewed as not living consistently with the traditional American way of life. The expertise involved in scheduling cannabis as among the most dangerous of all drugs available for human consumption was almost completely political and rhetorical rather than scientific and moral.

> Under the big drug bill Nixon was sending up to Congress, health officials and the surgeon general would no longer be responsible for ranking drugs according to their danger and potential for abuse. The job of "scheduling" drugs would fall to the attorney general and his chief narcotics officer. Cops, not doctors, would henceforth judge drugs' toxicity and also a "common loathing" by health professions in response to giving attorney general the power to schedule drugs. (Baum 1997, 25)

The process involved in actually scheduling drugs is itself a reminder of Escohotado's synthetic/non-synthetic distinction. During the actual process of scheduling drugs, pharmaceutical companies lobbied for various drugs in order to have them scheduled so as to ensure maximum availability and minimum regulation. One can only wonder whether or not the schedule assigned to cannabis would have been different with drug company commercial interests at stake (Grinspoon and Bakalar 1997, 14).

Suggesting cannabis had "no *recognized* therapeutic potential" Nixon had ducked the question of whether or not cannabis *actually* had therapeutic potential. Given that cannabis was not a part of the American pharmacaopia, therefore not of the standard of care for medical practice, it simply followed that cannabis did not, of course could not, have any "recognized" therapeutic effects. The Social Reality encourages the interpretation as meaning cannabis *actually* has no therapeutic benefits. This claim is just plain false given the ample evidence and history of the use of cannabis for various therapeutic purposes.[10]

Rubin in *Cannabis and Culture* presents a novel and informative scholarly report of the nature of ganja use. Booth recognizes the impact of this work:

> The drug being so very widely used on the island, despite being illegal, the Center for Studies of Narcotic and Drug Abuse of the US National Institute of Mental Health sponsored a medical anthropological research programme in 1970 to assess how chronic users were affected by it. The final results were published in full in 1975, written by Vera Rubin and Lamros Comitas and entitled simply, *Ganja in Jamaica*. The conclusions were fascinating.
>
> It was found that marijuana use was the reason for substantially lower levels of alcoholism than anywhere else in similar societies in the Caribbean, it did not cause any measurable brain or chromosomic damage, was not psychologically dangerous and there was no link between marijuana usage and crime, accepting that growing and using it were in themselves illegal acts. More interestingly, the study stated that the culture had in-built restraints which controlled the social effects of marijuana. The teenagers' decision as to whether or not a peer should join in smoking marijuana after his initiation prevented those who might suffer adversely from the experience from continuing with it. There were also widely held social rules which said that, for example, one should avoid the drug if not in a calm state of mind; another advised that ganja should never be used on an empty stomach (Booth 2004, 259–260).[11]

Consider the wide range of social and individual benefits of ganja included in this report:

1. lower levels of alcoholism
2. no measurable brain or chromosomic damage

3. not psychologically dangerous
4. not linked to crime
5. built-in restraints within culture to control social effects
6. respect for those who prefer not to use ganja

Again, in light of the accumulation argument that legalized cannabis would only add to the problems U.S. society already has with alcohol and tobacco, here it seems to subtract from the problem.

One country which in 1976 decided to ignore (but unable to legalize, given the UN Single Convention) minor possession and use of cannabis was the Netherlands. Booth points out:

> The government was being pragmatic by addressing the reality of the situation. The advantages of the *de facto* licensing of cannabis use were seen as considerable. Consumption could be controlled, drug education given, sales monitored, dealing done on officially specified premises and cannabis distribution separated from harder drugs. Furthermore, cannabis was no longer seen as deviant and anti-social by the predominantly young users. (Booth 2004, 281)

It seemed that in 1977 and the election of Jimmy Carter the U.S. federal government might move to legalize cannabis and treat it as a recreational substance as is alcohol.

> The election of Jimmy Carter to the White House in 1977 seemed to suggest there would be a move towards legalizing cannabis in the USA. In a speech to the US Congress on 2 August, in his first year in office, Carter was quite forthright: *Penalties against possession of a drug should not be more damaging to an individual than the use of the drug itself . . . Nowhere is this more clear than in the laws against possession of marijuana in private for personal use.* He wanted to remove all federal penalties for possession of less than an ounce of marijuana. (Booth 2004, 252–53)

However, several publicized political issues turned the public against Carter and awakened the Social Reality of cannabis use so that the United States experienced a major ideological swing from Carter to Reagan in the span of just a couple of years. This swing resulted in the introduction of hundreds of thousands of marijuana users into the criminal justice system. Before this happened, Carter's basic insight should be seriously considered, that penalties against possession of a drug should not be more dangerous than the use of a drug itself. Before the momentum swing and subsequent War on Drugs (taking us into the twenty-first century United States), consider that the states in the United States in the late 1970s were in a position quite similar to that of

2008 United States, with currently 12 recognizing medicinal exemptions to criminal or civil prosecution for cannabis use:

> By 1980, eleven states had removed all criminal penalties for possession. Alaska went so far as to declare that marijuana possession by adults in their own home was constitutionally protected under the laws of privacy. This remained in force until 1990 when the administration of President George Bush threatened to withhold major federal funding if the state did not reverse the decision. With this federal gun to its head, it did. (Booth 2004, 250)

War on Drugs: Social Reality Again Responds

Changes began in 1980 with the election of Ronald Reagan as U.S. president:

> Among those threatened by the post-Nixon slide toward easier marijuana laws was the Drug Enforcement Administration. Were marijuana legal, the country's problem with illegal drugs would shrink to the tiny number of heroin and cocaine users, obviating a federal drug-enforcement budget the size of the DEA's. So now that Peter Bourne was gone, the DEA began pushing for a harder line on marijuana.
>
> As soon as Bourne resigned, DEA administrator Peter Bensinger told reporters he wanted to see the federal penalties for marijuana increased, not eliminated. He also said any notion that marijuana is a valuable therapeutic drug—for reducing nausea in chemotherapy patents, for example—is hogwash. "The American Cancer Society," he said, "confirms that marijuana represents a more serious cancer threat than cigarettes."
>
> Which took the Cancer Society by surprise; it had said no such thing and in fact believed just the opposite. "We have no national policy on marijuana and cancer," a spokeswoman said in response to Bensinger. "We're interested in it, though, for treatment of pain for cancer victims.'" (Baum 1997, 126)

And further disregarding medical experts and their knowledge of the effects of cannabis:

> Lee Dogoloff and Dick Williams together effected the biggest change in drug policy since Nixon launched the Drug War. They took the leadership away from doctors and scientists and handed it to untrained, emotionally motivated parents. They then directed federal policy not at the most dangerous drugs, but at the one parents worried about as much for reasons of family politics and culture as health. (Baum 1997, 135)

Baum presents 1981 as the year in which a foundation was built for the change of drug policy that was to come. The change was from rehab and counseling to retribution and punishment: "To the extent criminals could be portrayed as a distinct population of inherently bad individuals, the easier it would be to justify cutting the social programs Reagan wanted eliminated or diminished" (Baum 1997, 138). And, "With the 1982 budget came the beginning of the end of the federally funded drug treatment network that four drug czars worked a decade to build" (Baum 1997, 144–45).

Reagan further acted against the essential nature of sentencing and administering justice, the tapering of the punishment to the specifics of the crime, by reintroducing mandatory minimum sentences for drug offences. As a result, "the prison population exploded. In 1970, 16 per cent of those held in federal penitentiaries were in for drug-related crimes. By 1994, the figure would be 62 per cent" (Booth 2004, 254).

Baum points out that Reagan simply overlooked racism and instead judged cannabis users as "bad" in more than a moral way, but bad in a way that was doing violence to society and therefore justified retribution:

> Reagan was redeploying the tactic Richard Nixon used to batter "root causes" in 1968: shift the blame for social problems away from inequality, racism, injustice, and the like and place it on the immoral acts of bad individuals. That way, government has no greater role than to mete out "swift and sure" retribution. (Baum 1997, 150)

Baum points out there were skeptics of the criminalization of cannabis use, especially the clear hypocrisy of such a policy in light of the legal and encouraged use of equally if not more dangerous substances:

> While nobody was saying that drawing hot, psychoactive smoke into the lungs was good for one's health (except perhaps in prescribed medical circumstances), many researchers were saying that a society that tolerates alcohol, tobacco, and bacon-double-cheeseburgers cannot on medical grounds justify jailing people for smoking marijuana. (Baum 1997, 152)

Indicating the war on drugs was viewed more as a game than as a matter of justifying the violation of moral rights of cannabis users, the Reagan presidency strategically refused to even discuss the matter:

> Dependent as it was on presenting marijuana as Public Drug Enemy Number One, Reagan's War on Drugs couldn't withstand scientific debate. Placed against heroin—or for that matter alcohol, tobacco, poor prenatal care, workplace accidents, and myriad other public health problems—marijuana pales by comparison. So rather than invite opponents onto the playing field of science and data, Turner and his colleagues attempted to ban the game altogether. (Baum 1997, 164)

> With marijuana a Schedule I illegal drug, the country had 45 million illegal drug users, and the DEA's budget reflected that. Were marijuana legal, the number of illegal drug users would slip to about 5 million. The "drug problem" would be reduced by some 90 percent, and the budget of the country's drug enforcement agency would likely be tailored accordingly. (Baum 1997, 258)

And, "The War on Drugs doubled the nation's prison population during the Reagan administration. The portion of state prisoners inside for drugs went from one in fifteen to one in three, and 85 percent of them were in for mere possession" (Baum 1997, 259).

> Through the 1980s, marijuana use declined but only at the expense of a rise in heroin and cocaine abuse which, unlike marijuana, ignited a sharp rise in violent crime and robberies. Marijuana dealers, who were mostly non-career or part-time criminals for whom the drug was their only criminal activity, withdrew from the market leaving their business open for take-over by hardened career criminals. Some of them continued to sell marijuana but most dropped it as uneconomic. Now, marijuana was in the hands of the heroin and cocaine pushers. (Booth 2004, 256)
>
> The decade of the eighties without a doubt covers the greatest institutional effort ever made to repress the use of illegal drugs. The crusade was already a phenomenon of global scale, and its result was an alarm without precedent. The American federal government alone—independently of state funds—spent millions on repression. Following the Reagan-Bush initiatives, it was not unheard of for children to report their parents or brothers for cultivating marijuana or possessing cocaine, or for parents to kill or wound their own children when they found them using an illicit drug. (Escohotado 1999, 146)

In 1989, William Bennett's legislation of morality focused only on certain vices while condemning others, oblivious to the arbitrary distinction being made between cannabis and alcohol. Consider his workings with the DEA and the basic strategy employed, again suggesting alcohol is a "social lubricant" and not a drug and also as significantly less harmful than cannabis:

> Alcohol was another problem. Bennett's drug office had no congressional mandate to address it, his mainstream constituency enjoyed it, and the multimillion-dollar alcohol lobby wouldn't stand for further restrictions on booze. So the drug office needed somehow to place alcohol on the "moral" side of the line. No small trick. Aside from the cirrhosis and highway deaths, booze was implicated in violent crime to a much greater degree than any illegal drug. The Justice Department found that half of those convicted of homicide in 1989 were using alcohol at the time of the killing, while fewer than 6 percent said they were on drugs alone.

> Bennett's men tiptoed through the minefield of alcohol and tobacco. John Walters took the position that marijuana, cocaine, and heroin "enslave people" and "prevent them from being free citizens" in a way that alcohol and tobacco do not. Bruce Carnes decided that drug taking was "life-denying" and "inward," but that using alcohol or tobacco was not. Illegal drugs, Bennett said in a speech that May, 'obliterate morals, value, character, our relations with each other, and our relation to God.' None of these conclusions was based on science, but collectively they had the effect of royal fiat.
>
> The Bennettistas also relied on a neat bit of tautology: marijuana, heroin, and cocaine are immoral because they are illegal. Why are they illegal? Because they are immoral. Compliance, not health, was the real issue. (Baum 1997, 265–66)

This is also a basic tenet of Social Reality: if cannabis use is illegal then it is immoral. As I will argue in the Part III Moral Assessment of cannabis use it is instead the moral that justifies the legal, not the legal which determines the moral.

Into the 1990s came a rise of the issue of medicinal cannabis, especially for MS patients and chemotherapy patients. Federal regulations demand cannabis is treated under an IND (investigational new drug) program and structure, one that would include placebos and thereby make the medical motivation of compassion secondary to the federal interest in proving in a rigorous scientific way the actual effectiveness of cannabis use. The problem is that this population of patients, although ideal for such a study, are actually suffering actual symptoms they want relieved.

> In 1992, after a rush of applications from AIDS sufferers, the administration of President George Bush shut down the IND programme, the director, James O. Mason, stating, *If it is perceived that Public Health Service is going around giving marijuana to folks, there would be a perception that this stuff can't be so bad.* At the time of its cessation, fewer than two dozen patients had qualified for state-issued marijuana in the entire USA.
>
> Through the 1990s, more terminally ill cancer, arthritis and MS patients broke US federal law. Some were jailed. In one case, a paraplegic was sentenced to life imprisonment plus sixteen years. In another, William Foster of Tulsa, Oklahoma, severely crippled with rheumatoid arthritis, was sent down for ninety-three years for growing ten cannabis plants and fifty-six cuttings, despite his defense proving that the Society of Neuroscience in Washington, DC, had shown marijuana to be an effective treatment for his disease. (Booth 2004, 296)

The federal government, with a conflict between two agencies, the FDA and Department of Justice, had the latter ultimately squash the FDA compassionate use program because the FDA program was inconsistent with the Department of Justice program. This was a clear example of the Social Reality exerting its power over the Scientific Reality of cannabis use. President Bush determined cannabis meant what the Department of Justice called it and therefore ignored the Scientific Reality.

Consider the reiteration of the Social Reality by the Clinton administration in 1996, going so far as to warn physicians to not discuss cannabis use with patients. In the 1990s there was a major movement to hydroponics in the illicit cannabis producing world, where cannabis users could use hydroponic equipment in their homes to grow not only their own cannabis, but cannabis of potent strains created by other users and suppliers. As of today it is believed that Mexico is no longer the sole producer but perhaps producer of half of the cannabis purchased and used in the United States.[12]

Booth goes on to consider how in Britain those arguing for legalization have recently focused upon the obvious double-standard existing between legalized alcohol and tobacco and illegal cannabis, again re-iterating the clear dangers to society of the former and unclear danger to society of the latter. He also points out recent incidences of civil disobedience (e.g., Colin Davies in Manchester opening a medicinal cannabis clinic and informing police of his doing so). The argument in Britain also considers a move to legalization would create billions of tax dollars and tens if not hundreds of thousands of jobs throughout the industry, small farmers could reap benefits, and the environmental advantages cannabis has on the land.

> In Britain, the British Medical Association (BMA) recommended in 1997 that medicinal cannabis be made legal. Twelve months later on 11 November 1998, the House of Lords Select Committee on Science and Technology released a report entitled *Cannabis: the Scientific and Medical Evidence*, having taken both verbal and written testimony from physicians and patients. The report included the statement that clinical trials of cannabis treatment for multiple sclerosis and chronic pain should be urgently conducted and the recommendation that cannabis be removed from Schedule 1 to Schedule 2 of the Misuse Drugs Regulations, allowing it to be provided by doctors under prescription. The Government rejected it. (Booth 2004, 297)

Booth presents an international move to decriminalize or legalize cannabis, one that seems to be leaving the United States and its Social Reality behind:

> Regardless of the strictures of the UN Single Convention, many other countries are moving in the same general direction. In western Europe, where it is reckoned at least a third of the adult population has used cannabis, Belgium, Italy, Luxembourg, Spain and Switzerland have all to some extent decriminalized it with certain basic and mostly public-order provisos unique to each. Portugal has acted likewise on all illicit drugs. (Booth 2004, 321–22)

And also,

> Estimates given by the United Nations International Drug Control Programme (UNDCP) suggest that 3.5 per cent of the world's adult population (being defined as those over the age of fifteen) was using cannabis in 2000. This is a total of 147 million people. The largest user population, in Asia, accounts for over 25 per cent of world cannabis consumption. Another 50 per cent or so is used in Africa and the Americas, in about equal quantities, with Europe accounting for a further 20 per cent, the remaining 5 per cent used elsewhere. (Booth 2004, 313)

Booth also explains Switzerland and Germany seem to allow selling of cannabis as long as it is not done so explicitly as an "intoxicant" but as "herbal tea, dried flowers, or pot pourri sachets" (Booth 2004, 322).

> Elsewhere in Europe, Ireland does not act against users but fines those found in possession; Denmark issues a police caution for possession of small amounts; Greece—which until recently had very harsh cannabis laws—acts likewise but insists apprehended smokers submit to counseling; Austria permits personal consumption and France carries out few prosecutions. (Booth 2004, 322)

Booth steps back from his comprehensive look at a variety of western European countries to see ambiguity in the overall situation. Different countries have different laws, again reinforcing the basic idea that the "truth" being considered is not a medical or scientific one but rather a social truth, one involving rhetoric, symbolism, and power.

The Netherlands' policy of allowing the use of cannabis has provided clear, concrete evidence against the gateway theory supposing a causal relationship between the use of cannabis and the subsequent use of "harder drugs." Booth relates the results of study of the Netherlands' cannabis users and specifically whether or not using cannabis has led them to harder drugs:

> Most cannabis users would not even consider graduating to harder drugs, any more than those who, for example, drank alcohol would. Surveys carried out in Amsterdam between 1987 and 1997 corroborated previous evidence that suggested that hard-drug abuse was not dependent upon preliminary soft-drug taking but the character of the individual and their preparedness to experiment. The wide availability of cannabis has not led to any greater increase in the use of harder drugs than that experienced in any other European country. (Booth 2004, 323–24)

Those who hold to the gateway theory bear a monumental burden of accounting for the fact that in Amsterdam legalization of cannabis has not affected rates of heroin use. Again it is clear that using cannabis does not cause one to use heroin or any other hard drugs. Consider the basic philosophical rationale guiding change in cannabis laws in Australia, citing the same principle cited by U.S. President Carter in his efforts to revise cannabis legislation:

> In 1994, a report by the Australian National Task Force on Cannabis stated, *Any social policy should be reviewed when there is reason to believe that the cost of administering it outweighs the harms reduced*, adding that Australia suffered more social harm from maintaining cannabis prohibition than from the drug itself. (Booth 2004, 324)

Civil disobedience in Ontario in 1995 by Christopher Clay (owner of Hemp Nation shop) had him challenge the law against cannabis possession and purchase because (as Booth puts it) he had "the desire to get buyers away from the black market, where there're no quality controls and no age restrictions, adding, "I'm also concerned about the thousands of Canadians who have criminal records just from marijuana possession" (Booth 2004, 325). It seems Canada as well as many other countries around the world are ready to decriminalize cannabis but for the U.S. federal government opposition and warning against such moves. Booth insightfully points out two "policy lynchpins" of the U.S. federal government:

> The first, user accountability, forced those using drugs to accept that, no matter what they were taking, someone somewhere was suffering as a result, be it an addict dying from an overdose or a Third World peasant being exploited. The second was zero tolerance, by which a drug offence, no matter how slight, was deemed as bad as the next, regardless of the substance involved or the culpability of the perpetrator. In the Anslinger tradition, a drug was a drug was a drug and, even if it was medicinally valid in other countries, it was still prohibited if it was in any way related to an illegal substance. (Booth 2004, 325–26)

So here are two current "lynchpins" of the Social Reality: first, using cannabis is hurting others even if there are no obvious others being harmed, and second using cannabis is just as dangerous as using heroin. Of course, the Scientific Reality completely rejects these "lynchpins" as simply not grounded in scientific research and understanding of drugs and drug use. The neurology chapter clearly distinguished different drugs physiologically; the DSM-IV-TR includes no withdrawal syndrome associated with cannabis use thereby distinguishing cannabis from other drugs with withdrawal syndromes. This all is apparently irrelevant to the zero tolerance principle. Also, there is the obvious hypocrisy in that alcohol is *tolerated* under the zero tolerance policy and pharmaceutical companies are working hand in glove with the health care industry. The result is not "zero tolerance" for drugs but rather the directive to citizens (and the "message being sent to youth") is to get drugs from pharmaceutical companies but not from anywhere else. Again, Escohotado's synthetic/non-synthetic distinction provides a hidden assumption behind the zero-tolerance policy.

> Dr. William Notcutt, a consultant anaesthetist at the James Paget Hospital in Great Yarmouth and director of the hospital's Pain Relief Clinic, stated in 2000, there appears to be a Puritanism concerning the use of cannabis in medicine, a reluctance to use it in case it leads to intoxication and a psycho-active reaction. This objection seems irrational to him. His argument is that, if someone is in pain and depressed, living a miserable life because of pain, why should a medicine that made them happier be proscribed. He pointed out that anti-depressants like Prozac are prescribed almost with abandon and yet they are also mind-altering drugs with a risk of severe side effects. Marijuana has few contra-indications and yet it is prohibited. (Booth 2004, 294)

As Booth points out, it is especially striking, internationally, that although the United States has a Bill of Rights and England does not, Britain has recognized what the United States and its Bill of Rights has not, that cannabis use is a matter of individual choice:

> In the fight against drugs, the federal authorities have deliberately created an atmosphere of fear. Whilst there are those who accept this as valid, it has still undermined the basic civil and human rights of tens of thousands of American citizens. The Bill of Rights has, in effect, been systematically abused with no opportunity for redress. (Booth 2004, 326)

And of the benefits Britain has found:

> Those in favour of legalization claim that it is up to the individual to decide what they do, want or need, but this is little more than a civil rights issue and, at least in Britain, there is no constitution or bill of rights under which to argue the point as, for example, exists in the USA. More pertinently, supporters of legalization argue that legalizing cannabis would remove it from the criminal sphere, allowing distribution to be regulated and even taxed. Permitting personal cultivation would also remove the criminal element. Regulation would ensure the quality of cannabis and remove the criminal risk of adulteration with hard drugs in order to ensnare and addict newer customers. The benefits of taxation are obvious although one aspect would have to be assessed. The value of the tax revenues would need to be balanced against the cost to society of cannabis use. What would have to be avoided would be the debacle caused by tobacco where the revenue raised does not meet the public-health cost of treating the resultant illness. (Booth 2004, 317)

Conclusion: Six Social Reality Beliefs about Cannabis

In this brief historical summary I have failed to discover clear and convincing reasons behind laws banning cannabis. It seems the federal government is simply insisting on cannabis being illegal and dismissing any talk of facts or scientific evidence, let alone suffering human beings.

> Regardless of criminal or civil law, marijuana use has steadily increased over the past fifteen years with the medicinal marijuana lobby furthering the public opinion that the drug is comparatively innocuous. DEA statistics in 2000 estimated thirty million Americans regularly used marijuana. (Booth 2004, 327)
>
> The number of marijuana arrests across the USA in 2000 stood at 734,498, 88 per cent of these for possession only; this figure was only slightly less than the combined total for murder, armed robbery, rape and assault; the fiscal national cost of policing specifically marijuana prohibition (as opposed to all controlled substances) was nine billion dollars annually; an estimated seventy million Americans, 24 per cent of the entire population, have tried cannabis; 12.9 per cent of all drug convicted prisoners in state prisons and 18.9 per cent in federal facilities (a total of approximately 38,300) were being held for cannabis related crimes, mostly only for possession; the average cost of housing marijuana convicts in prison was approximately $1.2 billion per annum. (Booth 2004, 328)

Booth, in the final pages of his exhaustively researched book on the history of hashish/cannabis/marijuana use in the world, offers some basic conclusions about the current U.S. federal policy on cannabis:

> Whatever the US government might want to do internationally, it has to accept that, in many countries, cannabis continues to be used, despite being officially banned, because it is traditional and to hope to stamp out its use is an arrogant assumption. It is akin to a teetotal Muslim country demanding America ban bourbon whiskey. In at least a dozen countries, cannabis occupies a cultural position as a religious sacrament. In India, it features in *puja*, the Hindu act of worship expressing devotion to the gods, and in major religious festivals such as Kumbh Mela, one of the greatest religious gatherings on earth. (Booth 2004, 329)

And Booth in the end captures the polarization which exists on the issue of cannabis use and law in the United States, complementing what I refer to as the Social Reality and Scientific Reality of cannabis use:

> Despite the many dozens of independent and government commissions, scientific investigations, sociological, pharmacological, criminological and medical sites, legislative assessments and political evaluations conducted throughout the world over the last hundred years, there is still no consensus of opinion. Either

cannabis is regarded as an innocuous social drug or as a serious danger to society. As soon as it is mentioned, argument—whether between individuals or governments—tends to become instantly polarized. That it can offer relief from some of the worst illnesses that afflict mankind is ignored. That it could provide a versatile and environmentally friendly new industrial material is dismissed. Instead, it is condemned and prohibited as being a problem not because it is harmful but because arbitrary moral decisions have decreed it to be so. (Booth 2004, 332)

Consider the events and Western reception of cannabis up to the twenty-first century in the United States as being supportive of the following beliefs:

Social Reality Belief 1: Asceticism (total denial of intoxication) regarding cannabis use.
Social Reality Belief 2: Cannabis use causes violence, aggression (assassin myth).
Social Reality Belief 3: Suspicion of foreign cultures and habits (anti-immigrant, specifically anti-Latino, Mexican, African American).
Social Reality Belief 4: Cannabis is a gateway drug leading to heroin use.
Social Reality Belief 5: Synthetic drugs are morally neutral and efficient while cannabis is natural and not safe.
Social Reality Belief 6: Cannabis is a dangerous drug with high abuse potential and no therapeutic uses.

Notes

1. Guiding me throughout my presentation of major historical events is *Cannabis: A History* (2004) by Martin Booth. Those who are more interested in the history of cannabis (of the events I introduce as well as others) are encouraged to begin with Booth's work. For my purposes in this book, I intend to only briefly present uncontroversial meanings of several major events grounding the current Social Reality of cannabis use.

2. However, more generally, in light of the state of the world in this early twenty-first-century United States, it is quite relevant to better understand and appreciate not merely the origins of the Islamic faith (and the meanings of the various sects involved) but it also allows an exercise of reason and openness to an Eastern culture, a culture within which the cannabis plant wa likely used for thousands of years.

3. This distinction and the underlying explanation for it goes beyond the purposes of this book, although it certainly seems one relevant to those with a serious interest in world peace across nations and specifically between the East and West. Acceptance of legalized cannabis in the United States, with the same legal status as alcohol currently enjoys, would indicate a move toward learning from the East, to defending

moral ideals while not quibbling about preferences and culturally accepted practices not directly harming those not of the culture.

4. This will be considered in chapter 9 and Old Testament consideration of cannabis, with God having the earth put forth plants on His Third day of creation, there is obvious tension between claims that plants are (in themselves) "evil" let alone created not by God but instead by the devil, the latter claim in obvious contradiction with the Genesis account of the Third Day of creation.

5. Consider also a very significant piece of technology, one which would foretell a massive twentieth-century cigarette industry, was the rolling machine: "The introduction of the cigarette-rolling machine in 1883 spurred cigarette consumption because cigarettes became cheaper than cigars. By 1885, a billion cigarettes a year were being produced. Americans consumed more than 815 billion cigarettes in 1988" (Hanson, Venturelli, and Fleckenstein 2002, 305).

6. Obviously, with cannabis laws still on the books now at the beginning of the twenty-first century in the U.S., and criminal law statistics commonly showing although there are more white than black users of cannabis, there are five times as many black cannabis users punished for cannabis use, the effect of the current law is the same as it was at its (racist) inception. A politician today who continues to reject cannabis legalization is more than likely just supporting the party line (e.g., holding firm to the seven beliefs of "Social Reality" to be articulated at the conclusion of this chapter), not paying much if any attention to the glaring implicit racism in these arrest statistics. This is also in addition to the strong argument concluding these laws actually violate the 10th Amendment, fail to recognize basic liberties clearly involved in Americans' "pursuit of happiness."

7. Perhaps a similar sentiment was also involved in alcohol prohibition in the United States, with the difference being the political power held by those immigrants who used alcohol were politically stronger than those who used marijuana, thereby leading to an ultimate repeal of prohibition. The Social Reality of the United States advocates alcohol but not cannabis. This cultural and political contingency, although logically irrelevant to the danger marijuana poses to individuals and to society as a medicine or as a recreational drug, became a basis for law prohibiting cannabis use and criminalizing its users. Possession of political power can be interpreted as the decisive factor in the ultimate failure of alcohol prohibition and success of marijuana prohibition.

8. There was a controversy involving the quality of writing the beat poets introduced to the world of literature, with some championing the spontaneous prose of the beats as revolutionary while others seeing it as inferior. Ezra Pound, for example, condemned beat prose by pointing out "Any damn fool can be spontaneous." Defenders of beat poetry and literature argue "The theory put into practice gets rid of "artificiality" by getting rid of art." Also, "And because the beats, unlike their French existentialist cousins and rather like the earlier Dadaists, see "the absurd" in its comic implications as fully as its tragic ones, a good deal of beat literature that fails as Art is quite enjoyable as Wisecrack" (Polsky 1985, 176).

9. "Altering consciousness" is the very definition of a psychoactive drug, thereby disallowing it to be used meaningfully as a standard with which to distinguish any drug from any other drug, or specifically to distinguish licit from illicit drugs.

10. Consider also Grinspoon and Bakalar, *Marihuana: The Forbidden Medicine*, pp. 15–17, on this same point of the DEA strategy of defining "accepted medical use" as standard of treatment, thereby in effect ruling out all Schedule I drugs.

11. Also in Jamaica originated in 1930s Rastafarianism in which herbs and marijuana are considered sacramental. Booth cites three scriptures in their justification for the use of marijuana: Psalms 104:14 (herb for service of man), Genesis 1:11 (God letting earth bring forth herb yielding seed), and Revelation 22:2 (leaves of the tree for healing). In Jamaica Rastafarians were suppressed using marijuana laws.

12. In chapter six, considering John Stuart Mill and utilitarianism, I will present data showing cannabis as being the major cash crop of the United States, worth many billions of dollars.

5

Revealing the Current Social Reality of Cannabis Use in the United States

THE SOCIAL REALITY IN THE UNITED STATES tolerates recreational use of alcohol as an intoxicant and yet prohibits even medicinal use of cannabis. Alcohol causes more individual and social harm than cannabis. In this chapter I first emphasize the high level of tolerance the Social Reality has for alcohol-related injuries and death. Second, I present "The Public and the War on Illicit Drugs" (Blendon and Young) showing where and how the public gets its information about cannabis specifically and to reiterate the public rejection of the legalization of cannabis for medicinal purposes. This study reveals the Social Reality regarding cannabis use in the United States. It further complements the historical events and resulting six foundational beliefs of the Social Reality on cannabis use.

The High Degree of Tolerance for Alcohol as a Recreational Drug in the United States

In *Drugs and Society*, Hanson Venturelli, and Fleckenstein name the second of two chapters on alcohol, "Alcohol: A Behavioral Perspective." Therein they include statistics and information about the use of alcohol specifically by adolescents and young adults. Consider, for example:

> In a 1998 survey conducted by the Substance Abuse and Mental Health Services Administration (SAMHSA), 113 million Americans age 12 and older who participated in the survey reported that they used alcohol at least once within the prior 30-day period (SAMHSA 1999). In the same survey, approximately 33 million

> reported engaged in binge drinking in the 30 days before the survey. A staggering 10.5 percent of current drinkers were under 21 in 1998. Of this underage group, 5.1 million engage in binge drinking, including 2.3 million who are classified as heavy drinkers. (heavy drinkers = five or more drinks on one occasion on 5 or more days during a given 30-day period) (Hanson, Venturelli, and Fleckenstein 2002, 202)

Among the many facts presented regarding "consumption patterns" of the U.S. society (from Newport 1999), consider the following of the several presented by Hanson, Venturelli, and Fleckenstein:

- To date, alcohol has been tried by 53 percent of 8th graders, 70 percent of 10th graders, 81 percent of 12th graders, and 89 percent of college students. Occasions of *heavy drinking* (five or more drinks in a row at least once before this survey was administered) occurred in 14 percent of the nation's 8th graders, 24 percent of the nation's 10th graders, and 32 percent of the nation's 12th graders (Hanson, Venturelli, and Fleckenstein 2002, 203).
- Estimated spending for health care services was $18.8 billion for alcohol problems and medical consequences of alcohol consumption and $9.9 billion for other types of drug problems (Hanson, Venturelli, and Fleckenstein 2002, 203).
- Whites have the highest rate of alcohol consumption at 86 percent, African Americans are second at 72 percent, and Hispanics are third at 69 percent (SAMHSA/OAS 1999) (Hanson, Venturelli, and Fleckenstein 2002, 203).
- With regard to 12th graders' consumption of alcohol, white underage students are much more likely to binge drink (36 percent) compared with African American students (12 percent) and Hispanic students (28 percent)" (Hanson, Venturelli, and Fleckenstein 2002, 204).
- Alcohol abuse is estimated to have contributed to 25 percent to 30 percent of violent crime (Hanson, Venturelli, and Fleckenstein 2002, 207).
- [A]lcohol is officially linked to at least half of all highway fatalities, and that figure includes only legal intoxication (Hanson, Venturelli, and Fleckenstein 2002, 207).

"I Don't Use Drugs I Only Drink."

The current Social Reality of the United States believes alcohol is not a drug. This assumption, false when considering alcohol is a sedative/depressant as per chapter 1, allows the Social Reality to use drugs without "owning up to it." In the section, "Cultural Influences," Hanson, Venturelli, and Fleckenstein point out: "The comment that 'I don't use and never would use drugs, I only drink' can easily be heard being espoused by a large portion of Americans, (probably a majority), who place alcohol in a completely separate category from drugs" (Hanson, Venturelli, and Fleckenstein 2002, 216).

> American culture in general views ethanol-containing beverages as sexy, mature, sophisticated, facilitating socializing, and enhancing status. Today, many of these beliefs are communicated through the mass media, and advertising is a key medium of communication. Advertising uses positive images in order to persuade observers to purchase a particular brand of alcohol. (Hanson, Venturelli, and Fleckenstein 2002, 216)

Again, the neurological reality of the effects of this drug does not change despite the irrational categorization of alcohol as a non-drug:

> Alcohol is a disinhibitor, which refers to depression of the cerebral cortex functions. When this occurs, it results in a suspension of rational or thoughtful constraints on impulsive behavior. *Inhibitions* (inner raw feelings and attitudes) are normally controlled through rationality and logical thought processes. (Hanson, Venturelli, and Fleckenstein 2002, 217)

Binge Drinking: Socially Tolerated Abuse

One quite visible acceptance of rampant legal drug abuse by millions of people is "binge drinking" among college students. "*Binge drinking* is defined as consumption of five or more drinks in one sitting or five or more drinks in short succession" (Hanson, Venturelli, and Fleckenstein 2002, 221). Consider that "Nearly half of all college students are binge drinkers" (Hanson, Venturelli, and Fleckenstein 2002, 221). Furthermore, in their section called, "College and University Students and Alcohol Use," they indicate, "As many as 360,000 of the nation's 12 million undergraduates will die from alcohol-related causes while in school. This is more than the number who will receive master's and doctorate degrees (Alcoholism Kills 2000)" (Hanson, Venturelli, and Fleckenstein 2002, 221). And as a final point indicating the extent to which college students use alcohol, Hanson, Venturelli, and Fleckenstein cite a CORE Institute Study:

> The CORE Institute survey is a validated survey instrument that has been administered to more than 1 million students—by far the largest sample of college students surveyed. The available figures from the CORE Institute survey (Presley et al. 1996) indicate that on average, approximately 83 percent of college students consume alcohol within the year this survey was given. The average number of

> drinks that students consume is 5.1 per week (Presley et al. 1996). Approximately 42 percent engaged in binge drinking 2 weeks before the CORE survey was administered. Of all the drugs reported, alcohol was the most heavily abused on college campuses, followed by tobacco 44 percent and marijuana 31 percent. (Hanson, Venturelli, and Fleckenstein 2002, 221)

My purpose in this section is to establish the fact that alcohol abuse is tolerated by the Social Reality in the United States. Of course the main question invited in the context of cannabis in the United States is, "What distinguishes binge-drinking college students as a cohort or population from those who use cannabis?" To stay focused on the level of tolerance the Social Reality has for alcohol abuse, consider that the negative effects of alcohol abuse and alcoholism assumed and absorbed by spouses, children, and communities of those who abuse alcohol. In their section on "The Role of Alcohol in Domestic Violence," Hanson, Venturelli, and Fleckenstein explain:

> The abuse of alcohol overwhelmingly emerges as a primary predictor of marital violence (De Jong 1995; Drug Strategies 1999). A study of 2000 American couples conduced in 1993 showed that rates of domestic violence were as much as 15 times higher in households where the husband was described as "often" being drunk, as opposed to "never" drunk (Collins and Messerschmidt 1993). The same study found that alcohol was present in more than half of all reported incidences of domestic abuse. (Hanson, Venturelli, and Fleckenstein 2002, 224)

And, reinforcing the significant negative effects of alcoholic parents on the habits and lives of their children, consider:

> It is estimated that out of 260 million Americans, 14 million are alcoholics. There are 28.6 million COAs [Children of Alcoholics] in the United States, and 6.6 million are under the age of 18 (Alcoholism Kills, 2000; NCADI 1992). Approximately 25 percent of American children are exposed before the age of 18 to at least one person in the family who is either an alcoholic or alcohol abuser. Children of alcoholics are at high risk of developing the same attachment to alcohol. Alcoholics are more likely than nonalcoholics to have an alcoholic parent, sibling, or other relative. (Hanson, Venturelli, and Fleckenstein 2002, 226)

To conclude this first section, it seems an understatement to claim alcohol is a dangerous drug. Although something could be legally done to criminalize alcohol abusers as are cannabis users, they are not likely to be so treated. This is quite relevant to cannabis in an argument citing the dangerousness of cannabis for users and/or for society as justifying its illegality. Such an argument must explain the legal availability of alcohol against the same criterion of dangerousness.

The Public View of Drugs and Cannabis: Confirmation of the Social Reality on Cannabis Use

"The Public and the War on Illicit Drugs" confirms and broadens defining beliefs of the Social Reality on cannabis use in the United States. The U.S. public rejection of cannabis reflects the twentieth-century propaganda and trust in the media as a primary source of information about cannabis. Blendon and Young pose four specific questions in their study: First, Where do Americans get their information about the extent of the nation's illegal drug problem and what are their experiences with it? Second, what worries Americans most about the country's illicit drug problems? Third, why do Americans think individuals use illegal drugs? Fourth, what are the public's views on various policy proposals to respond to the nations' drug problems, and what are their implications for the future? In addition, two more issues are considered: exchange of sterile needles and syringes of the used ones of injection drug users and the legalization of cannabis for medical treatments (Blendon and Young 1998, 827). The culmination of my application of main findings of this particular article will be with the sixth issue, considering the U.S. Public understanding of cannabis. The views revealed as a whole strengthen and make concrete the beliefs of the Social Reality.

1. Where Do Americans Get Their Information and What Are Their Experiences with It?

Although they oppose cannabis, most of the Social Reality have very little direct experience with it and get their information from the media. Blendon and Young, indicating an answer to their first study question and primary general point about the public view of the use of illegal drugs:

> Most members of the American public have very little direct experience with the illicit drug problem. Their views are largely shaped by the content and magnitude of media coverage on the issue. In the future, if health professionals want to change the direction of Americans' beliefs on particular drug policies they will have to devote significant resources to gaining media attention for their views.
>
> On this issue, it is not only the news media that will influence future public opinion. The public is likely to be swayed by what they see on weekly television health and crime drama series, by large paid-for advertising campaigns, and by public service advertisements that espouse a particular drug policy viewpoint. (Blendon and Young 1998, 831)

Note here especially in light of the history of propaganda started at the root of cannabis legislation by FBN director Anslinger that the media has continually been used to control public opinion to this day, creating adherence and support from a massive number of the public. The moral relevance of the public lack of personal experience with drugs, assuming this includes of cannabis, will be apparent in the Part III Moral Assessment chapters, specifically regarding qualified judges of pleasures.

2. What Worries Americans Most about the Country's Illicit Drug Problem?

In response to this second question, Blendon and Young reveal that

> Americans report that they worry about the effect of illicit drugs for the following 4 reasons: (1) linkage to high rates of crime, (2) negative effect on the national character, (3) morality, and (4) harmful health consequences for communities and individuals. (Blendon and Young 1998, 829)

Important for the Part III "Moral Assessment of Cannabis Use and Law" which is to follow, morality is one of the four reasons Americans worry about the effect of illicit drugs. Perhaps if the focus were merely on cannabis and not on "illicit drugs" as asked in the question posed the reasons would be fewer and morality would be primary. In any event, this particular response makes more important and compelling the analysis of the moral assessment of cannabis use which is to follow.

Further emphasizing morality, the "national character" and the "country's morals," half of all Americans view cannabis use as immoral and "not to be tolerated":

> The public also believes that the use of illicit drugs is a moral issue and thinks of it as a phenomenon that negatively affects the character and values of the country. Nearly three quarters (72 percent) see drug use as changing the national character, and 50 percent believe that it represents a fundamental breakdown in the country's morals. Even in the case of marijuana, which is thought to be less harmful by the public than other illicit drugs, 64 percent of adults describe its use as being morally wrong, and 51 percent think that it is morally wrong and should not be tolerated. (Blendon and Young 1998, 829)

Also revealed is that the Social Reality of cannabis use continues to support the gateway drug argument, one soundly and decisively rejected by the Scientific Reality of cannabis use (perhaps showing the power of media over the beliefs citizens will accept and defend). "Though seen as less risk, today, 63 percent of parents of teenagers and 76 percent of teenagers themselves say that marijuana leads to the use of other, more serious types of drugs" (Blendon and Young 1998, 829).

3. Why Do Americans Think Individuals Use Illegal Drugs?

> In a 1997 survey respondents were given a list of 10 possible reasons why some Americans might use illegal drugs. Only 3 factors were seen by a majority of Americans as a major reason for drug use. These included peer pressure, drug dealers trying to expand their markets, and poor parenting. Other surveys also show that poor parenting is seen as a significant factor by the public. Two thirds (66 percent) identify the disintegration of the family as a major cause, and 58 percent say that parents should share all or most of the blame for the increase in teenage drug use that occurred between 1992 and 1995. (Blendon and Young 1998, 829)

Note that the public does share the Scientific Reality belief that parents are largely responsible for teenage drug use. Peer pressure is also consistent with the findings of the risk to adolescents section of chapter 3, where peer influence along with parental inattention led to increased likelihood of cannabis use. Finally, although the Social Reality here cites "drug dealers trying to expand their markets" as significant (again, assuming also cannabis) there seems a lack of logical reasoning in also rejecting the legalization of cannabis. This is because legalization of cannabis would make cannabis less profitable to "drug dealers" and hence less likely to be peddled as widely and thoroughly as it is currently.

4. What Are the Public's Views on Various Policy Proposals to Respond to the Nations' Drug Problem?

> When looking at the future of American drug policy we see a paradox: most Americans (58 percent) do not see the nation's illegal drug problem getting better after years of increases in national spending, and they see the War on Drugs as having failed thus far (78 percent). Yet, despite this assessment, they continue to support greater resources being expended in generally the same policy direction as has been followed in the past. (Blendon and Young 1998, 830)

The public continues to support the Social Reality against drug use, and therefore are generally supportive of platforms and legislation promising on the face of them to decrease the prevalence of drug use (although in practice these initiatives are ineffective and work merely in a political way):

> Because Americans are very concerned about illegal drug use, they tend to indicate support for most of the approaches posed to them as options for reducing the use and effects of illegal drugs . . . among the approximately 19 policy choices they have been offered, there are 5 that are rejected by Americans: giving aid to farmers in foreign countries not to grow drug crops; giving aid to foreign governments to fight drug traffickers; legalizing marijuana for personal use; the death penalty for drug sales; and legalizing all illicit drugs. (Blendon and Young 1998, 830)

And now getting to the cannabis issue:

> The second issue, the legalized use of marijuana for medical purposes, has been discussed for over a decade. In early 1997, separate surveys reported that 62 percent and 60 percent of the American public supported a policy where physicians should be able to prescribe marijuana to their seriously and terminally ill patients. Moreover, 68 percent said that physicians should be able to prescribe marijuana for medical uses in states where it is allowed by law, and that the federal government should not prosecute medial doctors who do so. While opposing the use or legalization of marijuana for recreational purposes, the public apparently does not want to deny very ill patients access to a potentially helpful drug therapy if prescribed by their physicians. The public's support of marijuana for medical purposes is conditioned by their belief that marijuana would be used only in the treatment of serious medical conditions. (Blendon and Young 1998, 831)

There is the strong sense conveyed here that the Social Reality could in the right political climate compromise and allow cannabis for medicinal uses. The condition on granting this right to patients is that there would be no policy move to legalization of cannabis for recreational purposes (which will literally not be "tolerated"). That this condition exists can be understood through chapter 4 historical events of the twentieth century in the United States. There is also a sense in which the Social Reality assumes an inherent business philosophy, whereby when one has invested and committed enough into a belief there is no question of change and cutting losses. The public and U.S. federal government have committed too much to this war to budge on cannabis.

The "conditional" acceptance of medical marijuana by the Social Reality casts patients and advocates of medicinal marijuana as part of a "Trojan Horse" attack on the current law prohibiting cannabis use for recreational purposes. This often-used metaphor in reference to the legalization of cannabis is of war and sports, of defense, offense, of a game. As a philosopher, strikingly absent is a dispassionate search for the truth in order to create policy on cannabis.

Pew Research Center Social Trends Report, "A Barometer of Modern Morals: Sex, Drugs and the 1040"

Before concluding this chapter and this articulation of the Social Reality on cannabis use in the United States (completing Part II), consider a recent Pew Research Center Social Trends Report, "A Barometer of Modern Morals: Sex, Drugs and the 1040" (Pew Research Center, A Social Trends Report, March 28, 2006). The survey, "based on telephone interviews conducted with a nationally representative sample of adults, ages 18 years of age and older, living in continental U.S. telephone households," with 745 interviews conducted, was to rate various behaviors as "morally wrong," "morally acceptable, "not a moral issue," "depends," or "don't know." Results have as "morally wrong" the following percentages:

Married people having an affair: 88 percent
Not reporting all income on your taxes: 79 percent
Drinking alcohol excessively: 61 percent
Having an abortion: 52 percent
Smoking marijuana: 50 percent
Homosexual behavior: 50 percent
Telling a lie to spare someone's feelings: 43 percent
Sex between unmarried adults: 35 percent
Gambling: 35 percent
Overeating: 32 percent

Analyzing the responses to the moral status of cannabis use, of all adults 50 percent think it morally wrong, 10 percent think it morally acceptable, 35 percent that it is not a moral issue, 4 percent answer "depends," and 1 percent answered don't know. These most general numbers reflect a solid 50 percent who think using cannabis is morally wrong, consistent with the 52 percent in the study of Blendon and Young who find cannabis use "immoral and not to be tolerated." Also striking here is that 35 percent think it is not even a moral issue.[1] Of those who think cannabis use is morally wrong, the strongest correlations are with the following defining characteristics: age 65 or older (74 percent), white evangelical protestant (68 percent), church attendance weekly or more (66 percent), conservative ideology (65 percent), Republican Party identification (65 percent). Also striking is that of those whose family income is 75,000 or more marijuana use is "morally wrong" for 36 percent and not a moral issue for 54 percent, whereas for those whose family income is less than 30,000 cannabis use is "morally wrong" for 60 percent and is "not a moral issue" for 25 percent. Stereotypes which associate cannabis use with the lower economic classes would lead one to think that such use would be more tolerated by this class. However, the opposite is true, where, relatively speaking, the highest economic class reports the most tolerance.

As to the question of cannabis use relative to age, consider that for the age 18–49 group, 44 percent answer "morally wrong," and 41 percent that it is not a moral issue. For the 65+ age group, 74 percent answer "morally wrong," and only 16 percent not a moral issue. This is a huge 30 percent difference in judging morally the use of cannabis. Relative to education, 37 percent of college graduates answer morally wrong, 52 percent that it is not a moral issue. Significantly different, among those with high school or less, 63 percent answer "morally wrong" and only 20 percent that it is not a moral issue. Relative to ideology, cannabis use is "morally wrong" for 65 percent of conservatives, 48 percent of moderates, and 29 percent of liberals.

Note

1. This number will become quite relevant in several places within the Part III Moral Assessment, where distinctions between moral and non-moral cannabis use and between behaviors justly and unjustly punished action by human beings and citizens are more thoroughly considered.

III

A MORAL ASSESSMENT OF CANNABIS USE AND LAW

6
"Utilitarianism," "On Liberty," and Cannabis Use

In Part III addressed are three specific questions:

i. Is cannabis use ever morally justified? If so, how so?
ii. Is the law prohibiting the use of cannabis morally justified?
iii. Is the law criminalizing users of cannabis morally justified?

In answering these questions I enter into the primary text of several major theorists of moral philosophy. I begin with J. S. Mill and consider his "Utilitarianism" and "On Liberty," then Immanuel Kant and his moral philosophy (*Foundations of the Metaphysics of Morals, The Critique of Practical Reason,* and *The Metaphysics of Morals*), and third Aristotle and his *Nicomachean Ethics.* I then consider and apply the Old Testament and then the New Testament. I also develop a fuller Christian response to the three questions. At the conclusion of Part III, I present conclusions well supported by this variety of moral perspectives.

Mill's "Utilitarianism" as Applied to Cannabis Use and Law

The five chapters of Mill's "Utilitarianism":

chapter 1: General Remarks
chapter 2: What Utilitarianism Is
chapter 3: Sanctions of the Principle of Utility

chapter 4: Of What Sort of Proof the Principle of Utility Is Susceptible
chapter 5: On the Connection between Justice and Utility

Against Hedonism

After his "General Remarks," Mill moves into chapter 2 by providing for the utilitarian the foundation, the "greatest happiness principle":

> The creed which accepts as the foundation of morals "utility," or the "greatest happiness principle" holds that actions are right in proportion as they tend to promote happiness, wrong as they tend to produce the reverse of happiness. By happiness is intended pleasure, and the absence of pain; by unhappiness, pain, and the privation of pleasure. (Mill 1967b, 395)

The most basic statement of utilitarianism as a moral theory, the "greatest happiness principle," has us judge each action (and, as we will see, each law/policy) as moral ("right") or immoral (generally speaking, "wrong") depending upon the amount of overall happiness produced by the action. Moral actions are ones which promote a great amount of happiness, immoral actions are ones which produce a great amount of unhappiness. Actions which promote neither happiness nor unhappiness are morally neutral. It is necessary to keep in mind this basic greatest happiness principle as we move to cannabis use. For now, let us keep pace with Mill in his "Utilitarianism," moving with him to consider his justification for this foundational principle:

> Pleasure and freedom from pain are the only things desirable as ends; and that all desirable things (which are as numerous in the utilitarian as in any other scheme) are desirable either for the pleasure inherent in themselves, or as means to the promotion of pleasure and the prevention of pain. (Mill 1967b, 395)

The only desirable end is the furtherance of pleasure and freedom from pain. Although this may seem to imply hedonism, Mill will explain why he does *not* have in mind a hedonistic theory. He carefully makes clear the distinction between human beings and non-human animals, of faculties distinguishing human beings in kind (not merely in degree) from non-human animals. These more "elevated" faculties are beyond mere animal appetites and will lead him to consider this a qualitative difference. This move takes his moral philosophy beyond hedonism to a theory better understood as valuing the use and development of the "higher faculties":

> The comparison of the Epicurean life to that of beasts is felt as degrading, precisely because a beast's pleasures do not satisfy a human being's conceptions of happiness. Human beings have faculties more elevated than the animal appetites and, when once made conscious of them, do not regard anything as happiness which does not include their gratification. (Mill 1967b, 396)

Mill is indicating here that the life of hedonism is degrading, not satisfying human conceptions of happiness. A line is to be drawn between hedonistic pleasure and human happiness. Further acknowledging that some activities are qualitatively superior to others, thereby salvaging utilitarianism from being considered a hedonistic theory:

> It is quite compatible with the principle of utility to recognize the fact that some kinds of pleasure are more desirable and more valuable than others. It would be absurd that, while, in estimating all other things, quality is considered as well as quantity, the estimation of pleasures should be supposed to depend on quantity alone. (Mill 1967b, 396)

In light of cannabis use, this indicates it is important to understand whether an individual user is motivated by pleasure or by happiness, as these two are qualitatively different. The difference is in the faculties being used with each motivation. For example, there is a qualitative difference in the kind of pleasure experienced by a hedonistic user of cannabis who uses to extreme and excess, regularly dozing off, and the happiness of a cannabis user enjoying art and creating imaginative pieces of his own. Cannabis use to be assessed morally must be understood in light of a larger way of life for the individual involved. Adolescent cannabis users "going along with the crowd" and giving in to peer pressure is different than an adult cancer chemotherapy or AIDS Wasting Syndrome user is different than an artist (writer, guitar player, painter, actor, etc.) who considers cannabis use as enhancing their work. The quantity being used and the quality of the actions performed intoxicated are crucial factors in distinguishing between pleasure and happiness as a motivation for any cannabis user.

Mill provides a basic truth to those who trust experience as an irreplaceable teacher and source of knowledge about, among other things, cannabis use, intoxication, effects, and so on. Given that cannabis is the most used illicit drug in the United States and that there are an equal if not much larger number of alcohol users in the United States, a most interesting comparison would involve cannabis and alcohol, specifically as to why one drug is preferred over the other: "Of two pleasures, if there be one to which all or almost all who have experience of both give a decided preference, irrespective of a feeling of moral obligation to prefer it, that is the more desirable pleasure" (Mill 1967b, 396).

Of course, the trick here is to separate from a consideration of the merits of cannabis compared and contrasted to those of alcohol one's "feeling of moral obligation" to prefer the *legal* alcohol over the *illegal* cannabis.

Consider further text from Mill regarding competent judges of pleasures: "What means are there of determining which is the acutest of two pains, or the intensest of two pleasurable sensations, except the general suffrage of those who are familiar with both?" (Mill 1967b, 398). Relevant to the Social Reality of cannabis use, four-fifths of the public has no personal or family experience with drug use and abuse (including with cannabis; see chapter 5). These people are unable to measure the pleasure of cannabis intoxication against the pleasure of alcohol intoxication. The judgment of one who has only experienced either alcohol or cannabis but not both will on this view fail to be competent.

For Using Higher Faculties

Further pointing out the human capacity to enjoy higher pleasures, and continuing to distance himself from hedonism, Mill argues our unwillingness to trade our higher faculties for a life of lower faculties is revealed in our

> sense of dignity, which all human beings possess in one form or other, and in some, though by no means in exact, proportion to their higher faculties, and which is so essential a part of the happiness of those in whom it is strong that nothing which conflicts with it could be otherwise than momentarily an object of desire to them. (Mill 1967b, 397)

Here Mill invites the conclusion that a cannabis/alcohol user who is living a hedonistic existence would offend his own sense of dignity. Perhaps revealed in one apparently without a strong sense of dignity is the corresponding lack of awareness and development of the higher faculties. The culmination of Mill's distinguishing the pleasures uniquely human to those shared with nonhuman animals is found in his oft-cited lines:

> It is better to be a human being dissatisfied than a pig satisfied; better to be Socrates dissatisfied than a fool satisfied. And if the fool, or the pig, is of a different opinion, it is because they only know their own side of the question. The other party to the comparison knows both sides. (Mill 1967b, 397)

Mill moves on to emphasize the necessity of parents and society in general to engage a child and adolescent's higher faculties:

> Capacity for the nobler feelings is in most natures a very tender plant, easily killed, not only by hostile influences, but by mere want of sustenance; and in the majority of young persons it speedily dies away if the occupations to which their position in life has devoted them, and the society into which it has thrown them, are not favorable to keeping that higher capacity in exercise. (Mill 1967b, 398)

Consider the import of this sustenance in light of the chapter 3 consideration of adolescents as a significant "at risk" group because of the impact of negative parenting styles. The "tender plants" are those adolescents who come from places where opportunities for early experimentation and risk taking are ample. If Mill is right, the nobler feelings will "speedily die away" in a large number of youth whose higher faculties are not discovered, exercised, and consciously developed.

> Men lose their high aspirations as they lose their intellectual tastes, because they have not time or opportunity for indulging them; and they addict themselves to inferior pleasures, not because they deliberately prefer them, but because they are either the only ones to which they have access, or the only ones which they are any longer capable of enjoying. (Mill 1967b, 398)

Instead of an instantaneous loss of the use of higher faculties or intellectual tastes, what is described here by Mill is a losing of time and opportunity to use higher faculties as a development. Because of this lack of time and opportunity, persons "addict themselves to inferior pleasures." And they do this not out of deliberate choice, but rather because "they are the only ones to which they have access or only ones they are able to enjoy." Mill's words are applicable to today's youth who are not provided experience with the higher faculties and turn to inferior pleasures. These words also apply to young adults who are chronic cannabis users, living hedonistically; in this state of alienation and lethargy cannabis becomes the only pleasure they are able to enjoy (and perhaps not even cannabis if they become highly tolerant to its effects; again, Weil and Rosen's characterization of dependence at its worst). Such a scenario is implicitly tragic.

Mill more explicitly indicates how the distinction in kind between pleasures of the higher faculties and those of mere pleasure, giving more weight to happiness involving the higher faculties and less weight to pleasures of the animal nature:

> When, therefore, those feelings and judgment declare the pleasures derived from the higher faculties to be preferable *in kind*, apart from the question of intensity, to those of which the animal nature, disjoined from the higher faculties, is susceptible, they are entitled on this subject to the same regard. (Mill 1967b, 398)

Mill attempts to further articulate the kind of happiness he has in mind when actually applying the utilitarian theory to the way of life of which it is experienced:

> If by happiness be meant a continuity of highly pleasurable excitement, it is evident enough that this is impossible. . . . Of this the philosophers who have taught that happiness is the end of life were as fully aware as those who taught them. The happiness which they meant was not a life of rapture; but moments of such, in an existence made up of a few and transitory pains, many and various pleasures, with a decided predominance of the active over the passive, and having as the foundation of the whole not to expect more from life than it is capable of bestowing. (Mill 1967b, 399)

Mill would perhaps point out that those who are cannabis dependent and continually "high" are perhaps trying to be happy all the time in a way "expecting more from life than it is capable of bestowing." However, Mill here seems more applicable to the type of drug user who seeks an immediate, intense and pleasurable high and continually uses to remain in this state. Remember, however, from the chapter 3 DSM-IV-TR consideration of cannabis abuse and dependence that cannabis has no significant withdrawal symptoms and is at its worst a psychological dependence. In individual use, a drug with effects typically lasting three to four hours. The life of exercising the intellectual faculties, perhaps reading a book, takes a significant amount of time, patience, and commitment in order to reach the experience of pleasure of, for example, finishing a book (and subsequent pleasures involved in discussing the book with others who have also read the book). Cannabis use could enhance rather than detract from this active life of the higher faculties described by Mill.

Mill reflects on the question of why many people are unhappy, a unique moral line of thought having Mill explain that: "When people who are tolerably fortunate in their outward lot do not find in life sufficient enjoyment to make it valuable to them, the cause generally is caring for nobody but themselves" (Mill 1967b, 400). In other words, selfishness is here considered an essential cause of unhappiness. Consider this particular reason will make utilitarianism a much more acceptable theory, one advocating actions which benefit others as well as oneself in order to produce one's own happiness.

Mill continues to explain unhappiness by again revisiting the exercise of the intellectual faculties (here as the "cultivation of mind"):

> Next to selfishness, the principal cause which makes life unsatisfactory is want of mental cultivation. A cultivated mind—I do not mean that of a philosopher,

> but any mind to which the foundations of knowledge have been opened, and which has been taught, in any tolerable degree, to exercise its faculties—finds sources of inexhaustible interest in all that surrounds it: in the objects of nature, the achievements of art, the imaginations of poetry, the incidents of history, the ways of mankind, past and present, and their prospects in the future. (Mill 1967b, 400)

Here Mill provides further moral reason to deter adolescent cannabis use. To the extent that cannabis use is interfering with adolescents' discovery and exercise of higher faculties it is of extreme concern. Perhaps by the time of adolescence, for those whose lives already involve unaddressed conduct disorders and other risk factors, a move to cannabis, alcohol, sex, and other risky behavior indicates unhappiness *for want of mental cultivation.* Directing adolescents away from cannabis and other drug use involves getting them in touch with and actively engaging their higher faculties. This could involve explaining the lack of any clear end of or to the life revolving around the satisfaction of lower pleasures.

Consider furthermore here, in light of the earlier discussions of adolescent risk factors and parenting styles associated with drug abuse, a point both Mill and Kant emphasize: the importance of parental responsibility of taking care of a child upon bringing her into existence. As applied to the twenty-first-century United States, this would be directed against those who have "unwanted" children, who are having sex and risking pregnancy without having given any thought to what they would do were they to be a parent. Here, unlike with the use of cannabis, the law has seemingly respected the right of individuals to have sex, a culture a far way from those of the past with laws against adultery. Although the results of these irresponsible and careless actions result in significant disadvantages to the children who are brought into the world, Social Reality has not saw fit to wield the law against such "risky" behavior. A major point of this line of thought is cannabis law is not primarily about protecting children. Were protecting children the motivation behind law, parents who brought unwanted children into the world would be severely punished (or at least stigmatized in a negative way in society):

> It still remains unrecognized, that to bring a child into existence without a fair prospect of being able, not only to provide food for its body, but instruction and training for its mind, is a moral crime, both against the unfortunate offspring and against society; and that if the parent does not fulfill this obligation, the State ought to see it fulfilled, at the charge, as far as possible, of the parent. (Mill 1967a, 302)

This most basic responsibility, to provide not only food, clothes, shelter, but also training for a child's mind is owed to both the child and society. Mill demands strict penalties for the failure to fulfill this obligation. This is that of using the higher faculties, with a parent deliberately, intentionally bringing their children to an awareness of this power.

For Impartiality in Regards to My Happiness and That of Another

Mill emphasizes the necessity of the utilitarian remaining impartial. He cites as an example of impartiality the golden rule of Jesus, a model of strict impartiality in the sense of impartiality Mill has in mind:

> As between his own happiness and that of others, utilitarianism requires him to be as strictly impartial as a disinterested and benevolent spectator. In the golden rule of Jesus of Nazareth, we read the complete spirit of the ethics of utility. "To do as you would be done by," and "to love your neighbor as yourself," constitute the ideal perfection of utilitarian morality. (Mill 1967b, 402)

This ideal perfection can be realized in a society through its laws and social arrangements (relevant to cannabis prohibition and criminalization):

> As the means of making the nearest approach to this ideal, utility would enjoin, first, that laws and social arrangements should place the happiness, or (as speaking practically, it may be called) the interest of every individual as nearly as possible in harmony with the interest of the whole; and secondly, that education and opinion, which have so vast a power over human character, should so use that power as to establish in the mind of every individual an indissoluble association between his own happiness and the good of the whole. (Mill 1967b, 402)

Here Mill champions the ideal of impartiality in laws, social arrangements, education, and opinion and the facilitation of "a direct impulse to promote the general good as a habitual motive of action." As applied to the U.S. cannabis law, time and again those of the Scientific Reality have decried that the law criminalizing cannabis users causes more disharmony than does cannabis use itself. It is not clear the law is directly doing more than criminalizing 750,000 citizens a year (including medicinal users and those using in developing higher faculties). Furthermore, the law itself, not cannabis, is the more credibly demonstrated gateway to harder drugs (via criminal world, profit-motivated drug culture). With cannabis illegal, a vibrant black market creates countless situations where cannabis users are put at risk of harm they would not face were cannabis legalized.[1]

One obvious and often cited criticism of the utilitarian theory, as a tool to use to assess the morality or immorality of any particular action or decision is that the ultimate weight given to various interests involved often varies depending upon who is doing the weighing (and what personal interest they have in the outcome). The result is that the same action can be viewed as moral by some and immoral by others applying the same utilitarian theory. In an initial response to this criticism, one which can conclude ultimate relativity of the weights given to various actions, Mill clarifies this is not a criticism of the specific moral theory of utilitarianism but one of morality itself: "But difference of opinion on moral questions was not first introduced into the world by utilitarianism, while that doctrine does supply, if not always an easy, at all events a tangible and intelligible, mode of deciding such differences" (Mill 1967b, 405).

Mill clearly recognizes those who will simply write off without taking "a little trouble to understand" the interests of those who advocate cannabis legalization, those who hold an extreme and purposively uninformed position against cannabis use and legalization:

> Persons, even of considerable mental endowment, often give themselves so little trouble to understand the bearings of any opinion against which they entertain a prejudice, and men are in general so little conscious of this voluntary ignorance as a defect, that the vulgarest misunderstandings of ethical doctrines are continually met with in the deliberate writings of persons of the greatest pretensions both to high principle and to philosophy. (Mill 1967b, 405)

Pretensions to "high principle" (e.g., sending right messages to youth about cannabis) are ill-thought out, unreflective, dogmatic assertions against cannabis use, ignoring the strong minority of regular users and medicinal users, who represent the "opinion against which they entertain a prejudice." As prejudice the Social Reality on cannabis use may allude to morality (e.g., "protecting our children") and "high principle." But being ill-informed, it ultimately fails to be convincing to the growing number of the informed accepting the Scientific Reality on cannabis use.

Social Reality and cannabis laws prohibiting use reject the scientific truth about cannabis use. This rejection of scientific truth has very significant implications for any utilitarian. Mill surmises the stifling of truth (here "veracity") results in the stifling of civilization itself:

> But inasmuch as the cultivation in ourselves of a sensitive feeling on the subject of veracity is one of the most useful, and the enfeeblement of that feeling one of the most hurtful, things to which our conduct can be instrumental; and inasmuch as any, even unintentional, deviation from truth does that much towards weakening the trustworthiness of human assertion, which is not only the principal

> support of all present social well-being but the insufficiency of which does more than any one thing that can be named to keep back civilization, virtue, everything on which human happiness on the largest scale depends—we feel that the violation, for a present advantage, of a rule of such transcendent expediency is not expedient, and that he who, for the sake of a convenience to himself or to some other individual, does what depends on him to deprive mankind of the good, and inflict upon them the evil, involved in the greater or less reliance which they can place in each other's word, acts the part of one of their worst enemies. (Mill 1967b, 406)

The Social Reality of cannabis use as falsehoods propagated to justify continued prohibition of the use of cannabis makes Mill's claim applicable: the law prohibiting cannabis, and the continuing use of falsehoods to justify its existence, is "keeping back civilization, virtue, and the general happiness of society" and created for the "sake of convenience" for those who would rather not bother with revising unjust laws causing harms to certain minority groups.

Note Mill also provides a bridge between the utilitarian theory and deontological theories (i.e., one of general rules) such as that of Kant. General rules (e.g., do not lie) are valuable generalizations to use in day-to-day life as it is rarely the case one can justify a lie as producing more happiness than unhappiness. As a result, practically speaking, we can treat the general rule of not lying as a duty of sorts (although, of course, the "duties" of Mill, unlike those of Kant, are based upon the sole reason they generally produce overall happiness). In short, for a utilitarian's, duty (and "rules") plays a practical part of living as a utilitarian. "But to consider the rules of morality as improvable is one thing; to pass over the intermediate generalization entirely and endeavor to test each individual action directly by the first principle is another" (Mill 1967b, 407).

Further anticipating another primary criticism of a utilitarian theory of morality, similar to the above criticism of the relativity of the weights given to various effects of an action, Mill addresses the case of one who with evil intentions could justify acting on his evil intentions by manipulating the utilitarian theory. The only challenge to such an evil actor would be to weigh the happiness and unhappiness in a way so as to argue more unhappiness than happiness would result from doing evil. Mill counters:

> But is utility the only creed which is able to furnish us with excuses for evil doing, and means of cheating our own conscience? They are afforded in abundance by all doctrines which recognize as a fact in morals the existence of conflicting considerations, which all doctrines do that have been believed by sane persons. (Mill 1967b, 408)

So Mill here explains those with evil intentions can offer grossly inaccurate, biased weights to various interests effected by an action using the utilitarian theory, but can similarly misuse other theories of morality to similarly falsely justify their evil actions.

For Giving Weight to Conscience and Duty

Having distinguished utilitarianism from hedonism (distinguishing "higher faculties" from "animal desires"), cleared away two major criticisms of utilitarianism, and demonstrated Mill's awareness of and counters to these criticisms, he now moves into chapter 3 of his "Utilitarianism," "Of the Ultimate Sanction of the Principle of Utility." Further surprising to those who perhaps expect a purely mathematical calculation process in Mill's presentation of utilitarianism, consider his explicit awareness of "conscience" and an internal feeling of "duty":

> The internal sanction of duty, whatever our standard of duty may be, is one and the same—a feeling in our own mind; a pain, more or less intense, attendant on violation of duty, which in properly cultivated moral natures rises, in the more serious cases, into shrinking from it as an impossibility. This feeling, when disinterested and connecting itself with the pure idea of duty, and not with some particular form of it, or with any of the merely accessory circumstances, is the essence of conscience. (Mill 1967b, 409–10)

Careful to not commit himself to the existence of a non-material soul or spirit and consistent with the greatest happiness principle he describes conscience as a "feeling" and a "pain" connecting itself with the pure idea of duty. Reasonable to infer is that when we violate a duty we harm other people, and Mill would have us focus on the strong correlation between the violation of duties and the unhappiness generally produced by such actions to explain the essentially strong feeling of conscience. This peculiar sort of pain felt upon a disinterested analysis of an action, perhaps a desire to use cannabis in a situation where it would cause upset to significant others, would be described as one where conscience, a strong feeling against so acting, is experienced by one so reflecting, indicating one should not use in that situation.

Cannabis law criminalizes hundreds of thousands of citizens per year in the United States and is grounded in the racist 1937 Marihuana Tax Act. In this light the legalization of cannabis is a "political improvement":

> Every step in political improvement renders it more so, by removing the sources of opposition of interest and levelling those inequalities of legal privilege between

> individuals or classes, owing to which there are large portions of mankind whose happiness it is still practicable to disregard. (Mill 1967b, 413)

The double standard enforced by the U.S. federal government, allowing recreational use of alcohol but not of cannabis, seems a good example of "inequality of legal privilege between individuals or classes." Cannabis users also have a "happiness" which, with the Social Reality not budging on the prohibition of cannabis use, finds it "still practicable to disregard" (perhaps mostly so for politicians in general, finding it much more expedient to cite by rote the Social Reality beliefs to quash rational consideration of cannabis).

Further attempting to establish utilitarianism as a metaphysically viable theory, one getting to the ultimate reality of morality and a firm theoretical foundation, Mill cites a conviction as the "ultimate sanction" of the utilitarian theory, one which would serve as a (pseudo)metaphysical ground for accepting the Truth of the greatest happiness principle:

> The deeply rooted conception which every individual even now has of himself as a social being tends to make him feel it one of his natural wants that there should be harmony between his feelings and aims and those of his fellow creatures. . . . This conviction is the ultimate sanction of the greatest happiness morality. (Mill 1967b, 413)

This point also helps clarify the unhappiness suffered by cannabis users, otherwise law-abiding citizens, who but for their personal preference for cannabis are in harmony with their neighbors, and who deeply desire this harmony, to be merely treated as equal to recreational alcohol users.

In chapter 4 of "Utilitarianism," "Of What Sort of Proof the Principle of Utility Is Susceptible," the title itself suggests Mill's continuation of his argument for a justification, a foundation, or a proof to support utilitarianism as a viable theory. Once again Mill stresses what he assumes most everyone will agree with: "The utilitarian doctrine is that happiness is desirable, and the only thing desirable, as an end; all other things being only desirable as means to that end" (Mill 1967b, 414). Mill offers as a proof of the fact that general happiness is desirable the fact that individual happiness is desirable: "No reason can be given why the general happiness is desirable, except that each person, so far as he believes it to be attainable, desires his own happiness" (Mill 1967b, 414). Note Mill has moved here from an observation about individuals to a conclusion about the state, general population. This way of illustration was also used by Plato in his *Republic*, comparing the well-ordered soul of an individual to a well-ordered state of society. Such an argument is technically an analogy comparing two different types of things (individuals and societies) and therefore susceptible to rejection as fallacious if the two things being compared have significant differences. Obviously, individuals can be observed and are much different in significant ways than much more nebulous societies. Furthermore, and a more devastating criticism of Mill's utilitarianism as *the* moral theory, is what is called the "is/ought" problem: although something is in fact the case (e.g., happiness is desired by individuals) does not necessarily imply that this ought to be the case (e.g., happiness should be desired by individuals). This puts in question Mill's major justification of utilitarianism.

For Acting Virtuously

Mill recognizes virtue ethics as a viable opponent-theory of morality to his utilitarian theory. He counters the assumption by the virtue ethicist that acting for the sake of virtue is what makes one moral. Mill reiterates it is happiness that results from acting in a virtuous way that makes development of virtue recognized as moral by the virtue ethicist, and therefore happiness is the ultimate justification for virtue ethics.

> The principle of utility does not mean that any given pleasure, as music, for instance, or any given exception from pain, as for example health, are to be looked upon as means to a collective happiness, and to be directed on that account. They are desired and desirable in and for themselves; besides being means, they are a part of the end. Virtue, according to the utilitarian doctrine, is not naturally and originally part of the end, but it is capable of becoming so; and in those who love it disinterestedly it has become so, and is desired and cherished, not as a means to happiness, but as a part of their happiness. (Mill 1967b, 415)

Perhaps this is what happens through the habitual training through which one becomes moral as described by Aristotle (as will be considered in chapter 8). One comes to regard one's virtuous disposition and routine moral way of acting as fulfilling and necessary to the fulfillment achieved in life. This fulfillment is an essential part of happiness.

Further attempting to articulate the consistency between the greatest happiness principle and the development of virtuous traits of character, Mill considers virtue as "included in happiness," and virtues as "elements" of happiness.

> The desire of it is not a different thing from the desire of happiness any more than the love of music or the desire of health. They are included in happiness. They are some of the elements of which the desire of happiness is made up. Happiness is not an abstract idea, but a concrete whole; and these are some of its parts. (Mill 1967b, 416)

Mill further argues for the consistency between utilitarian morality and virtue ethics, especially in their shared moral rejection of those whose characters reflect "love of money, power, and fame":

> Virtue, according to the utilitarian conception, is a good of this description. There was no original desire of it, or motive to it, save its conduciveness to pleasure, and especially to protection from pain. But through the association thus formed it may be felt a good in itself, and desired as such with as great intensity as any other good; and with this difference between it and the love of money, of power, and of fame, that all of these may, and often do, render the individual noxious to the other members of the society to which he belongs, whereas there is nothing which makes him so much a blessing to them as the cultivation of the disinterested love of virtue. And consequently, the utilitarian standard . . . enjoins and requires the cultivation of the love of virtue up to the greatest strength possible, as being above all things important to the general happiness. (Mill 1967b, 416)

Note also Mill's claim here, the cultivation of the love of virtue is "above all things important to the general happiness." Love of virtue, disinterested love of virtue, makes a man a blessing to other members of society. However, morally speaking, beyond virtue ethics there is more deeply the maximization of happiness as the ultimate justification of the love of virtue. Utilitarianism is not synonymous with virtue ethics, as the latter is focused on individual development of excellences, moral and intellectual, as primary, while a utilitarian will in cases where the action which would promote the greatest amount of happiness were also inconsistent with how a virtuous actor would act would have a person maximize happiness of the whole although it took a non-virtuous action to bring about such happiness (although, to be fair to Mill, such actions may be rare).

Harkening back to the title of this book four of "Utilitarianism," and its question, Mill explains:

> We have now, then, an answer to the question, what sort of proof the principle of utility is susceptible. If the opinion which I have now stated is psychologically true—if human nature is so constituted as to desire nothing which is not either a part of happiness or a means of happiness, we can have no other proof, and we require no other, that these are the only things desirable. (Mill 1967b, 417)

Notice how Mill has, by earlier defining virtuous traits of character as "parts of happiness," subsumed virtue ethics within the larger utilitarian theory, making virtue ethics a part of utilitarian theory of morality.

Will, Desire, and the Development of Cannabis Dependence

Next Mill introduces the concept of the "will" and distinguishes it from desire[2]:

> Will, the active phenomenon, is a different thing from desire, the state of passive sensibility, and, though originally an offshoot from it, may in time take root and detach itself from the parent stock; so much so that in the case of an habitual purpose, instead of willing the thing because we desire it, we often desire it only because we will it. (Mill 1967b, 417)

Here Mill suggests a way of understanding cannabis dependence. Existing first is desire, a passive sensibility. Will is born out of desire, as "active phenomenon." In Mill's way of explaining it, the will can plant itself, metaphorically, apart from desire, so as to grow until a user willfully acts apart from or without desire. This would be using cannabis so much that one was no longer sensitive to its effects (e.g.). *Mill in so describing this state of a will separate from desire characterizes cannabis dependence.* This characterization of the state of will that has developed separately from desire is exemplified by a habitual user of cannabis who uses from morning to night, obsessively and primarily if not completely using cannabis out of habit. Mill further explains this conception of a will separate from desire: "will, like all other parts of our constitution, is amenable to habit, and that we may will from habit what we no longer desire for itself, or desire only because we will it" (Mill 1967b, 418).

Mill provides a way of "awakening" cannabis dependent-users to virtues. This way is consistent both with his incorporation of virtue ethics within the larger utilitarian theory and with the greatest happiness principle:

> How can the will be virtuous, where it does not exist in sufficient force, be implanted or awakened? Only by making the person *desire* virtue—by making them think of it in a pleasurable light, or of its absence as a painful one. It is by associating the doing right with pleasure, or the doing wrong with pain, or by eliciting and impressing and bringing home to the person's experience the pleasure naturally involved in the one or the pain in the other, that it is possible to call forth that will to be virtuous which, when confirmed, acts without any thought of either pleasure or pain. Will is the child of desire, and passes out of the dominion of its parent only to come under that of habit. (Mill 1967b, 418)

Here Mill describes the will as the "child of desire" who grows into adulthood to come under habit. Change from cannabis dependence to temperate user would have one associate temperance with pleasure, and self-indulgence with pain. By so associating, and specifically through "bringing home" these associations to the specific individual (and experiences) who is cannabis dependent, the cannabis dependent can desire to be virtuous and develop another sort of habit, likely to make him more happy himself and also making society more happy.

Mill makes explicit the point that the virtuous disposition is not intrinsically good, not good in itself, but good only insofar as it is a means of "attaining pleasure or averting pain."[3] As he explains: "this state of the will is a means to good, not intrinsically a good; and does not contradict the doctrine that nothing is a good to human beings but in so far as it is either itself pleasurable, or a means of attaining pleasure or averting pain" (Mill 1967b, 418).

The Right to Use Cannabis and Repugnance at Having This Right Legally Denied (the Basic Injustice of Cannabis Law)

At this point, before moving into chapter 5, the final chapter of "Utilitarianism," Mill has provided information relevant to the question of the morality of cannabis use but not much on the law prohibiting cannabis use. Utilitarianism is to be distinguished from hedonism, acting according to the higher faculties and not lower sensibilities as consistent with virtue ethics and careful to distinguish the will from desire. In the fifth and final chapter, the title alone—"On the Connection between Justice and Utility—indicates a possible move to a consideration of the legal prohibition of cannabis use:

> Our present object is to determine whether the reality to which the feeling of justice corresponds is one which needs any such special revelation, whether the justice or injustice of an action is a thing intrinsically peculiar and distinct from all its other qualities or only a combination of certain of those qualities presented under a peculiar aspect. (Mill 1967b, 419)

Suffice it to say for now that Mill intends to consider first the question of whether justice, specifically the "feeling" of justice (similar to the "feeling" of conscience), has to do with a sort of "revelation" or perhaps an intrinsic notion or innate idea with which we are born. And he will furthermore attempt to articulate justice by pursuing out various essential (necessary but not sufficient) "qualities" of this notion.

Extremely relevant to the issue of cannabis legalization and of a dominating rationale of those opposed to cannabis use, Mill considers the view of those who follow the law because it is the law (however unjust and immoral it may be). This opinion he considers as based in the motivation of "expediency" and preserving a "sentiment of submission to the law":

> Some maintain that no law, however bad, ought to be disobeyed by an individual citizen; that his opposition to it, if shown at all, should only be shown in endeavoring to get it altered by competent authority. This opinion (which condemns many of the most illustrious benefactors of mankind, and would often protect pernicious institutions against the only weapons which, in the state of things existing at the time, have any chance of succeeding against them) is defended by those who hold it on grounds of expediency; principally on that of the importance to the common interest of mankind, of maintaining inviolate the sentiment of submission to law. (Mill 1967b, 420)

The Social Reality of cannabis use expresses this interest of "maintaining inviolate the sentiment of submission to the law." Questioning the justice of U.S. cannabis law is in itself contrary to such submission. Mill also points out many of "most illustrious benefactors of mankind" (imagine here Jesus, Socrates, Thoreau) were recognized for just such action against the sentiment of submission to law. Mill also notes that when changes through "competent authority" have no chance of success there is necessitated resistance. Finally, here again he cites the use of "expediency" as an effective bureaucratic way to avoid addressing such issues as the legalization of cannabis.

Mill points out the problem with the position of those who would never disobey any law and who consider the law as the very standard of justice. Such people are thereby rejecting the fact there have existed and may exist unjust laws. It is rather obvious there have existed throughout history unjust laws. As Mill puts it, "it seems to be universally admitted that there may be unjust laws, and that law, consequently, is not the ultimate criterion of justice, but may give to one person a benefit, or impose on another an evil, which justice condemns" (Mill 1967b, 420). This point effectively counters those of the U.S. public who would argue that cannabis prohibition is just because it is the actual law currently enforced by the U.S. federal government. When pointing out historical examples of unjust laws this position would thereby fail logically for want of consistency. Furthermore, these very same people would just as ardently defend this right of adults to use cannabis were laws changed. This reveals (among other things) a position bereft of moral analysis and rational assessment of the actual justice of the laws in place. One who defines justice according to the law actually in place at any point in time is thereby committed to favoring *anything* and to a position whereby one arguably contradicts oneself, holding the same actions as both just and unjust.

Mill next presents the notion of "impartiality" (one he has already introduced early on in "Utilitarianism" in regards to how two pleasures were to be compared and contrasted). Here he explains this notion in light of the obligation of acknowledging "rights": "Impartiality where rights are concerned is of course obligatory, but this is involved in the more general obligation of giving to everyone his right" (Mill 1967b, 421). To counter the understanding of impartiality as indicating some intrinsically valuable quality of justice, Mill articulates impartiality as instead demanded in order to correctly calculate happiness involved in an action:

> Impartiality, in short, as an obligation of justice, may be said to mean being exclusively influenced by the considerations which it is supposed ought to influence the particular case in hand, and resisting solicitation of any motives which prompt to conduct different from what those considerations would dictate. (Mill 1967b, 421)

Prior to the 1937 Marihuana Tax Act, the fledgling Federal Bureau of Narcotics was led by Harry Anslinger, who was motivated to sustain funding for his agency (see chapter 4). He thereby launched his propaganda campaign against cannabis use (and users), the culmination of which was the passing of the Act. These personal, bureaucratic concerns exemplify precisely the type of motive that for justice's sake must be resisted. Failure to resist acting on such concerns results in unjust law. For utilitarian Mill this essentially means it does not promote the greatest amount of happiness and least amount of unhappiness for society.

Mill reflects upon the demonstration by the Greeks and Romans of an understanding of how the legislative process could create bad/unjust laws and how a sentiment of justice can be used to rectify these. This point opens the way to a rational assessment of the current federal law prohibiting cannabis use rather than refusing to do so because this law is (wrongly) believed to be infallible:

> But other nations, and in particular the Greeks and Romans, who knew that their laws had been made originally, and still continued to be made, by men, were not afraid to admit that those men might make bad laws; might do, by law, the same things, and from the same motives, which, if done by individuals without the sanction of law would be called unjust. And hence the sentiment of injustice came to be attached, not to all violations of law, but only to violations of such laws as *ought* to exist, including such as ought to exist but do not; and to laws themselves, if supposed to be contrary to what ought to be law. (Mill 1967b, 422)

The 1937 Marihuana Tax Act, legislation passed without scientific merit but from anti-Mexican, anti-immigrant motives was blatantly partial. Consider also that the "sentiment of injustice" is not felt about cannabis use in the way it is felt about physical assault, embezzlement, rape, murder, those actions where there exists a clear victim and harm to be rectified. The sentiment demands something be done to compensate for the harm done to another. In the case of cannabis use such harm and sentiment seems absent (as opposed to a different sort of sentiment propagated through the media).

This sentiment of justice and feeling will go so far as to utilize law to compel compliance: "When we think that a person is bound in justice to do a thing, it is an ordinary form of language to say that he ought to be compelled to do it" (Mill 1967b, 423). Mill proposes here three ways to compel in the name of justice (including law):

> We do not call anything wrong unless we mean to imply that a person ought to be punished in some way or other for doing it—if not by law, by the opinion of his fellow creatures; if not by opinion, by the reproaches of his own conscience. This seems the real turning point of the distinction between morality and simple expediency. (Mill 1967b, 423)

Punishment includes three forms here: law, social opinion, and conscience. In determining what, if any, of these should exist (e.g., in response to cannabis use) consider the crucial distinction between morality and justice and the appropriate type of coercion for each:

> duties of perfect obligation are those duties in virtue of which a correlative *right* resides in some person or persons; duties of imperfect obligation are those moral obligations which do not give birth to any right. I think it will be found that this distinction exactly coincides with that which exists between justice and the other obligations of morality. In our survey of the various popular acceptations of justice, the term appeared generally to involve the idea of a personal right—a claim on the part of one or more individuals, like that which the law gives when it confers a proprietary or other legal right. (Mill 1967b, 424)

At this point of his chapter 5, Mill has now made a move to considering justice as involving individual rights of others which clearly impact and make a claim on each of us: "Justice implies something which it is not only right to do, and wrong not to do, but which some individual person can claim from us as his moral right" (Mill 1967b, 424). In light of cannabis use, one major question is whether others can forbid cannabis use on the ground that some right of theirs is thereby violated.

Mill again cites the sentiment of justice as indicating when harm has been done:

> We have seen that the two essential ingredients in the sentiment of justice are the desire to punish a person who has done harm and the knowledge or belief that there is some definite individual or individuals to whom harm has been done.
>
> Now it appears to me that the desire to punish a person who has done harm to some individual is a spontaneous outgrowth from two sentiments, both in the highest degree natural and which either are or resemble instincts: the impulse of self-defense and the feeling of sympathy. (Mill 1967b, 425)

There would not be a felt sentiment of justice upon learning a fellow adult citizen is using cannabis, with no "definite individual or individuals to whom harm has been done." Without definite harmed individuals, it follows there is no clear reason one would experience either sympathy or self-defense any more than one would knowing an alcohol user was one's neighbor.

And of the way the sentiment of justice is tested or justified Mill characterizes the proper use of retaliation or vengeance. Perhaps those supporting prohibition (Social Reality on cannabis use) are "resenting a hurt to themselves," It is crucial, however, that merely being disagreeable to them is not enough. Their feeling, which must also be "moralized" or tested (otherwise, they are rejecting cannabis use only because they personally do not care for it without any reason) is:

> the natural feeling of retaliation or vengeance, rendered by intellect and sympathy applicable to those injuries, that is, to those hurts, which wound us through, or in common with, society at large. This sentiment, in itself, has nothing moral in it; what is moral is the exclusive subordination of it to the social sympathies, so as to wait on and obey their call. For the natural feeling would make us resent indiscriminately whatever anyone does that is disagreeable to us; but, when *moralized by* the social feeling, it only acts in the directions conformable to the general good: just persons resenting a hurt to society, though not otherwise a hurt to themselves, and not resenting a hurt to themselves, however painful, unless it be of the kind which society has a common interest with them in the repression of. (Mill 1967b, 425–26; emphasis added)

The sentiment of the Social Reality channels resentment against cannabis users and not against alcohol users. Cannabis users who otherwise act in harmony with the sentiment of justice find themselves questioning cannabis prohibition, as using cannabis is not demonstrably an activity society has "clear common interest to repress." Moral *resentment* is born of this utilitarian realization that cannabis use is being denied even though it does not clearly impede the common good. Again, Mill reinforces the point that mere feeling is not enough to act morally:

> It is common enough, certainly, though the reverse of commendable, to feel resentment merely because we have suffered pain; but a person whose resentment is really a moral feeling, that is, who considers whether an act is blamable before he allows himself to resent it—such a person, though he may not say expressly to himself that he is standing up for the interest of society, certainly does feel that he is asserting a rule which is for the benefit of others as well as for his own. If he is not feeling this, if he is regarding the act solely as it affects him individually,

> he is not consciously just; he is not concerning himself about the justice of his actions. This is admitted even by anti-utilitarian moralists. (Mill 1967b, 426)

Mill astutely recognizes two types of resentment (quite relevant to the issue of cannabis use and advocates of legalization). This is the distinction between one who individually enjoys cannabis and therefore advocates legality, and the other who has a "real moral feeling." The first considers the effects of cannabis use "solely as it affects him individually" and therefore has not formed a moral position. The second considers the effect cannabis legalization would have for others and overall happiness and therefore holds a moral position.

Giving a more terse articulation of a "right," Mill indicates the power of such a "valid claim" upon society (and upon utilitarians): "When we call anything a person's right, we mean that he has a valid claim on society to protect him in the possession of it, either by the force of law or by that of education and opinion" (Mill 1967b, 426). Cannabis users argue they have a right to use cannabis, a "valid claim on society to protect him in the possession of it." The question, however, is whether cannabis use would qualify as something for which one would have a "valid claim" upon U.S. society. If it can be argued that there is such a right, then the conclusion that follows is that everyone in the debate over cannabis legalization must acknowledge this valid claim and legalize cannabis. Furthermore, those who take rights seriously would defend cannabis users *whether the defenders themselves used cannabis or not*. This is a primary reason why the alcohol industry should *favor* cannabis legalization, further acknowledging *the right* of (adult) citizens to drink alcohol. "To have a right, then, is, I conceive, to have something which society ought to defend me in the possession of. If the objector goes on to ask why I ought, I can give him no other reason than general utility" (Mill 1967b, 427). Mill is loyal to the greatest happiness principle by respecting rights. Respecting rights furthers the happiness of society as a whole. This is a primary reason why policy-maker utilitarians must recognize (and craft laws that respect) rights.

Mill again uses the notion of the sentiment of justice by giving a concrete example of the type of action which excites this sentiment. These are the types of action indicating harm done to others. It is difficult to consider adult cannabis use as either wrongful aggression or wrongful withholding of something due someone else:

> The most marked cases of injustice, and those which give the tone to the feeling of repugnance which characterizes the sentiment, are acts of wrongful aggression or wrongful exercise of power over someone; the next are those which consist in wrongfully withholding from him something which is his due—in both cases inflicting on him a positive hurt, either in the form of direct suffering or of

> the privation of some good which he had reasonable ground, either of a physical or of a social kind, for counting upon. (Mill 1967b, 431)

The reason cannabis users experience *repugnance* is that they are subject to the unjustified aggression of the criminal law. First, denial of a cannabis user's right to use is a "privation of some good which he has reasonable ground for counting on." Second, Mill captures the repugnance felt by medicinal users specifically, wrongfully withholding from them "something" (cannabis/medicine) which is his due, "inflicting on him a positive hurt" (denying medical treatment), and the hurt as "privation of some good which he had reasonable ground, either of a physical or of a social kind, for counting upon." This last is particularly unjust, as users have a reasonable ground for believing that they would be legally permitted to use *any* medicine to ease pain and suffering.

To better understand and acknowledge the significant weight of the felt repugnance by cannabis users who are criminalized (disappointed in their government unjustly prohibiting cannabis use and criminalizing cannabis users), Mill explains it is the same repugnance underlying major moral wrongs of breaching friendship and promise: "The important rank, among human evils and wrongs, of the disappointment of expectation is shown in the fact that it constitutes the principal criminality of two such highly immoral acts as a breach of friendship and a breach of promise" (Mill 1967b, 432). Mill is a utilitarian and is therefore primarily interested in maximizing the most happiness and minimizing the most unhappiness through every action and law. He recognizes, in light of the introduction of rights as valid claims upon society, the need to explicitly indicate and "strictly construe" limits to rights in light of the general happiness of all:

> The equal claim of everybody to happiness, in the estimation of the moralist and the legislator, involves an equal claim to all the means of happiness except in so far as the inevitable conditions of human life and the general interest in which that of every individual is included set limits to the maxim; and those limits ought to be strictly construed. (Mill 1967b, 433)

Criminalizing cannabis users and refusing to recognize their right to use demands "strict construal" of the reasons for doing so, which at the minimum would require a clear articulation of the negative consequences averted and positive consequences accrued, and overall happiness promoted through cannabis prohibition.

Currently, with cannabis prohibited and cannabis users criminalized, many champions of justice for minorities and the oppressed completely ignore the injustice of cannabis criminalization. They instead simply assume this law as somehow, someway, conducive to the common social good (in addition to being expedient).Were cannabis legalized the realization of a "social injustice" that should not have been tolerated in the United States would likely come into public consciousness.

> And hence all social inequalities which have ceased to be considered expedient assume the character, not of simple inexpediency, but of injustice, and appear so tyrannical that people are apt to wonder how they ever could have been tolerated—forgetful that they themselves, perhaps, tolerate other inequalities under an equally mistaken notion of expediency, the correction of which would make that which they approve seem quite as monstrous as what they have at last learned to condemn. (Mill 1967b, 433–34)

At the end of his *Utilitarianism* and relevant to the question of whether or not U.S. cannabis law is just, Mill would have one consider whether the use of cannabis by adult citizens kindles in response a feeling of broken command demanding stern response or mild feeling which does not go so far as to justify legal punishment of cannabis users:

> Justice remains the appropriate name for certain social utilities which are vastly more important, and therefore more absolute and imperative, than any others are as a class (though not more so than others may be in particular class); and which, therefore, ought to be, as well as naturally are, guarded by a sentiment not only different in degree, but also in kind; distinguished from the milder feeling which attaches to the mere idea of promoting human pleasure or convenience at once by the more definite nature of its commands and by the sterner character of its sanctions. (Mill 1967b, 434)

For many who use cannabis there exists a deep sense of resentment, both constantly aware of the illegality of what they are doing while also aware of their own good sense and reason, using with an awareness of the Scientific Reality of cannabis use. Guilt of a user in this way can evidence not the wrongness of cannabis use but rather reluctance in breaking the law. Torn between the law and their most basic liberty as human beings (something they would never have forfeited in the first place to enter any society), hundreds of thousands of otherwise law-abiding citizens annually break the U.S. law.

"On Liberty" Applied to Cannabis Use and Law

Against Enforcement of a Common Morality

"On Liberty" demonstrates that for utilitarians there exist extremely compelling reasons against interfering with adult cannabis users. As a way of transitioning from Mill's "Utilitarianism" to his "On Liberty," consider the following from Alan Ryan's "Mill in a liberal landscape," a longish but very clear statement of what Mill took to be the limits of enforcing a "common morality":

> *Some* common morality must be generally enforced, and its features are just those that Mill suggests; but there is no reason to believe that a failure to secure uniformity of belief on disputed conceptions of the good life will bring about any harm other than whatever discomfort is attendant on being required to think for ourselves. Conversely, there is good reason to suppose that trying to enforce more than the basic morality Mill had in mind would result in the damage that *On Liberty* laments.
>
> It is sometimes suggested that a utilitarian defence of liberty is a non-starter; utilitarianism would license any degree of interference that gave enough pleasure to the majority. . . . Mill's response to this vulgar but not implausible argument was offered glancingly, in several places, and in three installments. One was an appeal to the intuitive idea that any claim that others should behave as I wish *just because* I wish them to do so has no merit. Mill knew that nobody *avowed* such a view. The buried premise of Mill's argument against it therefore was that where enough moral discord existed to excite the desire for uniformity, the demand that others should do anything in particular for the sake of a 'shared morality' is tantamount to the claim that they should think like me and act like me, because I want them to. This is what Mill denounced as his contemporaries' belief that their 'likings and dislikings' should be a universal guide. The second was . . . the content of the 'common morality' that any society must enforce was essentially limited to the defence of each of its members against a limited range of harms . . . the morality that underlies the making and keeping of contracts, the doing of jury duty, recognizing the obligation to go to work and earn a living, and so on. Any greater uniformity would do more harm than good. The third was essentially an elaboration on the conception of 'more harm' that was involved in such a response; that elaboration supplied the bulk of the positive argument of *On Liberty*. Mill denied that enforcing uniformity would be a good bargain in utilitarian terms, the entire essay was an argument to that effect, since it was an argument against yielding to the desire for uniformity of sentiment, whether for its own sake of for the sake of the general welfare. (Ryan 1998, 505–6)

Mill's "On Liberty" compliments "Utilitarianism," indicating individual rights should be respected so as to produce more social good and overall happiness. "On Liberty" provides several lines of thought quite relevant to the question of cannabis prohibition.

Consider the following from his fourth of five chapters of "On Liberty," "Of the Limits to the Authority of Society over the Individual":

> The interference of society to overrule his judgment and purposes in what only regards himself, must be grounded on general presumptions; which may be altogether wrong, and even if right, are as likely as not to be misapplied to indi-

> vidual cases, by persons no better acquainted with the circumstances of such cases than those are who look at them merely from without. (Mill 1967a, 277)

The law prohibiting cannabis use overrules the judgment of adults in purposes which only regard these users. The presuppositions of the U.S. federal government (e.g., cannabis use has no therapeutic value) "may be altogether wrong." *The Scientific Reality makes just this case against the Social Reality on cannabis use.* Furthermore the absolute prohibition of cannabis is a gross misapplication of law in light of individual cases (e.g., the criminalization of terminally ill patients). It is likely medicinal users are better acquainted with the effects of cannabis than are those of the U.S. Social Reality who look at them merely from without (or not at all).[4]

Further applying Mill here, cannabis law in effect tells therapeutic users that cannabis is not effective. The Scientific Reality of cannabis has been repeatedly ignored by government officials who themselves lack first-hand experience of cannabis use and effects. For many users cannabis has consistently been effective and predictable in effects. Suffering patients, if anyone, seem the best judges of the efficacy of their pain medications. "All errors which he is likely to commit against advice and warning, are far outweighed by the evil of allowing others to constrain him to what they deem his good" (Mill 1967a, 277).

For Natural Punishments

A major point captured by Mill (and Kant, Aristotle, and St. Augustine) concerns recognizing the natural punishment coming with dependence on or abuse of drugs. According to Kant there is the factor of "humiliation," for Aristotle the (quasi)virtue of "shame," and St. Augustine speaks of the compassionate response to one who is dependent on a substance and therefore hurting himself, punishing himself. Consider now Mill's quite democratic recognition of shame as a punishment of its own:

> Though doing no wrong to any one, a person may so act as to compel us to judge him, and feel to him, as a fool, or as a being of an inferior order: and since this judgment and feeling are a fact which he would prefer to avoid, it is doing him a service to warn him of it beforehand, as of any other disagreeable consequence to which he exposes himself. It would be well, indeed, if this good office were much more freely rendered than the common notions of politeness at present permit, and if one person could honestly point out to another that he thinks him in fault, without being considered unmannerly or presuming. (Mill 1967a, 278)

Here Mill would have adult cannabis users warned of "disagreeable consequences" of their use. Mill thinks justified no more than "unfavourable judgment" against those actions which concern one's own good but does not affect the interests of others in their relations with them.

Against Punishing Self-Regarding Actions

Relative to the notion of cannabis users as otherwise law-abiding citizens whose cannabis use is private and has no effect on the interests of others[5]:

> What I contend for is, that the inconveniences which are strictly inseparable from the unfavourable judgment of others, are the only ones to which a person should ever be subjected for that portion of his conduct and character which concerns his own good, but which does not affect the interests of others in their relations with him. Acts injurious to others require a totally different treatment. (Mill 1967a, 278–79)

Relevant to emphasize here is that subject to abuse is the line between self-regarding and other-regarding actions. Lawmakers who consider cannabis use as "other-regarding" stretch to an extreme degree the notion of harm. Practically speaking, it is not at all clear how an individual's cannabis use directly effects the interests of others (especially without other information about who, where, and how the individual is using). Peter Nicholson nicely captures this point:

> The distinction between self-regarding and other-regarding actions receives special attention. Bosanquet objected that if it was pressed, Mill's distinction "excludes individuality from every act of life that has an important social bearing"; and that it was arbitrary as a practical criterion because, every act being both self- and other-regarding, which aspect was fastened on in a particular case was 'a matter of mood and momentary urgency." The distinction Mill was attempting to describe was "practically recognized by every society," but it could not be made in Mill's terms. It should rather be drawn in terms Green had used: Mill was really after the distinction between actions where it was crucial that they be done for the right moral motive, so that they should not be subject to legal coercion, and actions whose performance was so important to society that they should be legally enforced, even if then not done for the right moral motive. (Nicholson 1998, 486–87)

As the Shafer Commission report speaks of the institutions of family and community as being essential to address the "drug problem," the same seems true when the line between legality and morality is kept clear. The government which respects liberty of citizens relies upon these other institutions in regards to moral matters. The government should not attempt to create shame where none existed nor clearly should exist. Instead, families, parents, communities must preserve the healthy experience of this moral feeling.

Beyond establishing cannabis use as at most a moral matter (generally self-regarding) not a legal matter (generally, other-regarding) Mill goes farther in drawing a further distinction in responding to self-regarding actions with which society disagrees (e.g., cannabis use). He presents a fine line between pity and dislike on the one hand and anger and resentment on the other:

> He may be to us an object of pity, perhaps of dislike, but not of anger or resentment; we shall not treat him like an enemy of society; the worst we shall think ourselves justified in doing is leaving him to himself, if we do not intervene benevolently by showing interest or concern for him. (Mill 1967a, 280)

A cannabis user may be an object of pity or dislike, but not anger or resentment (let alone legal punishment and criminalization). He should not be treated like an enemy of society. Here Mill indicates the essential injustice of the current U.S. federal policy prohibiting cannabis use. Mill would advise the government (and citizens generally) "to leave the cannabis user to himself" and at most intervene benevolently.

Mill recognizes in addition to matters of law and matters of morality those matters "merely contingent" and neither legal nor moral matters. This complements the distinction between pity and anger and further shows subtle differences in response to self-regarding behaviors with which others may disagree:

> Whenever, in short, there is a definite damage, or a definite risk of damage, either to an individual or to the public, the case is taken out of the province of liberty, and placed in that of morality or law.
>
> But with regard to the merely contingent, or, as it may be called, constructive injury which a person causes to society, by conduct which neither violates any specific duty to the public, nor occasions perceptible hurt to any assignable individual except himself; the inconvenience is one which society can afford to bear, for the sake of the greater good of human freedom. (Mill 1967a, 282)

The inconvenience of legalizing cannabis and respecting, not criminalizing, cannabis users, is one "which society can afford to bear, for the sake of the greater good of human freedom." Cannabis use, as at most harming the user himself, is of the province of liberty, not clearly moving into the province of law or even morality.

Negative Consequences of Treating Adults like Children

Mill explains that forbidding adult citizens from acting in ways without definite damage to others is to treat them like children. By so treating adults, a government ill-prepares citizens to act responsibly, to be mature and enterprising, instead producing grown-up children unable to think for themselves and further their own good once in a position to do so.

> If society lets any considerable number of its members grow up mere children, incapable of being acted on by rational consideration of distant motives, society has itself to blame for the consequences. Armed not only with all the powers of education, but with the ascendancy which the authority of a received opinion always exercises over the minds who are least fitted to judge for themselves; and aided by the *natural* penalties which cannot be prevented from falling on those who endure the distaste or the contempt of those who know them; let not society pretend that it needs, besides all this, the power to issue commands and enforce obedience in the personal concerns of individuals, in which, on all principles of justice and policy, the decision ought to rest with those who are to abide the consequences. (Mill 1967a, 282)

Mill here explains the essential problem with a government arresting and punishing users of cannabis. Cannabis users endure natural penalties in using cannabis. If users are willing to endure these (e.g., through a risk/benefit analysis which results in an individual benefiting more than being harmed) the government is insisting its member remain a child. Laws are not going to deter cannabis use, unlike an appreciation of a rick/benefit analysis that results in more harm than benefit as a result of using cannabis.

The U.S. Social Reality and set of beliefs are scientifically weak but well propagated in the media. They insist cannabis is not as benign as the hundreds of thousands of people who have actually used cannabis have concluded from their own experience. At the same time this same Social Reality also somehow justifies and continues to tolerate a right to use the drug alcohol.

> But the opinion of a similar majority, imposed as a law on the minority, on questions of self-regarding conduct, is quite as likely to be wrong as right; for in these cases public opinion means, at the best, some people's opinion of what is good or bad for other people; while very often it does not even mean that; the public, with the most perfect indifference, passing over the pleasure or convenience of those whose conduct they censure, and considering only their own preference. (Mill 1967a, 283)

Blendon and Young's "The Public and the War on Drugs" study (see chapter 5) revealed what Mill describes here. Eighty-one percent of the U.S. public claims no first-hand experience of drug abuse, little understanding of cannabis use, and consider their own preference only (alcohol) and not that of the minorities who are censured (cannabis). A moral thinker must judge impartially not preferentially. The conclusion invited here is that public opinion (and perhaps Social Reality itself) is merely an expression of its own preference and therefore not a moral judgment at all.

Mill relevantly brings up liquors and his major concern is with self-interested sellers controlling the market as opposed to a government provision of unmarketed and regulated liquors. In light of the legalization of cannabis, the government would regulate and control the production and sale of cannabis, perhaps not unlike the way liquor is currently sold in the United States in state liquor stores. Mill would point to cigarette (nicotine) marketing as an excellent twentieth-century example of what goes wrong when companies with profit interests are free to encourage the consumption of a drug. Beer commercialization and marketing continues to fuel rampant alcohol abuse, binge drinking, and morally speaking seems to ultimately leave alcoholics to simply suffer shame and humiliation upon recognition of their abuse of and dependence on alcohol. Mill emphasizes that once there is a profit motive and commercial interest, there is interest in *encouraging use*. Of course this will logically lead to more abuse and dependence in society as a whole. The system of sale and distribution of cannabis should eliminate a profit motive for those who sell it. The point of contact between a state licensed salesperson of cannabis and the cannabis purchaser/user is one of respectful and sanctioned, legal exchange. The difference between this experience and the experience of "scoring" cannabis through a friend or acquaintance (or a dealer and touching upon the criminal world) is monumental. The legalization of cannabis would remove this latter experience millions of times over for adult U.S. citizens.

In Mill's chapter 5, "Applications," he sets a standard which must be met in order to justify interfering with the liberty of another, the (unsafe) bridge example:

> If either a public officer or any one else saw a person attempting to cross a bridge which had been ascertained to be unsafe, and there were no time to warn him of his danger, they might seize him and turn him back, without any real infringement of his liberty; for liberty consists in doing what one desires, and he does not desire to fall into the river. Nevertheless, when there is not a certainty, but only a danger of mischief, no one but the person himself can judge of the sufficiency of the motive which may prompt him to incur the risk; in this case, therefore (unless he is a child, or delirious, or in some state of excitement or absorption incompatible with the full use of the reflecting faculty) he ought, I conceive, to be only warned of the danger; not forcibly prevented from exposing himself to it. (Mill 1967a, 294)

Applying the bridge example to cannabis use by an adult cancer chemotherapy patient who says he uses it to reduce nausea and vomiting, make treatment bearable, helping maintain the will to live, to grab the chemo patient by the arm and warn him of the dangers of cannabis dependence would be delusional *on the part of one so warning.* Such grabbing of this chemo patient's arm demonstrates a complete lack of compassion, of suffering with and as this fellow human being who is facing mortality, enduring chemo and the physical, psychological, and spiritual issues in this journey. Cannabis law used to coerce medical users seems more akin to a situation where the bridge does indeed exist intact, but has never been traveled by the one so warning.

For the Scientific Reality it seems uncontroversial to claim an individual's risk/benefit analysis may result in more perceived benefit in using rather than not using. Given the non-lethality and lack of any significant health risks, the effects of the majority of cannabis use, either in any particular instance of use or in a longer period of use, seems quite unlike unknowingly walking onto an unsafe bridge to fall into the river below. The warnings by those of the Social Reality, given their seven definitive beliefs, again indicate lack of reason (moral or scientific) and are a false alarm.

Mill goes on to say that when there is only a danger but not a certain "mischief," then "no one but the person himself can judge of the sufficiency of the motive which may prompt him to incur the risk." Here is a strong point justifying the legal availability of alcohol and cannabis. They are both potentially dangerous but not necessarily dangerous, so there is no "certain mischief" (neither "certain" nor "mischief" will likely result) as either harm to self or to others. Mill further explains in light of an individual's "choice of pleasures": "Their choice of pleasures, and their mode of expending their income, after satisfying their legal and moral obligations to the State and to individuals, are their own concern, and must rest with their own judgment" (Mill 1967a, 298). This is obviously not an assumption made in the United States regarding cannabis use. Mill qualifies this freedom to choose pleasures with "after satisfying their legal and moral obligations to the State and to individuals." This point reveals the deep moral wrong of criminalizing "Otherwise Law-Abiding Citizens." With responsibilities being met, the law reaches into a cannabis user's life and creates a problem where one does not exist. The current U.S. cannabis law violates the right of law-abiding citizens to choose their pleasures and way of expending their income. When the State does this it weakens itself, making a decision for citizens as a parent for a child.

Mill's reasons for the non-interference with others indicate why the questioning of current cannabis law is so pressing. This law eliminates liberty and enslaves citizens. A respect for a person's liberty respects his voluntary choice as itself proof that for this person the risk/benefit analysis comes out in favor of using cannabis. But to deny a person such decision-making capacity, he is thereby made a "slave." Perhaps this is felt most acutely by terminally ill and other medicinal users of cannabis who suddenly experience themselves as owned by the state, to the literal point of enduring pain and suffering in the name of the symbolism of cannabis prohibition to social order:

> The reason for not interfering, unless for the sake of others, with a person's voluntary acts, is consideration for his liberty. His voluntary choice is evidence that what he so chooses is desirable, or at the least endurable, to him, and his good is on the whole best provided for by allowing him to take his own means of pursuing it. But by selling himself for a slave, he abdicates his liberty; he foregoes any future use of it beyond that single act. He therefore defeats, in his own case, the very purpose which is the justification of allowing him to dispose of himself. He is no longer free; but is thenceforth in a position which has no longer the presumption in its favour, that would be afforded by his voluntarily remaining in it. The principle of freedom cannot require that he should be free not to be free. (Mill 1967a, 299–300)

One way to attempt to change the U.S. federal law on cannabis is civil disobedience. Responsible acts of civil disobedience first thoughtfully consider all legal options of changing the current law. The major problem in the attempt to change cannabis law is that the agencies through which this change would happen are the Social Reality itself. This once again touches upon the problem of policy dictating research instead of research dictating policy. As Mill too recognizes: "But where everything is done through the bureaucracy, nothing to which the bureaucracy is really adverse can be done at all" (Mill 1967a, 308)

Mill's conclusion to "On Liberty" seems a final summary of his general point throughout, that a State that denies basic liberty, such as legalized cannabis for adult citizens, makes them "dwarfs of men." In effect the State weakens itself by creating adult citizens who cannot think for themselves:

> A government cannot have too much of the kind of activity which does not impede, but aids and stimulates, individual exertion and development. The mischief begins when, instead of calling forth the activity and powers of individuals and bodies, it substitutes its own activity for theirs; when, instead of informing, advising, and, upon occasion, denouncing, it makes them work in fetters, or bids them stand aside and does their work instead of them. The worth of a State, in the long run, is the worth of the individuals composing it; and a State which postpones the interests of *their* mental expansion and elevation, to a little more

> of administrative skill, or of that semblance of it which practice gives, in the details of business; a State which dwarfs its men, in order that they may be more docile instruments in its hands even for beneficial purposes—will find that with small men no great thing can really be accomplished; and that the perfection of machinery to which it has sacrificed everything, will in the end avail it nothing, for want of the vital power which, in order that the machine might work more smoothly, it has preferred to banish.(Mill 1967a, 310)

Cannabis: Illicit Drug and Top U.S. Cash Crop

The way I read Mill has him advocating for the legalization of cannabis. By not heeding this argument more harm than good is done to society. The primary individuals harmed include medicinal cannabis users disallowed medicine and relief of pain and suffering, the 750,000 arrested for cannabis use every year in the United States, and more generally, as Mill concludes "On Liberty," citizens in general who are encouraged to think like children (to accept a law because it is the law without any rational or moral justification).

In this section presented are billions of dollars that could be taken from the current black market in cannabis. This market in the United States is widespread to the point that cannabis is currently the major cash crop of the United States Taxpayers are missing out on all of this income which is instead never taxed while an underworld of non-taxed cannabis growers and producers make substantial income. Consider, most relevant to a utilitarian consideration of the costs and benefits of cannabis prohibition, the following information regarding the current U.S. black market in cannabis by Jon Gettman ("Marijuana Production in the United States [2006]").

Contrary to the assumption that all cannabis comes from Mexico (or other foreign countries):

> American marijuana farmers grew 22.3 million pounds of marijuana in 2006 with a value of $35.8 billion. These figures, which include marijuana seized by law enforcement, include 56.4 million marijuana plants cultivated outdoors worth $31.7 billion and 11.7 million plants cultivated indoors worth 4.1 billion. Five states (California, Tennessee, Kentucky, Hawaii and Washington) had marijuana crops worth over $1 billion. (Gettman 2006, 11)

Consider next the following ranking of the average cash crop values in the United States from 2003 to 2005 (Gettman 2006, 13; I present here those above 2,500,000, numbers representing $1,000s), as evidence that cannabis is the major cash crop of the current United States:

TABLE 6.1
Annual Production Values (2003–2005)

Rank	*Crop*	*Average Production Value ($1000s)*
1.	Marijuana	$35,803,591
2.	Corn	$23,299,601
3.	Soybeans	$17,612,200
4.	Hay	$12,236,638
5.	Vegetables	$11,080,733
6.	Wheat	$7,450,907
7.	Cotton-All	$5,314,870
8.	Grapes	$2,876,547

Gettman, Jon. "Marijuana Production in the United States." The Bulletin of Cannabis Reform: 2006. www.drugscience.org/ber/index.html.

A utilitarian would most likely value very highly the potential social benefits of billions of dollars that currently exist in an illicit black market, untaxed and therefore providing no return to the public. Considering cannabis in the context of other crops (instead of other drugs) and yet also not making the move to considering the growing of hemp (not the focus of this book), the positive benefits of growing cannabis could also significantly strengthen U.S. farmers.

Further elaborating the meaning of the statistics regarding annual cannabis crops in the United States,

> Based on a comparison with average production values of other crops from 2003 to 2005 marijuana is the top cash crop in 12 states, one of the top 3 cash crops in 30 states, and one of the top 5 cash crops in 39 states. Marijuana is the largest cash crop in Alaska, Alabama, California, Connecticut, Hawaii, Kentucky, Maine, North Carolina, Oregon, South Carolina, Tennessee, and West Virginia. (Gettman 2006, 13)

In Tennessee, for example, the top crops are (in 1,000s):

Marijuana: $4,787,250
Soybeans $277,861
Hay $252,365
California
Marijuana $13, 848, 267
Vegetables $5, 668, 637
Grapes $2, 607, 181
(Gettman 2006, 14)

An economic analysis would also consider relevant the correlation of strong eradication measures with increased production (perhaps creating profit motive for citizens to enter the black market). This further supports the legalization of cannabis:

> The ten-fold growth of production over the last 25 years and its proliferation to every part of the country demonstrates the irrefutable reality that marijuana has become a pervasive and ineradicable part of the economy of the United States. The contribution of this market to the nation's gross domestic product is overlooked in the debate over effective control and discouragement of use by teenagers and children. Like all profitable agricultural crops marijuana adds resources and value to the economy. The focus for public policy should be how to effectively control this market through regulation and taxation in order to achieve immediate and realistic goals, such as reducing teenage access, rather than to continue to sacrifice achievable goals in exchange for unachievable long-term goals that have failed to materialize over the last 25 years. (Gettman 2006, 17)

Also recommended is generally a policy of control, similar to that used with tobacco and alcohol, in light of concerns with adolescent and underage access. As Gettman points out, by being illegal and criminalized, cannabis provides a profit motive for adolescents, one absent from alcohol and tobacco:

> It's time to debate the legalization of marijuana in the United States. Skeptics argue against legalization as a way of reducing teenage access, for example, by citing teenage access to alcohol and tobacco in a legal market despite age restrictions and related penalties. However unlike marijuana teens do not have a profit motive to sell tobacco and alcohol to one another. Effective control over production of tobacco and alcohol are prerequisites to both controlling access to those drugs by teenagers and the implementation of successful educational and discouragement campaigns. Replacing the façade of control provided by current policies with effective regulatory policies is also the first step in enacting effective policies to reduce teenage marijuana use. (Gettman 2006, 17–18)

Gettman suggests, again using what we already know about controlling alcohol and tobacco, "key elements" of cannabis legalization:

> Key elements of marijuana legalization policies should include federal and state excise taxes on production, distribution, and sales along with licensed market participation, age restrictions, and prohibitions on advertising and marketing to minors. Current regulatory models for tobacco and alcohol provide suitable examples upon which to base legislation to enact effective marijuana controls under federal and state laws. (Gettman 2006, 18)

Gettman concludes with an argument supporting the legalization of cannabis, claiming not doing so is a betrayal of the public trust.

> Under the policies of the last 25 years marijuana has become the most widely produced illegal drug in the United States and the nation's largest cash crop. The ten-fold increase in marijuana production from 1,000 metric tons in 1981 to the contemporary estimate of 10,000 metric tons undermines all drug control programs; with results like these it is difficult to take assurances of long-term effectiveness in any federal anti-drug program seriously. Taxation and regulation of marijuana is in the public interest. The refusal to implement a regulatory program for marijuana in the United States is irresponsible and a violation of the public trust. (Gettman 2006, 18)

Grow House Phenomenon: Evidence of the Impossibility of Enforcing Cannabis Law

In "Pot Growing Moves to Suburbs," John Ritter of *USA Today* reports on the current phenomenon of cannabis growers purchasing suburban homes to grow massive amounts of cannabis. This particular article focuses on five grow houses raided by DEA agents in Lathrop, California. Ritter reports "suburban pot-growing was found elsewhere—Merriville, Ind.; Westminster, Md.; Kankakee County, Ill.—though on a smaller scale than in Northern California and not necessarily tied to organized crime." Furthermore, "indoor pot seizures in California have skyrocketed . . . from 54,568 in 2004 to 196,000 last year, although it's unclear whether tougher enforcement or more growers is the reason." Further commenting on the continual growth and development of illegal cannabis production, Ritter reports,

> What is new is the size and sheer audacity found in the suburbs. The operations followed a similar pattern. . . . Growers paid up to $750,000 for houses in new subdivisions usually obtaining 100 percent financing and putting no money down. They gutted interiors and used every inch to grow pot, knocking down some walls and cutting holes in others to run water lines and ducts. They installed irrigation systems with timing devices and brought in water tanks, pumps, generators and power packs. They built scaffolding to raise plants 2 feet off the floor.
>
> To avoid suspicion from large power usage, growers by-passed a utility's electric meters and created their own circuit boxes. No one lived in the houses. (Ritter 2007)

The existence of such grow houses across the United States, their being undetected even among neighbors let alone DEA agents, reveals the black market in cannabis as unstoppable, thriving, and growing. Rather than crossing the Mexican border, paying off line attendants, hiring lookouts to spot long lines and good opportunities to cross the border with large loads, tunneling under the border, etc., cannabis production is being taken over by growers within the United States, making cannabis the top cash crop of the country. It stands to reason that utilitarians would not only factor in the billions of dollars currently being made by those of the black market, untaxed monies, but also the fact that federal cannabis law and perhaps the law itself is significantly sullied through the existence of unenforceable and ineffective laws.

Contamination of U.S. Cannabis: Further Utilitarian Reason for Cannabis Legalization

A final point regards the negative effects and production of significant unhappiness to many people. Consider that cannabis currently acquired through the black market is potentially contaminated with a fungus or mold potentially causing disease in the user. A continuing controversy in the Netherlands regards a perceived contrast in the quality of cannabis purchased at coffee houses versus that acquired through the official Office of Medicinal Cannabis (OMC). Although the OMC cannabis costs slightly more than the same purchased at a coffee house, this cost is said to be offset by the safety and integrity of the product, especially given carefully measured THC content and other compounds (e.g., CBD) and an environment in which the cannabis produced is kept uncontaminated. Hazekamp, in "An evaluation of the quality of medicinal grade cannabis in the Netherlands" demonstrates and concludes that "medicinal cannabis offered through the pharmacies is more reliable and safer for the health of medical users of cannabis." He also presents his results as "intended as a contribution to the discussion about the necessity or advantage of having a policy of centrally regulated production and distribution of medicinal grade cannabis" (Hazekamp 2006, 2). Of the Dutch policy, "largely formulated in the mid-seventies," "this policy does not moralise, but is based on the assumption that drug use is an undeniable fact and must be dealt with as practically as possible. The most important objective of this drug policy is therefore to prevent or to limit the risks and the harm associated with drug use, both to the user himself and to society" (Hazekamp 2006, 2). Distinctions between drugs are made on the basis of "harmfulness (cannabis products on the one hand, and drugs that represent an 'unacceptable' risk on the other)" (Hazekamp 2006, 2). Secondly, "the law differentiates on the basis of the nature of the offence, such as the distinction between possession of small quantities of drugs intended for personal use, and possession intended for dealing purposes. Possession of up to 30 grams of cannabis is a minor offense, while possession of more than 30 grams is a criminal offence. Drug use itself is not an offence" (Hazekamp 2006, 2).

Further describing the Dutch policy regarding cannabis, consider that although the policy is "tolerant" and based on the legal "expediency principle," whereby small-scale dealing is not prosecuted given the following conditions: "no advertising, no sales of hard-drugs, no nuisance must be caused in the neighbourhood, no admittance of and sales to minors (under the age of 18), and no sales exceeding 5 grams of cannabis per transaction. The stock of the coffeeshop should not exceed 500 grams of cannabis" (Hazekamp 2006, 2). The policy, again under the principle of "harm-reduction," recognizes users as "mainly young people experimenting with the drug—are not criminalized (they do not get a criminal record) and they are not forced to move in criminal circles, where the risk that they will be pressed to try more dangerous drugs such as heroin is much greater" (Hazekamp 2006, 2).

Further providing an idea of the way legalized cannabis would look in the United States, consider that there will be developed social norms of acceptable and unacceptable use (as in the Dutch experience here, also clearly demonstrable in the use of ganja in Jamaica):

> Tolerance does not mean that cannabis smokers can just light up a smoke anywhere they like outside a coffeeshop. Although no formal rules prohibit cannabis smoking in public places, such as bars, restaurants or concert halls, very few people do so. If they do, no sanctions are applied; but the person is likely to be asked by the personnel to put out the cigarette. The absence of formal regulations over the use of cannabis has opened the way for these informal norms, and their existence and effectiveness is an aspect of the Dutch drug policy that is often underestimated and difficult to grasp by foreigners. (Hazekamp 2006, 3)

This is quite similar to the norms regarding the consumption of alcohol. The norms in the United States have changed so that, while in the 1950s to 1970s drinking alcohol and driving was common, currently it is clear as a norm that using alcohol while driving a car is antisocial and not tolerated. A current norm is against having "open containers" of alcohol in public; something not in most places accepted nor condoned a norm which would likely develop upon cannabis legalization in the United States as well. Currently, cigarette smoking is being banned in public places (e.g., restaurants, bars) in the United States and has effectively removed smokers and smoking from these previously smoke-filled public places.

Consider that only in 2001 was the OMC created "in order to supply these patients with a safe and reliable source of high quality cannabis" (Hazekamp 2006, 3). And as for therapeutic uses recognized by the OMC:

> These are: nausea and loss of appetite resulting from chemotherapy, radiotherapy or HIV-combination therapy; palliative treatment for cancer and HIV

> patients; spasticity and pain associated with multiple sclerosis or spinal cord injury; chronic neurogenic pain; and physical or verbal tics caused by Tourette's syndrome. However, if they find it necessary in elected cases, medical professionals are allowed to prescribe cannabis for other indications as well. (Hazekamp 2006, 3)

Getting to the point of this particular study, to compare the quality of cannabis provided by coffeehouses to that provided by the OMC, in the visits to the coffeehouses chosen for the study, "The workers in most coffeeshops were found to have experience answering questions concerning the medicinal use of cannabis and were willing to offer advice on matters such as method and frequency of use, as well as on expected results" (Hazekamp 2006, 4). Furthermore, being short-changed common in the black market, consider that of the 10 grams paid for this study "less than 9.50 grams were present in the obtained package(s) in 5 out of the 11 cases," and "in one case (coffeeshop A) only 7.49 grams (-25 percent) were delivered" (Hazekamp 2006, 4).

The results from this study are most relevant to utilitarian considerations of the extent of the contamination problem currently in existence in the United States. These data from the Netherlands arguably imply a much greater problem in the United States with contamination than at coffeeshops. Unlike neighborhood growers and sellers in the United States's black market, Dutch coffeeshops would assumedly exercise control over their product as a business accountable to those who purchase their product. In short, these data indicate significant infections resulting from contaminated cannabis at coffeehouses and are therefore likely occurring at a significant rate in the United States:

> The EP requirements with regard to microbiological purity for inhalation preparations set the following limits for sample contamination: total molds and aerobic bacteria: < 10 colony forming units (CFU) per gram; total enterobacteria and gram-negative bacteria: < 100 CFU per gram. The infectious bacteria *Pseudomonas aeruginosa* and *Staphylococcus aureus* must be completely absent . . . all samples obtained from coffeeshops carried contamination levels of bacteria and/or fungi above these limits. In contrast, both cannabis varieties from the OMC were found to be clear of such contaminations. According to the OMC, rejection of its medicinal cannabis based on microbiological contamination has never occurred to date. (Hazekamp 2006, 6)

And of one particular sample further analyzed identified were "several known pathogens, including the intestinal bacterium Escherichia coli, and fungi of the Penicillium, Cladosporum and Aspergillus types" (Hazekamp 2006, 6). Revealing the presence of contaminants on "recreationally-used" cannabis: "The presence of potentially hazardous fungi on recreationally-used cannabis has been described routinely and increasingly these fungi are being acknowledged as an underestimated source of neurological toxicity or infections such as aspergillosis" (Hazekamp 2006, 6).[6]

In his conclusion, Hazekamp finds that "Delivery of medicinal cannabis to patients through the OMC and pharmacies results in a reliable product without the health risks commonly associated with coffeeshop cannabis" (Hazekamp 2006, 7). Furthermore, and speaking to current U.S. users as well (although they have no choice but to use black market cannabis):

> When patients choose to obtain cannabis from an uncontrolled source, they must realize that they do so with a certain risk to their health. In this test, we did not check for the presence of pesticides, fungicides or heavy metals, but there are plenty of indications that these are frequently present in cannabis samples from uncontrolled sources. (Hazekamp 2006, 7)

To conclude, given cannabis is the most used illicit substance in the United States, various infections may be transmitted and could be quite substantial (but, given the criminalization of cannabis users, is hidden in the "black market"). That this risk is substantial I argue by way of data from Netherlands coffeehouses. By considering the continuing controversy there regarding the merits, price, etc., of regulated cannabis versus cannabis acquired through coffee houses, it is shown that cannabis from the government is safe. If cannabis is unsafe in coffee houses in the Netherlands, it is almost certainly so in the United States through the black market, where unsafe production, storage, and handling of product ensures substantial disease.

Notes

1. Here the Social Reality would likely counter with a reaffirmation of its definitive beliefs. As indicated in the "Public and the War on Drugs" report, including cannabis legalization would lead to a weakening of the moral character of the country, perhaps in their utilitarian calculation a society where many were unhappy at the fact that their government allowed cannabis to be used by adults as they saw fit. This counter will be dealt with in the next section and Mill's "On Liberty."

2. A thorough philosophical consideration of cannabis use and cannabis law must employ this concept, one essentially justifying the belief in the existence of freedom (from physical determinism, e.g.) and also the ideas of personal responsibility and more generally morality. It is furthermore commonly used in reference to the use of cannabis (or any other substance) especially for those who abuse or are dependent upon cannabis (e.g., using or not using referred to as a matter of "will-power" in common vernacular).

3. This is a major distinction between Mill and both Kant and St. Augustine, the latter two conceiving of the good will as an ideal to attain in human morality.

4. As stated by Congressman David Obey (D-WI) in July 2006 after the U.S. House of Representatives rejection of the Hinchey-Rohrabacher amendment to prohibit federal government undermining of state cannabis laws: "If I am terminally ill, it is not anybody's business on this floor how I handle the pain or the illness or the sickness associated with that illness. With all due respect to all of you, butt out. I did not enter this world with the permission of the Justice Department, and I am certainly not going to depart it by seeking their permission or that of any other authority. The Congress has no business telling people that they cannot manage their illness or their pain any way they need to. I would trust any doctor in the country before I trust some of the daffy ducks in this institution to decide what I am supposed to do if I am terminally ill. . . . When is this Congress going to recognize that individuals in their private lives have a right to manage their problems as they see fit without the permission of the big guy in the White House or the big guy in the Justice Department or any of the Lilliputians on this congressional floor? Wake up!" (Drug Policy Alliance, July 10, 2006).

5. A qualification which could be quite broad reaching, although practically speaking, these effects seem captured by criteria of cannabis dependence.

6. Although beyond the scope of this present work, obviously with the United States there is further research to be done regarding the presence of these and other infections currently existent but not revealed for fear of legal retribution.

7

A Kantian Assessment of Cannabis Use and Law

IN A KANTIAN CONSIDERATION OF cannabis use and cannabis law I will rely on his three major works of morality: *Foundations of the Metaphysics of Morals* ("FMM"), *The Critique of Practical Reason* ("CPR"), and *The Metaphysics of Morals* ("MM," consisting of the Doctrine of Justice and the Doctrine of Virtue: "MMDJ," "MMDV"). A presentation of the distinction between virtue and justice (a major focus of MM, with part I of MM being the Doctrine of Justice and part II of MM being the Doctrine of Virtue) shows that for Kant cannabis use is properly considered not as a matter of justice but as a matter of virtue. It is clear that using the law to punish cannabis users is a misapplication of the law/justice. In considering cannabis use a matter of virtue, Kant provides a way to distinguish moral from immoral cannabis use. Most basically, moral cannabis use is done with a motive, or end served through use, while immoral cannabis use is done out of mere inclination with no (rational) end served through use. Kant values reason above all else, indicating any drug which incapacitates reasoning ability is a violation of one's duty to oneself as a rational, dignified being. Enabling reason and imagination would in this regard be a positive, valuable use of a drug (although Kant indicates many times in his moral philosophy it is quite difficult to name specific motivations involved and to completely rule out the involvement of inclinations).

Introduction to Kantian Moral Philosophy

Immanuel Kant continues to be one of the most influential thinkers in the academic study of morality. He captures an intuition that an act is (or at least can be) morally admirable even if no one benefits if it done out of a motivation of duty. Actions done for the sake of duty demonstrate what Kant calls a "law" of moral conduct. This "law" he compares to the physical laws of nature, with moral laws of nature applying to mental beings and physical laws of nature applying to physical objects. Kant emphasizes that by distinguishing physics from morality he thereby salvages human beings from determinism, a mechanistic and purely physical explanation of all human actions.

Consider how Kant divides "material philosophy" into ethics and physics:

> All rational knowledge is either material, and concerns some object, or formal, and is occupied merely with the form of understanding and reason itself and with the universal rules of thinking without regard to distinctions between objects. Formal philosophy is called logic. Material philosophy, however, which has to do with definite objects and the laws to which they are subject, is itself divided into two parts. This is because these laws are either laws of nature or laws of freedom. The science of the former is called physics and that of the latter ethics. The former is also called theory of nature and the latter theory of morals. (Kant 1959, 3)

Kant further distinguishes objects (of physics) from persons (of ethics) as one between the causality of natural necessity and the causality of freedom: "The concept of causality as natural necessity, unlike the concept of causality as freedom, concerns only the existence of things as far as it is determinable in time, and consequently as appearances in contrast to their causality as things in themselves" (Kant 1993, 98–99). And although some explain human actions using physicalistic, natural laws, the same laws used to explain the movements of inanimate objects, Kant emphasizes that in order to preserve freedom, human actions must be regarded as appearing to be deterministic (a matter of physics) but to also include an underlying reality of a thing in itself (implying the existence of a "realty" beyond what appears in space and time):

> Consequently, if we wish still to save it, no other course remains than to ascribe the existence of a thing so far as it is determinable in time, and accordingly its causality under the law of natural necessity, merely to appearance, and to attribute freedom to the same being as a thing in itself. This is absolutely unavoidable if one wishes to maintain both these mutually incompatible concepts; but in applying them, when one wishes to explain them as united in one and the same action and thus explain this union itself, great difficulties turn up, which seem to make such unification impossible. (Kant 1993, 99–100)

A most important concept of Kantian moral philosophy is the human "will." This is variously articulated by Kant as a "capacity for acting according to laws," "faculty" of choosing, equivalent to "practical reason," and that which allows rational beings to act according to principles in "practical" decision making. This faculty is what "recognizes the good" and therefore will be central to a Kantian moral assessment of cannabis use.

> Everything in nature works according to laws. Only a rational being has the capacity of acting according to the conception of laws, i.e., according to principles. This capacity is will. Since reason is required for the derivation of actions from laws, will is nothing else than practical reason. If reason infallibly determines the will, the actions which such a being recognizes as objectively necessary are also subjectively necessary. That is, the will is a faculty of choosing only that which reason, independently of inclination, recognizes as practically necessary, i.e., as good. (Kant 1959, 29)

Although inclinations are important to examine in light of cannabis use, let us instead continue to expand our understanding of Kant's moral world. In the moral world, unlike the physical world, the will is not merely free to act on principle but is free *only when* acting on principle. Consider that "independence from the determining causes of the world of senses (an independence which reason must always ascribe to it) is freedom" (Kant 1959, 71).[1]

Kant articulates freedom as a rational will directing a person's actions. Again, just as physical objects have causes for their movement in the natural world so persons have wills that enable them to cause themselves to act. Freedom is causing oneself to act rather than being caused to act by the natural world (as would happen to an object).

> As will is a kind of causality of living beings so far as they are rational, freedom would be that property of this causality by which it can be effective independently of foreign causes determining it, just as natural necessity is the property of the causality of all irrational beings by which they are determined in their activity by the influence of foreign causes. (Kant 1959, 64)

Freely using cannabis is willingly using and not using because caused to by the natural world, by impulse, out of mere desires and inclinations. Foreign causes here could perhaps be expanded to include a strong desire/appetite for cannabis intoxication (using "unwillingly"). Such causes are of the way of physics, the material world, and therefore resulting actions are not freely (therefore not morally) taken.

In considering any action, and specifically any moral action, Kant would have us understand that a will uses a "means" to attain an "end." For example, a chemotherapy patient uses the "means" of cannabis to attain the "ends" of a reduction of nausea and increased appetite.

> The will is thought of as a faculty of determining itself to action in accordance with the conception of certain laws. Such a faculty can be found only in rational beings. That which serves the will as the objective ground of its self-determination is an end, and, if it is given by reason alone, it must hold alike for all rational beings. On the other hand, that which contains the ground of the possibility of the action, whose result is an end, is called a means.

Moral Cannabis Use: Motivations and Not Mere Inclinations

Cannabis as a substance is a means which contains the ground of the possibility of action (using cannabis) in light of an end which, if rational, will hold for all rational beings. The action we are considering here is cannabis use. The ends of cannabis use, however, is quite varied. I earlier argued the simple dichotomy between medical and recreational use fails to account for several other ends (e.g., intellectual, spiritual).

> The end itself, the enjoyment we seek, is not a [moral] good but only well-being, not a concept of reason but an empirical concept of an object of sensation. Only the use of the means to it, i.e., the action, is called good (because reasonable deliberation is required for it). But, even so, the action is not absolutely good but good only in relation to our sensuous being and its feeling of pleasure or displeasure. The will whose maxims are affected by it is not a pure will, for the latter concerns itself only with that by which pure reason can of itself be practical. (Kant 1993, 65)

Kant would have us recognize as a semantic error labeling cannabis itself "evil" or "bad." For Kant the moral categories and concepts apply to actions and states of will of rational beings not to objects or things (or plants). The cannabis plant in itself is neither moral nor immoral. What is moral or immoral are actions and states of will (neither of which are possibly possessed by the cannabis plant).[2]

> *Good* or *evil* always indicates a relation to the will so far as it is determined by the law of reason to make something its object, for the will is never determined directly by the object and our representation of it; rather, the will is a faculty for making a rule of reason the motive of an action that can make an object real. Thus good or evil is properly referred to actions and not to the sensory state of the person. If something is to be, or is held to be, absolutely good or evil in all respects and without qualification, it could not be a thing but only the manner of acting, i.e., it could be only the maxim of the will, and consequently the acting person himself as a good or evil person. (Kant 1993, 62–63)

Here Kant indicates only a maxim can be absolutely good, with actors good insofar as they act in accordance to this maxim. And to further explain the Kantian concept of ends, consider that ends can be divided or categorized into incentives (desires) and motives (the will):

> The subjective ground of desire is the incentive, while the objective ground of volition is motive. Thus arises the distinction between subjective ends, which rest on incentives, and objective ends, which depend on motives valid for every rational being. (Kant 1959, 45)

In lieu of cannabis use, consider as incentives "euphoria and relaxation" while as motives "to increase interocular eye pressure so as to avoid glaucoma" or "to make art." These are quite different types of end. Consider the Social Reality on cannabis use in the United States It claims that although cannabis users may cite medical *motivations* they are really using cannabis out of *inclinations* and *desires.* It may seem to be on the surface impossible to distinguish cannabis use out of inclinations/desires with or without rational motive. However that the Scientific Reality evidence of motivations for cannabis use makes untenable such reduction of all motivations down to (hedonistic) inclinations.

Consider the distinction made by Kant between inclinations and freedom. This further indicates a contrast between inclinations and desires on the one hand and motivations, will, and freedom on the other:

> Freedom and the consciousness of freedom . . . are independent from inclinations, at least as motives determining (though not as affecting) our desiring; and, so far as I am conscious of freedom in obeying my moral maxims, it is the exclusive source of an unchanging contentment necessarily connected with it and resting on no particular feeling. This may be called intellectual contentment. Sensuous contentment (improperly so called) which rests on the satisfaction of inclinations, however, refined they may be, can never be adequate to that which is conceived under contentment. For inclinations vary; they grow with the indulgence we allow them, and they leave behind a greater void than the one we intended to fill. They are consequently always burdensome to a rational being, and, though he cannot put them aside, they nevertheless elicit from him the wish to be free of them. (Kant 1993, 124)

Kant here provides much to consider in distinguishing moral from immoral cannabis use. Cannabis is used morally if it is done out of motive and not merely inclination or desire. Notice for Kant "sensuous contentment" is an oxymoron, as the sensuous can never conceptually have "contentment." "Contentment" can only result from reason determining the actions of the will. Kant also explains relevant to immoral cannabis use that acting out of inclinations for sensuous pleasure without any use of intellect, "leaves behind a greater void than the one we intended to fill." This seems a major reason to present and discuss with youth at risk for cannabis abuse, inviting them to use their reason to understand the danger of sensuous pleasures as opposed to intellectual contentment. Kant also here reiterates criterion five of (cannabis) dependence: several unsuccessful attempts to quit using. He recognizes of such a person: "though he cannot put them aside, they nevertheless elicit from him the wish to be free of them."

The Moral Test for Cannabis Use: Universal Law

Moving from the general distinction between inclinations and motivations, acting according to desires versus reason and will, consider next that of various motivations the motivation of duty:

> It is an estimation of the worth which far outweighs all the worth of whatever is recommended by the inclinations, and that the necessity of my actions from pure respect of the practical law constitutes duty. To duty every other motive must give place, because duty is the condition of a will good in itself, whose worth transcends everything. (Kant 1959, 20)

Duty is "the condition of a will good in itself." Kant is not applying the term "good" to outcomes and specifically happiness produced (as would Mill). Rather, moral actions are willingly done for the sake of duty. These motivations and states of will produce good actions.

Maintaining the condition of a good will morally speaking trumps all and any inclinations. Kant describes the effect of the law, a command on an individual as "overpowering" inclinations:

> But that which is connected with my will merely as ground and not as a consequence, that which does not serve my inclination but overpowers it or at least excludes it from being considered in making a choice—in a word, law itself—can be an object of respect and thus a command. Now as an act from duty wholly excludes the influence of inclination and therewith every object of the will, nothing remains which can determine the will objectively except the law, and nothing subjectively except pure respect for this practical law. This subjective element is the maxim that I ought to follow such a law even if it thwarts all my inclinations. (Kant 1959, 17)

Here Kant indicates that law should itself determine the will in action even if doing so requires excluding any and all inclinations an individual may have in performing or not performing an action. Consider the distinction already made between inclinations and motivations, consider as mirroring the distinction between "maxims" and "the practical laws." Our maxims (inclinations) are to conform to the practical laws (motivations): A maxim is the subjective principle of volition. The objective principles (i.e., that which would serve all rational beings also subjectively as a practical principle if reason had full power over the faculty of desire) are practical law (Kant 1959, 17). The test all maxims must pass if they are to be morally justified maxims is to be sensibly applied as universal law (similar to the "laws" of physics in the other half of Kant's material philosophy). As Kant puts it: "I should never act in such a way that I could not also will that my maxim should be a universal law" (Kant 1959, 18).

And offering a concrete example of how one would articulate and then test the maxim involved in an action, Kant continues: "Let the question, for example, be: May I, when in distress, make a promise with the intention not to keep it?" (Kant 1959, 18).

To resolve this question, Kant morally reasons:

> The shortest but most infallible way to find the answer to the question as to whether a deceitful promise is consistent with duty is to ask myself: Would I be content that my maxim (of extracting myself from difficulty by a false promise) should hold as a universal law for myself as well as for others? (Kant 1959, 19)

Kant reasons he (as a rational, goal-directed human being) would not want his maxim of making deceitful promises into a universal law, as it would thereby invalidate the very meaning of a "promise" and hence would not make logical sense as a universal law.

Kant (1993) reiterates this test of subjective maxims, of their being sensibly applied as universal laws:

> Practical principles are propositions which contain a general determination of the will, having under it several practical rules. They are subjective, or maxims, when the condition is regarded by the subject as valid only for his will. They are objective, or practical laws, when the condition is recognized as objective, i.e., as valid for the will of every rational being. (Kant 1993, 17)

Continuing this line of thought, of justifying the maxims for our actions (e.g., cannabis use) Kant distinguishes between two types of imperatives under which to evaluate the maxims of our actions:

> If the action is good only as a means to something else, the imperative is hypothetical; but if it is thought of as good in itself, and hence as necessary in a will which of itself conforms to reason as the principle of this will, the imperative is categorical. (Kant 1959, 31)

So to keep a promise is good in itself, not good because it promotes happiness or pleasure of the agents. It is good because it is lawful, of the world of ends, a free act. Using cannabis, on the other hand, is not in itself good. Were all people to use cannabis the world would not thereby be moral or immural, unlike one in which all promises were kept or not kept. Instead, using cannabis is appropriately considered under the *hypothetical* imperative. *If* one has an end which would be furthered by using cannabis *then* using cannabis would be a sensible and beneficial appropriate imperative for one to follow (a "hypothetical" imperative assumes an end which is not held commonly by all rational wills).

Kant also articulates "The categorical imperative, which declares the action to be, of itself, objectively necessary without making any reference to a purpose, i.e., without having any other end" (Kant 1959, 32). Note here that the categorical imperative is necessary regardless of purposes involved. This is a law rational wills cannot break without thereby leaving the realm of morality for that of physics.

> Finally, there is one imperative which directly commands a certain conduct without making its condition some purpose to be reached by it. This imperative is categorical. It concerns not the material of the action and its intended result but the form and the principle from which it results. What is essentially good in it consists in the intention, the result bring what it may. This imperative may be called the imperative of morality. (Kant 1959, 33)

Later in CPR, quite relevant to the questions of the moral status of cannabis use and cannabis law, Kant points out satisfying inclinations (e.g., using cannabis to relax) is not a moral question *unless* "duty is in question":

> Pure practical reason does not require that we should renounce the claims to happiness; it requires only that we take no account of them *whenever duty is in question*. It can even be a duty in certain respects to provide for one's happiness, in part because (since it includes skill, health, and riches) it contains means to the fulfillment of one's duty and in part because the lack of it (e.g., poverty) contains temptations to transgress against duty. But to further one's happiness can never be a direct duty, and even less can it be a principle of all duty. (Kant 1993, 97; emphasis added)

Here Kant opens the door to a way of dealing with cannabis use. Cannabis use becomes morally relevant only "whenever duty is in question." He also acknowledges here the value of subjective inclinations, so that although they must always take a backseat to objective motivations and duties relevant to an action, when there are no such objective motivations or duties to be found an individual can with no moral problem use cannabis.[3]

Consider that cannabis users are using subjective maxims, principles, that in Kantian moral philosophy must conform to the categorical imperative in order to be considered moral. However, and extremely relevant to a Kantian assessment of cannabis use, the action in question *must first* be the type to which the categorical imperative applies.

> Maxims are thus indeed principles, but they are not imperatives. Imperatives themselves, however, when they are conditional, i.e., when they determine the will not as such but only in respect to a desired effect, are hypothetical imperatives, which are practical precepts but not laws. . . . They [laws] must thus be categorical; otherwise they would not be laws, for they would lack the necessity which, in order to be practical, must be completely independent of pathological conditions, i.e., conditions only contingently related to the will. (Kant 1993, 18)

This reiterates the place of each hypothetical and categorical imperative in Kantian moral philosophy. Hypothetical imperatives are seemingly as infinite as our subjective human inclinations. They become of moral concern when they involve the violation of moral duty (e.g., making a false promise). When such a violation happens, we therein find ourselves in the position of having to universalize actions that break duties, something Kant has already said is not possible in the world of ethics, where laws are absolute and never allow the violation of duty regardless of consequence.

As further concrete examples of actions involving each a hypothetical and a categorical imperative, Kant presents first an elder advising a youth to work and save his money in order not to want in his old age. Kant points out that such advice assumes (as an end) the youth wants to live to old age, something he does not necessarily have to do in order to have a good will and act as a rational will. Such saving for old age is therefore a *hypothetical* imperative, because it assumes of another rational will a specific object or inclination (rather than pointing out a duty being violated by not so saving). As an example of a categorical imperative, consider the earlier example of never making a deceitful promise. This imperative is categorical, according to Kant, as promises would not even exist were this a universal law, and so therefore it would be an imperative demanded of every individual as "categorical," referring only to the will, not to any object or inclination of the will of the individuals involved.

Using cannabis with various motivations or ends involved are actions that when taken by an adult, a rational, willing being, are correctly understood as matters for the hypothetical rather than categorical imperative. Any maxim made to universalize cannabis use for medicinal purposes, for recreational uses, etc., could be made, but not sensibly, practically made. This is because such a maxim assumes an inclination for using cannabis (rather than using other medicines or other therapy on the part of potential medical cannabis patients). In other words, one *can* will that cannabis use be made a universal law for several ends (that is, it is theoretically possible), whereas one cannot make a maxim universalizing false promises, as doing so would annihilate the very rational existence of promises (a rational being cannot make such a demand on every other rational will). Again cannabis use falls under the hypothetical imperative in that it depends on the individual and inclinations involved whereas making a false promise is categorical in that it does not depend on the existence of specific motivations on the part of the individual involved but rather applies to any rational (moral) being.

"To secure one's own happiness is at least indirectly a duty, for discontent with one's condition under pressure from many cares and amid unsatisfied wants could easily become a great temptation to transgress duties" (Kant 1959, 15). Here Kant presents the makings of an argument supporting cannabis use as a way for some people to "secure their happiness." One major effect of cannabis use is "relaxation," and Kant here points out one is to avoid "discontent with one's condition" (relax) because one may end up transgressing more duties than one would were one to simply secure one's own happiness. Consider also that Kant argues there simply exists no possible way to prescribe a way of life which would lead to happiness for all rational human beings.

> Now it is impossible even for a most clear-sighted and most capable but finite being to form here a definite concept of that which he really wills. If he wills riches, how much anxiety, envy, and intrigue might he not thereby draw upon his shoulders! If he wills much knowledge and vision, perhaps it might become only an eye that much sharper to show him as more dreadful the evils which are now hidden from him and which are yet unavoidable, or to burden his desires—which already sufficiently engage him—with even more needs! If he wills a long life, who guarantees that it will not be long misery? If he wills at least health, how often has not the discomfort of the body restrained him from excesses into which perfect health would have led him? In short, he is not capable, on any principle and with complete certainty, of ascertaining what would make him truly happy: omniscience would be needed for this. He cannot, therefore, act according to definite principles so as to be happy, but only according to empirical counsels, e.g., those of diet, economy, courtesy, restraint, etc., which are shown by experience best to promote welfare on the average. Hence the imperatives of prudence cannot, in the strict sense, command, i.e., present actions objectively as practically necessary; thus they are to be taken as counsels (*consilia*) rather than as commands (*praecepta*) of reason, and the task of determining infallibly and universally what actions will promote the happiness of a rational being is completely unsolvable. (Kant 1959, 36)

The reason Kant gives for not commanding strict obedience to a certain way of living in order to bring about happiness is that it would require omniscience to know such a way of life, one assuring the production of happiness for each and every individual. Kant considers matters of individual happiness, given the wide variety of preferences involved, ones of *prudence* not of morality; prudential imperatives are a type of hypothetical imperative and therefore presuppose certain ends of the individuals considering the imperative. Legally attempting to disallow the use of available empirical councils of cannabis use (e.g., Scientific Reality on cannabis use and its effects) is futile and in this Kantian line of argument, senseless. A major implication for cannabis prohibition given the Kantian claim there can be no way to objectively (legally) prescribe ways of life to bring happiness, is that it cannot be claimed cannabis must be prohibited *because it is inconsistent with a life of happiness.* This Kantian line of argument generally leads to tolerance for different inclinations and preferences of others. Tolerance in Kantian terms has one bear with the subjective inclinations of others (when those inclinations are not violating any duties in the process).

Cannabis Prohibition and Criminalization as Unjustified Violence

For Kant the proper place for consideration of cannabis use is in the *Doctrine of Virtue* and not in the *Doctrine of Justice*, as a moral issue rather than one of law. To enforce laws (justice) against cannabis use (ethics) is to enforce punishments against immoral actions rather than unjust actions. This is a misuse of justice. As Ladd puts it, duties of virtue and duties of justice are mutually exclusive:

> Only duties to others and those that are owed could satisfy this requirement of enforceability, for one obviously could not enforce duties to oneself and should not enforce duties the omission of which is not wrong. It follows from this that all duties that are not duties of justice are duties of virtue, and duties of justice and duties of virtue form two mutually exclusive classes of duties. (Ladd 1999, xx)

Ladd also explains the Kantian distinction between law and ethics:

> In sum, justice (Law) is distinguished from ethics in that (1) it is the subject of external legislation, (2) it relates only to duties of justice, and (3) it is concerned only with external actions in relation to others. Insofar as ethics is especially concerned with the duties of virtue, it excludes theory of justice; but insofar as, in ethical legislation, it is generally concerned with all duties whatsoever, it also includes theory of justice. (Ladd 1999, xx)

Cannabis use, as involving indirect duty to oneself and a concern of attaining virtue, is not a matter for justice at all. Furthermore, it is noted here ethics *includes* theory of justice. In other words, is inclusive of or on a higher level than. As such it can be used to assess and correct the theory of justice. Kant would eliminate both cannabis prohibition and criminalization in lieu of this logical distinction between duties of virtue and duties of justice. Consider Ladd's presentation of liberty "as demanding legitimate enforcement of justice/law":

> Kant's doctrine of justice and law turns on the concept of coercion. Law is conceived as a coercive order, and justice treats only what can be made a matter of coercion (that is, an object of external legislation). The principles of justice themselves determine the legitimate and illegitimate uses of coercion. The legitimate use of coercion is coercion that accords with liberty and the illegitimate use is one that transgresses liberty. The illegitimate use of coercion is called violence (*Gewalt*). (Ladd 1999, xxxv)

The law prohibiting the use of cannabis does violence to cannabis users. Cannabis prohibition and criminalization are *not in accord with* the liberty of cannabis users but rather *transgresses* their liberty. Ladd recognizes there also is a duty to obey political authorities (e.g., the law prohibiting cannabis use):

> The foundation of political authority, then, is a person's innate right to live in peace and freedom, which, incidentally, includes the right to have one's property secure and guaranteed. Everyone has a duty to obey the political authorities because they represent the rule of law, and, in obeying them, a person is *ipso facto* respecting the rights of others to live in peace and freedom. Accordingly, it is the rule of law that provides the final basis of political authority and political obedience, rather than, as for Locke, a presumed contractual relation among the citizens or between the people and the ruler (Kant doubts that such a contract every took place and maintains that, even if it had taken place, it could not provide the basis of political authority.) (Ladd 1999, xxxvi)

The "rule of law" preserves peace and freedom. Therefore any breach of the rule of law (e.g., illegal cannabis use) overtly threatens freedom and peace, rights of human beings that pre-exist civil societies. Perhaps the duty to not break U.S. federal law by using cannabis for any reason is being used by the Social Reality of cannabis use. In response, it is crucially important to recognize the duty to obey current public laws can be trumped by rights one has by virtue of being a person (aside from being born into and contributing to a particular civil society). These rights pre-exist political authority and any rule of law. As Ladd explains Kant's position:

> The main function of the civil state, therefore, is to maintain the rule of law, to guarantee and protect the rights of its subjects. This he calls the juridical condition of society, the state of public justice, legal justice. The individual rights to be secured are not, however, themselves, created by the civil society. They already exist in a state of nature, albeit only *provisionally* and not *peremptorily*. Hence, it is not the function of the state to create rights, but only to enforce them and to adjudicate disputes concerning them. (Ladd 1999, xxxviii)

And Ladd then points out there can be made laws (*Gesetze*) which may or may not coincide with the deeper sense of justice (*Recht*), and specifically with respect for human rights that pre-exist society and human-made laws:

> But that is not the whole of the story, because the state itself, as a law-making body (sovereignty), can make binding laws (*Gesetze*) for various purposes, including the common good, taxation, criminal justice, and so on. These come under the public Law (or justice) and may or may not coincide with justice in the sense of *Recht* (*ius*). (Ladd 1999, xxxviii)

Equality of Cannabis and Alcohol Users

Moving from Ladd into the *Doctrine of Justice* itself, consider the final section of Kant's own introduction in light of the double standard that currently exists in the United States between the use of alcohol (legal) and cannabis (illegal): "*Freedom* (independence from the constraints of another person's will), insofar as it [this freedom] is compatible with the freedom of everyone else in accordance with a universal law, is the one sole and original right belonging to every person by virtue of his humanity" (Kant 1999, 38).

And related,

> [This is] innate *equality*, that is, independence from being bound by others to do more than one can also reciprocally bind them to do. Thus, it is the property of a person's being his own master (*sui iuris*) comparable to being a respectable and innocent person (*iusti*), who, before any juridical act, has done no wrong to anyone. (Kant 1999, 38)

The otherwise law-abiding cannabis user who has "done no wrong to anyone" is being criminalized by a society whose alcohol use, rampant use of synthetic drugs, *he tolerates*. The inequality here is between the rights recognized of alcohol users and those not recognized of cannabis users.

As a further Kantian line of argument denouncing cannabis prohibition and criminalization, consider that Kant explicitly provides a way to morally-assess laws (allowing for another way of providing a Kantian assessment of current U.S. cannabis law and the criminalization of cannabis users). Kant puts forth a categorical imperative "concerning punishment" which must be met *by all laws:*

> Judicial punishment (*poena forensis*) is entirely distinct from natural punishment (*poena naturalis*). In natural punishment, vice punishes itself, and this fact is not taken into consideration by the legislator. Judicial punishment can never be used merely as a means to promote some other good for the criminal himself or for civil society, but instead it must in all cases be imposed on him only on the ground that he has committed a crime; for a human being can never be manipulated merely as a means to the purposes of someone else and can never be included among objects of the Law of things [*Sachenrecht*]. His innate Personality [that is, his right as a Person] protects him against such treatment, even though he may indeed be condemned to forfeit his civil Personality. He must first be found to be deserving of punishment before any consideration is given to the utility of this punishment for himself or for his fellow citizens. The law concerning punishment is a categorical imperative. (Kant 1999, 138)

As the U.S. federal government criminalizes cannabis users so as to "send a message" to citizens about the dangers of cannabis use, it thereby "manipulates them as a mere means." And of the very idea of legally punishing cannabis users, consider the standard to be used by Kant: "Only the Law of retribution (*ius talionis*) can determine exactly the kind and degree of punishment" (Kant 1999, 138). Of course, cannabis users are not harming others who are seeking compensation. The vast majority of cannabis arrests through the utilization of confidential informants, drug task forces, etc., and are not reported as having caused harm to others. The question begged by addressing cannabis use as an issue of law and specifically retribution is this: Who, exactly, is being compensated by criminalizing cannabis users? Without harms addressed, the Kantian conclusion here and throughout is that laws that prohibit rational adult human beings the use of cannabis and laws that criminalize and punish these rational human beings for using or merely possessing cannabis are both immoral.

Cannabis Use and Adolescents: Feeling Their Own Worth

In section 28 of the *Doctrine of Justice* (of MM) Kant also considers, relevant to cannabis use by adolescents, "The Rights of a Domestic Group—Second Subdivision, Parental Rights." Parents are the institution responsible for children by virtue of having chosen to create them:

> Just as from the duty of human beings to themselves, that is, to the humanity in their own Persons, arises the personal right of the two sexes mutually to acquire each other in a *real* way through marriage, so from the procreation in this union follows a duty to support and care for its products, that is, the children. As Persons, the children have thereby at the same time an original inborn (not an inherited) right to be cared for by their parents, until they are able to take care of themselves; actually this right comes directly from the law (*lege*) without any special juridical act being required for it. (Kant 1999, 91)

Kant would likely support positive reinforcement, interest, and involvement by parents in raising children. He would likely also oppose the parental styles associated with increased risk of cannabis use (i.e., alcoholic, non-consuming and condemning, over-demanding, overly protective) as they are not intended toward the end of providing the opportunity to feel their own dignity and moral worth, ultimately learning how to make (free) moral decisions on their own.

Kant advises parents to not merely expose children to a wide variety of activities but to also indicate those ends admirable themselves. Admirable actions are qualitatively different than those taken out of mere subjective inclinations and have different objects and ends. Parents should above all point out and emphasize the morality of acts done for the sake of duty, contrasted to those obviously done without motivation of duty:

> Since in early youth we do not know what ends may occur to us in the course of life, parents seek to let their children learn a great many things and provide for skill in the use of means to all sorts of arbitrary ends among which they cannot determine whether any one of them may later become an actual purpose of their pupil, though it is possible that he may some day have it as his actual purpose. And this anxiety is so great that they commonly neglect to form and correct their judgment on the worth of things which they may make their ends. (Kant 1959, 32–33)

Kant (1993) also indicates that teaching children to act according to duty (i.e., morally) they must be taught through what seem like two stages (also imagine the general applicability in a therapeutic setting):

> Certainly it cannot be denied that in order to bring either an as yet uneducated or a degraded mind into the path of the morally good, some preparatory guidance is needed to attract it by a view to its own advantage or to frighten it by fear of harm. As soon as this machinery, these leading strings, has had some effect, the pure moral motive must be brought to mind. This is not only because it is the sole ground of character (a consistent practical habit of mind according to unchangeable maxims) but also because, in teaching a man to feel his own

> worth, it gives his mind a power, unexpected even by himself, to pull himself loose from all sensuous attachments (so far as they would fain dominate him) and, in the independence of his intelligible nature and in the greatness of soul to which he sees himself called, to find himself richly compensated for the sacrifice he makes. (Kant 1993, 158)

This power to resist sensuous attachments and to feel one's own worth is essential for raising adolescents who will resist temptations to experiment with cannabis via peer pressure, alienation, and other associated risk factors. The greatness of soul and rich compensation should be celebrated in actions demonstrating these in the life an adolescent. Perhaps this is absent from parenting styles leading to cannabis experimentation (and riskier behaviors generally), as these adolescents have not discovered their power (of dignity and self-worth) to overcome peer pressure nor have they begun to develop a healthy acceptance of their duty (and faith in the long-term value of their currently dutiful actions).

This power to resist inclinations is a crucial part of Kantian morality training and of experiencing oneself as a dignified rational being of a kind different from mere natural objects. Wielding this power, utilizing the "strongest drive to the good," is crucial for moral actors:

> We should prove, by observations which anyone can make, that this property of our minds, this receptivity to a pure moral interest and the moving force in the pure thought of virtue when properly commended to the human heart, is the strongest drive to the good and indeed the only one when it is a question of continuous and meticulous obedience to moral maxims. (Kant 1993, 158)

Kant recommends to educators of youth the technique of making a game of recognizing good conduct (actions taken dutifully) and condemning bad conduct (inclinations overcoming duty). "By comparing similar actions under various circumstances, they could begin to exercise the moral judgment of their pupils in making the greater or lesser moral significance of the actions" (Kant 1993, 160). And rather than lecturing and "talking-down-to" children, parents should encourage children to exercise their newly acquired sense of power to make moral judgments, focused on their newly realized sense of duty.

> They would find that even very young people, who are not yet ready for speculation of other kinds, would soon become very acute and not a little interested, since they would feel the progress of their power of judgment; what is most important, they could confidently hope that frequent practice of knowing and approving of good conduct in all its purity, and of noting even the least deviation from it with sorrow or contempt, would leave a lasting impression of esteem for the one and disgust for the other, even though this practice is pursued only as a game of judgment in which children could compete with one another. By the

> mere habit of frequently looking upon actions as praiseworthy or blameworthy, a good foundation would be laid for righteousness in the future course of life. (Kant 1993, 160)

Relevant here are role models and specifically those role models encouraged and discouraged by parents. Aside from being role models themselves, the most powerful ones in the lives of children and young adolescents, the role models esteemed by parents indicate what is praiseworthy and what is blameworthy. Kant suggests that by learning to also discern praiseworthy actions a good foundation will be laid for righteousness in the future. It must be emphasized in light of cannabis use among adolescents that negative parenting styles seem to fail in having the child and adolescent feel his own self-worth, perhaps including morally lacking role models glorified by parents. A negative foundation laid may manifest itself in many of the 18–25- year-old age group, who currently shows the highest incidence of recreational cannabis use.

Kant explains how to use a story to teach a 10-year-old about the moral feeling, an introduction to pure virtue. In the story an honest man is offered substantial advantages and gain to act against a clearly recognized duty. If he does not violate duty, he suffers clear and substantial loss. If he violates the duty he will not be caught and experience substantial gain. In the story told he chooses to suffer and continue to do his duty even though he could by breaking his duty gain substantial advantages. "[A]t the moment when he wishes never to have lived to see the day which brings him such unutterable pain—think of him without any wavering or even a doubt remaining true to his resolution to be truthful" (Kant 1993, 162). A child who follows this story is invited to experience the emotions of the man and the reason for his decision to do his duty, and to imagine himself similarly choosing. Even though he suffers very significant negative consequences the goal is for the child to realize the same faculty of the will to act primarily for the sake of principle (not inclination or desire) exists in him. As Kant explains this point concerning the moral action of the man of the story, "Yet virtue is here worth so much only because it costs so much, not because it brings any advantage" (Kant 1993, 162). Kant emphasizes the intentional omission by the storyteller of any benefits to be accrued by the moral actor, "unmixed with any view to welfare, because it is in suffering that they most notably show themselves" (Kant 1993, 162). And as a conclusion here in the text: "Consequently, duty, not merit, has not only the most definite influence but, when seen in the true light of its inviolability, also the most penetrating influence on the mind" (Kant 1993, 163).

Again, Kantian training of children and adolescents would encourage a sort of morality game played with their parents. This sort of training leads to "make judging according to moral laws a natural occupation which accompanies our own free actions as well as our observations of those others, and to make it, as it were, a habit" (Kant 1993, 165). Kant explains that moral actions by definition go beyond mere inclination to a motivation to always act lawfully. In this way the action has moral worth as a disposition because of the maxim from which it was done" (Kant 1993, 166). The labor for the child in morality training involves experiencing pain in resisting inclinations:

> By this, the pupil's attention is held to the consciousness of his freedom; and, although this renunciation [of the sensuous] excites an initial feeling of pain, at the same time, by relieving him of the constraint even of his true needs it frees him from the manifold discontent in which all these needs involve him and makes his mind receptive to the feeling of contentment from other sources. (Kant 1993, 167)

The hoped-for result of this Kantian storytelling is a disposition whereby adolescents can feel their inner worth and power as members of the moral realm of ends possessing inherent dignity. Always acting with respect for dignity of rational beings (including ourselves) is at the core of Kantian morality. The challenge in teaching children and adolescents is to have them feel this, get in touch with this, experience this inner power of the will (and dignity, worth in themselves) at an early age, preparing them to use this feeling to guide them in their future (unsupervised) moral decision making. Kant suggests that such training will enable one to pass a major moral test of character, to act according to duty although one could easily and without detection benefit by violating that duty.

> In a case where I alone know that injustice lies in what I do, and where an open confession of it and an offer to make restitution is in direct conflict with vanity, selfishness, and an otherwise not illegitimate antipathy to the man whose rights I have impaired, if I can set aside all these considerations, there is consciousness of an independence from inclinations and circumstances and of the possibility of being sufficient to myself, which is salutary for me in yet other respects. The law of duty, through the positive worth which obedience to it makes us feel, finds easier access through the respect for ourselves in the consciousness of our freedom. If it is well established, so that a man fears nothing more than to find himself on self-examination to be worthless and contemptible in his own eyes, every good moral disposition can be grafted on to this self-respect, for the consciousness of freedom is the best, indeed the only, guard that can keep ignoble and corrupting influences from bursting in upon the mind. (Kant 1993, 167–68)

In the very brief conclusion to *The Doctrine of Virtue*, part II, "The Ethical Doctrine of Method," Kant presents an example of a "moral catechism" whereby a pupil is led through dialogue to understand moral duty in the proper way. After presenting an example of just such a dialogue, Kant explains (among other things) that:

> It is the *shamefulness* of vice, not its *harmfulness* (to the agent himself), that must be emphasized above all. For unless the dignity of virtue is exalted above everything else in actions, then the concept of duty itself vanishes and dissolves into mere pragmatic precepts, since man's consciousness of his own nobility then disappears and he is for sale and can be bought for a price that the seductive inclinations offer him. (Kant 1964, 156)

This is a very important point in light of teaching adolescents (and adults) about cannabis dependence. Rather than its harmfulness, Kant would recommend that the *shamefulness* of adolescent cannabis use (out of mere inclinations, peer pressure) must be emphasized above all else. Shame and self-respect, dignity and duty, rather than adverse consequences, are concepts of moral training qua Kant.

Consider in addition to shame the closely related concept of humiliation and the similar role it plays in training and teaching youth. Humiliation is an emotion which also indicates a sense of dignity and moral worth, without which one is bound to be led to develop a shameless type of existence.

> The moral law . . . completely excludes the influence of self-love from the highest practical principle and forever checks self-conceit, which decrees the subjective conditions of self-love as laws. If anything checks our self-conceit in our own judgment, it humiliates. Therefore, the moral law inevitably humbles every man when he compares the sensuous propensity of his nature with the law. Now if the idea of something as the motive of the will humiliates us in our self-consciousness, it awakens respect for itself so far as it is a positive motive. The moral law, therefore, is even subjectively a cause of respect. (Kant 1993, 77–78)

And further on this sense of dignity in part III, "On Servility," Kant states:

> But man regarded as a *person*—that is, as the subject of morally practical reason—is exalted above any price; for as such (*homo noumenon*) he is not to be valued as a mere means to the ends of others or even to his own ends, but as an end in himself. He possesses, in other words, a *dignity* (an absolute inner worth) by which he exacts *respect* for himself from all other rational beings in the world: he can measure himself with every other being of his kind and value himself on a footing of equality with them. (Kant 1964, 99)

Humility involves an appreciation for the power we have as persons to act in a dutiful way. As explained from the outset, properly understood, persons are only free when acting according to laws, morally acting when in accord with universalizable maxims. Kant captures this feeling of reverence for ourselves as inherently valuable and not for sale:

> True humility follows inevitably from our sincere and strict comparison of ourselves with the moral law (its holiness and strictness). But along with it comes exaltation and the highest self-esteem, as the feeling of our inner worth (*valor*), when we realize that we are capable of this inner legislation, and the (natural) man feels himself compelled to reverence the (moral) man in his own person. By virtue of this worth we are not for sale at any price (*pretium*) and possess an inalienable dignity (*dignitas interna*) which instills in us reverence (*reverentia*) for ourselves. (Kant 1964, 101)

The very experience of humiliation is a rough way of testing an action regarding its morality/immorality, especially in light of cannabis use. Some adult users may experience humiliation using cannabis while others may not. Perhaps humiliation reveals questionable inclinations of the cannabis user. This seems true if cannabis is being used for hedonistic reasons but not true for those using cannabis to rational ends. Given the humiliation insisted upon by the Social Reality in the United States at the very idea of using cannabis, users may be confused about whether or not they do or should experience humiliation at the use of cannabis.[4] Medicinal cannabis users who are not humiliated by their use are *resentful* of the Social Reality demand that they be humiliated. But for the U.S. policy they would not experience humiliation any more than others currently experience in their routine use of various medications or consumption of alcohol.

The point relevant to the question of moral cannabis use is that shamefulness and humiliation indicate a sense of dignity. By acknowledging and experiencing these emotions an individual is thereby able to wield a "power" of acting according to moral law, to the categorical imperative, and resist use inconsistent with the moral law. The categorical imperative, the putting into universal law the maxim for one's actions, provides a power to resist inclinations (utilizing humiliation to do so).

> Therefore, respect for the moral law must be regarded also as a positive but indirect effect of the law on feeling, in so far as the law weakens the hindering influence of the inclinations through humiliating self-conceit; consequently, we must see it as a subjective motive of activity, as a drive to obey the law and as the ground of maxims of a course of life conformable to the law. (Kant 1993, 82–83)

The categorical imperative *humiliates* self-conceit and therefore is itself a motive of activity. In other words, one motive of the several we may have in any particular situation is to resist actions that would have us experience "humiliating self-conceit." The law itself motivates us to resist acting in some particular way. Implied here is the sense of freedom one may have in choosing to act in a shameful and humiliating way is a false sense of freedom. Over-indulgence in cannabis may be just such a false sense of freedom. For Kant, overcoming such over-indulgent cannabis use would have one realize freedom is acting in a lawful, moral way. As a means of therapy and education for the cannabis dependent users, the development of a sense of shame and humiliation is crucial.

Direct Duty to Oneself: Against Immoderate Use of "Vegetable Products"

At this point I will present four types of duty articulated by Kant. In addition to better clarifying this concept the distinction allows a way to further locate cannabis use in Kantian moral philosophy and critically assess the use of laws/justice to prohibit use and criminalize users.

"We shall now enumerate some duties, adopting the usual division of them into duties to ourselves and to others and into perfect and imperfect duties" (Kant 1959, 39).

Direct Duty to Oneself

1. A man in despair wants to commit suicide. "One immediately sees a contradiction in a system of nature whose law would be to destroy life by the feeling whose special office is to impel the improvement of life" (Kant 1959, 40).

Direct Duty to Others

2. A man forced to borrow money, promises to repay even though he knows he will not be able to repay. "The maxim of his action would be as follows: When I believe myself to be in need of money, I will borrow money and promise to repay it, although I know I shall never do so." "It would make the promise itself and the end to be accomplished by it impossible" (Kant 1959, 40).

Indirect Duty to Oneself

3. "A third finds in himself a talent which could, by means of some cultivation, make him in many respects a useful man. But he finds himself in comfortable circumstances and prefers indulgence in pleasure to troubling himself with broadening and improving his fortunate natural gifts. Now, however, let him ask whether his maxim of neglecting his gifts, besides agreeing with his propensity to idle amusement, agrees also with what is called duty." "But he cannot possibly will that this should become a universal law of nature or that it should be implanted in us by a natural

instinct. For, as a rational being, he necessarily wills that all his faculties should be developed, inasmuch as they are given to him for all sorts of possible purposes" (Kant 1959, 41).

Indirect Duty to Others

4. A man sees others struggle with great hardships but has no desire to contribute to them; "For a will which resolved this would conflict with itself, since instances can often arise in which he would need the love and sympathy of others, and in which he would have robbed himself, by such a law of nature springing from his own will, of all hope of the aid he desires" (Kant 1959, 41).

Suicide here would violate a direct duty to oneself, a false promise a direct duty to others, the idler an indirect duty to oneself, and unsympathetic noncontributory an indirect duty to others. Cannabis use quite apparently involves a duty to oneself, whether direct or indirect. The third situation, of the idler, seems quite relevant to a moral assessment of cannabis use. Kant describes the idler (cannabis dependent?) in the following way: "in order to escape from burdensome circumstances, he destroys himself, he uses a person merely as a means to maintain a tolerable condition up to the end of life. . . . I cannot dispose of man in my own person so as to mutilate, corrupt, or kill him" (Kant 1959, 47). Roughly put, if cannabis use is merely pleasurable and an inclination but not being used to develop natural gifts toward the attainment of ends then it is immoral as a violation of one's duty to oneself.

The very fact that the most relevant duty involved is a duty to oneself has monumental implications for cannabis prohibition and criminalization (e.g., there exists no clear rationale for retributive justice; legislating violations of duties to ourselves would likely put most people in jail). Further, rather than applying to all cannabis users, it would seem to render immoral only abusers and users meeting most of the cannabis dependence criteria.

In DV, the second part of MM, we come to the most relevant part of Kant's moral philosophy regarding the question of when cannabis use is moral and immoral. As DV in part I dealt with the law, it is implicit in dealing now with virtue that enforceable punishment would be senseless. This is primarily because for Kant morality is essentially a question of proper motivation and free will, logically not something that can be legally forced. Of this second part of MM, there are two parts. Part I of DV is on "Duties to Oneself" and part II on "Duties of Virtue to Other Men." Kant explains there are two types of duty to oneself: self-preservation and perfecting oneself. As an animal and moral being a person has two different types of duty to oneself. As an animal being, persons have duties to preserve themselves, their species, and their ability to enjoy pleasures of life. Vices corresponding to these duties are "*self-murder*, the unnatural use of his *sexual desire*, and such *immoderate consumption of food and drink* as weakens his capacity for using his powers purposefully" (Kant 1964, 83). As a *moral* being man is "prohibited" against "robbing himself of a moral being's *prerogative*—that of acting in accordance with principles (i.e. inner freedom)—and so making himself a plaything of the mere inclinations and hence a thing" (Kant 1964, 83). The corresponding moral vices are lying, avarice, and false humility (servility). These six total vices are elaborated on by Kant and constitute the main content of part I of DV.

Beginning with the three animal vices generally and before moving to consider first self-murder, he explains again that acting against these duties can have one "depriving oneself (permanently or temporarily) of one's *capacity* for the natural *use* (and so indirectly the moral *use*) of one's powers" (Kant 1964, 84). He discusses each of these in turn, with article I "On Suicide," article II "On Carnal Self-Defilement," and article III "On Self-Stupefaction by the Immoderate Use of Food and Drink." The third article here (section 8 of DV) is arguably the most relevant text by Kant in his three works of moral philosophy directed at the specific question of when and why cannabis use becomes immoral (i.e., a violation of a duty to oneself). Before exploring this most important section, note that in addition to these three articles discussing natural duties to oneself as an animal being Kant goes on to consider the duties men have by virtue of their rationality and moral being, duties here against lying, avarice, and servility. None of these seems close to being as relevant to the question of moral cannabis use as is article III regarding the natural duty to ourselves as animal beings to refrain from immoderate use of food and drink. It is to this article III that I now turn.

Kant begins his explanation for why self-stupefaction, a "kind of intemperance," is a vice. He explains that it is not because one harms one's body, as this sort of reason is one concerning prudence and happiness, not morality. He instead explains, "Brutish intemperance in the use of food and drink is the misuse of the means of nourishment, whereby our ability to use them rationally is hindered or exhausted. *Drunkenness* and *gluttony* are the vices that come under this heading" (Kant 1964, 90). Kant considers it a violation of duty to oneself to put oneself in such a condition as to be rationally incapacitated as a result of consuming food or drink (or cannabis). Of drunkenness, Kant explains it "is commonly brought about by fermented drinks, but it can also result from other narcotics, such as opium and other vegetable products" (Kant 1964, 91). Kant is focused on the sedatives and opiates here, and although he brings in "vegetable products" he most likely intends very potent hashish (given the time and place of Kant's writing). Incapacitating oneself through the use of cannabis (perhaps as cannabis dependence, clinically speaking) is a violation of a direct duty to oneself as a rational (therefore moral, free) being.

Given my chapter 1 consideration of the five types of drugs, Kant seems less focused on the relaxation and potentially thought-provoking cannabis effects and more on those drugs that have one lose control, black out, and otherwise lose reasoning ability.

Of these drugs and the moral problem with their effects, Kant explains that "The temptation to use these lies it the fact that they produce, for a time, a state of fancied happiness, a freedom from care, and even illusory strength; but dejection and weakness follow and, worst of all, a need to repeat the narcotics and in so doing to increase them is established" (Kant 1964, 91). Kant demonstrates his understanding of drug use here, focusing on what clinicians would refer to as a felt need to use again, need to use more, and overall a temporary but illusory escape from care, followed by weakness. For those cannabis users who are motivated to escape, who meet criteria of cannabis abuse and/or dependence, Kant here condemns them as violating their duty to themselves.

Kant argues also that "Gluttony is even lower than drunkenness in so far as it engages merely sense as a passive condition and not, as does drunkenness, the imagination, which does afford an active play of representations and hence gluttony is even closer to the pleasure of cattle" (Kant 1964, 91). Here Kant seems to allow for moral cannabis use in so far as it "engages the imagination," consistent with spiritual, religious, philosophical, and artistic uses of cannabis. Kant also makes the same point made time and again by reports on cannabis by various appointed commissions in the twentieth century, namely that there is no clear rational line to be drawn in society between licit and illicit drugs. Currently the early twenty-first-century United States has a significant focus on the skyrocketing obesity rate and yet, morally speaking, one rarely if ever finds moral arguments made against rampant and habitual gluttony, a vice arguably more undutiful than cannabis use.

In addition to labeling different sections of DV as "articles" and dealing with each vice (failure to meet a duty to oneself as a rational being) he also follows up each of these with what he calls "Casuistical Questions." These sections essentially have Kant play a critic of the section he just presented, providing cases (hence "casuistry" or case-based reasoning) in which the points of the previous section are questioned. Following article III on Self-Stupefaction by the Immoderate Use of Food and Drink, the casuistical questions he provides seem to be a defense of drug use as what we currently would refer to as being a "social lubricant." He challenges the condemnation of drunkenness with the following: "Can we at least justify, if not extol, a use of wine bordering on intoxication, on the ground that it enlivens the company's conversation and combines it with frankness?" It is unclear what "bordering on" intoxication means, and I think instead Kant should have referred to one who is intoxicated (a "user" rather than "abuser") and thereby enlivened in conversation. In response to this line, a suspicious Kant warns: "But who can determine the measure for a man who is only too ready to pass into a state where he has no clear eye for *measuring*? The use of opium and spirits comes closer to degradation since the illusory state of well-being they procure makes the user silent, reticent, and withdrawn: they are therefore permissible only as medicines" (Kant 1964, 91). Again, Kant is suspicious of opiates as recreational drugs, moving beyond "wine" to focus on the harder drugs, harkening again to sedatives and opiates, away from cannabis. He provides the results of silence, reticence, and being withdrawn here as a further way of assessing the morality/immorality of cannabis use (but more appropriately other drug use). Note also that Kant explicitly recognizes the medicinal justification for such symptoms and a state (implicitly providing justification for medicinal use of drugs, cannabis). Kant concludes this article III with an explicit recognition of the virtue of temperance as essentially involved in the question of drug use: "intemperance, which is a violation of duty to oneself" (Kant 1964, 92).

Notes

1. Kant recognizes that he cannot prove this most basic metaphysical claim of there being a reality, a free will, beyond the physical world, what he refers to as "the idea of freedom." He acknowledges the "doubtful" nature of freedom: "freedom is only an idea of reason whose objective reality in itself is doubtful" (Kant 1959, 75) and also of the "Idea of freedom," . . . "how this presupposition itself is possible can never be discerned by any human reason" (Kant 1959, 80). Finally:

> Freedom is a mere idea. . . . It holds only as the necessary presupposition of reason in a being that believes itself conscious of a will, i.e., of a faculty different from the mere faculty of desire, or a faculty of determining itself to act as intelligence and thus according to laws of reason independently of natural instincts. (Kant 1959, 78–79)

2. Weil and Rosen (2004) would strongly agree with Kant here, frequently emphasizing one of his main points about drugs and drug use, that drugs themselves are not bad but (as he puts it) people's relationships to drugs are bad (of course, there could not for Kant be a "relationship" between an object and a person, but rather between two people in the "realm of ends"; this is not to imply Weil intends a literal sense of "relationship").

3. Perhaps this can be loosely described as a type of leisure or recreational time for free, dignified individuals pursuing happiness.

4. This given such an action, although illegal, could be universalized under various formulations of maxims, specifically regarding self-preservation, promotion of health, for example.

8

Aristotle on Cannabis Use and Law: The "Means" of Temperance and Justice

THE FOLLOWING CONSIDERATION OF Aristotelian virtue ethics will be applied to various aspects of cannabis use and the current U.S. federal law forbidding and criminalizing its use. The focus is on Aristotle's major work of morality, *Nichomachean Ethics* ("NE"), from which I provide relevant text, articulation, and application to the nature and morality of cannabis use as well as a consideration of the justice of cannabis law. Primary points relevant to cannabis use are made with Aristotle's presentation of two specific virtues, temperance and justice.

To approach temperance, I first point out the process of moral virtue development involves an individual, a soul we know through its attributes (or capacities, of nutrition/reproduction, sensation, appetite, reason). This development is intentionally aiming at a certain type of balanced relation between the various capacities, as a "disposition" or "character" which is and produces virtuous actions. Specifically applied to cannabis use is the virtue temperance. Temperance will be understood primarily as what Aristotle articulates as a "mean" or middle between two extremes, self-indulgence and boorishness. Immoral use of cannabis is "self-indulgent" while an attitude promoting absolute abstention is "boorishness."

The virtue most relevant to the central questions concerning cannabis law is justice. Before articulating and applying the Aristotelian idea of a mean to be attained for a *law* to be just, recognize for Aristotle the specific law (e.g., U.S. federal law prohibiting cannabis use) in place at any point in time has no bearing on whether or not it is just. Instead, a focused consideration must be made on whether a law is too extreme in retribution or in distribution, giving too much or too little of what one is due. In addition to the consideration of justice as a mean between extremes, Aristotle provides other points about justice relevant to cannabis law.

Nichomachean Ethics and Moral Virtue as Applied to Cannabis Use and Law

Humans are not born moral but rather become so only through repeatedly acting in a morally virtuous way. Again, given we are born with all possible faculties of the soul, but do not for many years discover and develop our practical and speculative powers, the need for experience in order to develop these is apparent. In book II of NE, "Moral Virtue, How Produced, in What Medium and In What Manner Exhibited," Aristotle concludes: "Neither by nature, then, nor contrary to nature do the virtues arise in us; rather we are adapted by nature to receive them, and are made perfect by habit" (NE, book II, section 1, 28). To be "adapted by nature" is to be capable of learning how to use the faculties we are born possessing (or will potentially develop through natural growth). Adapting involves learning how to control and direct our appetites and specifically desires. Learning such control is demonstrated by the exercise of practical reasoning and in considering implications of actions potentially taken before they are taken. Aristotle explains the process by which one becomes virtuous (e.g. temperate): "we become just by doing just acts, temperate by doing temperate acts, brave by doing brave acts" (NE, book II, section 1, 29).

In NE book II, section 2, on morally virtuous acts, Aristotle explains "These acts cannot be prescribed exactly, but must avoid excess and defect." Aristotle provides no "prescriptive" moral rules and duties (as, e.g., Old Testament Ten Commandments, Kantian categorical imperative) but rather *describes* (or characterizes) the morally virtuous actor. The definitive skill of the virtuous actor is to detect and act in accordance with the "mean" in any situation:

> Exercise either excessive or defective destroys the strength, and similarly drink or food which is above or below a certain amount destroys the health, while that which is proportionate both produces and increases and preserves it. So too is it, then, in the case of temperance and courage and the other virtues. For the man who flees from and fears everything and does not stand his ground against anything becomes a coward, and the man who fears nothing at all but goes to meet every danger becomes rash; and similarly the man who indulges in every pleasure and abstains from none becomes self-indulgent, while the man who shuns every pleasure, as boors do, becomes in a way insensible; temperance and courage, then, are destroyed by excess and defect, and preserved by the mean. (NE, book II, section 2, 30–31)

"Temperance" seems a most appropriate virtue with which to draw a general moral line between moral and immoral cannabis use. Here we can already say that excessive cannabis use would be inconsistent with the morally virtuous actor. Aristotle's position is clearly not one of total abstinence. He seems more consistent with the Scientific Reality than with the Social Reality in the cannabis debate. The main point is in using cannabis there is a mean to be found in order to use temperately. Note also that there is a basic choice for each individual, whether to be destroyed by excesses or to be preserved by routinely hitting the mean in life. There are many ways to go wrong and they all have in common that they are too extreme. Extremes destroy.[1]

The following, from NE book II, section 3, has Aristotle make a point relevant to the earlier consideration of adolescents and the primary importance of parental involvement, positive reinforcement, and avoidance of destructive "parenting styles." An implication here is that without a "right education" adolescents are likely to develop bad habits, habits having them "pained by and taking pleasure in" things they ought not. Within Aristotelian virtue training, learning to hit the mean and develop temperance, cannabis being legally prohibited is not clearly relevant. Rather, it is the parental demonstration of temperance (and other virtues, way of life) provided to a child and adolescent which is of crucial importance in effectively deterring adolescent cannabis use. Consider here the use of pleasure and pain in developing a foundation for moral excellence:

> For moral excellence is concerned with pleasures and pains; it is on account of the pleasure that we do bad things, and on account of the pain that we abstain from noble ones. Hence we ought to have been brought up in a particular way from our very youth, as Plato says, so as both to delight in and to be pained by the things that we ought; this is the right education. (NE, book II, section 3, 32)

Aristotle further suggests human beings make errors mostly on account of the pleasant, one of what he calls "three objects of choice" (pleasant, noble, the advantageous; their contraries the pains are the base, the injurious, the painful). Given what we have considered thus far from Aristotle, along with the detailed consideration of the "risk factors" for cannabis use among adolescents (chapter 3), we are able to understand adolescent cannabis use as likely involving no parental distinction being made between these objects and specifically not delighting in and being pained by things they ought. This leaves sensation and irrational appetite (desire) dictating choices and decisions of these adolescents. It would seem to follow that cannabis use by adolescents is merely appetitive by virtue of the lack of experience with the use of the faculty of reasoning. Adolescent experience with cannabis is more like the "base, injurous and painful" (in light of the faculty of the intellect being uninvolved in the use of cannabis) rather than pleasant, noble, and advantageous. However, a consideration of medicinal users of cannabis has their resulting state (contrasted with a state of pain and suffering) consistent with the "noble, pleasant, and advantageous."[2]

Three Characteristics of a Virtuous Actor

In NE book II, section 4, Aristotle adds that virtuous actions are performed by virtuous actors. Virtuous actors have already developed a character/disposition through previous experience and use in various contexts and situations of practical reasoning and decision making. Virtuous actions do not happen by accident or once in a while. Rather, they are habitual for those who regularly exercise and develop their practical reasoning faculty. Aristotle provides a most fruitful and rich characterization of the "certain condition" in which a virtuous actor acts:

> The agent also must be in a certain condition when he does them; in the first place he must have knowledge, secondly he must choose the acts, and choose them for their own sakes, and thirdly his action must proceed from a firm and unchangeable character." (NE, book II, section 4; 34)

For the temperate cannabis user, this will have him only using when "in a certain condition." First, he must have "knowledge," as including an understanding of the nature of cannabis intoxication, of what the user wants to attain as an end through the use of cannabis, of what it is he is doing individually and socially when he uses cannabis. Second, he must choose the acts for their own sakes. The virtuous cannabis user will not use for other people in response to peer pressure. The virtuous user will not generally act in a self-indulgent way. The type of action chosen "for its own sake" would for Aristotle be the ones which have the virtuous cannabis user hitting the "mean" and avoiding extremes in their use. Third, the actions must proceed from a firm and unchangeable character. As for the firm and unchangeable character, this is the goal of the morally virtuous actor, to attain such a state of perfection, one not ever clearly reachable as long as all human beings are subject to acting in extreme ways (e.g., cannabis use).

A relevant question in light of adolescent and young adult use of cannabis (and the common reason of "youthful foolishness") is the question of whether it is necessary for each human being to first inevitably act in extreme ways (e.g., getting carried away by an appetite or desire) in order to experience this effect and thereby (and perhaps *only* thereby) moving closer to becoming a morally virtuous actor, attaining a better sense of the "golden mean" (e.g., temperance in cannabis use). Aristotle would simply expect experimental use of cannabis on the part of young adults (as is the current case in early twenty-first-century United States). Keep in mind here that we are considering "use" and not "abuse" nor "dependence," although there would likely be in each individual's discovery of the mean for him or herself in developing temperance in cannabis use, a process of learning how much is too much, judging various strains and potencies, ways of using, how using is affected by eating, sleeping, everyday activities, and "settings," so that a temperate user results after years of experience, of the employment of "practical reasoning."

Doing One's Own Work Well

In NE book II, section 6, Aristotle elaborates further on the virtuous individual, moving to bring in the "man's own work" in addition to a general consideration of the state of a virtuous disposition: "the virtue of man also will be the state of character which makes a man good and which makes him do his own work well" (book II, section 6, 37). Consider here that the virtues state of character does two things: 1) makes a man good; 2) makes him do his own work well. Aristotle presents a way of understanding becoming virtuous that has individuals active, choosing and trying in order to develop a state of character so as to become "good" at "doing his own work well." Consider also the term "own" here. This opens the way for applying Aristotelian virtue ethics to a wide variety of human activities. Also implied is *not* working is not part of a morally virtuous disposition. A virtuous actor is active, is productive, and thus in light of the morality of cannabis use a tentative conclusion is that *moral* use of cannabis would not hamper one's doing his own work well. Cannabis use interfering with or keeping one from doing one's work well would not be virtuous.

Crucial in this consideration of a man's doing his "own work well" is the question of who is to judge "wellness." This could include the individual him/herself, society through its cultural standards, or some other measure. However, rather than reducing this question down into mere ambiguity, consider that a notion of doing one's work well would at least have all agree that there must involve some "work," so that at least cannabis users would have to have "work." Furthermore, they would have to at least make the claim that they were doing their work "well" on some standard of "well." These questions I have in mind for the cannabis-dependent user who is quite tolerant and unaware of the tolerance, showing symptoms of dependence. *The question to ask this person, from an Aristotelian perspective, would be whether or not cannabis use was helping them do their own work well.* This would be primarily revealing of the reality of the situation but would also provide the user an opportunity to assess his/her routine of use and their general way of life. Immoral use of cannabis would reveal itself as including no work being done at all; an unproductive life of little speculative or practical reasoning, a life lived for the desire for cannabis intoxication itself.

Intermediate Use of Cannabis

Consider the following by Aristotle, citing both an objective and subjective component to be considered in each instance of cannabis use. Aristotle here elaborates on the "mean" he has in mind, showing it as both an objective standard for all men as well as a unique individual subjective standard as well:

> In everything that is continuous and divisible it is possible to take more, less, or an equal amount and that either in terms of the thing itself or relatively to us; and the equal is an intermediate between excess and defect. By the intermediate in the object I mean that which is equidistant from each of the extremes, which is one and the same for all men; but the intermediate relatively to us that which is neither too much nor too little—and this is not one, nor the same for all. (NE book II, section 6, 37)

For cannabis users one and all, there is "extremely" high THC content in certain strains (in hashish vs. cannabis, e.g.), an "objective standard" exists to measure each strain as being more or less potent. However, there is also a subjective component, whereby some individual users may consider a particular THC content to be very potent, while another user may find the same THC content to be mild. The subjective element is further evident in light of the fact that some users may consider smoking every day excessive, while for a medicinal user, for example, such use would be moderate, producing a state of normalcy and freedom from significant negative symptoms. This point is again one revealing the relativity of cannabis use to particular users and the specific effects experienced through use. Aristotle concludes: "Thus a master of any art avoids excess and defect, but seeks the intermediate and chooses this—the intermediate not in the object but relatively to us" (NE, book II, section 6, 37).

Furthermore, consider the relevance of the passions as a way of assessing whether or not one was intermediate in use. Of moral virtue (and the way virtuous actors experience and respond to passions):

> For it is this that is concerned with passions and actions, and in these there is excess, defect, and the intermediate . . . to feel them at the right times, with refer-

> ence to the right objects, towards the right people, with the right motive, and in the right way, is what is both intermediate and best, and this is characteristic of virtue. (NE, book II, section 6, 38)

To assess the virtue of any particular instance of cannabis use, included would be a consideration of times of use, motivation for use (and why this object, cannabis, rather than others), with what people (if any) does one use, how or in what fashion or way does one use, etc. This has Aristotle take us back to a consideration of "set and setting" of use.[3]

In NE book II, section 7, Aristotle explains:

> With regard to pleasures and pains—not all of them, and not so much with regard to the pains—the mean is temperance, the excess self-indulgence. Persons deficient with regard to the pleasures are not often found; hence such persons have received no name. But let us call them "insensible." (NE, book II, section 7, 40)

So for the extreme of "boorishness" Aristotle here adds the descriptor of "insensible" and also notes this to be rare, strongly implying that most human beings struggle with temperance in light of some particular pleasure they are apt to excessively enjoy. This point is the reason why Aristotle will spend the majority of his time focusing on self-indulgence and not boorishness.

Aristotle introduces "Characteristics of the Extreme and Mean States: Practical Corollaries" and he notes "the temperate man appears self-indulgent relatively to the insensible man, insensible relatively to the self-indulgent" (NE book II, section 8, 44). He further measures in various ways the difference between extremes from each other and from the mean. This further demonstrates the way we each may use our own habits to judge others and seemingly unaware that we are considering our own use/non-use as the standard. So a weekly user of cannabis may look at a daily user of cannabis as immoderate, while a non-user of cannabis may see a weekly user of cannabis as immoderate, and so on. These should all be subordinated to the golden mean of temperance with both objective and subjective elemenets in mind.

In NE section 9, the last section of book II, Aristotle further emphasizes we are unique individuals and that we should each be especially cognizant of those things toward which we may be tend to act in too extreme a way. For cannabis users, this would be to be careful not to become too extreme in use (as per Weil and Rosen's description of things "getting away from" regular users, Mill's metaphor of a will coming to act apart from desire):

> But we must consider the thing towards which we ourselves also are easily carried away; for some of us tend to one thing, some to another; and this will be

> recognizable from the pleasure and the pain we feel. We must drag ourselves away to the contrary extreme; for we shall get into the intermediate state by drawing well away from error, as people do in straightening sticks that are bent. (NE, book II, section 9, 46)

And at the end of NE book II, section 9, Aristotle culminates in a main moral point applicable to the essential relativity of moral judgments concerning cannabis use. It is difficult to render a negative moral judgment on seemingly under control and temperate cannabis use:

> But up to what point and to what extent a man must deviate before he becomes blameworthy it is not easy to determine by reasoning, any more than anything else that is perceived by the senses; such things depend on particular acts, and the decision rests with perception. (NE, book II, section 9, 47)

Here it seems fair to conclude that any individual use of cannabis must be judged regarding the basic standard of hitting the mean and estimating whether or not the use is temperate. This shows unjust a U.S. federal law punishing and criminalizing *all* uses of cannabis as this includes temperate uses, and it is therefore punishing virtuous actors.

Temperance and Cannabis Use

Into NE book III, "Moral Virtue," where Aristotle considers conditions of responsibility for action, and in the case of cannabis users let us assume they are *voluntarily* using cannabis.[4] Here in NE Aristotle moves to consider the two specific virtues of courage and temperance. In NE book IV focus is on the specific virtues of Liberality, Magnificence, Pride, Good Temper, Friendliness, Truthfulness, Ready Wit, and the "quasi-virtue" Shame. Of these virtues, temperance seems most relevant to the question of the morality of cannabis use.

In NE book III, section 11, Aristotle begins by once again emphasizing the relativity of different sorts of appetites distinguished by their various objects. This most obviously is exemplified in the preference of some for cannabis, others for alcohol. Such differences are simply a brute fact about human beings. Aristotle also relevantly uses the term "craving" in reference to those appetites which seem to define individuals, not as in itself a bad feeling but rather of the nature of appetites themselves:

> Of the appetites some seem to be common, others to be peculiar to individuals and acquired . . . but not everyone cares for this or that kind of nourishment or love, nor for the same things. Hence such craving appears to be our very own. Yet

> it has of course something natural about it; for different things are pleasant to different kinds of people, and some things are more pleasant to everyone than chance objects. (NE, book III, section 11, 74–75)

As Aristotle moves into a consideration of the extreme of "self-indulgence" and what he would consider the essence of immoral cannabis use, consider his description of this lack of virtue:

> Plainly, then, excess with regard to pleasures is self-indulgence and is culpable; with regard to pains one is . . . so called because he is pained more than he ought at not getting pleasant things (even his pain being caused by pleasure), and the temperate man is so called because he is not pained at the absence of what is pleasant and at his abstinence from it. (NE, book III, section 11, 75)

And this:

> The self-indulgent man, then, craves for all pleasant things or those that are most pleasant, and is led by his appetite to choose these at the cost of everything else; hence he is pained both when he fails to get them and when he is merely craving for them (for appetite involves pain); but it seems absurd to be pained for the sake of pleasure. (NE, book III, section 11, 75)

Reconsider the DSM-IV-TR criteria for cannabis dependence (from chapter 3):

Criterion 1: Tolerance
Criterion 2a: Withdrawal: likely to take the substance to relieve or to avoid those symptoms (Criterion 2b).
Criterion 3: Going over Limit
Criterion 4: Many unsuccessful attempts at quitting.
Criterion 5: The individual may spend *a great deal of time* obtaining the substance, using the substance, or recovering from its effects.
Criterion 6. Important social, occupational, or recreational activities may be given up or reduced because of substance use.
Criterion 7: Despite recognizing the contributing role of the substance to a *psychological or physical problem* the person continues to use the substance.

The self-indulgent cannabis user meets criteria 5 and 6, "spending a great deal of time" and giving up "important social, occupational, or recreational goals," routinely and consistently choosing cannabis use "at the cost of everything else." Here Aristotle also points out the absurdity of being "pained for the sake of pleasure." This absurdity is that one is inducing pain in oneself in order to relieve it with cannabis, then to experience the effects and once again to crave cannabis, use and experience intoxication, going through this process instead of simply eliminating the assumed need of cannabis intoxication. Consider here also that the "self-indulgent" man craves not merely cannabis but "for all pleasant things." This may distinguish between one who uses only cannabis and otherwise is moderate versus a "polydrug user" or hedonist generally. The self-indulgent cannabis user has a life revolving around cannabis use and intoxication as an end in itself. Such a cannabis user is led by his appetite to choose getting high "at the cost of" everything else.[5] Here Aristotle again focuses on DSM-IV-TR criteria 5 and 6 as morally crucial. This is one of the places where Aristotle, through his description of the self-indulgent man, allows the establishment of a moral standard on cannabis use by providing a characterization of use which fails to be morally virtuous.[6]

Further, on the temperate cannabis user and what this would generally look like, consider another way reflected in the DSM-IV-TR of measuring immoderate use also presented by Aristotle, the ability to go without cannabis for a period of time. By doing this (perhaps along with a therapist, friend, or whomever) one can assess the nature and degree of the appetite and craving for cannabis intoxication. Of course there will be a desire for cannabis during this period of abstinence (as would be experienced upon stopping most any habit; cf. chapter 2 discussion of feelings of withdrawal upon cessation of eating carrots). The primary therapeutic, spiritual, and moral point of this exercise is to assess the primary motivations for use of cannabis, especially use which appears to meet criteria of dependence and appropriately described as "self-indulgent."[7]

In concluding this section on temperance:

> The temperate man occupies a middle position with regard to these objects. For he neither enjoys the things that the self-indulgent man enjoys most—but rather dislikes them—nor in general the things that he should not, nor anything of this sort to excess, nor does he feel pain or craving when they are absent, or does so only to a moderate degree, and not more than he should, nor when he should not, and so on; but the things that, being pleasant, make for health or for good condition, he will desire moderately and as he should, and also other pleasant things if they are not hindrances to these ends, or contrary to what is noble, or beyond his means. For he who neglects these conditions loves such pleasure more than they are worth, but the temperate man is not that sort of person, but the sort of person that the right rule prescribes. (NE, book III, section 11, 76)

Here note several things in applying to cannabis use this very fruitful text from NE. First, temperate cannabis users do not feel pain or craving when cannabis is absent, or "does so only to a moderate degree." Without a withdrawal syndrome associated with cannabis use and with only 10 percent of total users dependent, it seems much of cannabis use in the current United States could very well be temperate. Second, consider further as applied to cannabis use the Aristotelian question of whether cannabis is or is not "a hindrance to an individual's ends, or contrary to what is noble, or beyond his means." Reflecting the criteria of DSM-IV-TR for cannabis abuse and dependence, the "hindrance to ends" is cannabis becoming the center of a user's life, cannabis is not clearly beyond many people's means (even at grossly inflated black market prices) given that an ounce of cannabis could last for several weeks for the heaviest user coupled with the fact that there are not withdrawal symptoms that keep one purchasing more and more on a daily rate (as is the case with other "harder" drugs). The question of "what is noble" is obviously somewhat vague and general, but remember Aristotle earlier suggested (NE, book II, section 3, 32) human beings mostly make errors on account of the pleasant, one of what he calls "three objects of choice" (pleasant, noble, the advantageous), their contraries the pains are also three (the base, the injurious, the painful). The use of cannabis can be noble or base relative to the individual user. Aristotle inevitably stresses the "way of life" as applied to individual actions. Perhaps assessing cannabis use in light of the overall way of life, daily activities, and lifestyle, responsibilities, etc., is inevitable for virtue ethicist Aristotle. As such, an individual's cannabis use should be assessed in light of the overall lifestyle. This would tease out distinctions between hedonistic users and responsible, otherwise law-abiding citizens (among others).

At the conclusion of this consideration of temperance, Aristotle points out the importance of controlling appetites and further focuses on the overall way of life of which cannabis use plays a part:

> In an irrational being the desire for pleasure is insatiable even if it tries every source of gratification, and the exercise of appetite increases its innate force, and if appetites are strong and violent they even expel the power of calculation. Hence they should be moderate and few, and should in no way oppose the rational principle—and this is what we call an obedient and chastened state—and as the child should live according to the direction of his tutor, so the appetitive element should live according to rational principle. (NE, book III, section 12, 77–78)

A way of assessing cannabis use as moral or immoral is to ask whether one controls one's use/desire to be intoxicated as a tutor directing a child, or is the child running the classroom so that nothing is being accomplished (or something in the middle of these). Is one's desire for cannabis intoxication "insatiable"? Consider also Aristotle's concern for "strong and violent" appetites (unlike those described of virtually all cannabis users and more akin to physiological dependence of opiates, e.g.). The goal is an "obedient and chastened state," a state which would be demonstrated by moral users of cannabis.

The Virtue of Justice as Applied to Cannabis Law

Aristotle's explanation of the moral virtue justice is applicable to the question of the moral status of cannabis prohibition and criminalization. To begin, Aristotle characterizes a just man as law-abiding and of a certain character, as contrasted with the opposite:

> Let us take as a starting-point, then, the various meanings of 'an unjust man'. Both the lawless man and the grasping and unfair man are thought to be unjust, so that evidently both the law-abiding and the fair man will be just. The just, then, is the lawful and the fair, the unjust the unlawful and the unfair. (NE, book V, section 1, 107)

And from the characters involved to the actions taken, "Since the lawless man was seen to be unjust and the law-abiding man just, evidently all lawful acts are in sense just acts; for the acts laid down by the legislative art are lawful, and each of these, we say, is just" (NE, book V, section 1, 107–8).

Note that he refers to a man as "lawful," given that this is a man's character or general way of acting habitually, a lawful man. The federal law of the United States prohibiting cannabis use is a law which if followed leads to just acts, in the sense of justice that refers to the world's standard of justice, laws "laid down by the legislative art."

It is important for Aristotle to distinguish from justice in the sense of following the U.S. law against cannabis use and justice in the sense of meeting an "intermediate" which is something one skilled in the legislating art is able to create. The latter sense of justice is the moral sense of justice to be used to assess actually existing law.

> Of particular justice and that which is just in the corresponding sense, (A) one kind is that which is manifested in distributions of honour or money or the other things that fall to be divided among those who have a share in the constitution (for in these it is possible for one man to have a share either unequal or equal to that of another), and (B) one is that which plays a rectifying part in transactions between man and man. Of this there are two divisions; of transactions (1) some are voluntary and (2) others involuntary—voluntary such transactions as sale, purchase, loan for consumption, pledging, loan for use, depositing, letting (they are called voluntary because the *origin* of these transactions is voluntary), while of the involuntary (a) some are clandestine, such as theft, adultery, poisoning, procuring, enticement of slaves, assassination, false witness, and (b) others are violent, such as assault, imprisonment, murder, robbery with violence, mutilation, abuse, insult. (NE, book V, section 2, 111–12)

Most basically are here two types of justice: distributive and retributive. Considering first distributive justice, Aristotle explains that "the just is equal. . . . And since the equal is intermediate, the just will be an intermediate" (NE, book V, section 3, 112) and then, "the just, then, is a species of the proportionate" (NE, book V, section 3, 113) and "the unjust is what violates the proportion. Hence one term becomes too great, the other too small, as indeed happens in practice; for the man who acts unjustly has too much, and the man who is unjustly treated too little, of what is good" (NE, book V, section 3, 114). If one considers the prohibibion of cannabis use as compared to the right to use alcohol then the cannabis users under U.S. federal law currently receive "too little" of "what is good." Therefore, as cannabis users currently receive "too little" of what is good, namely the right to use cannabis and be free from criminal penalty for doing so cannabis prohibition and criminalization are unjust from the distributive justice perspective.

And into a consideration of retributive justice and therefore of criminalization of cannabis users. Aristotle presents the basic notion of "equality":

> This kind of injustice being an inequality, the judge tries to equalize it; for in the case also in which one has received and the other has inflicted a wound, or one has slain and the other been slain, the suffering and the action have been unequally distributed; but the judge tries to equalize things by means of the penalty, taking away from the gain of the assailant. (NE, book V, section 4, 115)

Applied to cannabis use there exists nothing to "equalize."[8] There is no "assailant" in cannabis use and therefore it is not clear how a judge is to assess the proper penalty for one who has used cannabis (e.g., two-hundred-dollar fine, driver's license suspended for six months). This further indicates cannabis criminalization is unjust.

Once into his consideration of the virtue of justice (as an intermediate between two extremes) Aristotle gives an explicit characterization of each extreme regarding "justice":

> We have now defined the unjust and the just. These having been marked off from each other, it is plain that just action is intermediate between acting unjustly and being unjustly treated: for the one is to have too much and the other to have too little. Justice is a kind of mean, but not in the same way as the other virtues, but because it relates to an intermediate amount, while injustice relates to the extremes. (NE, book V, section 5, 121)

Here Aristotle articulates justice and argues that the "*just action is intermediate between acting unjustly and being unjustly treated.*" Given that cannabis users are harming no one else (with no victims pressing charges against them) and at most harming themselves, it seems reasonable to conclude they are extremely unjustly treated.

Aristotle raises the question of "whether it is possible to treat oneself unjustly" (NE book V, section 9, 130). Perhaps cannabis prohibition can be justified by preventing a citizen's treating himself unjustly. Aristotle includes here the example of one who "voluntarily stabs himself" "and explains what makes this an unjust action is that it is a harm to the state. As this action is

> Contrary to the right rule of life, and this the law does not allow; therefore he is acting unjustly. But towards whom? Surely towards the state, not towards himself. For he suffers voluntarily, but no one is voluntarily treated unjustly. This is also the reason why the state punishes; a certain loss of civil rights attaches to the man who destroys himself, on the ground that he is treating the state unjustly. (NE, book V, section 11, 134)

Here the argument justifying the laws prohibiting use and criminalizing cannabis users would be grounded in the interest of the state. This interest is to protect all of its citizens. The state argues that given a person is a set of civil rights, to stab oneself is to stab these civil rights, to potentially eliminate the very existence of these civil rights, thereby a loss to the state. It is clearly a problem to use this argument as an analogy with cannabis use, as stabbing oneself is quite different as a much more serious type of injury than anything comparable to the effects of cannabis use. Also, given that illegal cannabis does much less physical harm than the legal alcohol and cigarettes, the argument is still left to justify their holding as a criterion "dangerousness" to disallow cannabis use. In fact, by allowing legal cigarettes and alcohol, they are doing an injustice to users of these substances by allowing massive harm to the state to go unchecked. Also, if the state argues it is protecting cannabis users against themselves, it still wrongly assumes cannabis users are in fact harming themselves. As demonstrated in the Scientific Reality of cannabis use, cannabis use has dangerousness akin to caffeine, no one ever died from using cannabis, few voluntarily enter treatment for cannabis dependence, after age 35 there is a sharp decline in cannabis use, and there is no withdrawal syndrome. All of this seems to tell against a state interest in protecting cannabis users from harming themselves or destroying a set of civil rights.

Grasping Happiness

After his consideration of the virtue of justice in NE, the next book (book VI) deals with intellectual virtue, not nearly as relevant to the questions of the morality of cannabis use and law as are the virtues of tolerance and justice.[9] Book VII deals with "Continence and Incontinence: Pleasure." Then books VIII and IX deal with "Friendship." Book X, the final book of NE, deals once again with Pleasure, and also Happiness. Rather than further delving into "continence" and distinguishing this state from the virtue of temperance, I move instead back to the point with which Aristotle began NE, the question of the end of human life and the answer of happiness. Relevant to cannabis use specifically is Aristotle's contrast of such a life with a life lived for pleasure. I will therefore move on to consider relevant points regarding pleasure and finally Aristotle's conclusion to NE regarding the nature of the life of happiness, applying his rationale to various ways of using cannabis.

Aristotle puts under careful and meticulous scrutiny what he takes to be a popularly assumed end to human life, pleasure itself, and the experience of pleasure. One argument Aristotle lodges against those who hold that pleasure is the good to human life is from his teacher Plato, who "proves the good not to be pleasure; he argues that the pleasant life is more desirable with wisdom than without, and that if the mixture is better, pleasure is not the good; for the good cannot become more desirable to the addition of anything of it" (NE, book X, section 2, 250). So if a cannabis user merely derived pleasure from use and argued this was enough and the good life, the key moral and therapeutic question is to *have this user imagine wisdom in addition to the current state of pleasure* and to weigh this state to that of mere pleasure. Such a tact may allow the user the opportunity to re-consider his hedonistic philosophy.

A further argument Aristotle makes against hedonism points out many things commonly considered good which do not bring pleasure. As he puts it: "there are many things we should be keen about even if they brought no pleasure, e.g., seeing, remembering, knowing, and possessing the virtues." He concludes, "It seems to be clear, then, that neither is pleasure the good nor is all pleasure desirable, and that some pleasures *are* desirable in themselves, differing in kind or in their source from the others" (NE, book X, section 3, 254).

Those who use cannabis solely for the pleasure it brings and who make getting high the only end to their lives, meeting many criteria of cannabis dependence when applying DSM-IV-TR, seem to be left attempting to respond to these powerful lines of argument presented by Aristotle against the moral justification for their hedonism. Aristotle would further suggest (as shown in his temperance chapter of NE) that such a life was self-indulgent more generally, not temperate and moderate.

In section 4, book X, Aristotle explains that pleasure "is a whole," existing at a point and time and complete in itself. In contrast a movement "takes time and is for the sake of an end, and is complete when it has made what it aims at" (NE, book X, section 4, 254). And further, "But of pleasure the form is complete at any and every time . . . for that which takes place in a moment is a whole" (NE, book X, section 4, 255). Here Aristotle is employing the contrast between pleasure and movement to emphasize the passivity and lack of achievement of hedonistic life aiming at pleasure as the ultimate end. There is nothing to getting high, when smoking and inhaling take only seconds to take effect, and the intoxication is the effect which simply happens to users. If that is all there is to it, if there is nothing done once intoxicated, there is no overall purpose to this use in light of an individual's life, then nothing is ever achieved.

Later in NE, book X, section 5, Aristotle once again points out the variability in what different individuals take to be pleasurable. This is especially true for us human beings who, with our reasoning faculty, can actively conceive and make meaning, and can therefore also choose a multitude of possible pleasures:

> So the pleasures of creatures different in kind differ in kind, and it is plausible to suppose that those of a single species do not differ. But they vary to no small extent, in the case of men at least; the same things delight some people and pain others, and are painful and odious to some, and pleasant and liked by others. (NE, book X, section 5, 260)

It seems rather obvious that there exist those who prefer alcohol and others cannabis. Rather than a problem to be eradicated, Aristotle here suggests this simply reflects the diversity of human nature.

As with judging the mean for specific individuals earlier described, here Aristotle presents a sort of good judge of pleasures. This establishes that the individual user is not the sole arbiter of whether or not they are actually hitting the mean, but the "good man" who has a view to the truth:

> That which appears to the good man is thought to be really so. If this is correct, as it seems to be, and virtue and the good man as such are the measure of each thing, those also will be pleasures which appear so to him, and those things pleasant which he enjoys. (NE, book X, section 5, 260)

Here is where the real intervention happens (and perhaps suggests why Aristotle speaks so much about friendship within NE within his main focus on virtues, moral and intellectual). *Friends* will confront and admonish, counsel about cannabis using habits, ask why they use cannabis and whether they can help in any way. They demonstrate their goodness in their friendly intervention, out of compassion and not retribution. More generally, they can have a significant impact in the life of a cannabis-dependent user can be made by introducing a "good man's" point of view (perhaps one of whom this particular individual knows and respects and would consider a "good man").

Finally, 'Whether, then, the perfect and supremely happy man has one or more activities, the pleasures that perfect these will be said in the strict sense to be pleasures proper to man, and the rest will be so in a secondary and fractional way, as are the activities" (NE, book X, section 5, 260). Perhaps here one could imagine jazz musicians, artists, performers, writers, and others using cannabis as "pleasures that perfect" such activities, and as such are the pleasures proper to these particular individuals. More generally, perhaps, the atmosphere of cannabis clubs could be ones of intellectual discussion and artistic expression, movement to further ends and not mere hedonism which settles for pleasure of cannabis intoxication itself.

The Social Reality of cannabis use recognizes alcohol as a social lubricant and cannabis as a mind-altering substance. This policy can lead citizens to simply comply with this federal government choice of acceptable intoxicant as if "from above." However, Aristotle points out how arbitrary and perhaps false is such an advocating of proper means of pleasant amusement:

> Pleasant amusements also are thought to be of this nature: we choose them not for the sake of other things; for we are injured rather than benefited by them, since we are led to neglect our bodies and our property. But most of the people who are deemed happy take refuge in such pastimes, which is the reason why those who are ready-witted at them are highly esteemed at the courts of tyrants; they make themselves pleasant companions in the tyrants' favourite pursuits, and that is the sort of man they want. Now these things are thought to be of the nature of happiness because the people in despotic positions spend their leisure in them, but perhaps such people prove nothing; for virtue and reason, from which good activities flow, do not depend on despotic position; nor, if these people, who have never tasted pure and generous pleasure, take refuge in the bodily pleasures, should they for that reason be thought more desirable; for boys, too, think the things that are valued among themselves the best. (NE, book X, section 6, 262)

Here Aristotle is perhaps characterizing those who know about drinking alcohol, as do the tyrants/despots of the Social Reality of cannabis use, and so able to reinforce their favorite pursuits. However, Aristotle also points out that just because tyrants favor one thing and disapprove of another thing (in the cannabis debate, the Social Reality acceptance of alcohol and rejection of cannabis) does not prove this is reasonable.

Continuing on the nature of amusement and its inferiority to happiness,

> Now to exert oneself and work for the sake of amusement seems silly and utterly childish. But to amuse oneself in order that one may exert oneself, as Anacharsis puts it, seems right; for amusement is a sort of relaxation, and we need relaxation

> because we cannot work continuously. Relaxation, then, is not an end; for it is taken for the sake of activity. (NE, book X, section 6, 262)

Here Aristotle both endorses relaxation as something we need and also that relaxation should not be (or become) an end in itself. Relative to cannabis use recall that one, if not the, primary effect of cannabis use is relaxation. So he would likely endorse cannabis use as an "amusement" but warn of cannabis dependence where "getting high" and relaxed becomes the sole end of use. Whether relaxing with alcohol or cannabis after work, here Aristotle would not clearly have much concern with distinguishing one from the other.

Into section 7 of book X, Aristotle reiterates that the activity and life of contemplation is the best life. His reasons for this:

> For, firstly, this activity is the best (since not only is reason the best thing in us, but the objects of reason are the best of knowable objects); and, secondly, it is the most continuous, since we can contemplate truth more continuously than we can do anything. And we think happiness ought to have pleasure mingled with it, but the activity of philosophic wisdom is admittedly the pleasantest of virtuous activities; at all events the pursuit of it is thought to offer pleasures marvelous for their purity and their enduringness, and it is to be expected that those who know will pass their time more pleasantly than those who inquire. Self-sufficiency must belong most to the contemplative activity. For while a philosopher, as well as a just man or one possessing any other virtue, needs the necessaries of life, when they are sufficiently equipped with things of that sort the just man needs people towards whom and with whom he shall act justly, and the temperate man, the brave man, and each of the others is in the same case, but the philosopher, even when by himself, can contemplate truth, and the better the wiser he is; he can perhaps do so better if he has fellow workers, but still he is the most self-sufficient. And this activity alone would seem to be loved for its own sake; for nothing arises from it apart from the contemplating, while from practical activities we gain more or less apart from the action.(in the cannabis debate, the Social Reality acceptance of alcohol and rejection of cannabis. (NE, book X, section 7, 264)

And "for man, therefore, the life according to reason is best and pleasantest, since reason more than anything else *is* man. This life therefore is also the happiest" (NE, book X, section 7, 266). Aristotle indicates a sort of measure for a life of happiness here, namely weighing the amount of "contemplation" involved in the life. As for cannabis use, this would have one assess the motivations of use and consider specifically the effect on contemplation of any individual's use. One can easily imagine an increase in quality and quantity of contemplation when using cannabis. One can also imagine a decrease in quality and quantity of contemplation for the user whose motivation is to go along with peer pressure or merely for hedonistic reasons. The latter, not exercising the highest faculty of reason, is not going to experience happiness through such use (and way of living).

As Aristotle puts it in NE book X, section 8:

> Happiness extends, then, just so far as contemplation does, and those to whom contemplation more fully belongs are more truly happy, not as a mere concomitant but in virtue of the contemplation; for this is in itself precious. Happiness, therefore, must be some form of contemplation.
>
> But, being a man, one will also need external prosperity; for our nature is not self-sufficient for the purpose of contemplation, but our body also must be healthy and must have food and other attention. (NE, book X, section 8, 268)

Conclusion

On the question of cannabis use, moral use is temperate use and done not for itself but within a larger life of movement, achievement, mobility, and doing one's own work well. Implicit is that cannabis use is not inherently immoral and the conceptual impossibility of consideration use of cannabis (or any activity) apart from some specific individual's way of life and disposition/character. Adolescent training is crucial to stem use by those experimenting and developing habitis of the lower human faculties. Applying the Aristotelian conception of justice shows that cannabis users do not get distributive justice (when contrasted with alcohol users) and suffer from a wrongly applied retributive justice, as there are no damages for which they are providing compensation.

Notes

1. As will be seen, this goes for cannabis use as well as for the legal prohibition and criminalization of cannabis use.

2. As pointed out throughout this work, once again here in the context of Aristotelian moral philosophy we acknowledge the relativity of cannabis use, of needing to know the "set and setting," and here specifically the "set" of the cannabis user.

3. Aristotle also makes the point in this section that some actions are inherently bad themselves and so are always excessive, yielding no mean or intermediate. Examples he gives are adultery, theft, and murder. It is not at all clear cannabis use, or any other recreational drug use including alcohol, is akin to such actions if for no other reason than these all necessarily involve direct and quite clear harms to other human beings.

4. I do not focus here on the distinction between voluntary and involuntary actions, as I have assumed throughout adult users of cannabis are using voluntarily. Given that U.S. federal law criminalizes any uses it would seem to needlessly "muddy

the waters" here to go further into an Aristotelian analysis of voluntary/involuntary actions. This assumption of freedom is also consistent with the consideration of cannabis use in the Kantian presentation of will, St. Augustine on will, and the description of human actions by Mill in his "On Liberty."

5. Here is the state both Kant and Mill describe as one whereby the will develops a habit apart from desire.

6. Although were such an individual also a medicinal user, the DSM-IV-TR would recommend through "Differential Diagnosis" to consider the use not as "cannabis dependence" but rather as a response to symptoms of an underlying disease (e.g., depression, epilepsy, multiple sclerosis).

7. It should also be re-emphasized that of the criteria of cannabis dependence, the one which is not recognized is cannabis withdrawal syndrome, and relatively minor trouble for most users to stop using if need be.

8. If anything, the harmed party is the U.S. citizen who is left no other choice but to purchase black market cannabis, not knowing where it is from or what is actually in it, and at two hundred dollars an ounce rather than twenty dollars an ounce. A black market exists "right under our noses," able to conduct billions of dollars worth of transactions tax free, in a sense taking money away from the taxpaying U.S. public.

9. There could potentially be fruitful application of these sections and topics to cannabis use. These sections deal with science, art, practical wisdom, intuitive reason, philosophical wisdom, relations between practical wisdom and political science, as well as more on practical wisdom in relation to political science and right rule.

9

Old Testament and Cannabis

HANSON, VENTURELLI, AND Fleckenstein (in *Drugs and Society*) and also Joy, Watson, and Benson, of the Institute of Medicine (IOM), in *Marijuana and Medicine: Assessing the Science Base* (1999), pose the same basic metaphysical question. This question goes beyond the beliefs of each of the Social Reality and the Scientific Reality and yet is an essential question for each, one that if left unanswered also leaves unanswered the deepest question concerning cannabis. The question is: Why are human and animal brains altered or affected *at all* by plant chemicals? The IOM report suggests an evolutionary explanation to account for the existence of cannabis receptors and the very existence of the plant/brain connection, specifically of the cannabis/cannabinoid receptor connection. The evolutionary theory would further hypothesize about the survival value of these receptors, perhaps including a way of use for human beings existing thousands upon thousands of years in the past, not to mention their existence in the various species of non-human animal.

> Cannabinoid receptors have been studied most in vertebrates, such as rats and mice. However, they're also found in invertebrates, such as leeches and mollusks. The evolutionary history of vertebrates and invertebrates diverged more than 500 million years ago, so cannabinoid receptors appear to have been conserved throughout evolution at least this long. This suggests that they serve an important and basic function in animal physiology. In general, cannabinoid receptor molecules are similar among different species. Thus, cannabinoid receptors likely fill many similar functions in a broad range of animals, including humans. (Joy, Watson, and Benson 1999, 42)

As for why a plant itself would have psychoactive substances such as THC, consider botanist Pollen: "No one knows for sure, but botanists offer several competing theories, and most of them have nothing to do with getting people high—at least not at the plant's beginnings" (Pollen 2001, 156). Pollen suggests from the "plant" perspective protection from ultraviolet radiation (hence higher THC at higher altitudes), protection from disease, and defense against pests.

The following analysis of cannabis and cannabis use provides an alternative to evolutionary theory employing relevant scripture from the Old Testament and assuming as divine creation both the cannabis plant and human beings/brains.

Seed-Bearing Plants Are for Food[1]

> *11* Then God said, "Let the land produce vegetation: seed-bearing plants and
> trees on the land that bear fruit with seed in it, according to their various kinds."
> And it was so. *12* The land produced vegetation: plants bearing seed according to
> their kinds and trees bearing fruit with seed in it according to their kinds. And
> God saw that it was good. *13* And there was evening, and there was morning—
> the third day. *Genesis 1:11–13*

From this scripture, it stands to reason that cannabis, a seed-bearing plant (specifically, the female plant), is one of those many plants God had the land bring forth. After this work on this third day of Creation, God "saw that it was good." God gave his approval of the cannabis plant. Consider Augustine's illumination of the meaning of such a divine judgment of goodness, not as divine "discovery" but rather divine "teaching," as God is not Himself finding anything but rather revealing something to human beings:

> For what else is to be understood by that invariable refrain, 'And God saw that it was good,' than the approval of the work in its design, which is the wisdom of God? For certainly God did not in the actual achievement of the work first learn that it was good, but, on the contrary, nothing would have been made had it not been first known by Him. While, therefore, He sees that that is good which, had He not seen it before it was made, would never have been made, it is plain that He is not discovering, but teaching that it is good. (Augustine 2000, 363)

The Bible speaks of 128 different plants, subdivided into fruit trees, field crops and garden plants, wild herbs, forest trees and shrubs, plants by rivers and marshes, plants of the wilderness, thorns and thistles, flowers of the field, and drugs, spices, incense, and perfume. The only passage that seems to stand in the way of the claim that cannabis is not explicitly named in either Old or New Testament regards whether cannabis was the "aromatic reed" used by

Moses and more generally in (some) Hebrew temples. Booth explains the ingredients of the oil produced by Moses can be considered as hemp reed and also indicates there are some who would argue Christ possibly used cannabis-based oils in his ministry:

> God instructed Moses to produce holy anointing oil with myrrh, cinnamon, kassia and kaneh bosm. The latter, Sula Benet (1936) claims "contains the root word kan (meaning both 'hemp' and 'reed') linked to the adjective bosm ('aromatic'), referred to cannabis. . . it has been suggested that cannabis was widely used in Hebrew temples in antiquity, up until the reign of King Josiah in 621 B.C., during which it was suppressed. (Booth 2004, 23)

History (e.g., as presented in chapter 4) bears out the rejection by westerners of the eastern plant of hashish/cannabis. Given the religious context during 621 B.C. the Minor Prophets foretelling the fall of Jerusalem, hemp came to be associated with Assyrian-like idol worship and disobedient lifestyle.

In addition to cannabis being created by God on the third day, consider also from Genesis the instruction to human beings that every plant yielding seed upon the face of the earth (therefore including cannabis) and every tree for fruit are both here to be consumed by human beings:

> *Genesis 1:29* Then God said, "I give you every seed-bearing plant on the face of the whole earth and every tree that has fruit with seed in it. They will be yours for food."

Cannabis can be eaten but is not customarily used as a staple of a diet as are other fruits and vegetables, various grains and corn, etc. in the U.S. diet. Still, this scripture, using "every seed-bearing plant" would seem on any interpretation to include the cannabis plant. Consider also that this scripture adds to what we know from the third day of Creation. We are here spoken to, advised to understand our essential relationship with the environment, namely for food/nutrition. Plants were given to human beings by God.

This scripture would fortify a biblical position against any view which would conclude cannabis is itself evil or ungodly. To forbid absolutely the use of cannabis as per current U.S. federal law is a rejection of God's creation, God's plant, what God has given. Those who respect the word of God are challenged in light of the cultural demands on them via media, press, and politicians whose position is a staunch and (ironically) righteous rejection of Genesis 1:29.

Further reinforcing the use of plants for food given by God (and not something to simply take for granted):

> I will provide for them a land renowned for its crops, and they will no longer be victims of famine in the land or bear the scorn of the nations. *Ezekiel 34:29*

Genesis 2:8–9: 8 Now the Lord God had planted a garden in the east, in Eden; and there he put the man he had formed. *9* And the Lord God made all kinds of trees grow out of the ground—trees that were pleasing to the eye and good for food. In the middle of the garden were the tree of life and the tree of the knowledge of good and evil.

The Garden of Eden is a blessedness we can scarcely imagine let alone know. Inheriting our sinfulness from Adam, we inherit his violation of the tree of knowledge of good and evil. It seems appropriate in light of current views on the use of cannabis to stop and recognize that trees and vegetative growth were used from the very beginning of Scripture as a symbol or tool to teach human beings.[2] Plants and trees we can rationally understand, thereby understanding the meaning of the use by God of plants and trees as symbolic of (the results of) proper and improper living. To communicate Truth through scripture, note the Garden of Eden having a tree of life and a tree of knowledge of good and evil. One may even go so far as to imagine cannabis somehow located among the rich and fruitful vegetation among these two trees of divine knowledge and eternal life.

God Created Growth

Moving into further relevant scripture to cannabis, consider that in His covenant with Noah, God graciously promises to never again curse the ground and that seedtime and harvest shall never cease:

Genesis 8:20–22:

20 Then Noah built an altar to the Lord and, taking some of all the clean animals and clean birds, he sacrificed burnt offerings on it. *21* The Lord smelled the pleasing aroma and said in his heart: "Never again will I curse the ground because of man, even though every inclination of his heart is evil from childhood. And never again will I destroy all living creatures, as I have done.

22 As long as the earth endures,
seedtime and harvest,
cold and heat,
summer and winter,
day and night,
will never cease."

Psalm 65: 9–13 presents the awesome way God cares for earth so that it annually provides water, grain, bounty, overflow of riches, so that the pastures, hills, meadows, valleys, all sing together. This Psalm further emphasizes the importance of stopping to "behold" what God has done:

9 You care for the land and water it;
    you enrich it abundantly.
The streams of God are filled with
        water
    to provide the people with grain,
    for so you have ordained it.
You drench its furrows
    and level its ridges;
you soften it with showers
    and bless its crops.
11 You crown the year with your bounty,
    and your carts overflow with
        abundance
12 The grasslands of the desert overflow;
    the hills are clothed with gladness.
13 The meadows are covered with flocks
    and the valleys are mantled with
        grain;
    they shout for joy and sing.

As the Creator and source of growth itself, let alone for the various uses of plants for human beings, consider also *Psalm 104:14–15,* where the writer seems primarily awestruck with the very ability to create the "very foundations of the earth" ("O Lord, how manifold are your works!"):

14 He makes grass grow for the cattle,
    and plants for man to cultivate—
    bringing forth food from the earth:
15 wine that gladdens the heart of man,
    oil to make his face shine,
    and bread that sustains his heart.

Here also note importantly in light of any who would defend asceticism, extreme self-discipline and self-denial, that God is praised for having given us wine to "gladden the human heart." This "gladdening" seems what we today would describe in physical and social terms as intoxication and recreational use.

The symbolism of flourishing like "green leaves" presents leaves as symbolic of God's awesome creation, of his creation and promise of regular seasons, of soil that yields life, green leaves flourishing in a strong environment, plenty of sun and water, seeming effortless in their being the plants they were designed to be.

Proverbs 11:28
28 Whoever trusts in his riches will fall,
but the righteous will thrive like a
green leaf.

God Created Medicines Not to Be Despised

Often applied scripture by currently existing Christian healers who promote the use of herbs and plants including cannabis are the "Minor Prophets" Sirach and Ezekiel. These are written at a time shortly after 800 B.C., during the migration of Aryans known as Scythians. "They brought cannabis with them and it is through contact with them that Europeans first came to know of it" (Booth 2004, 24). Consider from these two prophets support for the medicinal use of cannabis:

Sirach 38:4
The Lord created medicines out of the earth, and the sensible will not despise them.
Ezekiel 47:12
12 Fruit trees of all kinds will grow on both banks of the river. Their leaves will not wither, nor will their fruit fail. Every month they will bear, because the water from the sanctuary flows to them. Their fruit will serve for food and their leaves for healing.

Here "medicines" are indicated, beyond foods. The very fact of the divine creation of medicine indicates we are to use these to alleviate suffering rather than refuse medical treatment. Also, Ezekiel speaks of "leaves for healing," focusing specifically on a part of a plant, the leaf. Cannabis leaves and "buds" activate receptors in the brain, receptors related to, among other things, the experience of pain and suffering. The seeds of cannabis are nutritional while the leaves are where is located the bulk of psychoactive THC, so that the "fruit" of cannabis seeds are for food and the leaves of cannabis are for healing. A conservative conclusion here is that the very concept of using plants as medicine is revealed in Scripture. It also seems to follow that cannabis is a medicine of the earth whose leaves God has provided for "healing."

Note also that the "sensible" will not despise these medicines from the earth. "Despise" is a powerful term, related to hatred, passionate disapproval, perhaps going beyond what one can possibly know in order to make such a definitive judgment about a part of God's creation. Calling cannabis the "devil's weed" or "evil weed," to fervently and passionately stand behind the abolition of medicines of the earth such as cannabis, are violations of this warning in Ezekiel, more accurately a demonstration of non-sense, ignorance, on the part of such despisers. The current U.S. law makes illegal any use of cannabis and seems staunch and determined to continue to do so, including the explicit Schedule I rejection of use for healing purposes. Their hard line against cannabis has led to the demonizing of this plant. This way of treating God's healing plant is seemingly a form of *despising* this plant. The current U.S. federal policy and Social Reality of cannabis use are not "sensible" in a biblical sense.

Strengthening this emphasis and the attempt to understand the truth about cannabis and how to use cannabis in therapeutic ways, consider that part of the wisdom granted to Solomon by God was an understanding the varieties of plants and virtues of roots. In chapter 7 of *The Wisdom of Solomon* his attainment of wisdom includes all good things, friendship with God, and unerring knowledge of the world, the heavenly bodies, *and knowledge of plant and animal life.* Of the last, Solomon is given "unerring knowledge" of "the varieties of plants and the virtues of roots":

Wisdom of Solomon 7:15–22
15 May God grant me to speak with
judgment,
and to have thoughts worthy of
what I have received,
for he is the guide even of
wisdom
and the corrector of the wise.
16 For both we and our words are in
his hand,
as are all understanding and skill
in crafts.
17 For it is he who gave me unerring
knowledge of what exists,
to know the structure of the world
and the activity of the
elements;
18 the beginning and end and middle
of times,
the alternations of the solstices and
the changes of the seasons,
19 the cycles of the year and the
constellations of the stars,
20 the natures of animals and the
tempers of wild animals,
the powers of spirits and the
thoughts of human beings,
the varieties of plants and the
virtues of roots;

21 I learned both what is secret and
what is manifest,
22 for wisdom, the fashioner of all
things, taught me.

God Condemns Drunkards and Gluttons

No explicit mention is ever made of cannabis or cannabis intoxication in the Bible. Again, as presented in the history chapter, the plant is originally from the East, from China, and only came late into the geographical region through which the Old Testament accounts were lived and recorded (not until 800 B.C., right before the fall of the second kingdom). However, there is much to consider about the proper use of fermented grapes in the form of wine, and so I will attempt a general presentation of the use and abuse of wine in the Bible. From a consideration of the use and abuse of wine, I will analogize to the use and abuse of cannabis.

Although wine was above presented as something God provided to "gladden the heart," there are also very relevant limitations upon the meaning of "gladden." Distinct from being "gladdened" is a violent life fueled by wine. Assuming cannabis is a plant that in general creates a sense of euphoria for the user, consider the following scriptures as loosely applicable to cannabis use and specifically in drawing an Old Testament line between acceptable "gladdening" and disobedient abuse. Again, this acknowledgement of the gladdening of the heart also speaks against asceticism and absolute denial of the body.

Using cannabis merely to experience "pleasure" is a form of idolatry, replacing the passion for God for the passion for a worldly object. Such a person, according to the wisdom of Proverb 21, will lead to "want" and poverty:

Proverbs 21:17
Whoever loves pleasure will become
poor;
whoever loves wine and oil will
never be rich.

Proverbs 20 and "whoever is led astray" implies both risk of being harmed and causing harm by misusing wine and that not all are or will be led astray (otherwise, if all would be led astray, the command would be pointless).

Proverbs 20:1
Wine is a mocker and beer a
brawler,

and whoever is led astray by them is not
wise.

The effects of the use of wine are quite different from those of cannabis. Wine can lead to mocking, brawling. But again, implied is *misuse* and not the *mere use* of wine and drink to "gladden the heart."

Reinforcing the result of "poverty" from drinking wine, and also adding "gluttonous eaters of meat" to the same point as "winebibbers" (a point we in the twenty-first-century United States, with a concern with obesity-related diseases may do well to reconsider). It points to the rather arbitrary way we criminalize the use of cannabis while allowing the use of alcohol and encouraging consumption of massive amounts of food:

Proverbs 23: 20–21
20 Do not join those who drink too much
wine
or gorge themselves on meat,
21 for drunkards and gluttons become
poor,
and drowsiness clothes them in rags.

Proverbs 23 makes it becomes more apparent that wine becomes a problem for those who go too far or over a limit, a limit the drinker is apparently aware of and therefore responsible for, as the warning "do not look at wine when it is red" when it "goes down smoothly," stop drinking. These are signs or signals of a conscious awareness able to assess their state of mind and specifically of intoxication and therefore presenting a test of will to cease drinking.

Proverbs 23: 29–35
29 Who has woe? Who has sorrow?
Who has strife? Who has complaints?
Who has needless bruises? Who has
bloodshot eyes?
30 Those who linger over wine,
who go to sample bowls of mixed
wine.
31 Do not gaze at wine when it is red,
when it sparkles in the cup,
when it goes down smoothly!
32 In the end it bites like a snake
and poisons like a viper.
33 Your eyes will see strange sights
and your mind imagine confusing
things.

> *34* You will be like one sleeping on the
> high seas,
> lying on top of the rigging.
> *35* "They hit me," you will say, "But I'm
> not hurt!
> They beat me, but I don't feel it!
> When will I wake up
> so I can find another drink?"

In addition to not knowing when to stop drinking wine, one is stung and bitten, seeing strange things and uttering perverse things, ultimately in a state of disorder including a lack of feeling for physical injury. As if in a trance or utter obsession with wine, in the end waiting to awake to "seek another drink."

God Condemns Laws Contrary to Council and Advisors

Consider again Proverbs, as condemning laws criminalizing cannabis users as they do not harm other people:

> *Proverbs 3:30* Do not accuse a man for no reason—
> When he has done you no harm.
> *Proverbs 17:15* Acquitting the guilty and condemning
> the innocent—
> the Lord detests them both.

As for the history of the twentieth century in the United States, the use of false propaganda and the consistent rejection of the best available scientific evidence, expert testimony, and consistent conclusion that cannabis should be decriminalized (from the Indian Hemp Commission Report at the turn of the twentieth century, to the LaGuardia Report of 1944, to the Shafer Commission Report of 1973), consider the following in relation to the U.S. and the war on drugs:

> *Proverbs 11:14* For lack of guidance a nation falls,
> but many advisors make victory
> sure.
> *Proverbs 15:22* Plans fail for lack of counsel,
> but with many advisors they
> succeed.

It is a sign of weakness in a nation where the nation does not use many advisors therefore lacks guidance, therefore risks loss of victory. Rather than foretelling the fall of the United States, as applied to cannabis use perhaps this "falling" is the increasing disrespect and disregard for cannabis law (and therefore the law in general). Current policy not only leaves unutilized advisors but also uses coercive insistence that free adult citizens understand and accept the Social Reality of cannabis use. "Plans" or policies, laws, fail without many advisors, and the current U.S. Social Reality of cannabis use lacks and has always lacked just such advice.

God Condemns the Way of the Sluggard

Also in Proverbs is reiterated the outcome of those who become dependent upon cannabis use, who demonstrate many of the DSM-IV-TR criteria of dependence and live lives revolving around acquiring and using cannabis, citing specifically "thorns" as symbolic of the impediment in the way of activity, growth and development, fulfillment and fruitfulness:

> *Proverbs 15:19*
> The way of the sluggard is blocked
> with thorns,
> but the path of the upright is a
> highway.

Otherwise Law-Abiding Citizens . . . Deterred from Confession

Consider that cannabis prohibition punishes all cannabis users *including* otherwise law-abiding citizens. They go underground and into secrecy for fear of arrest and criminalization, loss of rights and status in society. In discussing cannabis use and the church with a pastor, I was told that there are many who use cannabis and therefore feel "too guilty" to attend church, even though they were otherwise law-abiding citizens and did not meet criteria of dependence nor abuse (e.g., "smoking a joint after coming home from work and going to bed"). This pastor informed me of the continuing need to invite such people to church, contrasting this rather benign behavior with that of those church attendees who live lives of revelry and binge drinking and without guilt attend church. Those who are concerned about the spiritual lives of cannabis users should consider that the U.S. cannabis law in essence *impedes* confession and redemption, poses a major obstacle in the way of otherwise law-abiding citizens who are inhibited from being fruitfully involved in a Church community:

> *Proverbs 28:13*
> He who conceals his sins does not
> prosper,

but whoever confesses and
renounces them finds mercy.

A Godly Plea for Terminally Ill Patients

Especially applicable to terminally ill patients, the wisdom of *Proverbs* reveals that by arresting and criminalizing cannabis-using terminally ill patients the government is acting contrary to the spirit of compassion called for by the Wisdom of God. Consider the place of wine here for the terminally ill, and the seemingly uncontroversial move to consider cannabis use as also called for by Proverb 31 (as it would help the dying person in the same way):

Proverbs 31:6–9
6 Give beer to those who are perishing,
wine to those who are in anguish;
7 let them drink and forget their poverty
and remember their misery no more.

8 Speak up for those who cannot speak
for themselves,
for the rights of all who are
destitute,
9 Speak up and judge fairly;
defend the rights of the poor and
needy.

The Social Reality remains in place in the United States, and 750,000 people are arrested annually for using cannabis, including those who derive therapeutic benefits (so that instead of introducing "thorns" into a life such use is removing thorns). Those who use cannabis are at this point "unable to speak for themselves" as the Social Reality is the press, media, FDA, criminal justice system, which provides the truth about the nature of cannabis for those who simply assume the law prohibiting cannabis use is just and moral.

Notes

1. Unless otherwise noted, the scriptures are from *Holy Bible* New International Version. Grand Rapids, MI: Zondervan 1986.
2. More broadly, this point leads to further consideration of the proper human concerns for the environment, ecology, and the natural world.

10

Christian Ethics and Cannabis Use

CANNABIS WAS SUMMONED FORTH from the earth by God on the third day of creation and He saw it was good. The sensible will not despise the cannabis plant. "Despise" involves hatred, passionate disapproval, a sanctimonious judgment, directed at this plant of God's creation. Referring to God's plant as the "devil's weed" or "evil weed" similarly has one despise. These words are not clearly fruits from the Spirit and invite one to question whether or not such hatred is consistent with the disposition Jesus Christ modeled while in human flesh. If God created medicines out of the earth He did so because of human (and animal) illnesses, diseases, and frailties. The concept of medicine itself implies disease and treatment of disease.

In this chapter I will build upon the Old Testament account of cannabis use and law and apply three specific New Testament scriptures, providing a way of answering from a Christian perspective the moral questions of this part III Moral Assessment. After applying these scriptures, I will next apply several concepts central to the morality of Christian theologian and philosopher St. Augustine, articulating and applying to cannabis use concepts including "will" and "inordinate desire." Third, and directly relevant to this part III Moral Assessment of cannabis use and law, I present and apply main points made by Corbett in his *Turned on by God*, specifically his chapter on marijuana. His coming from a Christian perspective and addressing issues still definitive of the current twenty-first-century U.S. debate provides responses to the part III Moral Assessment questions. I conclude this chapter by considering, contrary to the asceticism against cannabis use by the current U.S. Social Reality, the essential place of healing in the ministry of Christ and point out the consistency between this understanding of Christian life and the Scientific Reality on cannabis use.

Application of New Testament Scriptures

Moving into the Gospels from the Minor Prophets of the Old Testament, the goal is to use scriptures relevant to cannabis use to better appreciate how a Christian should understand and respond to such use.[1] Consider first from Matthew 15, concerning the distinction between "clean and unclean" actions and objects:

> *Matthew 15:10–11*
> *10* Jesus called the crowd to him and said, "Listen and understand. *11* What goes into a man's mouth does not make him 'unclean,' but what comes out of his mouth, that is what makes him 'unclean.'"

> And *Matthew 15:17–20*

> *17* "Don't you see that whatever enters the mouth goes into the stomach and then out of the body? *18* But the things that come out of the mouth come from the heart, and these make a man 'unclean.' *19* For out of the heart come evil thoughts, murder, adultery, sexual immorality, theft, false testimony, slander. *20* These are what make a man 'unclean'; but eating with unwashed hands does not make him 'unclean.'"

This point applied to the cannabis plant is consistent with the Old Testament point that God created all seed-bearing plants and so plants, inhaled or eaten or otherwise put into the body, do not make a person unclean. It is what comes out of the mouth which is to be judged to determine whether an individual action, way of life is "clean" or "unclean." Using the drug of alcohol as another example, it is not drinking the alcohol itself that defiles, but rather the violent, insensitive and destructive actions resulting from the irresponsible use of alcohol that defiles. In other words, one who drinks alcohol or smokes cannabis is not thereby defiled, but rather defilement depends upon what "comes out of the mouth."

Cannabis use, applying this particular scripture, can be morally assessed by studying and attending to "what comes out of the mouth" of one who uses cannabis. A person may under the effects of cannabis say things that defile. Uninhibited and ill-thought out talk can potentially hurt or cause harms to sensitive others and bring shame and sin on oneself. Cannabis use may also, however, result in a more sincere and loving interaction that would not have happened but for cannabis use.

A second relevant scripture, consistent with the Old Testament warning that the sensible will not despise cannabis employs the New Testament concept of "thanksgiving." Here emphasized is the way in which one should treat what God has created. The key concept is "thanksgiving," so that Christian cannabis use would be done in a way which demonstrated it was "to be received with thanksgiving by those who believe and know the truth with which we are called to accept it."

Timothy 4:1–5

The Spirit clearly says that in later times some will abandon the faith and follow deceiving spirits and things taught by demons. *2* Such teachings come through hypocritical liars, whose consciences have been seared as with a hot iron. *3* They forbid people to marry and order them to abstain from certain foods, which God created to be received with thanksgiving by those who believe and who know the truth. *4* For everything God created is good, and nothing is to be rejected if it is received with thanksgiving, *5* because it is consecrated by the word of God and prayer.

Here reinforced is the fact that everything God has created is good, including plants on the Third Day of Creation. However, also made clear is that what God has provided must be received with "thanksgiving."[2] The uncontroversial point is that rejecting the cannabis plant for any use at all is neither a "reception" nor an expression of "thanksgiving" in any sensible meaning of these terms. This point is evidence against the justice of the U.S. cannabis law. The moral assessment of use from a Christian perspective would include a consideration of whether use is with and without "thanksgiving."

Many medicinal users demonstrate this sort of "thanksgiving," in the relief of their pain, failing to have symptoms relieved by synthetic, legal drugs. The decision to break the law and use cannabis to relieve one's symptoms perhaps brings the citizen to the existence of a "higher law" and form of justice currently denied by a worldly government. Using cannabis in a hedonistic way oblivious to the fact that God created this plant demonstrates little respect for the process of intoxication (as a "gladdening of the heart"). Using in at least a "responsible" way if not in a way explicitly and humbly grateful to God for creating this plant is to use with thanksgiving. Although there are motivations not clearly with or without thanksgiving, many cannabis users can be considered as either using with or without thanksgiving. This is a major criterion to assess the use of cannabis from a Christian perspective.

Further applying this scripture, among those who use cannabis are "those who believe and know the truth." This truth is in God the Creator and of the inherent goodness of everything He has created. Knowing that God has provided cannabis for us human beings, some who "believe and know the truth" literally see right through politically motivated U.S. law prohibiting use and criminalizing users as encouraging society to consider cannabis a political symbol of the Social Reality. This is especially evident in light of the false propaganda and rhetoric throughout the criminalization of cannabis in the twentieth century and into the twenty-first century United States. The essential point is that there is a higher truth as God's law revealed through Christ with which the U.S. federal law must be consistent in order to be legitimate.

To expand on this thanksgiving-line of thought, Paul in Romans 14:23 states: But those who have doubts are condemned if they eat because they do not act from faith; for whatever does not proceed from faith is sin.

A Christian ethics directed at cannabis use should focus on the heart of the user. If the cannabis user thinks his/her use sinful (expressing shame, guilt, remorse, perhaps part of a more general lifestyle of reveling) then Christians should condemn that use. However, a user who experiences no guilt or doubt in use is at least not condemned by Paul here. Romans 14:23 is in the immediate context of Romans 14, with a primary theme of love bearing with the scruples and arbitrary choice of preferences unique to individuals. Explicitly condemned is passing judgment on a brother or sister for an eating preference. Two primary points relevant to cannabis use come to the fore from Romans 14:13 to the final chapter verse 23. First, Romans 14:16: "So do not let your good be spoken of as evil." Second, Romans 14:20: "It is wrong for you to make others fall by what you eat." Relevant to cannabis use, cannabis users are called upon to defend their use (especially given it passed the test of the heart of the user from Romans 14:23). But also, users must be very careful so as to not mislead other believers into unjustified use. These are both important facets of cannabis use as a Christian would understand it.

Prior to Romans 14, Romans 13 tells believers to be subject to and obey the authorities of the state. Although some may argue that all cannabis use is currently immoral and unjustified in the United States simply because the (worldly) authorizes say so, the effective counter to this line supporting total obedience to worldly authorities is revealed when those authorities demand action contrary to Scripture. This fact shows that although God has appointed all worldly authorities so that they would not have ruled let alone existed without Gods' allowance, not all actions, decisions, cannabis laws are thereby Godly. God can logically both appoint a worldly leader and allow this leader to freely choose un-Godly, unjust policy.

A third and final scripture I find relevant to cannabis use provides a further way from a Christian perspective of distinguishing between acceptable and unacceptable cannabis use:

Galatians 5:13–26
13 You, my brothers, were called to be free. But do not use your freedom to in-
dulge the sinful nature; rather, serve one another in love. *14* The entire law is
summed up in a single command: "Love your neighbor as yourself." *15* If you
keep on biting and devouring each other, watch out or you will be destroyed by
each other.
16 So I say, live by the Spirit, and you will not gratify the desires of the sinful
nature. *17* For the sinful nature desires what is contrary to the Spirit, and the
Spirit what is contrary to the sinful nature. They are in conflict with each other,
so that you do not do what you want. *18* But if you are led by the Spirit, you are
not under law.
19 The acts of the sinful nature are obvious: sexual immorality, impurity and
debauchery; *20* idolatry and witchcraft; hatred, discord, jealousy, fits of rage, self-
ish ambition, dissensions, factions *21* and envy; drunkenness, orgies, and the
like. I warn you, as I did before, that those who live like this will not inherit the
kingdom of God.
22 But the fruit of the Spirit is love, joy, peace, patience, kindness, goodness,
faithfulness, *23* gentleness and self-control. Against such things there is no law.
24 Those who belong to Christ Jesus have crucified the sinful nature with its pas-
sions and desires. *25* Since we live by the Spirit, let us keep in step with the Spirit.
26 Let us not become conceited, provoking and envying each other.

Verses 13 through 15 here present the concept of "freedom" from a Christian perspective; essentially a freedom from ultimate judgment for sins committed on the condition one believes that Jesus Christ is Savior. However, as will be seen with St. Augustine in the next section, this freedom is not demonstrated in a free reign to appetites, whereby the believer satisfies any and every desire. Instead, such a motivation evident in those who are supposedly dead to the flesh and free demonstrates something contrary to the freedom attained through Christ.

13 You, my brothers, were called to be free. But do not use your freedom to indulge
the sinful nature; rather, serve one another in love. *14* The entire law is summed up
in a single command: "Love your neighbor as yourself." *15* If you keep on biting
and devouring each other, watch out or you will be destroyed by each other.

Here is from a Christian perspective reason for resisting indulgence. Instead of being a slave to cannabis one should "love his neighbor as himself."[3] Christian freedom is also freedom from the law, primarily from judgment by the Old Testament Law of Moses and secondarily worldly laws. A Christian is dead to the world and alive to the Spirit: Spirit is freedom. However, the explicit warning in 13 is against "indulgence." Indulgence here has one focus and that is on one's own personal needs and desires and therefore not a consideration of the needs of others. Freedom from the law does not mean disrespect for the law. This freedom is only possible because of the humble recognition we inevitably break commandments (especially when they are robustly articulated and honestly applied). Instead of being judged guilty of our violating many of the commandments many times over (with merely one broken commandment would be grounds for God's punishing us with death) Christians are set free of the burden of being judged and found guilty; through recognizing their need for and accepting Christ they are dead to the (ultimate judgment of) Law and obsessively conforming to the law. Instead, the life is one of following the Spirit, being fruitful, striving for sanctification. This spiritual freedom can have one break a law, especially an unjust and hurtful law (e.g., current cannabis criminal law of the United States).

Continuing with Galatians and into 16–18:

> *16* So I say, live by the Spirit, and you will not gratify the desires of the sinful nature. *17* For the sinful nature desires what is contrary to the Spirit, and the Spirit what is contrary to the sinful nature. They are in conflict with each other, so that you do not do what you want. *18* But if you are led by the Spirit, you are not under law.

Here again the dichotomy between either living "by the Spirit" or to "gratify the desires of the sinful nature." Implied is that living by the Spirit has one at the same time opposing the gratification of desires of the flesh. The intentional use of cannabis hedonistically has one thereby live by the flesh and not by the Spirit. The use of cannabis for therapeutic purposes is not a use of cannabis for "gratifying the flesh" but rather is done in order to eliminate pains of the body. There is a difference between "body" and "flesh." The former is not sinful while the latter is, given the latter but not the former involves sinful desire and passion while the former is merely physicality akin to Aristotle's notion of "potentiality." This reading is strengthened by the claim by pain experts and psychologists, psychiatrists, neurologists, that using drugs for therapeutic purposes does not lead to nor is the equivalent to abuse or dependence (see DSM-IV-TR on Differential Diagnosis section of chapter 3 on dependence). As the use is not initiated by these people in order to "gratify the desires of the flesh," they are thereby continuing to live by the Spirit. In other words, therapeutic use, given the intentions of the user, is distinct from hedonistic use with the intention of short-term pleasure as an end in itself (merely gratifying the desires of the flesh). It may be that breaking a worldly law in order to follow the spirit is itself a test of faith for Christian believers who currently use cannabis.

Continuing with Galatians:

> *19* The acts of the sinful nature are obvious: sexual immorality, impurity and debauchery; *20* idolatry and witchcraft; hatred, discord, jealousy, fits of rage, self-

ish ambition, dissensions, factions *21* and envy; drunkenness, orgies, and the like. I warn you, as I did before, that those who live like this will not inherit the kingdom of God.

Considering the effects presented in chapter 2, both from the DSM-IV-TR regarding cannabis intoxication and from the phenomenological studies on the effects of cannabis intoxication, these acts of the sinful nature are not typical of cannabis users. Paul here states that the works of the flesh are "obvious." The terms "drunkenness" and "carousing" seem especially helpful ones to provide a sense of the reason why certain substance use is inconsistent with Christian faith. "Works" originating in drunkenness are often destructive, violent, impulsive, irrational, uninhibited, and demonstrating a general loss of control over one's will. Debauchery and carousing indicate a motivation for, need for, various hedonistic opportunities to satisfy short-term desires and having a mind bent on various pleasures and routinely performing shameless behaviors. Of these obvious works of the flesh, Paul lists: fornication, impurity, licentiousness, idolatry, sorcery, enmities, strife, jealousy, anger, quarrels, dissentions, factions, envy, drunkenness, carousing, and things like these. In assessing the use of cannabis of any particular person, these concepts provide another criterion for determining whether or not cannabis use is consistent with a Christian way of life. Using cannabis with a (mind)-set on such things as those listed here and intentionally putting oneself in a setting where they exist have one willingly perform works of the flesh, abiding in this general lifestyle. There may be a loose, spontaneous and false, fleshly sense of freedom more appropriately defined as impulsive and depraved, not freedom found in Christ the Savior.[4]

Legalization of cannabis in the United States will likely bring out in the open those who use cannabis in a mindless way, just to try it because it is now legally available, abusing it as a new "recreational drug" available on the legal carousing scene. However, other than those who are drunken carousers, it is less clear whether or not cannabis users whose intention is to relax, to have thoughtful interchange, to create and produce and perform, are producing works of the flesh.[5]

Continuing on Galatians, and considering the fruits of the Spirit:

22 But the fruit of the Spirit is love, joy, peace, patience, kindness, goodness, faithfulness, *23* gentleness and self-control. Against such things there is no law.

These fruit provide a way of analyzing cannabis use of any particular individual. The therapeutic users of cannabis clearly become more relaxed and at ease, peaceful, loving, and appreciative of those who help them live with their pain and suffering, showing kindness and generosity as they now can focus on something other than their physical and psychological ailments. This seems strong support for the therapeutic use of cannabis: its use can and does result in producing "fruits of the Spirit." It should be emphasized here also the last of the fruits, "self-control." The Aristotelian notion of temperance, the mean between two extremes, complements a Christian understanding of the moral cannabis user as one who demonstrates self-control.

Re-consider the seven criteria of cannabis dependence in light of each of the acts from the sinful nature and of the fruits of the Spirit. If a particular individual's use includes criteria of dependence such as interference with various role responsibilities, of a life revolving around cannabis use, then the scriptures here indicate the lack of fruits of the Spirit. Using cannabis is not in itself an expression of either of these lists of fruits. As has been a primary point made by all moral systems applied in the preceding chapters, what is necessary before making a judgment about a particular cannabis user is a consideration of specific motivations and inclinations of the user.

Continuing with Galatians, consider the consistency with other moral philosophers regarding the low status of "passions and desires," here as opposed to the Spirit:

> *24* Those who belong to Christ Jesus have crucified the sinful nature with its passions and desires. *25* Since we live by the Spirit, let us keep in step with the Spirit.
> *26* Let us not become conceited, provoking and envying each other.

So again, passions and desires of a carousing "old self" do not indicate a crucifixion of these. More generally such things are not the master of the life of a Christian who is by definition dead to just such fleshly passions and desires. Of course, we continue to experience such passions and desires, and the deeper idea here concerns the *type of life* we are called to lead, the character we are building through habitual actions and fruits produced. Cannabis use as a part of a larger life-style that has one "carousing" in a hedonistic, purely pleasure-seeking way is condemned as "fruitless" and lacking Spirit. Cannabis use by a depressed person who is thereby enabled to interact with others, to love them and open up to them, to serve them, is perhaps fruit of the Spirit and thereby justifies the use of cannabis.

St. Augustine on a Good Will and Inordinate Desire Applied to Cannabis Use

This brief presentation and application of St. Augustine provides extra detail to the general consideration of relevant Scripture from the Old Testament and

New Testament and complements the DSM-IV-TR presentation of cannabis dependence. As he presents his own youthful stealing of pears as one of "carousing" Augustine provides an especially vivid description of the essence of this disorder and of the way and attachment to worldly things, specifically cannabis, can be developed. Augustine assumes free will and personal responsibility of the adolescent in question, providing an additional angle to the assessment of adolescent cannabis use in chapter 3, where the focus was on the "risk factors" and generally outside influences on the adolescent user rather than holding the adolescent personally responsible. I conclude my brief application of Augustine by considering a good will, the object of a morality of St. Augustine, as one reflected in four particular virtues, prudence, fortitude, justice, and temperance. It is especially relevant in light of the part three Moral Assessment that temperance is once again the specific virtue most applicable to cannabis use from a moral-theoretical perspective.

Augustine can be understood as providing at least three ways of determining whether or not an individual cannabis user is immoral in that use. The first would assess the reasons motivating a user to use, to determine whether these reasons were for "pursuing an external thing" or were in order to serve God. The second way of assessing cannabis use is to determine whether or not the user is acting in an orderly way, where the focus is on the state of the will of the individual in question. This order has the mind/spirit in control of the other human faculties. The proper order of a will is central to the morality of Augustine, and can be alternatively understood as aiming toward the attainment of a "good will," which is characterized by four virtues: prudence, temperance, fortitude, justice. A third way Augustine provides for testing the morality of an action or individual habit is a practical one which has the user him/herself seriously imagine and portray an alternative life free from the (in this case) use of cannabis, if they were able to create it instantly (in current therapy, the so-called miracle exercise). What would the will involved in that life be like? This open and honest imaginative exercise reveals the idea we each have of an ordered will and is revealing to the user him/herself as ordered or disordered.

Orderly Will: The Augustinian Moral Standard and Cannabis Use

Augustine explains a "perfectly ordered" human being is one whose mind/spirit controls the other elements of one's nature[6]:

> Whatever this thing is in virtue of which human beings are superior to animals, whether we should call it 'mind' or 'spirit' or both (for both terms are used in

> Scripture), if it rules and controls the other things that constitute a human being, then that human being is perfectly ordered. (Augustine 1993, 14)

Augustine further elaborates upon the proper order of a soul, explaining "when reason, mind, or spirit controls the irrational impulses of the soul, a human being is ruled by the very thing that ought to rule according to the law that we have found to be eternal" (Augustine 1993, 14). Order, then, includes "mind/spirit" ruling irrational impulses, irrational impulses being sinful and directing passion to attain a temporal good and end. Appreciate also that "order" implies that mind/spirit can in fact control the desires. For example, in reference to "cupidity" Augustine explains that such fear of losing a temporal good is not stronger than the mind/spirit which can resist such a fear. He reasons that were this not so then "it would violate perfect order if the weaker controlled the stronger. Therefore, I think the mind must be more powerful than cupidity, precisely because it is right and just for the mind to rule over cupidity" (Augustine 1993, 16). And more generally, "And surely we do not doubt that every virtue is superior to every vice, so that the better and more sublime the virtue, the stronger and more invincible it is" (Augustine 1993, 16). This point is relevant to especially adolescent experimentation with cannabis, one which if grasped and believed by a youth can help protect him/her against peer pressure:

> Can a just spirit, a mind that is preserving its proper right and authority, take another mind that is ruling with the same equity and virtue, drive it from its stronghold, and subject it to inordinate desire?
>
> Not at all, for two reasons. First, each mind possesses the same degree of excellence. And second, any mind that would attempt such a thing must have already fallen from justice and become vicious, and therefore weaker. (Augustine 1993, 16)

Rather than being "subjected to" inordinate desire, one who acts in such a way (e.g., submits to peer-pressure and experiments with cannabis) has *already fallen* from justice in mind. Willing fleshly works happens only after this mental/spiritual fall. It is more likely (as research bore out in the chapter 3) that preexisting conduct disorders, criminal activity, and lack of adequate parental support have an adolescent already disordered in will prior to cannabis use.

Augustine points out that acting immorally, acting from inordinate desire, is harmful to the acting individual him/herself. Instead of vengefully attacking inordinate cannabis users as criminals Augustine would emphasize that inordinate desire is itself a punishment, a self-harming:

> Surely the very fact that inordinate desire rules the mind is itself no small punishment. Stripped by opposing forces of the splendid wealth of virtue, the mind is dragged by inordinate desire into ruin and poverty; now taking false things for

> true, and even defending those falsehoods repeatedly; not repudiating what it had once believed and nonetheless rushing headlong into still other falsehoods; now withholding assent and often shying away from clear arguments; now despairing completely of finding the truth and lingering in the shadows of folly; now trying to enter the light of understanding but reeling back in exhaustion. (Augustine 1993, 17)

Note how this description complements the distinction made in Galatians between "works of the flesh" and "fruits of the Spirit." The fleshly life is one of "defending falsehoods," rejecting clear arguments, "lingering in the shadows of folly," "ruin and poverty," and generally "taking false things for the true." These are consistent with cannabis abuse and dependence, including living a life revolving around cannabis for itself while not meeting role responsibilities and yet defending the life as a fulfilling of one's potential. Also note the text of "trying to enter the light of understanding," only to "reel back in exhaustion." Such cannabis users, perhaps those who meet the dependence criterion of "many previous attempts at quitting," are captured here by Augustine.

To complement this recognition of the self-harm and suffering involved in a life of inordinate desire, Augustine develops the argument that since human beings want to be happy they should therefore intentionally aim to develop a good will. By not developing a good will, one thereby harms oneself in making impossible the attainment of happiness. As we each have a free will, a will able to use reason to order and control desires and passions, we are morally speaking to act and intentionally attempt to develop a good will. A good will is generally defined by Augustine as "a will by which we desire to live upright and honorable lives and to attain the highest wisdom" (Augustine 1993, 19). Those who are of good will demonstrate four particular virtues: prudence, fortitude, temperance, and justice. Prudence is "the knowledge of what is to be desired and what is to be avoided," fortitude is an attribute that has one "patiently and calmly bear the absence of those things that it is not in our power to obtain or to keep," temperance is "the virtue that restrains inordinate desires," and justice is "the virtue by which each is rendered his or her due" (Augustine 1993).

A defining characteristic of the ordered will is living so as to attain eternal goods and not worldly goods. Augustine reasons "those who are happy on account of their love for eternal things live under the eternal law, while those who are unhappy are subject to the temporal law" (Augustine 1993, 25). Being good is to love eternal things, while to be bad is to love temporal things. Augustine cites the vast array of temporal things human beings cleave to in their cupidity.

1) this body (health, keen senses, strength, beauty, and other qualities)
2) "freedom" (Kantian sense/moral sense, of freedom as acting in accordance with the moral law, "autonomy")

3) free from worldly responsibilities
4) recognition by society (honors and praise and "popular acclaim")
5) property (for buying and selling)

Of the five categories of temporal things cannabis use can be considered as of the body (hedonism), moral freedom (using to demonstrate one's moral freedom, prove a point in the face of law prohibiting cannabis use), motivated by a desire to escape role responsibilities, used to gain popularity and "fit-in," or treated as a commodity to be bought and sold. The specific motivation for using cannabis would determine the temporal human goods involved in that particular use. An inability to stop using cannabis indicates potentially several of these temporal goods as involved in such disordered attachments. Augustine reminds that "it would be no punishment at all if human beings did not love things that can be lost against their will" (Augustine 1993, 26). Again, it is important to recognize it is a loving, clinging to, these things, not merely using them, considered here by Augustine.

Consider two examples of external things desired for their own sake rather than for serving God's purpose: a desire to accumulate money to get rich and a desire to consume cannabis to escape one's responsibilities. Money can be used to help feed the homeless, pay for indigent health care, or other eternal causes, and cannabis can be used to increase the appetite of cancer chemotherapy patients, relieve symptoms of Multiple Sclerosis, create poetry and inspire artistic performance. It is not the thing in itself (money, cannabis) but the way it is used that determines the morality of employing the thing.[7] Augustine makes this point employing the metaphor of a "limb of the soul." In light of the Moral Assessment theorists this is generally reason or spirit, humanity's highest faculty, overcome and under constant control of lower faculties, i.e., appetites and desires:

> They become good by being put to good use. And so someone who uses them well does not become attached to them. They don't become limbs of his soul, as it were (which is what happens when one loves them), so that when these things begin to be amputated he is not disfigured by any pain or decay. (Augustine 1993, 26)

The relevant question for ascertaining the order or disorder of a will is to assess whether one is attached to spending money or to using cannabis in such a way that one is disfigured if either is taken away. The term *disfigured* is crucial, and one that is worth applying to the diagnosis of cannabis dependence. Such a person's self-identity is dependent upon the accumulation of wealth or of habitually using cannabis.

Augustine also describes one who is not attached to external things:

> He is completely above such things, ready to possess and make us of them when there is need, and even readier to lose them and do without them. Since this is the case, you must realize that we should not find fault with silver and gold because of the greedy, or food because of gluttons, or wine because of drunkards, or womanly beauty because of fornicators and adulterers, and so on, especially since you know that fire can be used to heal and bread to poison. (Augustine 1993, 26)

Fear of losing things reveals a will cleaving to temporal goods. Cannabis use not acceptable on Augustine's account would be the type of use which had one "cleaving to" cannabis as an identity as opposed to being put to good fruitful use. Cannabis would be a "limb of the soul" of the immoral cannabis user.[8] Augustine describes the development of a habit in a way quite consistent with the development of cannabis dependence:

> The consequence of a distorted will is passion. By servitude to passion, habit is formed, and habit to which there is no resistance becomes necessity. By these links, as it were, connected one to another (hence my term a chain), a harsh bondage held me under restraint. The new will, which was beginning to be within me a will to serve you freely and to enjoy you, God, the only sure source of pleasure, was not yet strong enough to conquer my older will, which had the strength of old habit. So my two wills, one old, the other new, one carnal, the other spiritual, were in conflict with one another, and their discord robbed my soul of all concentration. (Augustine 1998, 140)

Here there is first a "distorted" will, then as a consequence is passion. Again, the initial experimentation with cannabis by an adolescent (or anyone, for that matter) cannot sensibly be driven by "passion" for the chemical effects of a substance never before experienced. Only after the distorted will is there passion. Then, by developing and serving the passion, by continuing to direct the will in use, a habit is formed. A habit is powerful and becomes a way of living. Here dependence is formed so that "habit" as described by Augustine is quite similar to dependence as per the DSM-IV-TR. Augustine also nicely captures the battle of wills within an individual dependent trying to quit but yet failing over and over again. Finally, note the resulting discord renders the individual unable to concentrate and the battle of the two wills consumes an individual's thoughts and plans (as per criteria of dependence, their "lives revolve around the substance"). This is the major harm and risk of cannabis use.

Stealing Pears as Smoking Weed . . . Understanding Adolescent Experimentation

One of Augustine's memorable confessions is an act of his "Adolescence" (book II, *Confessions*), of his being sixteen years old and stealing pears with his companions, "companions with whom I made my way through the streets of Babylon" (Augustine 1998, 28):

> I wanted to carry out an act of theft and did so, driven by no kind of need other than my inner lack of any sense of, or feeling for, justice. Wickedness filled me. I stole something which I had in plenty and of much better quality. My desire was to enjoy not what I sought by stealing but merely the excitement of thieving and the doing of what was wrong. There was a pear tree near our vineyard laden with fruit, though attractive in neither colour nor taste. To shake the fruit off the tree and carry off the pears, I and a gang of naughty adolescents set off late at night after (in our usual pestilential way) we had continued our game in the streets. We carried off a huge load of pears. But they were not for our feasts but merely to throw to the pigs. Even if we ate a few, nevertheless our pleasure lay in doing what was not allowed. (Augustine 1998, 29)

Augustine's immediate struggle in confessing his stealing of the pears is to articulate the motive for his act. He cannot accept as rationally plausible that he could choose and act without having been motivated by some reason or purpose. Augustine explains in *On Free Choice of the Will* "There are two sources of sin: one's own spontaneous thought, and someone else's persuasion" (Augustine 1993, 91).[9] It seems likely that stealing the pears involves persuasion by the members of the gang, a relationship common to generations of adolescents from Augustine's fifth century to our twenty-first century. Perhaps the pears/cannabis just happened to be the object of a dare or challenge to go along with the others as a member of the gang. Being a part of the gang, proving oneself worthy to go along with them is perhaps the motivation.

Augustine's personal confession of stealing the pears is followed by a recurrent and lengthy reflection on his state of mind at the time of stealing. He describes himself as having been full of wickedness, a state that had him act shamefully for its own sake. Acting shamefully for its own sake is perhaps the way adolescents act, especially given the major hormonal and social changes experienced during this time. Augustine reflects that stealing the pears was "not lovely or beautiful," not even in the way that "specious vices have a flawed reflection of beauty"(Augustine 1998, 31). He wonders whether it is possible "to take pleasure in what was illicit for no reason other than that it was not allowed" (Augustine 1998, 32). This same question could be asked of the cannabis-using adolescent, that he used cannabis "for no other reason than that it was not allowed," suggesting a "forbidden fruit effect" whereby a law itself and more generally the fact that cannabis use is considered by all to be an adult activity creates a desire for the forbidden object (e.g., cannabis).

Augustine in his continued reflection on the motivations involved in his choice to steal the pears realizes he would not have done so alone: "The theft itself was a nothing, and for that reason I was the more miserable. Yet had I been alone I would not have done it—I remember my state of mind to be thus at the time—alone I would never have done it"(Augustine 1998, 33). Augustine here recognizes his motivation, as one of fitting in, of going along, of conforming to social pressure.

> Out of a game and a jest came an avid desire to do injury and an appetite to inflict loss on someone else without any motive on my part of personal gain, and no pleasure in settling a score. As soon as the words are spoken "Let us go and do it," one is ashamed not to be shameless. (Augustine 1998, 34)

"One is ashamed not to be shameless." The "gang" and its challenges seem to involve an existential challenge, one of personal integrity and authenticity. Paradoxically, what is seen as a success in light of the gang is a nothing and choosing to not go along with the gang would be a godly success. Cannabis use, in this context, reveals one of many possible vices and adult objects a disordered adolescent, subject to peer pressure, may act upon.

It will likely be that just walking away from and avoiding Godless situations and challenges has one suffer from the ridicule of the disordered gang. But the one who does so demonstrates power in him/herself. The feeling of power, of righteousness, is grounded in Augustine's view that "a stronger thing cannot be corrupted by a weaker" unless the stronger willingly allows it to happen. Augustine pays special attention to his passivity in going along with the pear-stealing group. This reflection supports adolescents taking personal responsibility and demonstrating willingness to be held accountable for stealing pears or for using cannabis. Although he did have a choice to either join in the stealing of the pears or to turn from the situation once he realized what was going to be done, he passively went along. As he *acted* passively he is personally accountable to God for the action. Augustine realizes, "That there lay the cause of my sin I was now coming to recognize. I saw that when I acted against my wishes, I was passive rather than active; and this condition I judged to be not guilt but a punishment" (Augustine 1998, 114). It is crucial to recognize Augustine does not intend for passivity to be understood as mindless, unreflective, and animalistic going along with whatever the group was going to do. He clearly recognizes mental reflection *in the choice of* how to direct his will. This point is especially relevant in light of cannabis-using adolescents who demonstrate a myriad of risk factors for cannabis use; they are still free and responsible for the direction of their will. "The soul is not moved to abandon higher things and love inferior things unless it wills to do so" (Augustine 1993, 72).

Stealing pears, done first as a misguided passion, can lead to developing a habit experienced as a need for stealing pears. As the motivation involves a turning of the will to that of the satisfaction of others (popularity and playing a part in the gang), this leads to developing a habit for so acting. However, in this context cannabis experimentation is less about cannabis and its effects and more about the deeper motivation of "going-along-with" the gang (even when involving adult situations). "I inquired what wickedness is; and I did not find a substance but a perversity of will twisted away from the highest substance, you O God, towards inferior things, rejecting its own inner life (Eccles, 10: 10) and swelling with external matter" (Augustine 1998, 126).

Augustine acknowledges he lacked an eternal motivation for what he had done. The distinction between temporal and eternal goods provides the means for understanding the wrongness of our actions. Again, pears, money, alcohol, cannabis are not themselves inherently inferior things. These just happen to be the specific objects chosen and used in an individual's rejection of the inner life. A motivation of the will that is temporal is an "inferior thing." An "external" or "material" possession loved for its own sake is a clear indication of a lack of God rather than a love for God.

Virtues and Cannabis Use

A desire to act in an orderly way, motivated by eternal goods and not bound to temporal goods, has one develop four virtues:

1. Prudence—"knowledge of what is to be desired and what is to be avoided"
2. Fortitude—"the disposition of the soul by which we have no fear of misfortune or of the loss of things that are not in our power"
3. Temperance—"the disposition that checks and restrains the desire for things that it is wicked to desire"
4. Justice—"the virtue by which all people are given their due" (Augustine, 1993, 20)

Applied to cannabis use temperance is most applicable to cannabis use. In chapter 8, Aristotle was shown to articulate temperance as a mean between the extremes of self-indulgence and boorishness. Also applicable to cannabis use is prudence. This is similar to the "practical reasoning" ability described by Aristotle as requisite of the morally virtuous actor. One who has developed a stable disposition for acting prudently has done so consistently and in a variety of situations. Temperance and prudence as concepts provide another way of measuring our own will as orderly or disorderly, complimenting the more basic question of whether a user desires external things for themselves or to serve a Godly purpose. Less relevant in light of cannabis use are "justice" and "fortitude" as articulated here.

Still, fortitude and justice should not be strikingly absent in any cannabis user being assessed, as when one virtue is missing the others are also likely absent. Augustine claims "all four virtues . . . are present in those who love their own good will and value it highly" (Augustine 1993, 21). The implication is those who do not demonstrate prudence and temperance in using cannabis do not value their own good will. In light of adolescent users, this lack of value for their own good will is easy to observe and to understand, given the other factors correlated with such use (e.g., negative parenting styles). It is not at all clear *medicinal* users of cannabis do not love and value highly their good will in light of these four virtues. Fortitude in living with muscle spasms and incontinence, for example, may be trumped by prudence in using cannabis as it is effective in controlling these symptoms. Temperance would be less demonstrated by bearing treatable pain and suffering and a low quality of life than by using available medicines. Successful therapy further does justice to the interests of family, friends, and society, as a user who can attain a sense of normalcy and balance can therefore free up caregivers and allow the user to be more productive, less of a burden on others.

Overcoming a Disorderly Will

> "Nature is what grasps the commandment, the will is what obeys the commandment." (Augustine 1993, 119)
>
> ". . . they do not act piously; they are more eager to excuse than to confess their sins. Some people gladly believe that there is no divine providence in charge of human affairs. They put their bodies and their souls at the mercy of chance and give themselves up to be beaten and mangled by inordinate desires." (Augustine 1993, 73)

Augustine provides a useful account of how one overcomes inordinate desires such as non-virtuous cannabis use. A disordered will has one act to possess a temporal thing (wealth, beauty, success, cannabis intoxication) as an end in itself. In turning from future situations of stealing pears, Augustine will likely be labeled an outcast, as haughty or one who did not have what it took to be a part of the gang. Turning from the gang requires his own recognition that they are right—that he does not have the will to be a part of the gang, but rather a will to follow God. He may experience at this point an identity crisis, as in his personal story he is in-between identities, from pear thief (cannabis abuser) to something else. Augustine would have one consider and understand one cannot ever attain and keep *wealth, honors, pleasures,* or *physical beauty* by willing alone (Augustine 1998, 24). In this way one is reminded of destroying oneself through external things that cannot logically bring happiness. The realization which somehow happens during a life of short-term pleasure to short-term pleasure is that there is nothing to show, nothing created, nothing but the investment waste of a life that revolves around a substance. External things become attachments by requiring a continually increased commitment of tending and servicing. "For since the flaw is opposed to the nature, the more it destroys the integrity of the nature, the worse it is. Therefore, when you condemn a flaw, you are praising the thing whose integrity you miss. And to what does that integrity belong, if not to the nature?" (Augustine 1993, 99–100).

Augustine also invites the individual with a disorderly will to get in touch with, and to understand the integrity of his own nature. If an individual is able to condemn cannabis abuse or dependence as an attachment to a (unnecessary) temporal thing, in that very act he reveals (knowledge or evidence of) integrity and an orderly way of life. It was pointed out in chapter 3 when considering the seven criteria of cannabis dependence that one of the criteria was "many past failed attempts to quit cannabis use." If a particular user had tried to quit multiple times and so at least had met this criterion, then Augustine's point here is applicable, that there exists in one's doubt or questioning one's habit and way of using cannabis. In imagining another way of life one can potentially "re-order" one's life. Necessary for re-ordering a will is an authentic will to live a Godly life. Augustine's concluding reflection of the *Confessions* emphasizes the necessity of individuals themselves authentically asking for help:

> What angel can help a human being to grasp it? Only you can be asked, only you can be begged, only on your door can we knock (Matt. 7:7–8). Yes indeed, that is how it is received, how it is found, how the door is opened. (Augustine 1998, 305)

Scientific Realism and Christian Ethics

In a remarkable 1971 book called *Turned on by God*, J. Elliott Corbett applies a Christian perspective to three recreational drugs: marihuana, LSD, and heroin. The first chapter ("Marihuana: Is Our Nation in Danger of Going to Pot?") reinforces the moral arguments presented in part III (especially rejecting the law criminalizing users). He attempts to point out the importance for Christians to face and be advocates of scientific truth. The guiding theme of Corbett's application of the life of Christ is *redemption*, the redemption of every believer by Jesus Christ. As ideally imitators of Christ, Christians are encouraged by Corbett to be redemption-minded in understanding cannabis users.

Corbett begins this marihuana chapter: "In no area of public controversy are falsehoods as mixed with facts as they are with respect to marihuana" (Corbett 1971, 13). Corbett provides his reflection at a time in U.S. society (1971) when there was a visible and observable "gap" between an older and a younger generation.

> It has become a symbol of rejection of the contemporary order. The older generation has passed marihuana laws which cannot be enforced or applied equally; they have established a penalty system which informed and objective observers regard as unjust. Thus a mockery has been made of the law, and youth are quick to perceive this. Through smoking marihuana, a young person may feel he can show his despite for the draft, the entire Vietnam operation, the "white racist power structure," etc. (Corbett 1971, 23)

Here Corbett points out several things *still true* in twenty-first-century United States: the cannabis laws are unenforceable (as use is rampant and a black market exists making cannabis widely available, not to mention the 1990s boom in hydroponics and large grow operations in houses being used by cannabis producers discreetly and seemingly free from detection), not applied equally (although whites use cannabis more than Latinos or African Americans, the latter two groups are criminalized, arrested more than whites), and the penalty system as "unjust" (in light of the context of Corbett, there has been an improvement from the 2–10 year minimum sentence for cannabis possession, wrecking many lives as a result; however, the "otherwise law-abiding citizen" would argue any penalty for possession is unjust). As a result, a "mockery" has been made of the law. The moral arguments of Kant, Mill, Aristotle, and Augustine would all be used against a law attempting to use mere rhetoric and scare tactics and the law as a tool to oppress rather than provide retributive justice. Also, "youth are quick to perceive this" false propaganda regarding cannabis use, available to almost half of 10th graders and almost all 12th graders in the current U.S.

Continuing with Corbett:

> In a recent Massachusetts Court decision (*Massachusetts v. Leis and Weiss*), the court decided that alcohol is used to relax in the face of tensions induced by participating in contemporary society and is therefore acceptable. But marihuana is used purely for pleasure and in order to get "high" and thus deserves its illegal and criminal status. . . . As someone has said, with this kind of self-righteous stance, it is as though the older generation were saying to the younger, "I've got mine, Jack, but we are not going to let you have yours." (Corbett 1971, 23)

Here Corbett exposes nicely the alcohol/cannabis double-standard, one obviously arbitrary if not patently unjust. This has the effect of making righteous the "younger generation" and power-motivated the "older generation." Corbett cites Dr. Robert Gould further on this generational conflict and the deeper symbolism of cannabis amid a society in which all use some type of drugs:

> Since today's youngsters have grown up in this society, they cannot help identifying with it—like us, they take drugs daily and routinely for release from the same kinds of tension. But if alcohol is the adults' chosen thing for his purposes, youth, as usual, need to choose something else to be their own thing. By choosing marihuana, a youngster is thus able to imitate his parents while at the same time rebelling against them—a remarkable achievement, in fact. (Corbett 1971, 24)

Corbett characterizes what sounds much like what has been called "amotivational syndrome" or perhaps symptoms associated with cannabis dependence. This most morally questionable way of using cannabis is here, as has emerged throughout this part III Moral Assessment of cannabis use, described as "hedonistic."

> Another real problem which marihuana presents is the tendency on the part of users to withdraw, to become reticent and reflective instead of actively seeking to solve the pressing problems of our present society. Even apart from any effects upon the mind, just to enjoy smoking marihuana takes several hours out of one's day. Except for some vague benefits in terms of creativity, persons do not take marihuana to become more effective on their jobs; they take it for recreational use. Also, no one rationally tries to make a case for marihuana's sharpening the mind, as bridge or chess might do, or for its improving oneself physically, as tennis or swimming.
>
> There real issue focuses on apathy and loss of motivation, says Dr. David Smith, director of the Haight-Ashbury Free Clinic in San Francisco. How do we overcome this and avoid withdrawal from participation in the real world? Some marihuana users undoubtedly "cop out" for hedonistic reasons—it is pleasurable to do so. Others may find life in our tension-ridden, problem-laden culture painful. Withdrawal seems necessary. (Corbett 1971, 24–25)

Such hedonistic users would not generate a successful moral defense of their actions from the moral perspectives already considered, and Corbett employs nicely the nomenclature of his day in separating out and morally condemning those users who are "copping out."

After presenting basic information about cannabis Corbett's next section, "Marihuana and Christian Concern," has him preface his consideration with a goal: "In the paragraphs that follow, we shall focus our attention on the Christian's concern about marihuana: in connection with goals, intentions, means, and consequences" (Corbett 1971, 25). As for the "goals" of a Christian examining the issue of cannabis use, Corbett begins:

> Certainly one of these would be to discover the truth about the drug. If Christians are to exhibit a healthy respect for realism, it will be necessary to strip away all the folklore and old wives' tales concerning cannabis and to face harsh or pleasant facts about the hemp plant as research reveals them. (Corbett 1971, 25)

It is fairly evident that the current Social Reality of cannabis use in the United States does not (and has not in the past century) demonstrate such a "healthy respect for realism." The U.S. federal government has used false propaganda and a pretended ignorance of the benign nature of the effects of cannabis, and most importantly rejects the Scientific Reality of cannabis use.

Corbett stresses the need to be honest and upfront with youth in educational campaigns in the school system. As he puts it:

> No scare campaign based on undocumented anecdotes and newspaper clippings will do. We must possess the confidence that youth will respond to the truth and that their feelings, rather than being manipulated, may be positively formed if informed by reality. (Corbett 1971, 26)

Such respect for the ability of today's youth to responsibly resist opportunities to use cannabis is lacking. The U.S. federal government continues to refuse to recognize the right of adults to use cannabis. A major reason given for this refusal is that such legalization would "send the wrong message to youth" (and result in a rampant cannabis problem among children and adolescents, heroin addiction skyrocketing as per the gateway drug argument). This assumes the youth depend upon the federal government to know the nature and dangers of cannabis use. This is an assumption not at all born out in consideration of the major risk factors of adolescent cannabis use. This is furthermore ironic given that youth seem to have little problem "getting the message" about the dangers of legalized drugs of nicotine/cigarettes and alcohol. "Scare campaigns" are the essence of the Social Reality approach to educating youth, one based upon fear and not rational thought and willed action, setting a precedent for similar mindless following of authorities into adulthood.

As for "intentions" and cannabis use, Corbett poses the question, Why do youth turn to marihuana? Citing psychiatrist Robert Gould, who has experience working with New York City users of cannabis and other drugs, Corbett presents four basic groups or types of motivation of users among youth:

1) curiosity, adventurousness, and desire to conform to group
2) expression of mild rebellion and growing-up pains

3) withdrawal, passivity, shyness, inhibitions, feelings of inadequacy and insecurity
4) hippies (looking for an inner truth, salvation through love, and a way to avoid hypocrisy, the rat race, competitiveness, and false values of society) (Corbett 1971, 28)

Of the first group Corbett explains: "If, from a Christian perspective, one considers reasons given for smoking marihuana, several of these are cause for special concern. 'The desire to conform to the group' stands in sharp contradiction with the counsel of St. Paul: 'Do not be conformed to this world' (Rom 12:2)" (Corbett 1971, 29). And further, "Apparently many students are conforming and will conform; they follow the lead of their peer group. The pertinent question facing the concerned Christian at this point is, How do you influence the peer group?" (Corbett 1971, 30).

I would suggest instead of directly "influencing" the peer group the recognition and steering clear of such a group (indirectly influencing them by demonstrating an alternative to going along with the gang). As for the second and third groups, Corbett hopes a Christian would reach out to and address "mild rebelling and growing pains" as well as those who are characterized by "withdrawal, passivity, shyness, inhibitions, feelings of inadequacy and insecurity." He hopes such youth can be effectively offered Christian faith as a source of fulfillment instead of cannabis use. The "hippies" are not much dealt with by Corbett here (indirectly through "drug expert" Richard H. Blum) but it seems consistent with these expressed concerns by Corbett that he would be similarly concerned about a youth (under 18 years of age, let us suppose) who was living a hippie lifestyle including the use of cannabis. In light of these four groups, there seem very few uses by adolescents of cannabis that would be acceptable from a Christian perspective (other than perhaps medical uses).

In his next section, "Means, Marihuana, and Christian Concern," and in the subsection called "Law Enforcement," Corbett reminds the current readers of this work of the penalties that existed for cannabis possession in the 1950s and most of the 1960s in the United States, ones that gave more prison time to cannabis users than to rapists and murderers. It may be that this deeply ingrained position against the use or possession of marijuana continues to exist as the current Social Reality in the United States:

> Under the Narcotics Control Act of 1956, imprisonment of two to ten years and a possible maximum fine of $10,000 were provided for a first offense for marihuana possession. However, in the case of first offenders on a possession conviction, it has been possible to secure a suspended sentence and receive probation. In 1970 a bill (H.R. 18583) passed the Congress which eliminated mandatory

> sentences for possession of marihuana and reduced the penalty to no more than one year in prison and a fine of $5,000. (Corbett 1971, 31)

Again, Corbett published this book in 1971, shortly after which Nixon would deem cannabis Schedule I. However, further considering the legal state of affairs from the 1950s and 1960s (perhaps shining light on the strongly held moral convictions of the "older generation" even into the twenty-first-century United States):

> State laws for marihuana possession and sale are often much harsher. In some cases penalties range up to twenty years on a first offense for possession. Thus it is obvious that a system of invoking harsh penalties has been used as the primary deterrent in dealing with the marihuana user. (Corbett 1971, 31)

This is the Social Reality way to deal with cannabis users, to wield the criminal law to punish them. Consider this situation from the perspective of a cannabis user and "otherwise law-abiding citizen," who is faced with the obvious double-standard of Social Reality accepting recreational intoxicant alcohol while condemning recreational intoxicant cannabis.

It is often difficult for marihuana users to understand why such severe penalties are imposed against possession of the drug while no penalties are rendered for alcohol possession. Yet half of the criminal homicides and a large percentage of other serious crimes, such as rape and assault, are committed by persons under the influence of alcohol. Sociologist Alfred R. Lindesmith explains how this may have come to pass:

> The upper social classes from which the lawmakers are generally drawn usually use alcohol as their favorite narcotic and until recently knew little or nothing from direct observation or experience about marihuana. It is therefore quite easy to understand that they should be very gentle with the user of alcohol and very severe with the marihuana user. (Corbett 1971, 33)

Corbett summarizes five points which should make Christians "concerned about using the law enforcement approach to deal with the marihuana user," including:

1. the legal penalty structure is unjust
2. "when one considers laws regulating users of alcohol, the marihuana user does not appear to enjoy his constitutional rights to equal protection under the law."
3. With cannabis the legal focus is on "judgment rather than on correction or rehabilitation"

4. "the Christian is led to question a law which doesn't work, is unenforceable, and tends to weaken the fabric of the legal system since it invites disobedience."
5. not fair to prevent "the vast majority from using a drug harmless to them" because of "only a few" who suffer "temporary psychotic episodes or commit crimes in connection with marihuana use" (Corbett 1971, 33).

Into his "Research" section, Corbett moves beyond law enforcement to consider this way of "meeting problems connected with marihuana use." Into the twenty-first century, the U.S. federal government has stifled and hindered research on the medicinal effects of cannabis. Consider the problems existing in 1971 and thereabouts, problems we have inherited entering the twenty-first century:

> Another means of meeting problems connected with marihuana use has been intensive research on some of the questions that remain unanswered. Such research has been severely handicapped by the general public. Therefore, while federal agencies are glad to receive funds for research on marihuana, they may be hesitant to publicize any studies which discount the drug's evil effects for fear that such publicity might place in jeopardy other desired research financing. The public and Congress tend to take this kind of attitude: "Here are some funds for research on marihuana. But be sure you come up with the right answers. For we know in advance it's responsible for creating a lot of pot-headed dope fiends." (Corbett 1971, 34)

Here Corbett highlights the hesitancy to publicize results from cannabis studies that counter what I have called the Social Reality of cannabis use. This attitude seems to be borne out in the recent study on American attitudes in chapter 5. The public continues to base its views on cannabis from the media and federal government, and the federal government is basing its policy decisions on the Social Reality.

The current reluctance if not sheer and utter rejection of the therapeutic and medicinal uses of cannabis contrasts with how a Christian should approach the uses:

> The Christian would certainly applaud the means of research as one avenue in dealing with the marihuana problem. Emphasizing realism and seeking out God's truth locked in the universe, the Christian welcomes any steps which bring accurate knowledge to those placed in decision-making roles. The Christian faith also stands in judgment of any reluctance by federal bodies to announce the results of research which is contrary to long-cherished views of the general public. Further, the Christian would have to call into question the tardiness with which the government and other public bodies have sought to develop research re-

> garding marihuana usage. Perhaps this has been due to the vicious circle described by researchers Weil and Zinberg: "Because it [marihuana] is dangerous, they are reluctant to allow work to be done on it. Because no work is done, people continue to think of it as dangerous." (Corbett 1971, 35)

If Christians would think of research as at least necessary (but not sufficient) for dealing with cannabis use, then they should be dissatisfied with the fact that in the forty years since Corbett's book, nothing has changed. Rejection of cannabis has included the federal government's discontinuing its own IND program for cannabis in 1992, not because it was ineffective but because it conflicted with the message the government thinks itself obliged to "send" to the public regarding the effects of cannabis (implying the mere scientific truth would be ineffective).

In addition to the legal and research approaches, Corbett moves to the educational approach. Here he once again emphasizes truth and accurate information, not false propaganda:

> Whenever educational efforts are based on facts and sound research, communicated through professional techniques, and implemented through the use of trained personnel in whom students can place their trust, then Christians will support these efforts. Not only is truth at stake in this instance but also respect for the one to be educated. Educators will demonstrate such respect by refusing to propagate known falsehoods, use inferior methods of instruction, or enlist teachers pupils will automatically turn off. On the latter point, young people today, especially the older ones, are unlikely to accept information presented by law enforcement officials. Public health authorities are more likely to be given a responsive hearing. (Corbett 1971, 36–37)

This message has been largely unheeded by the U.S. federal government, continuing to present cannabis use as per the Social Reality and accompanying myths, presenting cannabis to youths in a way that has demonstrated no resulting effect in trends of experimentation among adolescents. Again emphasized by Corbett is respect for youth, telling them the truth and trusting them in their decision-making.

Onto to a consideration of "Consequences," where Corbett prefaces his consideration with: "So let us consider what happens to those convicted, those who suffer psychological damage, those who use marihuana over a long term, and others" (Corbett 1971, 37). Of those arrested, consider as justification for the title and a major motivation for writing my own current book Corbett's recognition here:

> There is little question that marihuana laws have often made criminals out of otherwise law-abiding citizens. That is, those convicted of marihuana possession

> charges and subsequently jailed have often not committed any other crime, nor have they done any harm to other human beings. (Corbett 1971, 37)

And Corbett cites further harm produced by criminalizing cannabis users:

> For a first offender, the fact that our criminal processes are not at all good for reforming people is not too significant. His arrest for marihuana, however, may mark the beginning of a more serious criminal career. Not only will his arrest record make his obtaining a job that much more difficult, but an arrest, together with having to put up bail and go through any further stages of the criminal process for a crime which he believes almost every young person commits and is no way wrong, can only increase his bitterness and alienation from society. (Corbett 1971, 37)

Corbett also presents several arrested for cannabis possession who at the time were receiving sentences 20 times as great as those for rape, robbery, arson, kidnapping, or second-degree murder. (Corbett 1971, 38) Corbett's plea to Christians regarding the harsh penalization of cannabis users rests on the basic Christian principles of justice:

> In terms of human waste and degradation, no sensitive Christian can view the severe consequences of harsh penalties for marihuana-connected "crime" and believe that our nation is moving constructively. The imposition of long sentences for minor offenses in no way coincides with basic Christian principles of justice. The results of imprisonment due to mandatory minimums cannot be squared with the kind of redemptive response the Christian gospel requires of its adherents. Is there a serious Christian alive who believes that a Christ who offered redemption to a criminal on the cross (Luke 23:43) would not want his followers to opt for a redemptive rather than a punitive approach to a minor drug user? (Corbett 1971, 39)

This redemptive approach is central to Corbett's application of Christian belief in response to cannabis use, one in contrast with the Social Reality and current U.S. federal government staunch and retributive stance.

In his next sub-section, "The generation gap," Corbett presents several points that help elucidate the Beat-Hippie subculture and specifically the attitude of those who portray a certain "attitude" toward society (similar to Polsky's description of the Beats in chapter 4). Dr. Robert Gould is cited as stating: "These youngsters might be helped if they could trust adult authorities. They can't trust us if we use unjust or hypocritical laws to control them" (Corbett 1971, 40). Citing scripture relevant to cannabis laws, Corbett points out the judgment to come for those who hypocritically legitimate alcohol while condemning cannabis (knowing the significant penalties incurred unfairly by users of the latter):

> If present legal prescriptions regarding marihuana have compartmentalized and polarized our society and ruined its redemptive role, then there is cause for Christian concern. Any system which puts men at odds with their brothers—whether the division be national, racial, or generational—must be called into question.
>
> When youth look about them and see that, aside from age requirements, there are no restrictions for possession of alcohol—a drug related to more crime and more highway accidents than any other drug—then they tend to feel that they system has placed a halo on hypocrisy. We know that Matthew took a whole chapter to record Jesus' stinging attack upon the hypocrisy of the cotemporary Establishment. In six sections of chapter 23 Jesus leads off with "Woe to you, scribes and Pharisees, hypocrites!" Thus current charges of sanctimoniousness must be examined seriously by the Christian. Pompous pretense will not save anyone. (Corbett 1971, 40–41)

Here again the hypocrisy in advocating legalization of alcohol while criminalizing the use of cannabis, a hypocrisy Corbett here interprets as the same kind of hypocrisy condemned by Christ. Furthermore, it seems each Christian, before rendering a personal verdict on the legalization of cannabis, must examine him/herself for "sanctimoniousness," especially in light of this double-standard advocating the right to use alcohol while criminalizing the use of cannabis.

Corbett also clearly rejects the gateway argument concluding cannabis use leads to "harder drugs" (e.g., heroin):

> From a Christian perspective, if it could be shown that marihuana use leads to heroin addiction, this would be cause for alarm by the man of faith. Since the truth seems to be overwhelmingly otherwise, the Christian, who bows to the truth, accepts this conclusion. (Corbett 1971, 42)

Corbett rejects the gateway argument and advises Christians to do the same. This is a staple of the Social Reality of cannabis use, one the federal government will not likely relinquish regardless of the overwhelming evidence to the contrary. As has been seen throughout previous chapters, the gateway theory simply fails. There is a decisive contrast between the Scientific and Social Reality on this particular point.

In his last two pages of this section, before moving toward his conclusion and along his most essentially redemptive approach Corbett insightfully presents a sub-section called "Crimes against Oneself." Corbett begins:

> One issue not treated as yet is a philosophical one, yet an issue very directly related to *consequences.* That question is, Should persons guilty of crimes without victims (crimes against oneself) be charged with a criminal offense and be subject to severe penalties? "After all," says the regular marihuana user, "what's it to

you? I'm not hurting anyone else; if there are ill effects, I'm only injuring myself." (Corbett 1971, 48)

Perhaps this argument can be considered the "what's it to you?" defense of cannabis use. Just as a current alcohol user, cigarette smoker (or any other risky actor), would respond were their drug prohibited by the Social Reality, "what's it to you?" you (fellow citizen, dignified human being) cannot tell me whether or not I can use cannabis. Corbett also cites two further lines of sub-argument to support the "what's it to you" argument. First, "many persons, who do harm to themselves regularly — smoke three packs of cigarettes a day, overuse sleeping pills, use bizarre weight control methods, etc.—are not adjudged criminals and jailed" (Corbett 1971, 48). Here, Corbett is using the reason that just because something is harmful to the user does not mean it should be criminalized.[10] Second, to counter those who would cite a danger of having cannabis users intoxicated while driving motor vehicles:

> Furthermore, the marihuana users may say, "If I drive a car when I'm stoned and get into an accident where others are hurt, then, of course, I should be charged. Or if I go off my rocker when I'm high and assault someone—although I don't expect to—then I would not resent a criminal indictment. But if I'm minding my own business, don't bother anyone and smoke grass because I like grass, then society should have no complaint against me. After all, it's my life." (Corbett 1971, 48)

Corbett cannot find the question of self-harm specifically being addressed by scripture but attempts to apply the Christian faith in the general to cannabis use:

> The Christian faith does not provide specific guidance on such a matter as this. Nevertheless, Christ's Great Commandment, "Love . . . your neighbor as *yourself*" (Luke 10:27, italics mine), ought to be saying something to us here. Self-love, self-respect, and self-dignity are at the heart of the Christian gospel. . . .
>
> If a regular marihuana user is engaging in self-hate or making use of a self-destructive device, the sensitive Christian, who covets fulfillment for him too, should be concerned. Though he would not likely be so judgmentally concerned as to desire the application of stiff penalties, at the same time he ought to be redemptively concerned enough to encourage redirection of the pot smoker's life. (Corbett 1971, 49)

Here the strategy of a Christian for one who is cannabis dependent is redemptive, "encouraging redirection." This is quite dissimilar from the Social Reality strategy of retributive justice. Corbett continues:

> Beyond this, there is the question of criminal versus civil offense. In terms of consequences, it would be difficult for any Christian to take the position that a

> marihuana user—if he has not harmed anyone else—should be subject to severe criminal penalties. A criminal record, even for a minor offense, has a way of haunting a person by closing off to him future educational and vocational opportunities. In view of this, should any charge be made, a nonvengeful position would require that such a charge be placed in the civil courts. (Corbett 1971, 49)

Here Corbett advocates a "nonvengeful" position, one in contrast with the Social Reality of cannabis use. He perceptively points out the real negative effects on a cannabis user's life, the legal consequences, ones currently experienced by students and young adults in the twenty-first-century United States disqualified for student loans as well as various occupations because of cannabis convictions. Here again it is recognized that the criminal offense and practical results are out of balance with the damage done (if any) by the offense itself.

In his final section of this chapter on cannabis Corbett presents "Taking the Redemptive Initiative." He begins by summarizing his foregoing analysis (much of which I have presented above). Complementing my current approach of using various disciplines to view the meaning of cannabis use, Corbett points out the necessity of considering cannabis from multiple disciplinary perspectives in order to get to the truth of cannabis use:

> In the light of all this, in what direction does the redemptive initiative lie? Of one thing we may be sure: a common effort of people in all fields involved in drug abuse is required—law enforcement personnel, researchers, educators, medical scientists, psychiatrists, legislators, sociologists, and clergymen. As Dr. Robert Gould has stated so clearly, "Any single discipline trying to provide the full answer to the drug problem will inevitably fail, since in all likelihood the causes of drug abuse are multidetermined and therefore require a many-sided approach." (Corbett 1971, 50)

Corbett's sub-sections of this final section include "Reducing Penalties Now," "Research," "Education," "Using Public Health as a Model," "Should Marihuana Be Legalized?" "Transforming Society," and "Role of the Church." Corbett reinforces his foregoing presentation of cannabis and the Christian response, advocating a public health model to educate about cannabis use, legalization with accompanying educational and rehabilitation program, developing ("transforming") society in a way which had people not interested in turning to cannabis for escape or withdrawal, and the church becoming innovative and open to ways of connecting with youthful generations.

Corbett expresses what I take to be further support for a focus on the Beats, the hippies, and alienated sub-cultures in general. Corbett imagines a different type of U.S. society, a "transformed" society, one inspired in part by the conclusion of Dr. Stanley Yolles: "if we are ever to solve the problem of drug abuse, it is crucial for us to focus on and try to solve the root causes of alienation." And after this Yolles conclusion, Corbett continues with thoughts quite challenging to the twenty-first-century situation:

> Marihuana has become a symbol of rebellion against society—with its corrupting Vietnam War, economically debilitating nuclear arms race, highly competitive business system, impersonal technology, inflexible and entrenched institutions. So how do we change the social structure of our nation to make it more in keeping with our cultural norms? How do we create the kind of society youth will not want to rebel against but embrace, will not want to withdraw from but participate in?
>
> A part of the redemptive initiative then would be to attempt to develop the kind of society represented by less tension, more means to reconciliation, more basic equity and opportunities for fulfillment, less competition and more cooperation, more freedom and less oppression. In such a society no man would be cast in a mold. In this society citizens would want to participate, not escape; they would find acceptance by brothers of divergent views and feel at ease with friends and neighbors of contrasting stripe. (Corbett 1971, 51)

And in concluding this chapter on cannabis, Corbett's final two paragraphs:

> Drug abuse is a multidimensional problem requiring a multidimensional answer. There is no use in pretending that the whole answer will be miraculously provided by religion or the church. For some of the answers, we must look to legislators, researchers, educators, health specialists, and social reformers.
>
> But if most marihuana users are afflicted with anomie, and suffer disorientation, normlessness, anxiety, and isolation, the Christian faith, working through the instrument of the church, could help. Drug users could receive guidance, discover norms, overcome frustration, and find that they belong. Indeed, through the new high of worship, they could be turned on by God. (Corbett 1971, 64)

Healing, Christian Faith, and Cannabis

To conclude this chapter and Christian response to the question of the morality of cannabis use and cannabis law, consider the question of cannabis use for medicinal purposes, specifically in light of the more general Christian consideration of the proper place of healing in the ministry of Jesus and therefore Christian ethics. Morton Kelsey's *Healing and Christianity in Ancient Thought and Modern Times* compliments Escohotado's presentation both of the Greeks central importance in how medicine was most basically understood and the twentieth-century synthetic/non-synthetic distinction. Kelsey's major purpose in his book is to better understand the place of medical interventions in Christian life. By application I will apply several of Kelsey's points to a Christian position regarding cannabis use for therapeutic purposes.

Adding to the scriptural analysis of the cannabis plant from the Old Testament consider now the meaning of sickness and suffering for the people and cultures of the Old Testament. In chapter 3, "Religious Healing in the Ancient World", Kelsey points out that

> In the Old Testament generally there was little thought of any need for stop-and-go signals on God's power for life and death. Deuteronomy 32:39 pretty well summarizes the basic attitude of most of the Old Testament: "It is I who deal death and life; when I have struck it is I who heal (and none can deliver from my hand)." (Kelsey 1973, 33–34)

A belief that is perhaps still existent within the Social Reality on cannabis use is the Old Testament view that sickness is "God's rebuke for man's sin" (Kelsey 1973, 34) and "there was really no end to the ailments Yahweh could produce for the benefit of men who did not obey him to the letter" (Kelsey 1973, 35). "Again and again one is told that to follow wisdom and the law will bring health and long life, while to do otherwise will result in misery, misfortune, sickness, and death" (Kelsey 1973, 38).

So the Old Testament view of sickness and ailments was as punishments for disobedience to God. It is not hard to see why there would exist, therefore, people shunned and negatively stigmatized for their suffering and disease, as given this basic belief that sickness was retributive punishment by God, the suffering was justified and therefore righteous and to be endured.

To elaborate further on the Old Testament meaning of sickness, consider that this view of sickness as punishment complimented two essential factors of the Old Testament Israelites, first the importance of obedience to God for their very survival as a people called by God and second as a way of rejecting popular explanations of sickness as involving other gods or evil spirits:

> Back of this concern with the disciplinary effect of disease rather than with healing were two most important factors. First was the stress upon the group. In much of the Old Testament there was so much emphasis upon the people Israel as a whole that what happened to the individual was a secondary matter.... The other principal reason for neglect of individual healing was the fact that any idea of evil spirits as the cause of sickness and harm was rejected. The belief was common among most peoples at the time of the early Hebrews. Both the Egyptians and the Babylonians held that sickness resulted from the demonic ill will of various gods or evil spirits. The Persians with their well-developed dualism looked on diseases as one activity of the powers of darkness. In the Vedic writings it is sometimes even difficult to decide whether a noun refers to a sickness or to the demon who

> caused it, so closely are the two related. But much of the Old Testament was an attempt to bring the people of Israel to a worship of Yahweh alone, who was seen as the sole source of both good and evil, of sickness as well as health. (Kelsey 1973, 38)

Now moving to a consideration of asceticism in the form of Gnosticism, a type of belief system assumed by the Social Reality in regards to cannabis use. Absolute abstinence from cannabis use as per Social Reality is in line with an assumed Gnostic goal of total denial of intoxication (of any and all pleasures and appetites). Kelsey presents Gnosticism in historical context as influenced by a central tenet of those who believed in Greek gods and then attempted to assimilate the gospel of Christ while denying Christ was actually in bodily, physical, human form:

> (of Greek gods, e.g. Aesclepius) these various separate gods of healing portray one of the most basic and imbedded ideas of ancient Greek culture. This is the notion of the dichotomy of mind and body, of *nous* and *physis*, known as Gnosticism. Out of this came a theory of the origin of man which held that men had been made when the *nous* somehow became entrapped in the grosser body, the *physis*. This material part was nonessential. Later, as Gnosticism matured, the body came to be viewed as positively evil, and salvation was seen as the liberation of the mind-soul from it, so that the valuable part of man might have freedom and bliss.
>
> The combination of Greek thinking and Greek healing cults did not offer a resolution of this division in man. And so in Gnosticism a point of view emerged in which healing of the body was clearly a relatively unimportant matter. In some Gnostic asceticism the body was practically destroyed. Until the Council of Nicaea the church fathers were constantly fighting the influences of the Gnostic point of view on Christianity because its low valuation of the body resulted in a split in man's being. In a later chapter we shall consider how far the Gnostic point of view has crept back into the teaching and practice of the church. (Kelsey 1973, 49–50)

Here Kelsey not only emphasizes the basic Gnostic belief in a complete split between mind and body, but also belief in a myth whereby the mind is in a separate vessel of body, with the latter being only an impediment to the true reality of pure mind/soul free from the body. Kelsey promises to get back to this point as he discusses the modern church, and for our purposes we will consider the possibility that Christians assume this Gnostic belief in rejecting all cannabis use and that the Social Reality of cannabis use is essentially Gnostic in regards to cannabis use.

Moving into a focus on the ministry of Jesus and the question of what place healing and the use of medicine should play in the life of a Christian, Kelsey starts with Scripture. In his chapter, The Unique Healing Ministry of Jesus of Nazareth, he points out: "nearly one-fifth of the entire Gospels are devoted to Jesus' healing and the discussions occasioned by it. Except for miracles in general, this is by far the greatest emphasis given to any one kind of experience in the narrative" (Kelsey 1973, 54). Further explaining the centrality of healing to the ministry of Jesus, Kelsey explains consistency between agape love and healing:

> The ministry of healing of Jesus is certainly in line with the constant emphasis in his teachings upon compassion and caring about one's neighbor. Certainly it is not out of character with that teaching. This stress on the importance of *agape* love, is a most basic aspect of his teaching. One of the most concrete ways of expressing that love is through concern about another's physical and emotional condition, and the removal of torturing infirmities, physical hindrances, and mental or emotional illness. (Kelsey 1973, 57)

Kelsey contrasts this emphasis on agape love and compassion to that of not only the Old Testament but also of Aristotle:

> Aristotle saw no basic change in the popular theory, which was also the personality theory of most of the Old Testament, reaching its ultimate expression in the book of Proverbs. Here wisdom is enough; if you get wisdom, and exalt wisdom, then you shall be brought to honor. For the Jews in general, morality was a relatively simple matter of education and good will, and fear a most useful instrument to enforce the right way when good will was not present.
>
> Jesus, on the other hand, treated human beings as much more complex. He believed and taught that, up to a point, men do have conscious control of personality and that it should be exercised and developed. (Kelsey 1973, 62)

Although important to discipline one's mind and one's body, there was also the question of the state of the *spirit*, a state integral to the health of the individual human being as a whole. Addressing the way the spirit could cause sickness:

> Demonic spirits made people sick physically, mentally, and morally. They could not be controlled by the conscious will of the individual, once it had been set aside by the alien power. The persons' powers of knowing were not impaired; he knew that he was possessed but could do nothing about it. It was a matter of possessing the will, not of knowledge alone. (Kelsey 1973, 63)

This idea of the will being "possessed" is one inviting a mental picture of the immoral user of cannabis, of being so impaired (or "dependent") on cannabis that she did virtually nothing else than use cannabis. In this sense, cannabis "owns" that person in that the person works for the use of the drug for itself, as an end in itself. Although on an Aristotelian view, one's bad disposition and poorly developed character would logically lead to dependence and by using in such an "extreme" (self-indulgent) way, would have one fail to attain happiness. In the Old Testament, one possessed by cannabis would suffer poverty and want. Christ however can heal the spirit and thereby simply annihilate this long-developed bad disposition or sickness of mental and physical nature.[11]

Jesus recognized man's essential inability to defeat the demonic and therefore the need of each individual for spiritual help. Jesus' healing of the sick was in a sense cooperative with the sick individual, helping them to expel demonic spirits. Love was the cure:

> Man by his own humanity, his own will, cannot deal with the depth and complication of the psychic life in which he participates; single-handed, humanity cannot stand against the demonic. One reason Jesus was so responsive to sickness and sin was his sense that they result from men's domination by alien spirits, to which his whole being was antagonistic. The only way to drive them out—to bring health of body, mind, and soul—was through the Spirit of God, the Holy Spirit. This is characterized by love, by agape. Thus the injunction of Jesus that we love one another as he loved is not just an ethical maxim. It also has healing implications. Only a life characterized by love can give hospitality to the Spirit of God. (Kelsey 1973, 64)

Jesus' way of healing the sick was cognizant of the person's being possessed, controlled, living a life they really did not want to live and from which Jesus could free them through His spiritual healing. In light of cannabis use and specifically of those dependent upon cannabis, Jesus, response of agape love is in stark contrast to that of the Social Reality and that of the U.S. federal government. St. Augustine seems influenced by this same healing spirit of Christ by recognizing that one who has some inordinate desire is to be primarily pitied and compassionately considered, as they are damaging or harming themselves.

Perhaps the cannabis-dependent person is being possessed by a demonic spirit. Assuming this for the sake of application of Kelsey's line of reasoning here, consider first that: "Nowhere in the Gospels is there any suggestion of Jesus asking a sick person what he had done or whether he had sinned before healing him. Instead he took direct action to meet the need" (Kelsey 1973, 65). Unlike the moral condemnation and criminalization of the Social Reality of cannabis use in the United States, Jesus compassionately counseled and healed persons without judgment. Consider:

> Jesus knew the reality of alien and evil "spirits" that can possess men (today we might often call this condition a mental complex) and also how the reality of God can touch an individual and not only drive out such a spirit but put something else in its place. According to his point of view, man cannot always by his own will fight off the infiltration of alien, evil personality constellations that somehow or other takes possession of him. (Kelsey 1973, 65)

To assume that the cannabis dependent need to be punished and criminalized because they have willed to put themselves in such a state is to ignore the spiritual element of cannabis dependence (or any dependence). Of Jesus' response to such a misunderstanding, one consistent with the Scientific Reality on cannabis use, Kelsey points out: "Thus he made clear that men in their present condition do not deserve or need judgment and punishment, which only drive them further into despair and defeat" (Kelsey 1973, 65). "Men who were sick and in trouble morally needed understanding and compassion, not judgment and punishment. They were up against realities or forces which the human will could not handle on its own; they needed help, and Jesus responded to their need" (Kelsey 1973, 66).

The Christian response is of "help" and of "responding to their need." This echoes the same point made from sociological, psychological perspectives in pointing out that more damage is done to cannabis users by the law than is done by the use itself.

> He was also able to demonstrate the reality of his point of view in opposition to almost the entire Judaic and Greek culture of his time. At least six of his healings were done on the Sabbath to show his own people how important it was to set aside statutes of external observance when there was an opportunity to help a sick or disabled person. Thus Jesus' treatment of men was not just his own unique approach. It was intended as a general way for men to treat one another. As such, it was (and still is) a radically new attitude toward men, with all sorts of implications beyond the healing ministry. (Kelsey 1973, 66)

Consider the metaphors used by Kelsey in reference to Jesus the healer, of a "rescuer" and of a "ladder":

> If Jesus had any one mission, it was to bring the power and healing of God's creative, loving Spirit to bear upon the moral, mental, and physical illnesses of the people around him. It was a matter of rescuing man from a situation in which he could not help himself. Jesus disclosed a new power, a ladder to bring him out of the pit of his brokenness and sin. Leaving man in his wretched condition so as to learn from it makes no sense in this psychological framework. Judgment and punishment only add to a burden already intolerable. (Kelsey 1973, 67)

Punishing cannabis users through retribution with the plan of having the user "learn from his mistakes" makes no sense from a Christian perspective. It is akin to kicking a man when he is down, punishing someone who is already suffering self-induced punishment (e.g., of a life revolving around cannabis use, or perhaps more generally of a life of conduct disorders in adolescents preceding cannabis use, of alienation and lack of motivation in 18–25-year-olds). Christ, in his love and compassion, is the "ladder" leading out of the pit. The Christian conclusion regarding public policy would include such a ladder in easy access to therapy and rehabilitation for such users, not forfeiture of money, dignity, school and job prospects, for what is not a crime but a sickness.

This consideration of cannabis dependence as a sickness (as per DSM-IV-TR, AMA) is one advocated by physicians and unites both Christians and the medical establishment against the Social Reality of cannabis use and federal policy prohibiting cannabis use.

> Jesus' healing actions flowed from his psychological awareness of man's nature and his experiences of sonship with God. Modern medicine has adopted the same nonjudgmental attitude towards healing. The sick person is not to blame. Unless one understands the view Jesus had of man, it is difficult if not impossible to understand his healing ministry. (Kelsey 1973, 67)

Getting into specifics about Jesus' healing ministry is Kelsey's chapter 6, "What, How, and Why Did Jesus Heal?" He here points out, using categories of modern medicine to interpret the types of illnesses healed by Jesus:

> There are broad medical categories which can be helpful in understanding the New Testament descriptions [of healings]. Looked at in terms of the human organism itself, we find three basically different classes of human illness. First, there is organic disease in which the structure or tissue of the body is damaged in some way. Second are the functional disorders, in which sickness results because one organ or part of the body is not working properly. And third, there is psychic or mental illness, which shows up as a disturbance of the personality, and here brain disease is usually included, although there is some question as to how much ordinary mental illness can be blamed on brain damage. (Kelsey 1973, 73)

Of organic disorders, Kelsey explains "these disorders include wounds, foreign bodies, lesions, and resulting blood clots or hemorrhages; bacterial and viral infections, and growths of one kind or another. This group also embraces the deterioration that follows these invasions as well as that which results from long functional disturbance" (Kelsey 1973, 74). Of the second grouping he considers all organs and common diseases, and of the third mental illness, including psychosis, neurosis, or hysteria. He then explains: "It is perfectly clear that the healings of Jesus occurred in all three of these medical categories of disease. But even more interesting is the fact that they occurred predominantly in the first and last groups" (Kelsey 1973, 75).

Not apparently using any medicines or chemicals, herbs (including cannabis) in his ministry, Jesus' "most common means of healing was by speaking words and touching the sick person with his hand" (Kelsey 1973, 79). Jesus' words and touch did two things:

> They awakened the spirit that lay deep within these people, waiting to be touched. And at the same time his actions, words, and attitudes brought contact with the Spirit of God, the creative force of reality, which sets men's minds and bodies aright and recreates them. (Kelsey 1973, 86–87)

Christian healing of cannabis dependence would essentially involve "awakening the spirit that lay deep within these people, waiting to be touched." This could be done by Christians demonstrating the Spirit of God through actions, words, and attitudes. These are all grounded in agape love and are non-judgmental and compassionate. This Christian way of healing can by awakening the spirit of a cannabis dependent person (e.g., rediscovery of spiritual gifts and God's will for his/her life) and through a "creative force" set men's minds and bodies aright, recreating them. Here, perhaps less relevant to law, seems the essence of Christian therapy with cannabis dependenence (and more generally any other dependence problem). The point is that this change was a spiritual change, one that brought health to body and mind as well.

Further debunking asceticism, Christian Kelsey comes back to this point he earlier addressed in light of the prominent Old Testament view of sickness as being punishment from God for sinfulness. It seems reasonable to conclude from Kelsey here that those who defend either Gnosticism or sickness as punishment from God under the name of Christianity are confused. Consider Kelsey on this point, further demonstrating the connection between Christianity and the medical establishment, one sometimes not reflected in the modern Church:

> The "Christian" attitude that glories in sickness is completely alien to that of Jesus of Nazareth; it is aligned on the side of what he was fighting against. I very much suspect that anyone who glories in the benefits of illness has either known little of it in himself or those dear to him, or else has serious masochistic tendencies. Sickness is a destructive and evil phenomenon, and Christ as the incarnation of creativity was dead set against it. Modern medical practice is a monument to the attitude of Jesus; it practices in his way as the churches often do not. (Kelsey 1973, 90)

Especially relevant to the current Social Reality of cannabis use in the United States as intentionally "standing in the way of" healing the multitude of illnesses considered in the therapeutic effects chapter, something which "angers" Jesus, Kelsey applies Mark 3:4, where Jesus "is angry at those who would stand in the way of a healing act; their hearts are hard because they are more interested in religious rules than in human beings. Again we see real hostility toward sickness and the forces that cause it, including those who obstruct healing" (Kelsey 1973, 92). Perhaps the ardent rejection of even legal medicinal cannabis uses is a modern-day example of giving precedence to secular rules rather than to human beings.

Kelsey contrasts Jesus's view with the Old Testament view of illness. He points out:

> Yet although some illness is caused by sin, Jesus did not have any illusion that therefore it all originates in sin. Nor did he hold that once a man had stepped off the way and was suffering for it, he ought to be made to endure the full burden of his mistake. (Kelsey 1973, 94)

The view of sickness being a result of sinfulness of the sick person is one of the Old Testament and yet is for some reason seemingly held by some under the guise of Christianity. Kelsey presents this view as having endured from the medieval period through the Reformation:

> This attitude—the modern feeling that most sickness must result from some basic error or fault on the part of the sick person—comes to us directly from the Reformation. This is one area of medieval thinking the reformers didn't reform. Instead they firmly preserved the medieval idea about man and his need for healing. The thirteenth-century church, for instance, carefully kept a sick man from seeing a doctor until after the priest had come to hear and forgive his sins. Church authorities in nineteenth-century England still thought this decree "wisely made." And English clergy were given detailed instructions, based on references to Calvin, on how to bring a sick man to realize God's purposes in making him suffer. Today many sincere Christians assume that somehow illness, borne properly, makes stronger and better Christians, without questioning why they believed such a thing. (Kelsey 1973, 95–96)

Kelsey firmly states a major point of his work *Healing and Christianity* by rejecting once and for all asceticism from a Christian perspective: "The coming of Jesus, if indeed he was the incarnation of God, wipes out once and for all the notion that God put sickness upon men because he is angry with them. Jesus' ministry of healing embodies the exact antithesis of this idea" (Kelsey 1973, 97).

Conclusion

Throughout the moral assessment of cannabis use there have been revealed several points of convergence and agreement among Mill, Kant, Aristotle, and Christian Ethics. Consider the following points of agreement:

1. *Immoral use of cannabis is one of habitual use without desire.*
   Mill introduced the conception of a will growing apart from desire, so that one uses cannabis without enjoying the effects but rather using purely out of habit (what Weil and Rosen refer to as an "unproductive habit"). Kant would characterize such use as done from mere inclination without motivation, thereby not free and not moral. Aristotle characterizes such a user as extreme and self-indulgent, "pained for the sake of pleasure." Christian ethics has Augustine emphasize inordinate desire growing into a habitual use apart from desire, one which has one "led astray."
2. *Immoral cannabis use fails to engage the "higher faculties" of human beings.*
   Mill in "Utilitarianism" goes to great pains to distinguish hedonism from happiness, the latter having one engaged in the qualitatively higher faculty of intellect. Aristotle too emphasizes the necessity of a virtuous actor engaging the intellect, an active faculty as opposed to the passive faculty of sensation. Kant likewise articulates freedom as acting according to laws and motivations, not according to mere inclinations. Augustine emphasizes employment of the higher faculties in seeking eternal and not temporal goods.
3. *Pleasures preferred vary among human beings and these are not a matter of prescription or legal enforcement.*
   Mill speaks of the utilitarian import of allowing people liberty in self-regarding actions. Kant would have us understand that cannabis use is not typically a matter for applying the categorical imperative but rather a matter for consideration in light of hypothetical imperatives held by specific individuals. As such the preference for cannabis would presuppose some end being met by use. He would also offer as relevant the imperfect duty to oneself to secure one's happiness including choice of pleasure.
4. *Moral use of cannabis must be considered in light of the human sense of dignity and worth, especially relevant to adolescent use of cannabis.*
   Mill explains the import of imparting to youth a sense of their own dignity and moral worth above and beyond a life of satisfying mere animal appetites. Kant offers in detail training exercises and a way of teaching

children what it feels like to act for the sake of duty and the feeling of power and freedom in such action. He also would emphasize the import of humiliation and shame for coming to appreciate this faculty. Aristotle emphasizes parenting as involving teaching children in proper pleasure and pain, experiencing these in the proper ways with regards to the proper objects. Christian ethics would emphasize the difference between acting for temporal goods as opposed to for eternal goods, emphasizing latter as consistent with spiritual life.

5. *Adolescent cannabis use is almost always immoral.*
   Mill would likely find adolescent users ones without an understanding of their higher intellectual faculties and instead developing unproductive habits, the only ones that they perceive as available to them. Adolescents are also likely hedonistic or acting out of peer pressure and therefore not freely choosing but rather going along with the crowd. The Christian ethics of St. Augustine captures nicely this sort of action in his own confession of stealing pears with the gang of his day. Kant too would not likely find adolescent cannabis users employing motivations for their use but rather being moved by mere inclinations, similarly lacking employment of the higher faculties and therefore immoral in use.
6. *Laws prohibiting cannabis use are unjust.*
   Mill would have us appreciate the import of allowing people freedom in self-regarding actions to choose for themselves. This is because of the overall happiness resulting from such respect. To prohibit use (without reason) is to treat adult citizens like children, stunting their growth and weakening the civilization. Kant would have us understand such laws as treating adult citizens as a means to an ends held by the government rather than as an ends in themselves, thereby disrespecting these citizens in a most fundamental way. For Kant, it is simply illogical (and bound to failure) to apply laws to matters of virtue and ethics, essentially dealing with imperfect duties to oneself. Aristotle would have us focus on the lack of distributive justice apparent in cannabis prohibition, especially in a society which tolerates the much more dangerous recreational drug of alcohol. A Christian ethics (Corbett section) would have us appreciate the sense of injustice and hypocrisy in the false propaganda used to support prohibition of cannabis while legalizing and illogically accepting the drug alcohol.
7. *Laws criminalizing cannabis users do violence to citizens.*
   Mill would have us appreciate the partiality evident in cannabis laws, the more appropriate use of opinion and conscience rather than of law to punish users, and perhaps go so far as to condemn current cannabis law as continuing to preserve unjust law in the name of "expediency." He

would have us see these laws as a form of aggression on the part of the government toward cannabis users. Kant would similarly have us appreciate the violence of such laws toward cannabis users, once again emphasizing the conceptual impossibility of using laws to dictate virtue. Corbett similarly emphasizes that a Christian could see the hypocrisy and propaganda supporting cannabis law and criminalization, prescribing a redemptive attitude rather than one of punitive punishment.

Notes

1. Of course, this is inevitably a selective and not exhaustive process. I welcome further discussion of various other relevant scriptures regarding the use of cannabis, although I would be somewhat surprised were those New Testament scriptures to contradict the message and interpretation provided of the three I use here (in addition to those used in the previous chapter from the Old Testament).

2. The context of the early Church, and here of the "order" to "abstain from certain foods," is most likely dealing with asceticism and is rejecting this position. In light of cannabis use, the main application I am making here is to the "order" of the U.S. federal government to "abstain" from cannabis use. There is obvious contrast between the U.S. federal government legal ban on cannabis and those who "know the truth."

3. Although it could be a false dichotomy to assume one is either a slave to cannabis or to others, as some could perhaps display temperance in their cannabis use and also love and genuinely support one's neighbors. Furthermore, this command involves not merely loving others but also loving oneself. Medicinal users of cannabis, caring for and preserving themselves, and also who are using cannabis in a way which is beneficial to their own particular way of life, are perhaps loving themselves as per this command and would not condemn others who similarly chose to use cannabis.

4. Kant would emphasize humiliation as what should properly be felt by individuals who performed actions consistent with all or most of these terms listed by Paul. Mill would similarly emphasize shame as what must ultimately be focused upon in light of those living in such a way.

5. This list of characteristics also seems to return us to a consideration of the heart, the motivating reasons of the user. Again, "It is not what goes into the mouth that defiles, but what comes out of the mouth that defiles."

6. Similar to Aristotle whose language emphasizes various "faculties" of the soul with the rational faculty ideally controlling the lower faculties, and Kant with the rational categorical imperative is freedom.

7. This is a major moral point in the part III Moral Assessment of cannabis use. This is particularly true of the Christian ethic and of the scriptures cited in the previous section.

8. Again, the criteria of cannabis dependence seem to nicely complement this Augustinian idea.

9. In reflecting on this point, Augustine cites Catiline, a person who had committed many crimes popularly considered unmotivated. In response to this example Augustine reasons, "No one would commit murder without a motive, merely because he took pleasure in killing." Augustine believes Cataline's objective to be "to capture the city by violent crimes to obtain honours, government, and wealth" (Augustine 1998, 30).

10. Since his work in 1971, 2007 U.S. has added many additional harms to self tolerated in society (e.g., high-fat, high-cholesterol foods and obesity, diabetes).

11. This he does also to emphasize the more important power was the forgiveness of sins, not the healing of the body.

Conclusion: The Essence of Cannabis Law: Avoiding Change at All Costs

In theory the Schedule I status of cannabis could be changed in the United States Cannabis would be controlled, regulated, and distributed as is alcohol. However, in practice, the Social Reality on cannabis use is entrenched and unquestioned by those who actually create and revise U.S. law. There is probably not much going to change the Schedule I status of cannabis any time soon.

Moral arguments have all concluded cannabis prohibition and criminalization are both immoral. Cannabis prohibition denies distributive justice and cannabis criminalization is a misuse of retributive justice, the latter committing a harm on "otherwise law-abiding citizens" who have not harmed anyone. As for using cannabis, moral theories above applied have shown cannabis use in itself to be neither moral nor immoral, but moral or immoral depending upon the way in which it is used. This way is particularly focused on the motivations and the disposition of the user in question, and more generally on the specific faculties of the soul in the user. Temperance is the definitive virtue and central to all moral theories on the subject of intoxication (alcohol and cannabis in particular). Aristotelian is reasoning inherent in the criteria of the clinical diagnoses of dependence and abuse. For Aristotle, the goal is to achieve moderation in all of our actions, with cannabis use this means avoiding the extremes of self-indulgence and boorishness in order to achieve a temperate disposition.

Although cannabis users can furthermore articulate a cogent and convincing Scientific Reality of cannabis use, rendering cannabis relatively as safe as caffeine and certainly safer than the legal "social lubricant" alcohol, the fact of the matter is that the federal government and those who serve it are dedicated to uphold the seven traditional beliefs of the Social Reality. These beliefs make the Social Reality blind to the immorality and injustice which, once these beliefs are questioned (as frequently happens with medicinal users who find relief from cannabis), is quite apparent in the current Schedule I status imposed upon cannabis.

My conclusion will move beyond the moral conclusions reached on cannabis use and cannabis law. I aim to get to the very essence of the Social Reality. I submit that cannabis use is not essentially a moral issue as assumed by a large percentage of each the Social Reality and the Scientific Reality. Instead, the essence of the cannabis controversy is political in nature with a moral majority using the criminal law to punish harmless wrongdoing in order to preserve their view of the traditional American way of life. The current state of affairs reflects precisely what Tocqueville observed of the U.S. public, their irrational assumption that their leaders are inhuman and uncorrupt, somehow not subject to the same moral challenges and flaws of character they demonstrate when not acting in their official government capacity. This assumption is shown in the U.S. public's unquestioning allegiance to the U.S. law forbidding cannabis use.

I begin this final chapter by first considering the obvious expected response to the existence of an unjust law (from the perspective of a moral philosopher), civil disobedience. As has already been pointed out, cannabis is currently the most widely used illicit drug in the United States and is the highest grossing cash crop of the United States Civil disobedience requires intentional and open resistance and acceptance of legal penalties. The majority of cannabis users are apparently reluctant to make such a political stand.

Civil Disobedience to Cannabis Laws: Justified Actions and Will to Suffer for the Right to Use Cannabis

The moral argument to be made for civil disobedience is grounded in justice. There exists both an unfair distribution (more accurately, a lack of *recognition of* human rights) and an abuse of retributive justice in criminalizing "otherwise law-abiding citizens." The moral arguments are much more powerful with pressing interests of medicinal users who continue to give personal claims about the positive experienced effects, claims consistent with what is understood about the neurology of cannabis in the plant/brain interaction as well as what has been concluded by commissions appointed to examine cannabis since the 1894 Indian Hemp Commission Report. Denying a human being relief of pain and suffering denies basic human dignity. To think people whose pain and suffering can be relieved through using cannabis will not use it for the mere sake of a federal law is to demonstrate one's own lack of personal experience with pain and suffering. Many who are terminally ill and facing their own mortality and ultimate death cite their fear of being in pain as their primary fear beyond their fear of dying. If one would rather die than be in pain, what law can possibly deter such a person from relieving their pain and suffering? Perhaps here the point is the one Kant captured in his distinction between issues of "virtue" and issues of "justice," explaining that to apply the categories of justice to matters of virtue is to attempt to do something conceptually impossible. Without legal means of obtaining cannabis, otherwise law-abiding citizens find themselves facing the decision of either procuring cannabis through illegal means or continuing to suffer and experience pain. This situation would be eliminated were cannabis legalized.

Thoreau, in "On the Duty of Civil Disobedience," presents several observations to consider in light of unjust cannabis laws, particularly for medicinal users of cannabis. Thoreau's view of government generally comes with a suspicion and a feeling that its powers must be limited from in intruding on people's lives. As he puts it, "For government is an expedient by which men would fain succeed in letting one another alone" (Thoreau 1960, 223).

Reminding us of our human substance, that which is the very source of our liberty, our conscience, our deeply-felt convictions about right and wrong, Thoreau asks:

> Must the citizen ever for a moment, or in the least degree, resign his conscience to the legislator? Why has every man a conscience, then? I think that we should be men first, and subjects afterward. It is not desirable to cultivate a respect for the law, so much as for the right. (Thoreau 1960, 223)

And to the illusion that a law prohibiting cannabis and criminalizing users somehow makes them more (or less) just, Thoreau echoes Kant: "Law never made men a whit more just" (Thoreau 1960, 223).

Thoreau reflects upon a position similar to many in the current United States aiming to preserve cannabis criminalization, those who follow any and every law for the mere reason that they are the laws. Thoreau's example has him consider a bureaucratic work from his day Paley's "Duty of Submission to Civil Government." Thoreau ultimately condemns Paley as he "resolves all civil obligation into expediency." This sort of assumed bureaucratic ignorance, the same as the Social Reality of cannabis use in the United States, can be defeated and overcome by what Thoreau refers to as "action from principle": "Action from principle—the perception and the performance of right,—changes things and relations; it is essentially revolutionary, and does not consist wholly with any thing which was" (Thoreau 1960, 228). And acknowledging the fact unjust laws exist (e.g. current U.S. cannabis laws), Thoreau poses the question which frames the basic options for cannabis users convinced neither cannabis prohibition nor criminalization is morally justified: "Unjust laws exist; shall we be content to obey them, or shall we endeavor to amend them, and obey them until we have succeeded, or shall we transgress them at once?" (Thoreau 1960, 228).

The options here include just persevering and continuing to obey unjust laws, something a mass of the public of the United States is willing to do. But those who are convinced by both the Scientific Reality as well as the conclusions reached in the Moral Assessment, simply going along is an unacceptable option, given the issue involves conscience and truth. The next option is to "endeavor to amend them." In light of the currently entrenched Social Reality of cannabis use in the United States, seems politically impossible. The United States is faithful to synthetic medicines for therapy and alcohol for relaxation. Tocqueville captures the essential problem with denying cannabis users their rights and instead insisting they work through legal means and legal recourse.

> When an individual or a party is wronged in the United States, to whom can he apply for redress? If to public opinion, public opinion constitutes the majority; if to the legislature it represents the majority, and implicitly obeys its injunctions; if to the executive power, it is appointed by the majority and remains a passive tool in its hands; the public troops consist of the majority under arms; the jury is the majority invested with the right of hearing of judicial cases; and in certain States even the judges are elected by the majority. However iniquitous or absurd the evil of which you complain may be, you must submit to it as well as you can. (Stone and Mennell 1980, 101)

As a third option in response to an unjust law, Thoreau considers "transgressing them at once," and this seems the primary response by cannabis users of early twenty-first-century Americ. Given that cannabis is the primary cash crop of our country while at the same time under a criminal law prohibiting its every use, hundreds of thousands if not millions are currently repeatedly transgressing these laws, and are actually being exploited for substantial profit by untaxed and unregulated producers, distributors, sellers on various levels, in virtually every part of the United States.

Thoreau would perhaps probe further into the nature of the cannabis situation in the United States at this turn of the twenty-first century. He would almost certainly advocate physicians' prescribing cannabis for conditions if they thought it would improve through canabis use. It is surprising that the U.S. public has not vocally condemned the arrest and criminalization of terminally ill patients who use cannabis, but this shows how powerful an allegiance a bulk of the U.S. public has for the Social Reality of cannabis use. Consider Thoreau as speaking to current health care workers: "but if it is of such a nature that it requires you to be the agent of injustice to another, then, I say, break the law. Let your life be a counter friction to stop the machine. What I have to do is to see, at any rate, that I do not lend myself to the wrong which I condemn" (Thoreau 1960, 229). And for those who choose to intentionally subvert an unjust law, Thoreau reminds each individual counts and that being arrested for such a thing would in a sense be acting in a quite meaningful, eternal way: "For it matters not how small the beginning may seem to be: what is once well done is done for ever" (Thoreau 1960, 230).

More notably from Thoreau, each citizen should consider the law which punishes anyone unjustly potentially punishes that citizen him/herself unjustly. This is a major reason for *every citizen* in the United States to advocate for the rights of cannabis users regardless of whether or not he/she is a cannabis user (but an alcohol user, tobacco user, cheeseburger user, or user of other potentially prohibited harmless activities): "Under a government which imprisons any unjustly, the true place for a just man is also a prison" (Thoreau 1960, 230). The Social Reality in the United States is powerful, and the minority of those who advocate for the legalization of cannabis use is powerless *only when* it just goes along with the Social Reality: "A minority is powerless while it conforms to the majority; it is not even a minority then; but it is irresistible when it clogs by its whole weight" (Thoreau 1960, 231).

In response to those who fear for losing their jobs, their careers, their lives as they know them, Thoreau, instead of consoling, asks about the alternative to so acting, and the damage done by acting against conscience[1]:

> When the subject has refused allegiance, and the officer has resigned his office, then the revolution is accomplished. But even suppose blood should flow. Is there not a sort of blood shed when the conscience is wounded? Through this wound a man's real manhood and immortality flow out, and he bleeds to an everlasting death. I see this blood flowing now. (Thoreau 1960, 231)

This is the sort of "blood" which was a major point of consideration in the moral assessment chapters. Kant spoke of the dignity of human beings and would be a strong supporter of doing one's moral duty "though the heavens may fall" (therefore, "though one may get arrested"). For those who possess and protect this sense of moral conscience, of "being one's own man" as a human being, Thoreau's point will cause pause. However, many if not most people will be unmoved, not much different now than in Thoreau's time, as he says of his neighbors, "they dread the consequences of disobedience to their property and families" (Thoreau 1960, 232).

Reiterating this inability on the part of his neighbors to demonstrate an understanding of this most basic point, of being in touch with one's basic sense of dignity and self-ownership and control, he recognizes, "if there was a wall of stone between me and my townsmen, there was a still more difficult one to climb or break through, before they could get to be as free as I was" (Thoreau 1960, 233).[2] On the meaning and importance of civil disobedience for human beings everywhere on this planet under every form of government, Thoreau explains: "It costs me less in every sense to incur the penalty of disobedience to the State, than it would to obey. I should feel as if I were worth less in that case" (Thoreau 1960, 232).

And in his concluding paragraph of civil disobedience:

> The progress from an absolute to a limited monarchy, from a limited monarchy to a democracy, is a progress toward a true respect for the individual. Even the Chinese philosopher was wise enough to regard the individual as the basis of the empire. Is a democracy, such as we know it, the last improvement possible in government? Is it not possible to take a step further towards recognizing and organizing the rights of man? (Thoreau 1960, 240)

Perhaps the cannabis issue indicates whether the U.S. democracy will forge forward and continue to develop and improve upon its living up to its basic principles or whether it will inevitably regress back into a limited monarchy where the few govern the many in practice.

Civil disobedience within the context of medical practice would be a strategic step to demand recognition of the moral right of patients to use cannabis.[3] Recently in the *Hastings Center Report*, Robert Macauley (in "The Hippocratic Underground: Civil Disobedience and Health Care Reform") focuses on health care reform and the impact of false billing for patients' welfare. He relevantly recognizes cannabis:

> As it relates to the practice of medicine, civil disobedience has historically been carried out to support minority groups who either were ignored by the majority . . . or were simply unable to speak for themselves. . . . The same can be said for other areas of medicine that, though they fall outside the scope of this paper, might lend themselves to civil disobedience, such as the use of medical marijuana. (Macauley 2005, 41)

Macauley presents three criteria for civil disobedience: openness, nonviolence, and submission. As to what this would look like in actual practice, he anticipates physicians who prescribe cannabis for medicinal purposes to do so openly and nonviolently, offering themselves up to federal government authorities by doing so:

> In light of the recent rejection of state initiatives to allow for the legal prescription of medicinal marijuana, perhaps physicians in those states will eventually decide to openly and nonviolently make it known they do prescribe medicinal marijuana for appropriate patients, submitting to the federal authorities and peacefully accepting the negative consequences for doing so. (Macauley 2005, 40)

And furthermore, "physicians engaging in direct civil disobedience would violate federal laws precisely in order to procure medications and services for people who need them and would otherwise be deprived of them" (Macauley 2005, 40).

Macauley also cites three "preconditions" that must be met to justify an act of civil disobedience: first, "the collection of the facts to determine whether injustices are alive." If the scientific and moral arguments presented in this book have made this case, then this condition is met by laws prohibiting the use of cannabis and also laws criminalizing users. Second, "normal appeals to the political majority have already been made in good faith and that they have failed" (Macauley 2005, 40). It could be argued that the current state initiatives providing for the legal medicinal use of marijuana rejected by the federal government is evidence of such a failed good faith effort. Macauley also notes here, "Yet even if some legal options remain, this does not preempt civil disobedience" (Macauley 2005, 40). In other words, the state initiatives may be enough to meet the second condition, as opposed to continuing to confront, for example, federal legislators who still cite the archaic gateway drug argument and the comparative benefits of the seriously problematic Marinol drug, etc. The Social Reality of cannabis use is openly advocating beliefs that do not hold up under rational investigation. Social Reality is the justice system. Furthermore, throughout the twentieth century in the United States, the "legal options" are treated according to political ends and so harnessed and legalistically stalled or rejected so that researchers who want to simply investigate the actual effects of cannabis in a controlled, scientific way are disallowed "official" cannabis to use. Arguably this second criterion of justifiable civil disobedience has been met in U.S. federal cannabis law.

Third, "the specific form of civil disobedience being considered must carry with it some reasonable possibility of success . . . care must be taken to see that it is understood"(Macauley 2005, 41). Here is where the media would play an important role, putting into the national consciousness the stories of patients suffering from terminal illnesses, cancer chemotherapy, AIDS, MS, glaucoma, neuropathic, and other illnesses and who experience relief by using cannabis. The challenge involves seeing clearly through myth and rhetoric to the real life stories of those who have moved beyond the narrow visions of the cannabis plant as a threat to democracy and instead accept the clear evidence of its effectiveness.

In light of actions of direct disobedience, Macauley explains that "collectivity is the strongest defense" (of physicians willing to disobey an unjust law) and that "the federal government almost certainly would not prevent a substantial number of physicians from practicing medicine in a way that attempts to meet the needs of a selectively underserved population" (Macauley 2005,

43). This has just recently happened with the ACP endorsing therapeutic cannabis (see p. 54). However, given current tension between the federal government and states expressed initiatives and continued acceptance of the moral right to medicinal cannabis, perhaps Macauley's puts too much faith in the power of collectivity to sway the U.S. federal government.

Macauley also cites another type of civil disobedience relevant to medicinal cannabis, the term "evasive noncompliance" (borrowed from Childress). This involves the direct violation of laws but is neither open nor submissive. Perhaps, given the severe punishments threatened by the federal government for prescribing medicinal cannabis (e.g., loss of medical license), "evasive noncompliance" is practically employed. State and local law enforcement officials, especially in areas where initiatives have been successfully passed, may be reluctant to punish therapeutic users as they are also citizens of these communities and perhaps are personally a part of the consensus that passed initiatives. It seems that currently there exists use of evasive noncompliance, whereby physicians recommend cannabis and explain its therapeutic potential while not calling this to the attention of federal authorities.

To finish this brief consideration of civil disobedience in light of unjust cannabis laws, consider Barnes concludes his philosophical discussion of the legalization of cannabis with justification for acts of civil disobedience on the part of states as entities refusing to enforce federal drug laws.

> My primary claim will be that even if one grants that the United States federal government properly has authority over drug legalization and that the government has a significant interest in preventing the recreational use of marijuana, other states should follow Arizona and California in legalizing the medicinal use of marijuana (along with its production, distribution, and prescription). (Barnes 2000, 17)

Barnes thinks it important for states to pass laws allowing therapeutic use of cannabis for two reasons: first, "state law enforcement officials are less likely to aid in enforcing federal laws when their own state laws contradict federal law"; second, "states can effectively protest the obstructionist position of the federal government by passing these laws. This form of protest is analogous in many respects to civil disobedience" (Barnes 2000, 40). Here, Barnes compliments the strategy of "evasive noncompliance," on the part of the states in response to the federal government.

Criminalizing Harmless Wrongdoing: The Essence of Marijuana Law

"There is little question that marihuana laws have often made criminals out of otherwise law-abiding citizens" (Corbett 1971, 37).

In this section I move closer to articulating the essence of the Social Reality of cannabis use, beyond the seven beliefs of Social Reality already articulated. This deeper essence is grounded in moral conservatism having the federal government prohibit conduct for the reason that it is not traditional nor popular. Cannabis use is basically disliked by many in U.S. society (although these are not directly harmed or injured by cannabis use).

As capturing the essence of U.S. prohibition of cannabis use, I articulate and apply positions presented in Joel Feinberg's *Harmless Wrongdoing*. This, Feinberg's fourth volume of his *Moral Limits of the Criminal Law*, presents a "Synopsis of Volumes One, Two, and Three," where he articulates four principles justifying "liberty-limiting" (or "coercion-legitimizing") principles. The "*harm to others principle*" is "the principle that the need to prevent harm to persons other than the actor is always a morally relevant reason in support of proposed state coercion," the "*offense principle*" is the principle that "it is necessary to prevent hurt or offence (as opposed to injury or harm) to others," *legal paternalism* holds the principle that "it is necessary to prevent harm to the very person it prohibits from acting, as opposed to 'others,'" and *legal moralism* is the principle holding "it is necessary to prevent inherently immoral conduct whether or not such conduct is harmful or offensive to anyone" (Feinberg 1988, ix). Cannabis users denied legalized use of and criminalized because of the use of cannabis treated under either legal paternalism or legal moralism. This, given they are at most harming themselves. Major implications of using these two terms in reference to cannabis law will be developed further in what follows.

Within his chapter 29, "Moral Conservatism: Preserving a Way of Life," Feinberg provides much for understanding how the reason of preserving the moral character of society is used to reject the legalization of cannabis (as revealed in the Public and War on Drugs study in chapter 6). Consider first Feinberg's definition of "moral conservative": "persons who would use the criminal law to prevent deviant or eccentric conduct whether or not it is harmful or offensive" (Feinberg 1988, 39). He also cites H. L. A. Hart defining "the conservative thesis," "the thesis that it can be morally legitimate to preserve a society's traditional way of life from radical or essential change by means of legal coercion" (Feinberg 1988, 43). Some try to broaden their justification for using the criminal law beyond harm to self by citing indirect and vague long-term harms that would result (to society) from the conduct in question. Feinberg explains, of those who employ such a strategy, they cite

> explicitly or tacitly the *offense principle*, and argue against legal impunity for discreetly private immoralities on the ground that they would come to be directly offensive anyway, their original privacy notwithstanding. . . . As the "immoralities"

spread, it is claimed, their presence will inevitably be felt in subtle but pervasive ways that shock or disgust the ordinary person" (Feinberg 1988, 43–44).

A further way of broadening the offense principle would hold that "certain types of genuine immoralities, even when private and harmless, are such evident and odious evils that they should be forbidden on that ground alone" (Feinberg 1988, 44).

The Social Reality of cannabis use has been and continues to be defended through the employment of a moral conservative argument. Current cannabis law prevents cannabis use even though it is neither harmful nor universally offensive (both sides of the debate acknowledge significant social use despite absolute legal prohibition). Applying Hart's definition of moral conservativism to U.S. federal cannabis prohibition, the criminal law is used to preserve the "traditional way of life." Feinberg helps to illuminate this Social Reality justification for cannabis prohibition by employing the concept of a "way of life." He points out that by utilizing this concept the Social Reality (and those supporting cannabis prohibition) *need not even posses a moral argument to support such a prohibition.* Here is the crucial move from morality to preference, a broader category of actions which are akin to those concerning each individual's pursuit of happiness as s/he articulates "happiness": "It bears repetition that a group's moral code is only part of its "way of life," and by no means the only part that the conservative wishes to preserve. The conservative argument would apply just as well to whatever other elements are central to a way of life" (Feinberg 1988, 44). Further elaborating on the same basic justification for limiting the liberty of cannabis users in the United States, Feinberg refers to the early twentieth century temperance movement as wielding a "way of life" rationale for alcohol prohibition, specifically against deviant lifestyles:

> The temperance movement that succeeded in imposing Prohibition on the country was only partly concerned to prevent the harms caused by excessive drinking, and the forms of its arguments were not typically paternalistic. One of its primary targets was the spreading influence of life-styles that deviated from the traditional norms the movement represented, on the one hand the free-wheeling style of the sophisticated cocktail-swigging urban or suburban middle classes, on the other the ethnic customs of immigrant workers of Catholic and Lutheran backgrounds in which the social drinking of whiskey or beer played a large role. (Feinberg 1988, 45–46)

Feinberg explains that this use of a "way of life" rationale is not grounded in morality or justice but rather reflect the motivation of many to maintain their "cultural dominance." Citing Joseph Gusfield on this point: "The process of deviance designation in drinking must be seen in terms of the cultural dominance rather than as reflecting necessities of social control" (Feinberg 1988, 46).

Feinberg points out that it is not clear that moral norms or laws that do not prevent harms but merely preserve tradition are threatened by nonconforming action (e.g., cannabis use): "Moral and nonmoral norms that do not prevent harms so much as preserve a traditional way of life are not themselves threatened by every kind of nonconforming action" (Feinberg 1988, 47). He again cites Gusfield in distinguishing between four types of deviant, expanding only the last as a threat to the traditional way of life. It is the last I contend have been and continue to be produced in more and more numbers by cannabis law in the United States. First is the "repentant deviant." He "never doubts the legitimacy of the norm but breaks it in a morally weak moment." These seem primarily represented by those who experiment with cannabis in early adulthood, likely one of the many who use cannabis once or infrequently. Second, the "sick deviant" is "thought to be unable to help himself." Here may be included those who obsessively use cannabis (10 percent of total users) and who are diagnosed as cannabis dependent. Third, the "cynical deviant" "who is self-seeking, amoral, and unrepentant." Here may be the individual with early conduct disorders, use of cannabis along with other illegal drugs. The three of these are no real threat to the norms of society (Feinberg 1988, 47). However, "the real threat to the norm itself" is the 'enemy deviant" "He accepts his own behavior as proper and derogates the public norm as illegitimate." Further, "one is not likely to encounter much guilt about marijuana smoking in the subculture where it prevails" (Feinberg 1988, 47, citing Gusfield).

It is relevant Feinberg here cites cannabis smoking in particular for his example of the enemy deviant. The implication is that the rampant and unstoppable current U.S. black market in cannabis use includes hundreds of thousands of *enemy deviants* who derogate the public norms (Social Reality) as illegitimate. In the case of cannabis use, the moral arguments provided by Kant, Mill, Aristotle, Old and New Testament, the Scientific Reality having one conclude cannabis is not dangerous relative to other drugs and has therapeutic effects and benefits provides strong justification for such "derogation." As such, to know the most widely used illicit drug in the United States is cannabis is not surprising. The effects of the existence of this large number of enemy deviants are difficult to calculate.

The situation in the early twenty-first-century United States is such that the federal government Schedule I policy forbidding cannabis has created hundreds of thousands of cannabis users who are enemy deviants (by the mere fact of using cannabis, regardless of the intention of the user). More will utilize cannabis and simply reject as false and "illegitimate" the law banning the use of cannabis for any purpose, medicinal or recreational. Enemy deviants exist because of cannabis law. Resentment and ill-will toward the law result from unwillingly becoming enemy deviants. "Otherwise law-abiding citizens" are because of cannabis law alone wary of the law in general, paying grossly inflated prices (e.g., $200 instead of $20/ounce) from dealers with no recompense for short-changing, risking the use of adulterated product, etc. With the billions of dollars annually fueling cannabis sales as the leading cash crop in the United States it stands to reason that there is a substantial view within the U.S. society that cannabis is an acceptable recreational substance.

Preserving the Traditional American Way of Life

Feinberg casts the conservative position (one I consider as the basis of the position against legalization of cannabis) as attempting to preserve a "traditional way of life." Preserving the "traditional way of life" has individuals attempt to stop any (significant) social change from taking place. Feinberg characterizes them as not merely conservative but also "aging," implying these are older people particularly defending the conservative position: "So in the end, the aging conservative feels that he is not only an alien in his own land, but a stranger in his own family" (Feinberg 1988, 49). Conservatives defend as justified the use of the criminal law to resist social changes "because these changes are contrary to the will of the majority, and therefore illicit in their origins"(Feinberg 1988, 50). Here, the conservative argument is that the will of the majority is the law and therefore anything counter to that law is by definition "illicit."

The essence of this argument is the same as that heavily criticized by moral philosophers, particularly Mill, who sees it as quite evident that as human beings are themselves subject to corruption, there is no clear reason why institutions conducted by individuals would not be subject to the same abuses. The 1937 Marihuana Tax Act is an obvious example of a gross injustice done to Mexicans in the United States, based upon falsehoods and propaganda. In the war on drugs from Nixon to the present discussion of cannabis use has simply been cut off. Here, in the context of moral conservatives we can understand why and how the criminal law has been used to arrest social change *without moral grounds for doing so.* Cannabis prohibition is not based on science or the fruits of an authentic search for truth.

As a way of buttressing the moral conservatism argument, Feinberg explains that those who hold this position make

> an appeal to the rights of an overwhelming majority, as such, to prevent unwanted changes in its traditional way of life . . . is essentially based on fairness, for it concludes that it is unfair (and hence morally illegitimate) to alter the

> moral environment of a community without the consent of the majority (or at least a quite substantial minority) of its members. (Feinberg 1988, 50)

The majority have a sort of agreement, in the case of cannabis prohibition, that cannabis use will never be legitimated by the federal government. Furthermore on this fairness line of argument, "Many or most of the unwilling majority, it is said, have genuine interests, investments of their own personal well-being, in the perpetuation of the traditional ways, so that an abandonment of those ways, through either abrupt or gradual changes, would be a set back to that interest" (Feinberg 1988, 50–51). This argument has as the harm to conservatives a "setback of their interest" to live in a United States without legalized cannabis.

In response to this fairness line of argument buttressing the conservative, Feinberg counters by arguing that such a position would justify too much coercion and would likely come back on the conservative to threaten some activities s/he would her/himself be unwilling to relinquish. Feinberg also explains why it is so hard for moral minorities to effect change through persuading the moral majority, a point particularly relevant to the current state of cannabis law in the United States:

> Trying to become a majority presumably requires efforts to *persuade* one's fellows to join one's cause, but that opportunity is hardly open to the person whose favored activities are deemed criminal and banned on pain of punishment. . . . "Moral minorities" do not necessarily even wish to persuade a majority to their styles of life, but only to persuade the majority to leave them in peace. (Feinberg 1988, 53)

This last comment strikes me as not asking much of the moral majority, to be left in peace, one consistently expressed as a desire of "otherwise law-abiding citizens" who use cannabis. Feinberg next provides reasons why the precedent set by laws such as those forbidding cannabis use logically support similar (and totalitarian) restrictions, from legislating morality to legislating religion on the basis of the same "traditional way of life" rationale:

> Whatever principle of fairness the moral conservative uses to justify the legal prohibition of unestablished minorities styles of life, he will be hard put to explain why the principle doesn't establish with equal cogency the fairness of sweeping totalitarian restrictions. In particular, if it is fair to enforce moral conformity on conservative grounds, why is it not fair to enforce religious conformity in religiously homogeneous communities on the same grounds. . . . So the argument for the need to preserve a way of life would apply *a fortiori* to religious nonconformity. (Feinberg 1988, 53)

And also indicating how close the prohibition of cannabis use comes to the violation of a most (perhaps the most) basic right of free speech: "It would be impossible, moreover, for the conservative argument to stop short of crossing the line between the prohibition of a disapproved sort of conduct and the prohibition of speech advocating that conduct, or even speech advocating the permissibility or the legalizing, of that kind of conduct" (Feinberg 1988, 53). Consider as an example of this move already having been made over this line to the prohibition of speech the warning by President Clinton and his DHHS director to physicians and health care workers to not even discuss or mention cannabis use with patients. Such imposition violates the very heart of the physician/patient relationship, not to mention imposing a certain cultural belief and symbolism upon medical experts by bureaucrats of the federal government who are not themselves experts on cannabis use. Beyond speech, that the conservative can stop any change *because it is a change*, using the criminal law in the name of not morality but preference and tradition. With maintenance of the "traditional way of life" eliminates privacy and independent judgment from the life of citizens:

> Once more, how is the conservative argument to stop short of justifying, again on grounds of 'fairness,' the enforced regulation of hairstyle and the prohibition of long beards and styles of clothing of those who advertise themselves as nonconformists? Do not these *visible* deviations from prevailing standards weaken those norms as much as the existence of deviant attitudes, tastes, sex lives, and reading and entertainment preferences that are only indulged in private? (Feinberg 1988, 53–54)

And consider that such laws are essentially "a form of discrimination as arbitrary as racial prejudice."

> Considerations of fairness, when they do have a bearing on these issues, seem to oppose rather than reinforce the conservative argument. If we assume, as seems natural, that human nature comes in different sizes and shapes, so to speak, that there are deep and morally significant differences among normal people in respect to basic temperament and emotional needs, then to insist that only some of these types of character, even if they are the most common ones, are entitled to their satisfaction, would seem to be unfair to others, a form of discrimination as arbitrary as racial prejudice. (Feinberg 1988, 54)

Here Feinberg reveals a prevalent thought of cannabis users, particularly in light of a U.S. society that tolerates alcohol use. Some people prefer to use cannabis instead of drinking alcohol; both "social lubricants," both in moderation relaxing and yet use of cannabis is illegal, taboo, and socially forbidden, while alcohol is widely advertised and enjoyed to the satisfaction of those of the majority. There is no reason to justify this distinction but rather it is just the way it is and cannabis users have to just accept the fact of their criminality. This is grossly unfair to cannabis users, especially otherwise law-abiding citizens.

Feinberg moves back to the conservative claim of being "harmed" by the change of a law and further develops this argument:

> Some disapproved-of private conduct wrongs them, they claim, precisely because it *harms* them, and harms them because it sets back a genuine, at least partly other-regarding interest they have in living in a certain kind of (homogeneous) community, namely a community in which persons do not behave in the disapproved-of way, even in private. Preventing such harm to them, they claim, legitimizes criminal prohibitions of the disapproved-of conduct of the others, under the harm principle. (Feinberg 1988, 56)

Feinberg addresses a situation roughly similar to that of the moral majority in the United States defending the Social Reality of cannabis prohibition. Applying Feinberg's symbolism, consider the Social Reality cannabis prohibitionist neighbor as "A" and private cannabis user as "B."

> Let us focus then on a distinction between two ways A can have an other-regarding interest in B. On the one hand, A's interest in B might be . . . a *vicarious interest*, an interest in B's well-being as an end-in-itself (as in love) or in B's ill-being. . . . On the other hand, A's other-regarding interest in B may be an interest in some state or condition of B other than the advancement of B's own interests. What A wants for B and has an interest in bringing about in that case is quite independent of what B wants for himself or what is in B's interest, though A may have an independent (vicarious) or derivative (instrumental) interest in B's concurrence as well. We can characterize A's ulterior interest in B's life-style as a predominantly *external interest*, and one that may well be in conflict with B's own personal interest. (Feinberg 1988, 60)

Consider, for example, the use of cannabis by private citizens in their own homes. A neighbor does not want to know that such a thing is going on, and so this neighbor is interested in stopping such activity from happening. However, the cannabis user has a personal interest in using cannabis in the privacy of his home. This pits the external interest of neighbor against a personal interest of the cannabis user. "When two persons each have interests in how one of them lives his life, the interests of the one whose life it is are the more important. I should think that this denial of his judgment is virtually tantamount to a denial of that person's autonomy" (Feinberg 1988, 61)

This denial of autonomy is quite similar to the Kantian rejection of cannabis prohibition as violating the dignity and inherent value of persons or "ends in themselves." The moral conservative holds that his external interest in a neighbor's not legally acquiring and using cannabis outweighs any personal interests a rational adult citizen has in obtaining and using cannabis.

Consider Feinberg's quite similar example of drinking a bottle of beer as analogous to using cannabis: "What of my interest in being able to drink a bottle of beer whenever I feel like it, when that interest clashes with the puritan's more widely held interest, of equal vitality and innocence, in living in an alcohol-free society?" (Feinberg 1988, 63) Some may argue that a distinction between these two interests involves a desire to drink (or use cannabis) as merely self-indulgent. However, consider Feinberg's counter:

> If the desire to drink beer (or to masturbate, or to eat pickled ham) is to be dismissed as "merely" self-indulgent, though its moral innocence is otherwise duly acknowledged, then we might with equal justification dismiss the puritan's interest that beer not be drunk . . . as officious busybodies' interests or gratuitous meddlers' interests, for it is difficult to understand why a desire for a pure society could become so powerful as to make its object a component of a person's own good, without an element of that morally unsavory sort. (Feinberg 1988, 64–65)

To call any cannabis use "self-indulgent" and hold an extreme prohibitionist stance is to demonstrate a "meddler's interest." It furthermore ironically demonstrates the individual who makes such a judgment is perhaps likewise "self-indulgent" (in their extreme position passionately and dogmatically held, purposely ignoring scientific evidence and moral reflection). Feinberg explains the injustice of "arresting cultural change" (e.g., to legalized cannabis): "invasions of the interest that persons are presumed to have in their own liberty, if done in order to arrest cultural change, cannot be justified on the grounds that individuals must be protected from harm, nuisance, or unjust exploitation" (Feinberg 1988, 65). And, "The characteristic conservative argument . . . is not that any given way of life is uniquely rational, but rather that any severe change in a traditional culture is evil as such, even though it might seem on other grounds to be an improvement" (Feinberg 1988, 65).

I suspect those of the Social Reality are against cannabis use simply because it is illegal and assume there must be good reasons for this law otherwise it would not exist. Feinberg presents Lord Thurlow, a nineteenth-century English Lord Chancellor, in a way which adequately represents the absurdity of such a position:

> Lord Thurlow, a nineteenth-century English Lord Chancellor . . . said to a group of dissenters: "I'm against you by God, Sir, I'm in favor of the established church; and, if you'll get your damn religion established, I'll be in favor of that." Quite explicitly it was the *establishment* as such that Lord Thurlow was "in favor of," not any particular set of religious doctrines. (Feinberg 1988, 65)

Those for whom the "establishment" dictates morality would support *either* legalized or prohibited cannabis, depending upon the law which was in place at the time and in the place in which they found themselves. Although currently prohibitionist, with legalization they will immediately and decisively accept the use of cannabis as up to the discretion of adult individual citizens (as is alcohol use).

Feinberg's next line for reasoning explains why current cannabis prohibition takes away the personal autonomy of cannabis users (echoing the significant moral concerns of both Mill and Kant):

> If I am forbidden on pain of criminal punishment and public humiliation from acting as a I prefer in ways that harm no one, in places where I offend no one, on the ground that in so doing I would be subtly changing the moral environment of my fellow citizens, I am being asked to acquiesce to a demand that would utterly demean my autonomy. Surely a person's autonomy, whatever else it may consist in, precludes his thinking of his activities, practices, beliefs, and preferences as no more than part of others' "environments." How can I have any personal autonomy if my neighbors can claim a *right* to have me think, feel, and privately behave only in ways they approve? There is nothing offensive to autonomy in the practice of limiting some people's liberty for the sake of other people's interests; using persons as "means to an end" can be inoffensive when the "end" is the protection of other persons, but morally odious when the "end" is anything else. (Feinberg 1988, 67–68)

Remembering Kant and our duty to treat others as ends in themselves, consider that cannabis users are treated as mere means or things by the law forbidding their using cannabis (while allowing the use of alcohol, thereby clearly using an arbitrary double-standard grounded in the "traditional way of life" argument).

> I confess that I cannot see how a person whose interests have not been adversely affected, and who is still able to live a good life, can have any personal grievance against the people in his "social environment" when they discreetly live their own lives and form their own views in ways that he finds regrettable. (Feinberg 1988, 68)
>
> A more plausible way of arguing for a grievance even without harm is to argue that persons brought up in a traditional way of life often order their own lives in all good faith in reliance on the old ways being continued. Emotionally unprepared, then, for drastic changes, they are left high and dry in their declining years, not only disappointed but righteously embittered by changes which are in their eyes betrayals. (Feinberg 1988, 68)
>
> The sense of grievance in these cases is understandable, even when the aggrieved party can show no genuine harm to his interests or rude affronts to his sensibility. Understandable, perhaps, but justifiable? I think not. No one ever signed a "social contract" with such people, or made a solemn vow, or even an

> informal promise, to keep things unchanged. If aggrieved parties believe otherwise on ideological grounds, then they are victims, in a way, of their own conservatism. (Feinberg 1988, 68–69)

Tocqueville's Prophecy Realized in U.S. Cannabis Law

> Once an opinion has spread on American soil and taken root there, it would seem that no power on earth can eradicate it. In the United States general doctrines concerning religion, philosophy, morality, and even politics do not vary at all, or at least are only modified by the slow and often unconscious working of some hidden process. Even the very crudest prejudices take an unconscionable time to efface, in spite of all the froth and stir of men and things.
>
> One hears people say that it is inherent in the habits and nature of democracies to change feelings and thoughts at every moment. That may have been true of such small democratic nations as those of antiquity, carried away by an orator's eloquence. But I have never seen anything like that happening in the great democracy on the other side of our ocean. What struck me most in the United States was the difficulty experienced in getting an idea, once conceived, out of the head of the majority and stopping their following the man of their choice. Neither writings nor speeches can have much success in that; only experience can do it, and that too must sometimes be repeated. (Tocqueville 1966, 615)

It may be that having presented the Scientific Reality of cannabis use and supporting moral arguments is futile in light of the fact that existent is a powerful moral majority in the United States, along with a federal government strongly opposed to any discussion of cannabis. However, although applying Tocqueville here, neither "speaking nor writing" can make the Scientific Reality of cannabis use the basis for a new U.S. federal policy legalizing cannabis, "experience will avail," although it must be "repeated." Perhaps this is in part because of the stark contrast between the effects routinely experienced and expected by regular cannabis users from most walks of life to the way the federal government demonizes cannabis and criminalizes cannabis users. Repeated experience is needed to be sure that these effects are in fact as controllable as they seem, as innocuous as they seem, in order to question the Schedule I status of cannabis use. The "otherwise law-abiding citizens" who are criminals only because of their cannabis use are opposed by a moral majority by and large lacks any personal experience with cannabis use and gets its information about cannabis effects from the media and federal government. The deeply held conviction against cannabis use and legalization in the United States is just the type of opinion Tocqueville describes.

Tocqueville also relevantly recognizes of the tendency of the federal government to keep the public in "perpetual childhood," and to be the "sole arbiter" of their happiness, in his section called "Democratic Despotism":

> Above this race of men stands an immense and tutelary power, which takes upon itself alone to secure their gratifications, and to watch over their fate. That power is absolute, minute, regular, provident, and mild. It would be like the authority of a parent, if, like that authority, its object was to prepare men for manhood; but it seeks on the contrary to keep them in perpetual childhood: it is well content that the people should rejoice, provided they think of nothing but rejoicing. For their happiness such a government willingly labours, but it chooses to be the sole agent and the only arbiter of that happiness: it provides for their security, foresees and supplies their necessities, facilitates their pleasures, manages their principal concerns, directs their industry, regulates the descent of property, and subdivides their inheritances—what remains, but to spare them all the care of thinking and all the trouble of living? (Stone and Mennell 1980, 375)[4]

In light of cannabis prohibition, it may be that those of this silent and complacent public may respond to those defending cannabis legalization, why raise all the fuss? Alcohol is legal and you may drink as much as you like, or what would motivate a citizen to question the parent/federal government? These are rhetorical questions for those who realize their own dignity, liberty, and inherent value as individual human beings (hopefully at least reasonable questions for those who have lost touch with their own dignity and humanness).

Continuing his thoughts on this tendency of paternalism on the part of the federal government, consider particularly the effect on the "will" of the individual, the same "will" essential to distinguishing for Kant persons from things, for St. Augustine the crucial element of an individual to be "ordered" and the essence of the liberty championed in democratic society:

> Thus it every day renders the exercise of the free agency of man less useful and less frequent; it circumscribes the will within a narrower range, and gradually robs a man of all the uses of himself. The principle of equality has prepared men for these things: it has predisposed men to endure them, and oftentimes to look on them as benefits.
>
> After having thus successively taken each member of the community in its powerful grasp, and fashioned them at will, the supreme power then extends its arm over the whole community. It covers the surface of society with a network of small complicated rules, minute and uniform, through which the most original minds and the most energetic characters cannot penetrate, to rise above the crowd. The will of man is not shattered, but softened, bent, and guided: men are seldom forced by it to act, but they are constantly restrained from acting: such a power does not destroy, but it prevents existence; it does not tyrannize, but it

> compresses, enervates, extinguishes, and stupefies a people, till each nation is reduced to be nothing better than a flock of timid and industrious animals, of which the government is the shepherd. (Stone and Mennell 1980, 375–76)

An alternative translation to "robs a man of all the uses of himself" is "robs each citizen of the proper use of his own faculties" (Mayer and Lerner translation). "Faculties" is more consistent with the Moral Assessment presentation of Kant, Aristotle, and Mill. It was seen that all three distinguish between appetite, sensation, intellect, and other faculties, with all indicating a qualitative superiority to the intellect guiding the other faculties, controlling and directing them. As applied to cannabis use, the United States federal law prohibiting the use of cannabis in essence makes the choice for each citizen, regardless of the reasoning process and control of the faculties of the individual involved. As such the government thereby "robs" citizens of the use of their own faculty of reason.

Tocqueville's description of the "despotism that democratic nations have to fear" characterizes accurately the current cannabis prohibition by the federal government of the United States. The law is imposed upon the public as a flock of timid and industrious animals, a significant number of whom trust that cannabis prohibition can be scientifically and morally justified. The very lack of question of the Schedule I status of cannabis, let alone the regular criminalization of citizens who use it for therapeutic purposes, seem evidence of a "stupefied" people.

Consider further that many of the U.S. public seemingly believe that if something is legal then it is necessarily moral, that the laws citizens follow are not subject to any conception of a higher sort of justice which, although difficult to articulate, allows a way of rationally considering and improving the continually evolving laws of the land. Consider Tocqueville's observation of this sort of blind obedience to the law:

> The Americans hold that in every state the supreme power ought to emanate from the people; but when once that power is constituted, they can conceive, as it were, no limits to it, and are ready to admit that it has the right to do whatever it pleases. They have not the slightest notion of peculiar privileges granted to cities, families, or persons: their minds appear never to have foreseen that it might be possible not to apply with strict uniformity the same laws to every part, and to all the inhabitants. (Stone and Mennell 1980, 86)[5]

Here is the same point made throughout the morality chapters, namely that since individuals make up legislative bodies, they are subject to the same corrupting forces as individuals outside of these legislative bodies. This point has been particularly emphasized in the political Social Reality rejection of medicinal marijuana, showing that policy has dictated research rather than research dictating policy. Furthermore, the cannabis laws were in their very origin prejudicial, based on no good reasons or scientific evidence, and directed against Mexicans particularly and so-called deviants of U.S. society more generally. Cannabis was removed on the sly from the U.S. pharmacopia by Anslinger, basically on his own personal, individual, and bureaucratic, initiative. Nixon simply ignored the Shafer Commission Report in making cannabis a Schedule I drug, and from that time to the present day the U.S. federal government stance stays the same. It seems that it only needs to somehow "occur to someone" that cannabis prohibition may not be based upon any good scientific or moral reasons for them to realize and perhaps express their concern about the injustice of this law. Although the media controls the public opinion on this issue, medicinal marijuana patients continue to realize the therapeutic effectiveness and that the Social Reality is unscientific and immoral in criminalizing cannabis users. As this segment of the U.S. public grows (more chronic illnesses in United States, baby boomers aging), perhaps some legislators will personally realize the injustice of the U.S. federal policy and Schedule I status of cannabis, and cannabis legalization will be a possibility.

Tocqueville, in his section called "The Tyranny of the Majority," provides an appropriate conclusion to *Otherwise Law-Abiding Citizens: A Scientific and Moral Assessment of Cannabis Use.* For many cannabis users the issue is one of morality and basic human rights, things for which the law exists and without which the law is worthless and not worth respecting:

> When I refuse to obey an unjust law, I by no means deny the majority's right to give orders; I only appeal from the sovereignty of the people to the sovereignty of the human race.
>
> There are those not afraid to say that in matters which only concern itself a nation cannot go completely beyond the bounds of justice and reason and that there is therefore no need to fear giving total power to the majority representing it. But that is the language of a slave.
>
> What is a majority, in its collective capacity, if not an individual with opinions, and usually with interests, contrary to those of another individual, called the minority? Now, if you admit that a man vested with omnipotence can abuse it against his adversaries, why not admit the same concerning a majority? Have men, by joining together, changed their character? By becoming stronger, have they become more patient of obstacles? For my part, I cannot believe that, and I will never grant to several that power to do everything which I refuse to a single man. (Mayer and Lerner 1966, 231–32)

Here is captured the current situation for the hundreds of thousands of cannabis users in the United States. In not respecting the unjust law prohibiting cannabis use and punishing "otherwise law-abiding citizens" they at the same time make an "appeal to the sovereignty of the human race."

Cannabis is the most used illicit drug in the United States and the primary cash crop of the country for the last several years. The use of this drug is at most a moral issue, perhaps not even a moral issue, but certainly not an issue with which the law should be concerned (assuming a democratic form of law and government). Given the irrational and immoral criminalization of harmless wrongdoing and unjustified prohibition of cannabis use (especially given the double standard of the U.S. culture tolerating alcohol use, abuse, dependence, and significant harms to individuals themselves as well as to many innocent others) the obvious direction U.S. federal lawmakers should take is one which acknowledges cannabis as a recreational drug of choice for many "otherwise law-abiding citizens."

Notes

1. Note too that to lack an appreciation of what Thoreau is talking about here is good evidence of one's having lost touch with one's dignity, liberty, sense of social and political freedom.
2. Quite similar to the reception of the newly sighted prisoner of Plato's "Allegory of the Cave."
3. "Medical Marijuana Clinics Face Crackdown" Andrew Glazer, Associated Press. *N.Y. Times* March 11, 2007.
4. See also Tocqueville, *Democracy in America*, part II, book 4, chapter 6 "The Sort of Despotism That Democratic Nations Have to Fear," 667.
5. See also Mayer and Lerner translation, *Democracy in America*, part II, book IV, chapter 2 "Why the Ideas of Democratic Peoples about Government Naturally Favor the Concentration of Political Power," 655.

Bibliography

Aggarwal, Sunil, Gregory T. Carter, and Jeffrey J. Steinborn. "Clearing the Air: What the Latest Supreme Court Decision Regarding Medical Marijuana Really Means." *American Journal of Hospice and Palliative Care* 22(2005): 327–29.

Agres, Ted. "The Future of the FDA." *The Scientist* 12(2006): 46.

Alakbarov, Farid U. "Medicinal Properties of Cannabis According to Medieval Manuscripts of Azerbaijan." *Journal of Cannabis Therapeutics* 1(2001): 3–14.

Alger, Bradley E. "Endocannabinoids: Getting the Message Across." *Proceedings of the National Academy of Science* 101: 8512–13.

American College of Physicians. "Supporting Research into the Therapeutic Role of Marijuana." A Position Paper, 2008.

Amtmann, Dagmar, Patrick Weydt, Kurt L. Johnson, Mark P. Jensen, and Gregory T. Carter. "Survey of Cannabis Use in Patients with Amyotrophic Lateral Sclerosis." *American Journal of Hospice and Palliative Care* 21(2004): 95–104.

Anthony, James. "Death of the 'Stepping Stone' Hypothesis and the "Gateway' Model? Comments on Morral *et al.*" *Addiction* 97 (2002): 1505–08.

Archambault, D. "Adolescence, A Physiological, Cultural and Psychological No Man's Land" in *Adolescent Substance Abuse, Etiology, Treatment and Prevention.* Ed. G. Lawson and A. Lawson, 11–28. Gaithersburg, MD: Aspen, 1992.

Aristotle. *De Anima.* Translated by R. D. Hicks. New York: Prometheus, 1991.

Aristotle. *Nicomachean Ethics.* translated by David Ross. Revised by J. L. Ackrill and J. O. Urmson. New York: Oxford University Press, 1988.

Augustine. *On Free Choice of the Will.* Translated by Thomas Williams. Indianapolis: Hackett Publishing Company, 1993.

———. *Confessions.* Translated by Henry Chadwick. Oxford: Oxford University Press, 1998.

———. *The City of God.* Translated by Marcus Dods. New York: The Modern Library, 2000.

Ault, Alicia. "Institute of Medicine Says Marijuana Has Benefits." *The Lancet* 353(1999): 1077.

Baker, David, Gareth Pryce, Gavin Giovannoni, and Alan J. Thompson. "The Therapeutic Potential of Cannabis." *The Lancet* (Neurology) 2(2003): 291–98.

Barnes, R. Eric. "Reefer Madness: Legal & Moral Issues Surrounding the Medical Prescription of Marijuana." *Bioethics* 14(2000): 16–41.

Baum, Dan. *Smoke and Mirrors. The War on Drugs and the Politics of Failure.* New York: Little, Brown and Company, 1997.

Bello, Joan. *The Benefits of Marijuana: Physical, Psychological and Spiritual.* Boca Raton, FL: Lifeservices Press, 1996.

Benjamin, Walter. *On Hashish.* Translated by Howard Eiland, et al. Cambridge, MA: The Belknap Press, 2006.

Berg, Jessica. "Smokescreen." *Hastings Center Report* 36(2006).

Berger, Peter, and Thomas Luckmann. *The Social Construction of Reality: A Treatise in the Sociology of Knowledge.* New York: Anchor Books, 1966.

Birba, Baron Ernst von. *Plant Intoxicants: A Classic Text on the Use of Mind-Altering Plants.* Rochester, VT: Healing Arts Press, 1995.

Biskupic, Joan. "Court: Let Congress Legalize It." *USA Today* June 7, 2005.

———. "Patients Who Use Marijuana Fear Worst if Forced to Stop." *USA Today.* June 7, 2005.

Blendon, Robert J., and John T. Young. "The Public and the War on Illicit Drugs." *JAMA* 279(1998): 827–32.

Blows, Stephanie, Rebecca Q. Ivers, Jennie Connor, Shanthi Ameratunga, Mark Woodward, and Robyn Norton. "Marijuana Use and Car Crash Injury." *Addiction* 100(2005): 605–11.

Boire, Richard Glen. *Marijuana Law.* 2nd ed. Berkeley, CA: Ronin Publishing, Inc., 1996.

Bonnie, Richard, and Charles Whitebread II. *The Marijuana Conviction: A History of Marijuana Prohibition in the United States.* New York: The Lindesmith Center, 1999.

"Boomers Don't Raise Potheads." *Journal of the American Medical Association* 286(2001): 1306.

Booth, Martin. *Cannabis. A History.* New York: St. Martin's Press, 2004.

Bovard, James. *Lost Rights: The Destruction of American Liberty.* New York: St. Martin's Griffin, 1995.

Bradbury, Jane. "Small Part of Cannabis Puzzle Solved by Animal Studies." *The Lancet* 358(2001): 302.

Brook, Judith, Elinor Balka, Martin Whiteman. "The Risks for Late Adolescence of Early Adolescent Marijuana Use." *American Journal of Public Health* 89(1999): 1549–54.

Burstein, Sumner. "In Humans Ajulemic Acid Has a More Favorable Side-effect Profile than THC for the Treatment of Chronic Neuropathic Pain." *Cannabinoids* 2(2007): 1–2.

Butrica, James L. "The Medical Use of Cannabis among the Greeks and Romans." *Journal of Cannabis Therapeutics* 2(2002): 51–70.

Camf, Jordi, and Magi Farre. "Mechanisms of Disease: Drug Addiction." Review Article, *New England Journal of Medicine* 349(2003): 975–86.

Carter, Gregory T., and Bill S. Rosen. "Marijuana in the Management of Amyotrophic Lateral Sclerosis." *American Journal of Hospice and Palliative Care* 18(2001): 264–70.

Chen, Chuan-Yu, Carla L. Storr, and James C. Anthony. "Influences of Parenting Practices on the Risk of Having a Chance to Try Cannabis." *Pediatrics* 115(2005): 1631–39.

Clarke, Robert C., and David Paul Watson. "Botany of Natural *Cannabis* Medicines." In *Cannabis and Cannabinoids: Pharmacology, Toxicology, and Therapeutic Potential,* edited by Franjo Grotenhermen and Ethan Russo. New York: The Haworth Integrative Healing Press, 2002.

Cooper, Terry. *Sin, Pride & Self-Acceptance.* Downers Grove: InterVarsity Press 2003.

Corbett, J. Elliott. *Turned On by God.* Richmond, VA: John Knox Press, 1971.

Corey, S. "Recent Developments in the Therapeutic Potential of Cannabinoids." *P R Health Science Journal* 24(2005): 19–26.

Cotkin, George. *Existential America.* Baltimore: The Johns Hopkins University Press, 2003.

Crawford, Viviane. "The 'Homelie Herbe.'" *History Today* 2002: 40–41.

Crowley, Aleister. *Diary of a Drug Fiend.* York Beach, ME: Samuel Weiser, Inc., 1995.

Davidoff, Frank. "Sex, Politics, and Morality at the FDA: Reflections on the Plan B Decision." *Hastings Center Report* 36(2006): 20–25.

Degenhardt, Louisa, Wayne Hall, and Michael Lynskey. "Exploring the Association between Cannabis Use and Depression." *Addiction* 98(2003): 1493–1504.

Deakle, David. "Simeon Seth on Cannabis (Cognoscenti of Cannabis II)." *Journal of Cannabis Therapeutics* 1(2001): 15–20.

Demmer, Bryon. "Arrest Suffering, Not Medical Marijuana Patients." *The Humanist* Nov/Dec 2001: 35–36.

Denson, Thomas, and Mitchell Earleywine. "Decreased Depression in Marijuana Users." *Addictive Behaviors* 31(2006): 738–42.

DePalma, Anthony. "Canadians Lean toward Easing Marijuana Laws." *New York Times* June 17, 2001.

Doblin, R., and M. A. R. Kleiman. "Marijuana as Antiemetic Medicine: A Survey of Oncologists' Attitudes and Experiences." *Journal of Clinical Oncology* 9(1991) 1314–1319.

Doweiko, Harold E. *Concepts of Chemical Dependency.* 3rd ed. Pacific Grove, CA: Brooks/Cole, 1996.

Dreher, Melanie. "Crack Heads and Roots Daughters: The Therapeutic Use of Cannabis in Jamaica." *Journal of Cannabis Therapeutics* 2(2002): 121–33.

Dreher, Melanie Creagan. *Working Men and Ganja: Marihuana Use in Rural Jamaica.* Institute for the Study of Human Issues, 1982.

Drug Policy Alliance. "Slow Progress for Medical Marijuana in Congress." Thursday, July 29, 2006, www.drugpolicy.org/news/062906hinchey.cfm.

Drug Use in America: Problem in Perspective; Second Report of the National Commission on Marijuana and Drug Abuse, March 1973 (Shafer Commission Report).

DSM-IV-TR. American Psychiatric Association. *Diagnostic and Statistical Manual of Mental Disorders*. 4th ed. Text Revision. VA: Arlington, 2000.

Dworkin, Ronald. *Taking Rights Seriously*. Cambridge, MA: Harvard University Press, 1978.

Earlywine, Mitch. "Marijuana Arrests and Increase in Marijuana Use Disorders." *Journal of the American Medical Association* 292(2004): 802.

ElSohly, Mahmoud A. "Chemical Constituents of *Cannabis*." In *Cannabis and Cannabinoids: Pharmacology, Toxicology, and Therapeutic Potential*, edited by Franjo Grotenhermen and Ethan Russo. New York: The Haworth Integrative Healing Press, 2002.

Engle, John. "Culture's Unacknowledged Iron Grip." *Chronicle of Higher Education* February 2, 2007.

Escohotado, Antonio. *A Brief History of Drugs: From the Stone Age to the Stoned Age*. Rochester, VT: Park Street Press, 1999.

Feinberg, Joel. *The Moral Limits of the Criminal Law. Vol. 3, Harm to Self*. New York: Oxford University Press, 1986.

———. *The Moral Limits of the Criminal Law. Vol. 4, Harmless Wrongdoing*. New York: Oxford University Press, 1988.

Ferdinand, Robert F., Frouke Sondeijker, Jan van der Ende, Jean-Paul Selten, Anja Huizink, and Frank C. Verhulst. "Cannabis Use Predicts Future Psychotic Symptoms, and Vice Versa." Research Report *Addiction* 100(2005): 612–18.

Festenstein, Matthew. *Pragmatism & Political Theory: From Dewey to Rorty*. Chicago: University of Chicago Press, 1997.

Foster, Stephen, and James A. Duke. *The Peterson Field Guide Series. A Field Guide to Medicinal Plants and Herbs of Eastern and Central North America*. 2nd ed. New York: Houghton Mifflin Co., 2000.

Frank, Mel. *Marijuana Grower's Guide*. Deluxe Ed. Los Angeles, CA: Red Eye Press, 1997.

Freking, Kevin. "Boston, Boulder Lead Nation in Use of Marijuana." *The Courier* June 17, 2005.

Fried, Peter A. "The Consequences of Marijuana Use during Pregnancy: A Review of the Human Literature." *Journal of Cannabis Therapeutics* 2(2002): 85–104.

Gahlinger, Paul. *Illegal Drugs: A Complete Guide to Their History, Chemistry, Use, and Abuse*. New York: Plume, 2004.

Gallagher, Romayne, J. Allan Best, Gilliam Fyles, Pippa Hawley, and Wendy Yeomans. "Attitudes and Beliefs about the Use of Cannabis for Symptom Control in a Palliative Population." *Journal of Cannabis Therapeutics* 3(2003): 41–50.

Gaskin, Stephen. *Cannabis Spirituality*. NY: High Times Books, 1996.

Gettman, Jon. "Marijuana Production in the United States." *The Bulletin of Cannabis Reform: 2006*. www.drugscience.org/ber/index.html.

Gieringer, Dale H. "The Acceptance of Medicinal Marijuana in the U.S." *Journal of Cannabis Therapeutics* 3(2003): 53–65.

Glazer, Andrew. "Medical Marijuana Clinics Face Crackdown." *New York Times*, March 11, 2007.

Giuffrida, Andrea, F. Markus Leweke, Christoph W. Gerth, Daniela Schreiber, Dagmar Koethe, Johannes Faulhaber, Joachim Klosterkotter, and Daniele Piomelli. "Cerebrospinal Anadamide Levels Are Elevated in Acute Schizophrenia and Are Inversely Correlated with Psychotic Symptoms." *Neuropsychopharmacology* 29(2004): 2108–14.

Gray, Mike. *Drug Crazy. How We Got into This Mess and How We Can Get Out.* New York: Routledge, 2000.

Green, Bob, David Kavanagh, and Ross Young. "Being Stoned: A Review of Self-reported Cannabis Effects." *Drug and Alcohol Review* 22 (2003): 453–60.

Green, Brian, and Christian Ritter. "Marijuana Use and Depression." *Journal of Health and Social Behavior* 41(2000): 40–49.

Grinspoon, Lester. "On the Future of Cannabis as Medicine." *Cannabinoids* 2(2007): 13–15.

Grinspoon, Lester, and James B. Bakalar. *Marihuana: The Forbidden Medicine.* Revised and expanded edition. New Haven, CT: Yale University Press, 1997.

Grotenhermen, Franjo. "Review of Therapeutic Effects." In *Cannabis and Cannabinoids: Pharmacology, Toxicology, and Therapeutic Potential,* edited by Franjo Grotenhermen and Ethan Russo. New York: The Haworth Integrative Healing Press, 2002.

Grotenhermen, Franjo. "How to Prevent Cannabis-induced Psychological Distress . . . in Politicians." *The Lancet* 363(2004): 1568–69.

———. "Cannabinoids and the Endocannabinoid System." *Cannabinoids* 1(2006): 10–14.

———. "Therapeutic Use of Cannabis." *The Lancet* 351(1998): 758–59.

Grotenhermen, Franjo, and Ethan Russo, eds. *Cannabis and Cannabinoids: Pharmacology, Toxicology, and Therapeutic Potential.* New York: The Haworth Integrative Healing Press, 2002.

Hall, Wayne. "Getting the Cannabis Withdrawal Question into Proper Perspective: Comments on Smith." *Addiction* 97(2002): 754.

Hall, Wayne, and Louisa Degenhardt. "Cannabis Use and Psychosis: A Review of Clinical and Epidemiological Evidence." *Australian and New Zealand Journal of Psychiatry* 34(2000): 26–34.

———. "Medical Marijuana Initiatives. Are They Justified? How Successful Are They Likely to Be?" *CNS Drugs* 17 (2003): 689–97.

Hall, Wayne, MacDonald Christie, and David Currow. "Cannabinoids and Cancer: Causation, Remediation, and Palliation." *The Lancet* (Oncology) 6(2005): 35–41.

Hall, Wayne, and Nadia Solowij. "Adverse Effects of Cannabis." *The Lancet* 352(1998): 1611–16.

Hanson, Glen, Peter J. Venturelli, and Annette Fleckenstein. *Drugs and Society.* 7th ed. Boston: Jones and Bartlett Pub., 2002.

Hashibe, Mia, Hal Morgenstern, Yan Cui, Donald Tashkin, Zuo-Feng Zhang, Wendy Cozen, Thomas Mack, and Sander Greenland. "Marijuana Use and the Risk of Lung and Upper Aerodigestive Tract Cancers: Results of a Population-Based Case-Control Study." *Cancer Epidemiology Biomarkers and Prevention* 15(2006): 1829–34.

Hazekamp, Arno. "An Evaluation of the Quality of Medicinal Grade Cannabis in the Netherlands." *Cannabinoids* 1(2006): 1–9.

Herer, Jack. *The Emperor Wears No Clothes: Cannabis and the Conspiracy against Marijuana.* 11th ed. Phoenix, AZ: Paper Master Trade Printing, 1998.

Hill, Matthew, Sachin Patel, Erica Carrier, David Rademacher, Brandi Ormerod, Cecilia Hillard, and Boris Gorzalka. "Down Regulation of Endocannabinoid Signaling in the Hippocampus Following Chronic Unpredictable Stress." *Neuropsychopharmacology* 30(2005): 508–15.

Hillig, Karl and Paul Mahlberg. "A Chemotaxonomic Analysis of Cannabinoid Variation in *Cannabis* (Cannabaceae)." *American Journal of Botany* 91(2004): 966–75.

Hobbs, W., T. Rall, and T. Verdoorn. "Hypnotics and Sedatives: Ethanol" in The Pharmacological Basis of Therapeutics, 9th ed., ed. J. Hardman and L. Limbird, 361–96. New York: McGraw Hill, 1995.

Hodges, Clare. "Personal Account of Medical Use of Cannabis." *Journal of Cannabis Therapeutics* 2(2002): 155–60.

Hollister, Leo E. "Marijuana (Cannabis) as Medicine." *Journal of Cannabis Therapeutics* 1(2001): 5–27.

Holy Bible. New International Version. Grand Rapids, MI: Zondervan, 1986.

Husak, Douglas. *Legalize This! The Case for Decriminalizing Drugs.* New York: Verso, 2002.

Jansen, Mila, and Robbie Terris. "One Woman's Work in the Use of Hashish in a Medical Context." *Journal of Cannabis Therapeutics* 2(2002): 135–43.

Johnston, L. D., P. M. O'Malley, J. G. Bachman and J. E. Schulenberg. *Monitoring the Future National Results on Adolescent Drug Use: Overview of Key Findings, 2007* (NIH Publication No. 08-6418). Bethesda, MD: National Institute on Drug Abuse, 2007.

Joy, Janet, Stanley Watson, Jr., and John Benson, Jr., eds. *Marijuana and Medicine. Assessing the Science Base.* Division of Neuroscience and Behavioral Health Institute of Medicine. Washington, DC: National Academy Press, 1999.

Kant, Immanuel. *Foundations of the Metaphysics of Morals.* Translated by Lewis White Beck. New York: The Liberal Arts Press, Inc., 1959.

———. *The Doctrine of Virtue*, part II of *The Metaphysic of Morals.* Translated by Mary Gregor. New York: Harper and Row, 1964.

———. *Critique of Practical Reason.* Translated by Lewis White Beck. Upper, Saddle River, NJ: Prentice-Hall, Inc. 1993.

———. *Metaphysical Elements of Justice.* 2nd ed. In *The Metaphysics of Morals*, Part I. translated by John Ladd. Indianapolis: Hackett Publishing Company, 1999.

Kapp, Clare. "Swiss Debate whether to Legalise Cannabis." *The Lancet* 362(2003): 970.

Kelsey, Morton T. *Healing and Christianity in Ancient Thought and Modern Times.* New York: Harper and Row, 1973.

Kendall, Robert. *Cannabis Condemned.* "The Proscription of Indian Hemp." *Addiction* 98(2003): 143–51.

Kenkel, Donald, and Alan Mathios. "'Gateway Effects': Insights from Economics Needed." *Addiction* 97(2002): 1505.

Ladd, John. Introduction. *Metaphysical Elements of Justice* by Immanuel Kant. Translated by John Ladd. Indianapolis: Hackett, 1999.

Lambert, Didier M. Editorial. "Cannabis and Endocannabinoids: 'The Old Man and the Teenagers.'" *Chemistry and Biodiversity* 4(2007): 1609–1613.

Leinwand, Donna. "Anti-drug Advertising Campaign a Failure, GAO Report Says." *USA Today* August 29, 2006.

———. "College Drug Use, Binge Drinking Rise." *USA Today* March 15, 2007.

Leweke, F. Markus, Christoph W. Gerth, and Joachim Klosterkotter. "Cannabis-Associated Psychosis: Current Status of Research." *CNS Drugs* 18(2004): 895–910.

Lewin, Louis. *Phantastica: A Classic Survey on the Use and Abuse of Mind-Altering Plants.* Rochester, VT: Park Street Press, 1998.

"Looking Back on the Millennium in Medicine." *New England Journal of Medicine* January 6, 2000.

Lowenstein, Edward, and Sidney Wanzer. "The U.S. Attorney General's Intrusion Into Medical Practice." *New England Journal of Medicine* 346(2002): 447–48.

Lynskey, Michael. "An Alternative Model is Feasible, but the Gateway Hypothesis Has Not Been Invalidated: Comments on Morral et al." *Addiction* 97(2002): 1508-1509.

Lynskey, Michael, Carolyn Coffey, Louisa Degenhardt, John Carlin, and George Patton. "A Longitudinal Study of the Effects of Adolescent Cannabis use on High School Completion." *Addiction* 98(2003): 685–92.

———. "Research Report: A Longitudinal Study of the Effects of Adolescent Cannabis Use on High School Completion." *Addiction* 98(2003): 685–92.

Macauley, Robert. "The Hippocratic Underground: Civil Disobedience and Health Care Reform." *Hastings Center Report* 35(2005): 38–45.

Macleod, John, Rachel Oakes, Alex Copello, Ilana Crome, Mattias Egger, Matthew Hickman, Helen Stokes-Lampard, and George Davey Smith. "Psychological and Social Sequelae of Cannabis and Other Illicit Drug Use by Young People: A Systematic Review of Longitudinal, General Population Studies." *The Lancet* 363(2004): 1579–88.

Marsicano, Giovanni, Carsten Wotjak, Shahnaz Azad, Tiziana Bisogno, Gerhard Rammis, Maria Cascio, Heiko Hermann, Jianrong Tang, Clementine Hefmann, Walter Ziegigansherger, Vincenzo Marzo, and Beat Lutz. "The Endogenous Cannabis System and Extinction of Aversive Memories." *Nature* 418(2002): 530–31.

Mathre, Mary Lynn. "Cannabis and Harm Reduction: A Nursing Perspective." *Journal of Cannabis Therapeutics* 2(2002): 105–20.

Mayer, J. P. and Max Lerner, eds. *Democracy in America.* A New Translation by George Lawrence. Harper and Row: 1966

McGee, Rob, Sheila Williams, Rechic Poulton, and Terrie Moffitt. "A Longitudinal Study of Cannabis Use and Mental Health from Adolescence to Early Adulthood." *Addiction* 95(2000): 491–503.

McPartland, John, and Ethan Russo. Cannabis and Cannabis Extracts: Greater Than the Sum of Their Parts. *Journal of Cannabis Therapeutics* 1(2002): 103–32.

McWilliams, Peter. *Ain't Nobody's Business If You Do: The Absurdity of Consensual Crimes in Our Free Country.* Los Angeles, CA: Prelude Press, 1996.

Mikuriya, Tod H. "Cannabis as a Substitute for Alcohol: A Harm-Reduction Approach." *Journal of Cannabis Therapeutics.* 4(2004): 79–93.

Mill, John Stuart. "On Liberty." In *Ethical Theories: A Book of Readings.* 2nd ed., A. I. Melden, ed. Upper Saddle River, NJ: Prentice-Hall, 1967a.

Mill, John Stuart. "Utilitarianism." In *Ethical Theories: A Book of Readings.* 2nd ed., A. I. Melden, ed. New Jersey: Prentice-Hall, Inc., 1967b.

Miller, David. *Brassey's Book of the Crusades.* Dulles, VA: Brassey's, Inc., 2001.

Mirken, Bruce, and Mitch Earlywine. "The Cannabis and Psychosis Connection Questioned: A Comment on Fergusson et al. 2005." *Addiction* (2005): 714–15.

Monfreid, Henri de, and Ida Treat. *Pearls, Arms and Hashish: Pages from the Life of a Red Sea Navigator, Henri De Monfreid.* New York: Coward-McCann, Inc., 1930.

Moore, Jr., John A., and Myron Roberts. *The Pursuit of Happiness. Government and Politics in America.* 4th ed. New York: Macmillan Pub. Co., 1989.

Morgan, Edmund S., ed. *Puritan Political Ideas, 1558–1794.* Cambridge, MA: Hackett Pub. Co., 2003.

Morral, Andrew, Daniel McCaffrey, and Susan Paddock. "Reassessing the Marijuana Gateway Effect." *Addiction* 97(2002): 1493–1504.

Morral, Andrew, Daniel McCaffrey, and Susan Paddock. "Evidence Does Not Favor Marijuana Gateway Effects over a Common-Factor Interpretation: Responses to Anthony, Kenkel and Mathios and Lynskey." *Addiction* 97(2002): 1509–10.

Muller-Vahl, Kirsten, Hans Kolbe, Udo Schneider, and Hinderk Emrich. "Movement Disorders" 205–13 in Grotenhermen, Franjo and Ethan Russo, editors. *Cannabis and Cannabinoids: Pharmacology, Toxicology, and Therapeutic Potential.* New York: The Haworth Integrative Healing Press, 2002.

Musty, Richard E., and Rita Rossi. "Effects of Smoked Cannabis and Oral Delta9-Tetrahydrocannabinol on Nausea and Emesis after Cancer Chemotherapy: A Review of State Clinical Trials." *Journal of Cannabis Therapeutics* 1(2001): 43–56.

Nathan, K., W. Bresnick, and S. Battei. "Cocaine Abuse and Dependence" *CNS Drugs* 10(1998): 43–59.

National Institute on Alcohol Abuse and Alcoholism. (NIAAA). Publication 21(1997). Available http://silk.nih.gov/silk/niaaal/publications/15221-1.htm.

Nicholson, Peter. "The Reception and Early Reputation of Mill's Political Thought," In *Cambridge Companion to Mill.* Cambridge: Cambridge University Press, 1998.

Nutt, David, Leslie King, William Saulsbury, and Colin Blakemore. "Development of a rational scale to assess the harm of drugs of potential misuse" *The Lancet* 369(2007): 1047–53.

Palladino, Paolo. *Plants, Patients and the Historian. (Re)membering in the Age of Genetic Engineering.* Piscataway, NJ: Rutgers University Press, 2003.

Papanastassiou, Alex M., Howard L. Fields, and Ian D. Meng. "Local application of the cannabinoid receptor agonist, WIN 55,212-2, to spinal trigeminal nucleus caudalis differentially affects nociceptive and non-nociceptive neurons." *Pain* 107 (2004): 267–75.

Pate, David. "Glaucoma and Cannabinoids," 215–24 in Grotenhermen, Franjo and Ethan Russo, editors. *Cannabis and Cannabinoids. Pharmacology, Toxicology, and Therapeutic Potential.* New York: The Haworth Integrative Healing Press, 2002.

Patton, George C., Barbara J. McMorris, John W. Toumbourou, Sheryl A. Hemphill, Susan Donath, and Richard F. Catalano. "Puberty and the Onset of Substance Use and Abuse." *Pediatrics* 114(2004): e300–e306.

Patton, George C., Carolyn Coffey, John Carlin, Louisa Degenhardt, Michael Lynsky, and Wayne Hall. "Cannabis Use and Mental Health in Young People: Cohort Study." *British Medical Journal* 325(2002): 1195–98.

Percy, Andrew, Siobhan McAlister, Kathryn Higgins, Patrick McCrystal and Maeve Thornton. "Response Consistency in Young Adolescents' Drug Use Self-reports: A Recanting Rate Analysis." *Addiction* 100(2005): 189–96.

Perkenigg, Axel, Roselind Lieb, Michael Hofler, Peter Schuster, Holger Sonntag, and Hans-Ulrich Wittchen. "Patterns of Cannabis Use, Abuse and Dependence over Time: Incidence, Progression and Stability in a Sample of 1228 Adolescents." *Addiction* 94(1999): 1663–78.

Petro, Denis J. "Cannabis in Multiple Sclerosis: Women's Health Concerns." *Journal of Cannabis Therapeutics* 2(2002): 161–75.

Pew Research Center. Social Trends Report. "A Barometer of Modern Morals: Sex, Drugs and the 1040." Pew Research Center, 2006.

Pollen, Michael. *The Botany of Desire: A Plant's-Eye View of the World.* New York: Random House, 2001.

Polsky, Ned. *Hustlers, Beats and Others.* Chicago: University of Chicago Press, 1985 (orig. 1967).

Pope, Jr., Harrison G. "Cannabis, Cognition, and Residual Confounding." *Journal of the American Medical Association* 287(2002): 1172–74.

Ridenour, Ty, Linda Cottler, Compton Wilson, Edward Sptznagel, and Renee Cunningham-Williams. "Is There a Progression from Abuse Disorders to Dependence Disorders?" *Addiction* 98(2003): 635–44.

Ritter, John. "Pot Growing Moves to Suburbs." *USA Today* February 2, 2007.

Rosenthal, Ed, and Steve Kubby. *Why Marijuana Should Be Legal.* New York: Thunder's Mouth Press, 2003.

Rosenthal, Ed, Dale Gieringer, and Tod Mikuriya. *Marijuana Medical Handbook: A Guide to Therapeutic Use.* Oakland, CA: Quick American Archives, 1997.

Rubin, Vera (ed.) *Cannabis and Culture,* Mouton, The Hague, 1975.

Russo, Ethan. "Cannabis Treatments in Obstetrics and Gynecology: A Historical Review." *Journal of Cannabis Therapeutics* 2(2002a): 5–35.

Russo, Ethan. "Hemp for Headache: An In-Depth Historical and Scientific Review of Cannabis in Migraine Treatment." *Journal of Cannabis Therapeutics* 1(2002b): 21–92.

Russo, Ethan. "Migraine." In *Cannabis and Cannabinoids: Pharmacology, Toxicology, and Therapeutic Potential.* Edited by Franjo Grotenhermen and Ethan Russo. New York: The Haworth Integrative Healing Press, 2002c.

Russo, Ethan. "Cannabis: From Pariah to Prescription." *Journal of Cannabis Therapeutics* 3(2003): 1–29.

Russo, Ethan. "Clinical Endocannabinoid Deficiency (CECD): Can this Concept Explain Therapeutic Benefits of Cannabis in Migraine, Fibromyalgia, Irritable Bowel Syndrome and Other Treatment-Resistant Conditions?" *Neuroendocrinology Letters* 25(2004a): 31–39.

Russo, Ethan. Editorial. *Journal of Cannabis Therapeutics.* 4(2004b): 1–6.

Russo, Ethan. "Letter: Cannabinoid Medicines and the Need for the Scientific Method." *Cannabinoids* 2(2007): 16–19.

Russo, Ethan, Mary Lynn Mathre, Al Byrne, Robert Velin, Paul Bach, Juan Sanchez-Ramos, and Kristin Kirlin. *Journal of Cannabis Therapeutics* 2(2002), 3–57.

Ryan, Alan. "Mill in a Liberal Landscape," In *Cambridge Companion to Mill.* Cambridge: Cambridge University Press, 1998.

Satel, Sally. "A Whiff of 'Reefer Madness' in U.S. Drug Policy." *New York Times* August 16, 2005.

Scholten, Willem K. "Guidelines for Cultivating Cannabis for Medicinal Purposes." *Journal of Cannabis Therapeutics* 3(2003): 51–61.

Schnelle, Martin, and Florian Strasser. "Anorexia and Cachexia." In *Cannabis and Cannabinoids: Pharmacology, Toxicology, and Therapeutic Potential.* Edited by Franjo Grotenhermen and Ethan Russo. New York: The Haworth Integrative Healing Press, 2002.

"Scientists Say Government Blocking Marijuana Research," Findlay, OH: *The Courier*, July 21, 2004.

Sharp, David. "Highs and Lows of Cannabis" *The Lancet* 363(2004): 344.

Shorter Oxford English Dictionary. 5th ed. Oxford: Oxford University Press, 2002.

Skager, Rodney. "Findings and Recommendations for More Effective Drug Education for Youth: Honesty, Respect and Assistance When Needed." *Safety First* (2004): 1–6. www.safety1st.org.

Sloman, Larry. *Reefer Madness: The History of Marijuana in America.* New York: St. Martin's Griffin, 1998.

Smith, Neil T. "A Review of the Published Literature into Cannabis Withdrawal Symptoms in Human Users." *Addiction* 97(2002): 621–32.

———. "Cannabis, Carrots and Common Experiences: A Reply to Comments on Smith." *Addiction* 97(2002b): 916.

Stephens, Robert S., Roger A. Roffman, Stephanie A. Fearer, Carl Williams, Joseph F. Picciano, and Randy S. Burke. "The Marijuana Check-up: Reaching Users Who Are Ambivalent about Change." *Addiction* 99(2004): 1323–32.

Stone, John, and Stephen Mennell, eds. *Alexis de Tocqueville: On Democracy, Revolution, and Society.* Chicago University of Chicago Press, 1980.

Strohbeck-Kuchner, Gisela Skopp, Rainer Mattern. "Cannabis Improves Symptoms of ADHD." *Cannabinoids* 3(2008): 1–3.

Taskin, D. P. American Thoracic Society, International Conference of 2006, "Marijuana Use and Lung Cancer: Results of a Case Control Study." May 24, 2006.

Thoreau, Henry David. "On the Duty of Civil Disobedience." In *Walden; or, Life in the Woods and On the Duty of Civil Disobedience.* Chicago: Signet, 1960.

Tierney, John. "Marijuana Pipe Dreams." *New York Times* August 27, 2005.

Tims, Frank M., Michael L. Dennis, Nancy Hamilton, Betty J. Buchan, Guy Diamond, Rod Funk, and Laura B. Brantley. "Characteristics and problems of 600 Adolescent Cannabis Abusers in Outpatient Treatment." *Addiction* 97 (2002 Suppl. 1): 46–57.

Tocqueville, Alexis de. *Democracy in America.* Edited by J. P. Mayer and Max Lerner. New York: Harper and Row, 1966.

Vastag, Brian. "Medical Marijuana Center Opens Doors." *Journal of the American Medical Association* 290(2003): 877–79.

Voelker, Rebecca. "NIH Panel Says More Study is Needed to Assess Marijuana's Medicinal Use." *Journal of the American Medical Association* 277(1997): 867–68.

Weil, Andrew, and Winifred Rosen. *From Chocolate to Morphine: Everything You Need to Know about Mind-altering Drugs.* Revised edition. New York: Houghton Mifflin Company, 2004.

Werner, Clinton A. "Medical Marijuana and the AIDS Crisis." *Journal of Cannabis Therapeutics* 1(2001): 17–33.

Wingerchuk, Dean. "Cannabis for Medical Purposes: Cultivating Science, Weeding Outthe Fiction." *The Lancet* 364(2004): 315–16.

Wodak, Alex, and Annie Cooney. "Should Cannabis be Taxed and Regulated?" *Drug and Alcohol Review* 23(2004): 139–41.

Woolridge, Emily, Simon Barton, Jonathon Samuel, Jess Osorio, Andrew Dougherty, and Anita Holdcroft. "Cannabis Use in HIV for Pain and Other Medical Symptoms." *ournal of Pain and Symptom Management* 29(2005): 358–67.

Zajicek, John, Patrick Fox, Hilary Sanders, David Wright, Jane Vickery, Andrew Nunn, and Alan Thompson. "Cannabinoids for Treatment of Spasticity and Other Symptoms Related to Multiple Sclerosis (CAMS Study): Multicentre Randomized Placebo-controlled Trial." *The Lancet* 362(2003): 1517–26.

Zeppetella, Giovanbattista. "The Palliation of Dyspnea in Terminal Disease." *American Journal of Hospice and Palliative Care* 1998: 322–28.

Zohary, Michael. *Plants of the Bible.* New York: Cambridge University Press, 1982.

Index

About the Author

Matt Stolick is currently in his tenth year at the University of Findlay. An associate professor of philosophy, he regularly teaches courses in applied ethics (health care, environmental, animal, sports) and introduction to philosophy, as well as courses in epistemology, metaphysics, and aesthetics. He is a dynamic teacher who prefers working from great books and primary texts; training young minds in an open, respectful learning environment; and pushing students to better know themselves and think critically. He regularly provides ethics perspectives for the *American Journal of Hospice and Palliative Medicine*. He is editor of the Bioethics Network of Ohio newsletter (*BIO Quarterly*), as well as on the Board of Trustees of the organization, and is a member of the Blanchard Valley Regional Health Center ethics committee. Stolick received his BA in philosophy from Westminster College (PA), and MA and PhD in philosophy at the University of Tennessee–Knoxville. His dissertation was titled, "Training Medical Students to Care Compassionately." Matt and his wife of ten years, Randi, have three children: daughters Van (5) and Simone (3) and son Moses (1). They reside in Findlay, Ohio.